Yearbook of International Humanitarian Law

Volume 26

Editor-in-Chief

Heike Krieger, Department of Law/Public Law, Free University of Berlin, Berlin, Germany

Series Editors

Pablo Kalmanovitz, Department of International Studies, Instituto Tecnológico Autonómo de México (ITAM), Mexico City, Mexico

Eliav Lieblich, Buchmann Faculty of Law, Tel Aviv University, Tel Aviv, Israel

Stavros Evdokimos Pantazopoulos, National and Kapodistrian University of Athens, Athens, Greece

The *Yearbook of International Humanitarian Law* is a leading annual publication devoted to the study of international humanitarian law. It provides a truly international forum for high-quality, peer-reviewed academic articles focusing on this crucial branch of international law. Distinguished by contemporary relevance, the Yearbook of International Humanitarian Law bridges the gap between theory and practice and serves as a useful reference tool for scholars, practitioners, military personnel, civil servants, diplomats, human rights workers and students.

Heike Krieger · Pablo Kalmanovitz ·
Eliav Lieblich · Stavros Evdokimos Pantazopoulos
Editors

Yearbook of International Humanitarian Law, Volume 26 (2023)

Humanitarian Actors

Editors

Heike Krieger
Department of Law/Public Law
Free University of Berlin
Berlin, Germany

Eliav Lieblich
Buchmann Faculty of Law
Tel Aviv University
Tel Aviv, Israel

Pablo Kalmanovitz
Department of International Studies
Instituto Tecnológico Autonómo de México
(ITAM)
Mexico City, Mexico

Stavros Evdokimos Pantazopoulos
National and Kapodistrian University
of Athens
Athens, Greece

The views expressed in this *Yearbook* are not necessarily those of the members of the Editorial Board, the Board of Advisors to the Editorial Board, the Board of Recommendation and/or those institutions they represent, including the T.M.C. Asser Instituut and T.M.C. ASSER PRESS.

ISSN 1389-1359   ISSN 1574-096X (electronic)
Yearbook of International Humanitarian Law
ISBN 978-94-6265-662-8   ISBN 978-94-6265-663-5 (eBook)
https://doi.org/10.1007/978-94-6265-663-5

Published by T.M.C. ASSER PRESS, The Hague, The Netherlands www.asserpress.nl
Produced and distributed for T.M.C. ASSER PRESS by Springer-Verlag Berlin Heidelberg

© T.M.C. ASSER PRESS and the authors 2025

No part of this work may be reproduced, stored in a retrieval system, or transmitted in any form or by any means, electronic, mechanical, photocopying, microfilming, recording or otherwise, without written permission from the Publisher, with the exception of any material supplied specifically for the purpose of being entered and executed on a computer system, for exclusive use by the purchaser of the work.
The use of general descriptive names, registered names, trademarks, service marks, etc. in this publication does not imply, even in the absence of a specific statement, that such names are exempt from the relevant protective laws and regulations and therefore free for general use.

Cover art: ivanastar via iStock by Getty Images (https://www.istockphoto.com/nl/foto/moderne-abstra cte-achtergrond-met-kleurovergang-gm980931798-266452279)

This T.M.C. ASSER PRESS imprint is published by the registered company Springer-Verlag GmbH, DE, part of Springer Nature.
The registered company address is: Heidelberger Platz 3, 14197 Berlin, Germany

If disposing of this product, please recycle the paper.

Editorial Board

General Editors

Prof. Heike Krieger (Editor-in-Chief), Free University of Berlin
Prof. Pablo Kalmanovitz (Editor), Instituto Tecnológico Autónomo de México (ITAM), Mexico City
Prof. Eliav Lieblich (Editor), Tel Aviv University

Managing Editor

Dr. Stavros Evdokimos Pantazopoulos, National and Kapodistrian University of Athens

Editorial Assistant

Baptiste Beurrier, T.M.C. Asser Instituut, The Hague

Board of Advisors to the Editorial Board

Dr. Louise Arimatsu, Centre for Women, Peace and Security, London School of Economics
Dr. William Boothby, Geneva Centre for Security Policy
Prof. Geoffrey Corn, Texas Tech University School of Law
Dr. Hanne Cuyckens, Leiden University College
Dr. Cordula Droege, International Committee of the Red Cross
BGen. Prof. Paul Ducheine, Netherlands Defence Academy/University of Amsterdam
Prof. Robin Geiß, United Nations Institute for Disarmament Research
Prof. Dr. Wolff Heintschel von Heinegg, Europa Universität Viadrina, Frankfurt (Oder)
Prof. Dr. Jann K. Kleffner LL.M., Swedish Defence University
Prof. Dr. Nils Melzer, International Committee of the Red Cross/University of Glasgow
Prof. Dr. Héctor Olasolo, University of El Rosario, Colombia/The Hague University of Applied Sciences
Dr. Christophe Paulussen, T.M.C. Asser Instituut, The Hague
Jelena Pejic, Lieber Institute West Point/Just Security
Dr. Kinga Tibori-Szabó, UN Iraq
BGen Kenneth W. Watkin (Ret'd)/Former Judge Advocate General, Canada
Prof. Dr. Gentian Zyberi, Norwegian Centre for Human Rights

Board of Recommendation

HRH Princess Margriet of the Netherlands, Honorary President of the Netherlands Red Cross
Prof. Dr. Tim McCormack, University of Tasmania/Special Adviser on International Humanitarian Law to the Prosecutor of the International Criminal Court
Prof. em. Dr. Horst Fischer, University of Leiden
Dr. Dieter Fleck, Honorary President of the International Society for Military Law and the Law of War
Prof. Terry D. Gill, University of Amsterdam
H. E. Judge Christopher Greenwood, Master at Magdalene College, University of Cambridge
Dr. Theodor Meron, Former Judge of the International Residual Mechanism for Criminal Tribunals
H. E. Judge Dr. Fausto Pocar, International Court of Justice
Prof. Dr. Michael N. Schmitt, University of Reading

Guest Reviewers

Prof. Dr. Constantine Antonopoulos, Democritus University of Thrace
Dr. Douglas Cubie, University College Cork
Dr. Grant Dawson, Wildlife Justice Commission
Prof. Dr. Treasa Dunworth, University of Auckland
Prof. Dr. Patrycja Grzebyk, University of Warsaw
Dr. Alonso Gurmendi Dunkelberg, London School of Economics and Political Science
Magistrate Dr. Julieta Lemaitre Ripoll, Special Jurisdiction for Peace
Dr. Alexander Wentker, Max Planck Institute for Comparative Public Law and International Law

Preface

International Humanitarian Law (IHL) arguably originates with the neutralization of battlefield medical assistance in the late nineteenth century. Since then, humanitarian actors have diversified and amplified their work and mission far beyond their founders' imagination, in a process that has contributed fundamentally to shaping contemporary IHL. Most notably, the International Red Cross and Red Crescent Movement has played fundamental roles in the drafting and enforcement of IHL instruments and has expanded its membership and mandate globally to cover humanitarian crises directly or indirectly linked to armed conflicts all over the world.

For volume 26, the *Yearbook of International Humanitarian Law* invited contributions that investigate the law, history, and politics of humanitarian action in armed conflicts and beyond. Common to the complex contemporary constellation of humanitarian actors is the espousal of a historically distinctive set of fundamental principles: humanity, neutrality, impartiality, and independence. In keeping with these principles, humanitarian actors have prioritized access to populations in need in conflict areas, often operating with discretion and confidentially. All humanitarian actors are forced to engage with *de facto* powers of various sorts in conflict areas, including High Contracting Parties, non-state opposition groups, terrorist organizations, and drug trafficking cartels with military capabilities. How is loyalty to humanitarian principles maintained in contexts that bear so little resemblance with historical battlefields—and in a political and legal world that increasingly demands criminal accountability and counter-terrorist action? Are the efforts of humanitarian actors excessively restricted by applicable legal frameworks?

The two contributions to the special theme address these questions and more. David Matyas's article conveys a rich sense of the legal complexity surrounding the work of humanitarian actors on the ground. Focusing on international non-governmental organizations, international humanitarian organizations, and civil society actors, and drawing on interviews with humanitarian practitioners in Africa, the Middle East, Europe, and the United Kingdom, the author reconstructs the intricate configurations of international, domestic, and foreign state laws and jurisdictions; public and private laws; soft law standards and regulations, which constitute, constrain and enable, the "everyday work" of humanitarian actors. In the process,

Matyas reveals the insufficiency of traditional legal approaches to humanitarian governance, which are framed within areas of public international law, and relativizes the role and practical importance of IHL in humanitarian action.

While Matyas's analysis of humanitarian legal governance focuses on non-state actors, Oscar Gómez's contribution looks at the state as a humanitarian actor. Challenging the perceived centrality of non-state actors in humanitarian practice, in which states appear as either benevolent funders or dysfunctional structures, Gómez shows the crucial importance of state agencies in aid-receiving states as effective providers of humanitarian relief and protection. Through a case study of Colombia's highly developed state humanitarian agencies, which have been dedicated to addressing the humanitarian impact of decades-long armed conflict, the article shows why we should see the state as a key humanitarian actor, not simply as either benevolent funder or helpless receiver.

In the general submissions section, Neil Davison looks at the exemption in the Chemical Weapons Convention for law enforcement operations, notably for "domestic riot control purposes." As Davison shows, while the CCW drafters had mainly tear gas in mind when introducing the law enforcement exemption, ambiguities in the treaty left open the question whether other toxic chemicals could be permissibly used in law enforcement, in particular aerosolized chemicals acting on the central nervous system. Davison's article reconstructs and reflects on the legal clarification introduced by the CCW Conference of the Parties in 2021, whereby the use of this type of chemicals was excluded from the law enforcement exemption. Davison highlights the crucial role of the ICRC in this clarification and identifies remaining ambiguities and open questions in the treaty.

The Russian aggression against Ukraine has brought the question to the fore of when a third state turns into a co-party to an international armed conflict because of the provision of support to a belligerent. In his contribution, Robin Sebastiaan David Sinnige digs into the specific case of the provision of processed satellite imagery. He argues that such a kind of intelligence support operates in a legal grey area because the pertinent standards are unclear in practice and in literature. Against this background, he proposes a new test consisting of three elements: the extent of the support, the causal link, and the intent. Based on this definition he concludes that in some instances the provision of tactical intelligence support entails a co-party status.

The Yearbook concludes with the Year in Review section, written by Belén Guerrero Romero, Wamika Sachdev, and Baptiste Beurrier.

We are grateful to the authors for their engagement with the Yearbook. Huge thanks are due to the peer-reviewers and to Baptiste Beurrier for his support with the editing process. We hope this edition contributes to the manifold discourses in international humanitarian law.

Mexico City, Mexico	Pablo Kalmanovitz
Berlin, Germany	Heike Krieger
Tel Aviv, Israel	Eliav Lieblich

Contents

Part I Humanitarian Actors

1 Humanitarians and Their Law(s): A Comprehensive Inquiry 3
David Matyas

**2 The State as a Humanitarian Actor: Opportunities
and Challenges in Decolonizing Humanitarianism** 43
Oscar A. Gómez

Part II Other Articles

**3 Nerve Agents by Another Name: The Thirty-Year Effort
to Close a Loophole on Chemical Weapons** 77
Neil Davison

4 On the Sideline or on the Pitch? *The Classification of Third
States Supporting Active Belligerents in an International Armed
Conflict with Satellite Imagery* 109
Robin Sebastiaan David Sinnige

Part III Year in Review

5 Year in Review 2023 157
Belén Guerrero Romero, Wamika Sachdev, and Baptiste Beurrier

Part I
Humanitarian Actors

Chapter 1
Humanitarians and Their Law(s): A Comprehensive Inquiry

David Matyas

Contents

1.1	Introduction	4
1.2	The Traditional International Legal Starting Point	7
	1.2.1 Areas of International Law with Bearing on Humanitarian Assistance	7
	1.2.2 Questioning the Traditional Starting Point	11
1.3	Reconstructing the Field from the Perspective of Humanitarian Practitioners: Towards A Comprehensive Inquiry	14
	1.3.1 Domestic Public Laws	16
	1.3.2 Private Law	23
	1.3.3 Self-governance: Humanitarians as Norm-Makers	29
1.4	Conclusion: Where Can A Comprehensive View Provide Insights?	32
References		35

Abstract Legal considerations play a key role in humanitarian assistance. Humanitarians may look to law to answer questions such as "what is permissible aid", "who is an authorized humanitarian", "what determines access to an affected context", and "who can claim humanitarian protections and immunities". But what are the specific areas of law with bearing on humanitarians in their everyday work? Is public international law—as traditionally advanced—the most appropriate field for this inquiry? This chapter argues for a reconstruction of the laws of humanitarian assistance from the perspective of humanitarian practitioners. From this viewpoint, it shows how prominent areas of public international law—such as international humanitarian law (IHL)—become relativized, and multiple other strands of law—public and private, international and domestic, hard and soft—are brought to the fore. Taking such a perspective helps to better understand the everyday practices of humanitarian assistance, including the strategic priorities of humanitarian actors, and the legal obstacles they face.

Keywords Humanitarian assistance · International humanitarian law · International disaster law · Disasters · Armed conflict · Qualitative

---

D. Matyas (✉)
Faculty of Law, University of New Brunswick, Fredericton, Canada
e-mail: david.matyas@unb.ca

© T.M.C. ASSER PRESS and the authors 2025
H. Krieger et al. (eds.), *Yearbook of International Humanitarian Law, Volume 26 (2023)*,
Yearbook of International Humanitarian Law 26,
https://doi.org/10.1007/978-94-6265-663-5_1

1.1 Introduction

Humanitarian needs represent a longstanding, diverse and growing set of challenges. The United Nations Office for the Coordination of Humanitarian Affairs (OCHA) estimated that in 2024, 299 million individuals would need humanitarian assistance,[1] up from the 62 million people in need in 2012.[2] These numbers reflect compounding challenges such as the increasing frequency, intensity, spatial extent and duration of weather and extreme events,[3] and the entrenchment of international and non-international armed conflicts worldwide.[4]

For humanitarian actors[5] navigating these contexts, theirs is an "espace humanitaire"[6] or "humanitarian space",[7] shaped by a "spectrum of political, institutional, economic and social"[8] as well as military and pragmatic considerations.[9] Among these, legal considerations are of central importance. Humanitarians may look to law to answer questions such as "what is permissible aid", "who is an authorized humanitarian", "what determines access to an affected context", and "who can claim humanitarian protections and immunities". Though law is not the exclusive force framing humanitarian assistance, humanitarian actors face numerous issues with decidedly legal characteristics and on which a legal perspective offers unique insights.

To date, the importance of law in shaping humanitarian assistance has featured in a rich legal literature, prominent in journals such as *The International Review of the Red Cross, The Journal of International Humanitarian Legal Studies*, the *Yearbook of International Disaster Law* and the *Yearbook of International Humanitarian Law*, with articles considering core questions such as the relationship between international human rights and relief,[10] the consent requirement for humanitarian assistance,[11] the role of different United Nations organs in shaping assistance,[12] and possible clashes between relief, sovereignty,[13] and territorial control.[14]

---

[1] OCHA 2023, p. 4.

[2] OCHA 2020, p. 66.

[3] IPCC 2012, p. 111.

[4] OCHA 2020, pp. 8–9.

[5] By humanitarians, I variously discuss humanitarian individuals and humanitarian organizations. As detailed further below, my focus is on non-state actors involved in the provision of humanitarian assistance.

[6] Brauman 1996, p. 43.

[7] See e.g., Collinson and Elhaway 2012; Herman 2015, p. 29; Thürer 2007; Lohne and Bergtora Sandvik 2017, p. 5; Hilhorst and Jansen 2010.

[8] Herman 2015, p. 30.

[9] Collinson and Elhaway 2012, p. 2.

[10] Creta 2012; Hesselman 2018, p. 201; Barber 2009.

[11] Ryngaert 2013; Sivakumaran 2015; Helton 1992.

[12] Zimmermann 2017; Zwitter 2011; Barber 2020.

[13] Kuijt 2015.

[14] Gal 2017.

1 Humanitarians and Their Law(s): A Comprehensive Inquiry

Amidst these studies and perspectives, a question that has received less treatment is *what law* or *areas of law* should be canvassed to understand the everyday work of humanitarian actors? Across the varied contexts in which humanitarians engage, is public international law—as traditionally advanced[15]—the most appropriate field for this inquiry? Could a broader consideration of additional areas of law provide distinct insights into how humanitarian assistance is facilitated and constrained?

In response, this chapter's central contribution is to lay out the broader field of laws as they appear to humanitarian practitioners. The chapter thus represents a reconstruction of the fields of law from the perspective of humanitarian practitioners. From this viewpoint, prominent areas of public international law—such as international humanitarian law (IHL)—become relativized, and multiple other strands of law—public and private, international and domestic, hard and soft—are brought to the fore. Such a comprehensive perspective is required, I argue, to understand the everyday practices of humanitarian assistance, including the strategic priorities of humanitarian actors, and the legal obstacles they face. Additionally, this chapter makes a methodological contribution by exploring this reconstructed field through a mixed-method approach,[16] combining doctrinal analysis with qualitative empirical analysis. It draws on 22 semi-structured interviews—variously conducted in-person in Nairobi, Kenya and remotely with individuals in East and Central Africa, the Middle East, the UK, and Europe—in order to put humanitarian practitioner perspectives in conversation with black letter laws.[17]

---

[15] The preponderance of the legal scholarship on humanitarian assistance is explored through the lens of public international law. However, there is some scholarship which looks more closely at domestic laws in humanitarian assistance, particularly within the international disaster law scholarship (for instance Fisher 2007 and Zwitter et al. 2015). More programmatically, the IFRC's Disaster Law program has focussed extensively on operationalizing international disaster law in domestic statutes (IFRC 2022), as discussed further below.

[16] Some important existing socio-legal studies of humanitarian assistance with an empirical approach to the relationship between humanitarian assistance and law include Sutton 2020 and 2021.

[17] Interviewees were selected based on a "snowball sampling" approach (Kirchherr and Charles 2018). They were humanitarian actors from non-governmental organizations (13 interviews), international organizations (7 interviews), and government (1 donor interview and 1 state receiving humanitarian assistance), predominantly occupying the roles of country directors and regional humanitarian directors within their organizations. Initial contacts acted as "gatekeepers" (Hammersley and Atkinson 2007, pp. 49–53) for identifying other individuals from whom the snowball sampling proceeded. Relying on a snowball sampling shaped the types of individuals interviewed, their geographic locations, and the type of humanitarian responses in which they were involved. For instance, at the time of interview, all respondents were international staff members. While some interviewees drew on experiences from earlier in their careers when they were employed as national staff, a larger study could valuably delve more explicitly into the distinct perspectives of national staff (see for instance James 2020). Further, at the time on interview, respondents were based in the above-noted regions, and not in other important humanitarian contexts—like Asia, Latin America, or the Caribbean, for instance. That said, the mobility of many interviewees over their careers meant that they were able to share experiences from times working in other regions. Those interviewed had also been active in a variety of different humanitarian contexts—including disasters, armed conflicts, and work with refugees and internally displaced persons. The mobility of those interviewed thus also meant that several of them had worked in a variety of these contexts over their

Notably, this study focuses on the work of "auxiliary", non-state humanitarian actors, rather than the laws of humanitarian assistance at large. In the face of humanitarian shocks, the affected state—its national emergency and health authorities, military, etc.—has the primary obligation to provide relief under public international law.[18] This study focuses on the humanitarian actors who come next—those who provide relief when affected states are unable (or unwilling) to do so. The actors of interest thus include prominent non-governmental organizations and international organizations in the humanitarian cluster system, along with other non-state assistance-providing actors, such as private corporations, diasporas, and local civil society organizations. The humanitarian assistance provided directly by foreign states is not considered. Contextually, this study considers these actors in the diversity of environments in which they provide assistance, looking beyond armed conflicts to also consider humanitarian situations such as disasters and refugee contexts.

The chapter first considers the public international laws of humanitarian assistance that are the traditional starting and focal point for legal inquiries into humanitarian assistance (Sect. 1.1). Following from how respondent humanitarian actors identify the areas of laws most applicable to them, Sect. 1.2 then reconstructs the field of laws from the perspective of humanitarian practitioners. It considers a comprehensive field of laws applicable to humanitarian assistance which additionally includes domestic public laws, private laws, and forms of self-governance. Finally, Sect. 1.3 concludes by exploring how a comprehensive view can provide insights for more effective humanitarian assistance.

---

careers. Importantly, the role of those individuals interviewed within their organizations would also have shaped the types of legal issues they encountered, and responses may have been different had individuals with different roles in their organizations—such as general counsels—been interviewed. Such interviews, however, were beyond the scope of this study. Interviewees gave their consent to be quoted directly, paraphrased, and/or have information from the interview referred to—and the information in this chapter is presented according to that consent.

[18] There are numerous international law sources that establish this position. See e.g. Geneva Convention Relative to the Protection of Civilians in Time of War, opened for signature 12 August 1949, 75 UNTS 287 (entered into force 21 October 1950) (Geneva Convention IV), Article 3; International Covenant on Economic, Social and Cultural Rights, opened for signature 16 December 1966, UNTS 993 p. 3 (entered into force 3 January 1976) (ICESCR), Articles 6, 9; UN General Assembly (1991) Resolution 46/182, UN Doc. A/RES/46/182, Guiding Principle 4; Tampere Convention on the Provision of Telecommunication Resources for Disaster Mitigation and Relief Operations, opened for signature 18 June 1998, 2296 UNTS 5 (entered into force 8 January 2005), Article 4; African Union Convention for the Protection and Assistance of Internally Displaced Persons in Africa, opened for signatures 23 October 2009, UNTS 3014 (entered into force 6 December 2012) (Kampala Convention), Article 5(1); International Law Commission (2016) Draft Articles on the Protection of Persons in the Event of Disasters, with Commentaries, UN Doc. A/71/10, Article 10; Constitution of the World Health Organization, opened for signatures 22 July 1946, UNTS 14, 185 (entered into force 7 April 1948), Article 21. For additional commentary see Valencia-Ospina E (2010) Third Report on the Protection of Persons in the Event of Disasters, UN Doc. A/CN/4/629, para 76; Sivakumaran 2015, pp. 502, 515–516; Akande and Gillard 2016a, p. 11; ICRC 1987, para 4871.

1.2 The Traditional International Legal Starting Point

To start our inquiry into the applicable laws of humanitarian assistance let us begin with a thought experiment.

> Imagine a field base in eastern Niger, where an Australian national is employed as country director for a major international humanitarian organization. The organization has been in Niger for a decade and has a longstanding Memorandum of Understanding with the Government regarding the scope of their work in the country. More recently, there has been an armed conflict in the region with a non-state armed group that is proscribed as a terrorist organization by the U.S. Government.

> Now, imagine a flood occurs in an area which is home to a population of internally displaced persons, controlled by that non-state armed group, and designated as a "proscribed area" by the Government of Australia.

> To provide assistance, the country director will deliver a grant contracted with a public United States donor. To enter the area, she will have to negotiate access with the non-state armed group and pay a transit fee. Additionally, Niger has declared a State of Emergency which includes a requirement that humanitarian actors wishing to travel to that area go with an armed escort.

What laws shape how this humanitarian actor works? Are these questions of international law? Domestic law? Public law? Private law? We will return to this thought experiment throughout this chapter, but for now, let us consider what *public international law* can say about this situation, the traditional area of law relied upon for such an inquiry. This section begins by looking at the areas of public international law with bearing on humanitarian assistance before challenging whether public international law is the most appropriate domain for this inquiry.

1.2.1 Areas of International Law with Bearing on Humanitarian Assistance

In public international law, there is no overarching humanitarian assistance convention. Instead, an array of sources and areas of law shape the legal landscape navigated by humanitarians.

To begin, from our hypothetical fact pattern above, we know that there is an armed conflict, which tells us that we are in the sphere of international humanitarian law (IHL). We also know that the armed conflict is of a non-international character, engaging Article 3 Common to the Geneva Conventions and Protocol II Additional to the Geneva Conventions.[19] Article 3(2) Common to the Geneva Conventions, says that "[a]n impartial humanitarian body, such as the International Committee of the Red Cross, may offer its services to the Parties to the conflict."[20] Article 18 of Protocol II Additional to Geneva Conventions provides more detailed information about relief

---

[19] Indeed, Niger ratified APII in 1979 (see ICRC-IHL Databases).

[20] Geneva Convention IV, above n 28, Article 3(2).

societies and relief actions, such as offers of assistance, the character and content of assistance, and who may consent to that relief.[21] Further, customary international law contains rules related to access for humanitarian relief to civilians in need[22] and the freedom of movement of humanitarian relief personnel.[23] IHL can thus guide us through several issues in our thought experiment such as the requirement of consent to provide relief, the obligation of Niger to allow and facilitate assistance, as well as Niger's right to establish checks and controls over that assistance (often referred to as "technical arrangements").

Going beyond the armed conflict, we also know with the flood, and the flood response, that we may simultaneously be in the sphere of international disaster law (IDL—also at times referred to as international disaster response law (IDRL)). Treaty law here is less developed and more "scattered" than in IHL[24] and, where it does exist, it is narrower (such as being focussing on telecommunications in disasters[25]). But we do have a very good subsidiary source in the International Law Commission's *Draft Articles on the Protection of Persons in the Event of Disasters.*[26]

Furthermore, broader areas of international law, such as international human rights law (IHRL), can be applicable in the context of our thought experiment—such as general human rights related to the protection of life, the provision of food, health, and shelter.[27] These rights are derived from sources such as the ICESCR[28] and the ICCPR.[29] Additionally, there are human rights instruments with provisions focussed more explicitly on humanitarian assistance. These include the *Convention on the*

---

[21] Protocol Additional to the Geneva Conventions of 12 August 1949, and relating to the Protection of Victims of Non-International Armed Conflicts, opened for signature 8 June 1977, 1125 UNTS 609 (entered into force December 1978) (Additional Protocol II), Article 18.

[22] ICRC Rule 55.

[23] ICRC Rule 56.

[24] Fisher 2007, p. 353. See also Nakjavani Bookmiller 2016; Cubie 2022.

[25] Tampere Convention, above n 28.

[26] International Law Commission (2016) Draft Articles on the Protection of Persons in the Event of Disasters, with Commentaries, UN Doc. A/71/10.

[27] The Inter-Agency Standing Committee, for instance, identifies four groups of international human rights with relevance for the protection of persons in the event of disasters: (1) rights related to the protection of life; security and physical integrity of the person; and family ties, (2) rights related to the provision of food; health; shelter; and education, (3) rights related to housing, land and property, livelihoods and secondary and higher education, and (4) rights related to documentation; movement; re-establishment of family ties; expression and opinion; and elections (IASC 2011); see also Cubie 2019, pp. 158–173.

[28] International Covenant on Economic, Social and Cultural Rights, opened for signature 16 December 1966, UNTS 993, p. 3 (entered into force 3 January 1976) (ICESCR).

[29] International Covenant on Civil and Political Rights, opened for signature 16 December 1966, UNTS 999, p. 171 (entered into force 23 March 1977) (ICCPR).

Rights of the Child,[30] the *Convention on the Rights of Persons with Disabilities*,[31] and the *African Charter on the Rights and Welfare of the Child*.[32]

Given the diverse legal domains relevant to humanitarian assistance, there is considerable scope for overlap, interaction, and potential contradiction between these different public international law regimes.

Though IHL may have once been considered the "default" law of humanitarian assistance, this position has changed[33] towards one that views legal domains of humanitarian assistance more broadly and contends with intersections such as IHL and IDL—such as in the above thought experiment—where disasters and conflicts overlap.[34]

Article 18 of the ILC's *Draft Articles*, accounts for this interaction stating that "the present draft articles do not apply to the extent that the response to a disaster is governed by the rules of international humanitarian law."[35] Article 18 accordingly holds that while IHL is the *lex specialis* in the event of overlap, the Draft Articles can apply to the extent that the legal issues they raise, are not already covered by IHL.[36] IDL can thus offer specificity where IHL is silent (or overly general) on issues such as the initiation of assistance, the entry of goods and equipment, or professional standards and work permits related to relief personnel.[37] In our thought experiment, IDL may thus provide useful specificity regarding the issuance of work permits or customs clearance for required goods and equipment.[38]

Similarly, IHL and IHRL are generally viewed in the context of humanitarian assistance as "complementary and not mutually exclusive."[39] As stated by the ICJ in *Wall* advisory opinion, "the protection offered by human rights conventions does not cease in case of armed conflicts".[40] The question for humanitarians, accordingly, is not "*whether* human rights law is indeed directly applicable in times of armed conflicts, but *how* this law is applicable in relation to international humanitarian

---

[30] Convention on the Rights of the Child, opened for signature 20 November 1989, UNTS 1577, p. 3 (entered into force 2 September 1990), Article 22(1).

[31] Convention on the Rights of Persons with Disabilities, opened for signature 13 December 2006, UNTS 2515, p. 3 (entered into force 2 May 2008), Article 11.

[32] African Charter on the Rights and Welfare of the Child, opened for signature 11 July 1990 CAB/LEG/24.9/49 (entered into force 29 November 1999), Article 23(1).

[33] See e.g., Lohne and Bergtora Sandvik 2017, pp. 5, 12, 14, 19.

[34] Kuijt 2014, p. 65.

[35] International Law Commission (2016) Draft Articles on the Protection of Persons in the Event of Disasters, with Commentaries, UN Doc. A/71/10, Article 18.

[36] International Law Commission (2016) Draft Articles on the Protection of Persons in the Event of Disasters, with Commentaries, UN Doc. A/71/10, Article 18, para 9.

[37] Gavshon 2009, pp. 258–260; See also Williams and Simm 2018, pp. 54–55.

[38] International Law Commission (2016) Draft Articles on the Protection of Persons in the Event of Disasters, with Commentaries, UN Doc. A/71/10, Articles 15(1)(a) and 15(1)(b).

[39] Schwendimann 2011, p. 1003.

[40] ICJ Legal Consequences of the Constriction of a Wall in the Occupied Palestinian Territory, Advisory Opinion, 9 July 2004, [2004] ICJ Rep 136, para 106. See also ICJ Legality of the Threat of Use of Nuclear Weapons, Advisory Opinion, 8 July 1996, [1996] ICJ Rep 226, para 25.

law."[41] IHRL can, for instance, assist in interpreting IHL provisions and help answer questions such as what denials of consent to provide humanitarian assistance might be viewed as arbitrary, and what forms of relief are legitimate under the cover of IHL.[42]

Beyond these multilateral treaties, there are also regional and bilateral treaties that may be relevant to our thought experiment. In this case, the existence of internally displaced persons means that we might look to the African Union Convention for the Protection and Assistance of Internally Displaced Persons in Africa (Kampala Convention). Niger ratified the Kampala Convention in 2012, being the first country in Africa to incorporate it into their domestic law in 2018.[43] It contains provisions on humanitarian issues such as on allowing and facilitating humanitarian assistance[44] as well as obligations relating to humanitarian agencies more generally.[45] In other contexts, there may similarly be bilateral assistance agreements and peace agreements with relevant provisions on humanitarian assistance.[46]

Finally, to qualify as a humanitarian in this context, hard and soft norms of international law suggest that the Country Director in our earlier thought experiment may[47] need to adhere to the humanitarian principles of humanity, impartiality, neutrality, and independence.[48] Humanity, described as the "essential principle"[49] of humanitarian assistance, is often expressed practically as the provision of assistance to protect life and health, alleviate suffering, and safeguard human dignity.[50] Impartiality refers to humanitarian action "carried out on the basis of need alone, giving priority to the most urgent cases of distress and making no distinctions on the basis of nationality, race, gender, religious belief, class or political opinions."[51] Neutrality, the third humanitarian principle, is about not taking sides in hostilities or other controversies.[52] Finally, independence describes humanitarian actors' freedom from

---

[41] Kuijt 2014, p. 74.

[42] Akande and Gillard 2016b, pp. 504–505.

[43] UNHCR 2018.

[44] Kampala Convention, above n 28, Articles 3(1)(J) and 5(7).

[45] Kampala Convention, above n 28, Article 6.

[46] See for instance Intergovernmental Authority on Development (2018) Revitalised Agreement on the Resolution of the Conflict in the Republic of South Sudan (R-ARCSS). https://www.peaceagreements.org/viewmasterdocument/2112. Accessed 9 December 2023, Chap. 3.

[47] I intentionally use the word "may" here given works by authors such as Weller 1997 and Sharpe 2023 on the relativity of humanitarian principles, a position discussed in further detail below.

[48] See e.g. OCHA 2012; Kampala Convention, above n 28, Article 6(3); UN General Assembly (2020) Resolution 75/127, UN Doc. A/RES/75/127, p. 1; UN General Assembly (2021) Agenda Item 75(a), UN Doc. A/76/L.23, p. 1.

[49] Pictet 1979, p. 135.

[50] OCHA 2012; ICRC 2016a; on human dignity see ICTY, *Prosecutor v Aleksoveski*, Judgment, 25 June 1999, Case No. IT-95-14/1-T, T.Ch., para 49; Sphere 2018, p. 28; ICJ, *Military and Paramilitary Activities in and against Nicaragua (Nicaragua v United States of America)*, Judgment, 27 June 1986, [1986], ICJ Rep 392, paras 242–243.

[51] See e.g. OCHA 2012; see also ICRC 2016a, 2021, para 1343.

[52] OCHA 2012.

1 Humanitarians and Their Law(s): A Comprehensive Inquiry

the influence of actors such as states and donors.[53] In our thought experiment, the principle of neutrality may conflict with the use of an armed escort provided by one Party to the conflict, or the payment of a transit fee to another, while the principle of independence could clash with elements of the US donor contract.

1.2.2 Questioning the Traditional Starting Point

As discussed in the previous sub-section, public international laws provide key insights into why humanitarian assistance unfolds as it does, and pathways for it to occur more smoothly. Generally, public international laws offer insight into the relationship between humanitarians and states, including the obligations owed by states to humanitarian actors, and those of humanitarian actors towards states. But, in the everyday legal lives of humanitarian actors, are these the types of issues of central importance to humanitarian actors? Are there questions that public international law fails to pose about humanitarian assistance? What other everyday legal issues exist for humanitarian actors outside the scope of public international law? Thinking back to our thought experiment, this sub-section points to the need for a more comprehensive reconstruction of the fields of humanitarian assistance law from the perspective of humanitarian practitioners.[54] Here, I begin bringing in the perspectives of the humanitarians interviewed as part of this study.

To begin, the influence of public international laws are not of consistent importance—or consistent *perceived* importance—across different humanitarian contexts. One respondent went so far as to say, "I don't know if anyone in the access field will say that IHL is useful"[55] while another suggested, that areas of international law such as IHL might be "at best an argument"[56] for humanitarian practitioners. In the context of humanitarian negotiation, Sutton similarly describes "a general scepticism of law's relevance to frontline humanitarian negotiations."[57]

---

[53] See e.g. OCHA 2012; see also ICRC 2016a.

[54] It is important to acknowledge that the varied perspectives of different actors can influence one another and are in no ways watertight compartments. In instances where a state's perspective privileges international law, for instance, it can influence how they interact with humanitarian actors and, by extension, influence humanitarian perceptions about the relative importance of international law. The *perspective* of the actors involved in humanitarian assistance is thus a key consideration in determining the relative importance of different areas of law in shaping humanitarian assistance.

[55] NGO3.

[56] IGO1.

[57] Sutton 2023, p. 109.

While such perspectives from practitioners must be considered alongside instances where public international laws *do* provide vital protections, such as prohibitions on targeting, and general protections of, civilians, they demonstrate an apprehension amongst some humanitarians of the full operational value of public international laws across different humanitarian contexts. Indeed for many other respondents, international law was recognized as an important form of normative order, but only as one sitting alongside others.

Next, a focus on international law can privilege certain types of humanitarians over others. The ICRC, for instance, is named explicitly in several IHL treaties.[58] These references do not exclude other relief organizations from providing assistance— indeed the 1987 Commentary to APII notes that the Red Cross "does not have a monopoly on humanitarian activities".[59] However, as noted in the 1952 Commentary to GCI, the ICRC is not only listed by virtue of its unique status, but also "as an example of what is meant by an "impartial humanitarian organization.""[60] The 2016 Commentary to GCI further adds "[f]or the drafters of the Conventions, the ICRC *epitomizes the essential characteristics of* an impartial humanitarian organization."[61] Public international law thus seems to view humanitarians as *ICRC-approximating* actors. This perception suggests that all humanitarians should work in ways that are near the benchmark set by the characteristics of the ICRC. However, there are also non-ICRC approximating humanitarians operating in this context—such as domestic civil society actors, private contractors, or ideologically partial humanitarians—who may be overlooked when focussing on ICRC-approximating actors.

Furthermore, a focus on ICRC-approximating humanitarians may make it seem as though rules applicable to the Red Cross are equally applicable to other humanitarian actors. For instance, whereas the Red Cross is "constitutionally obliged to comply" with the humanitarian principles[62] based on its founding charter and by-laws,[63] this is not necessarily true of other humanitarian actors, as the below analysis shows. Ultimately, the relevance of international law to different actors is conditioned by factors such as context, the law applicable in that context, the type of actors operating in that context, and the strength of domestic laws. As one respondent noted,

> there was never a situation clearer to me than Syria on how useful it was not to be bound by international law. The ICRC and the UN were tied to Damascus. It was almost torturous to watch. [...] While at the same time, [an NGO] started [...] facilities [in X] because the ICRC couldn't make it there.[64]

---

[58] See for instance Protocol Additional to the Geneva Convention of 12 August 1949, and relating to the Protection of Victims of International Armed Conflicts, opened for signature 8 June 1977, 1125 UNTS 3 (entered into force December 1978 (Additional Protocol 1) Article 81; Additional Protocol II, above n 31, Article 18.

[59] ICRC 1987, para 4872.

[60] ICRC 1952, p. 108.

[61] ICRC 2016b, para 1153 (my emphasis).

[62] Weller 1997, p. 449.

[63] Weller 1997, p. 444; See also Sharpe 2023.

[64] NGO1.

1 Humanitarians and Their Law(s): A Comprehensive Inquiry

Here the respondent is describing a situation, where the UN and ICRC actors would not operate without the consent of the Assad regime over concerns related to sovereignty and territorial integrity, whereas other international humanitarians felt more able to operate in opposition-controlled areas in the north of Syria in the absence of that consent.[65] This perspective reinforces how the relevance of different legal sources in humanitarian assistance is both *contextual* and *relative*.

Additionally, a focus on international law can over-emphasize legal issues with international characteristics. For instance, as one respondent noted, "most of the literature is […] concerned with the question of access from a third state without the consent of the concerned state. […] But in Niger it was not at all that question which was at stake".[66] The consent requirement is indeed a heavily canvassed question in the scholarship on the laws of humanitarian assistance.[67] And, while the consent requirement is a question that international law is particularly well-suited to address, it is also a rare occurrence in humanitarian assistance. For instance, a 2010 study of 77 sudden-onset disasters found that only 19 had some degree of actual or threatened assistance refusal, or delayed acceptance, and of those, eight had refused assistance from only one to two sources, and a mere two had refused assistance from more than two sources.[68] This data thus highlights how denials of consent are infrequent, and where they do occur, are usually partial—only applying to a limited set of actors. Another respondent elaborated, "I have been in a situation of minor [access] issues, [but] I wouldn't say I've been in a situation where there are no NGOs in the country and there was no consent totally"[69] while another stated, "I had a very rare occasion in which the government really imposes [a] "no". They are [instead] imposing a number of elements that are making [it] very difficult [for you] to proceed and to progress".[70]

Finally, not all humanitarian legal opportunities and constraints are visible from the perspective of public international law. Domestic laws may undercut humanitarian goals in ways only superficially evident through international law. As one respondent shared,

> we keep looking very much at […] the traditional humanitarian complexity of the armed conflict [ ] But what is amazing is [this] new area in which we are completely unprepared. And the way we were negotiating with the border guards between Turkey and Greece during the push for migrants from Turkey to Greece, or at the border between Northern Macedonia and Hungary […] are having huge implications from a human right as well as from a

---

[65] This position is discussed in the Oxford Guidance, which notes that "Private actors [such as non-governmental organizations] are not directly bound by these rules [of public international law on sovereignty and territorial integrity] and thus humanitarian relief operations they conduct without the consent of the relevant states will not necessarily be a violation of *international law*." Akande and Gillard 2016a, pp. 51–52; Ryngaert makes a similar argument, Ryngaert 2013, pp. 12–13.

[66] IGO7.

[67] Ryngaert 2013; Sivakumaran 2015; Helton 1992.

[68] Nelson 2010, pp. 391–392.

[69] NGO8.

[70] IGO3.

humanitarian point of view. But the humanitarian organizations, from a [legal] point of view, are unprepared.[71]

As the humanitarian field expands and grapples with emerging issues such as migration and counterterrorism, questions arise which demand an expanded view of the diversity of laws relevant to contemporary humanitarian concerns. The following section continues this expanded inquiry.

1.3 Reconstructing the Field from the Perspective of Humanitarian Practitioners: Towards A Comprehensive Inquiry

By a comprehensive inquiry into the laws of humanitarian assistance, I mean a more holistic approach; one that moves beyond public international law to additionally consider the impacts of areas such as domestic law, private law, and soft law.

International lawyers are, of course, aware of the interplay between international and domestic laws. But in taking an international legal perspective, there is a tendency to ask particular questions of domestic law—such as "have the laws of humanitarian assistance been incorporated into domestic law?" or "how are domestic laws contributing to customary rules of humanitarian assistance?" While these are valuable inquiries, they are not the ones considered here. A comprehensive inquiry analyses instead, how other areas of law *independently* shape humanitarian assistance. It recognizes that other areas of law ask *different* questions of humanitarians and ones that do not necessarily overlap with public international law. Further, it acknowledges that there can be tensions and even clashes of norms between different regimes.

Such a comprehensive view is not an entirely aberrant approach, considering how law shapes humanitarian assistance. Comprehensive views have been both *implicitly* relied on by some authors working on humanitarian assistance and even referenced more *explicitly* by others. Modirzadeh and Lewis' work on humanitarian assistance and counterterrorism, for instance, considers how public international laws, domestic statutes, private laws, and administrative regulations bear on humanitarian assistance in the domain of counterterrorism,[72] thus implicitly employing a comprehensive view of the laws of humanitarian assistance. Similarly, Mackintosh looks at how US domestic counterterrorism legislation, UNSC sanction regimes, and donor contracts impact MSF's humanitarian operations and operational neutrality.[73] Wynn-Pope et al. rely on an implicit comprehensive view in discussing the intersection of Australian counterterrorism laws with the humanitarian principles.[74] In the context of rescues at sea in the Mediterranean, several authors employ implicitly comprehensive views

---

[71] IGO4.

[72] Lewis and Modirzadeh 2021; Modirzadeh et al. 2011; Modirzadeh and Lewis 2021, pp. 408–410.

[73] Mackintosh 2011.

[74] Wynn-Pope et al. 2016.

by commenting on overlapping domestic and international legal regimes,[75] whereas in the context of the Sahel, Ferraro illustrates how international legal norms rub up against domestic states of emergency and regulations which demand that humanitarians use armed escorts.[76] Fisher, probing IHL and IDL, also delves into the role of domestic regulations in shaping humanitarian assistance in the context of disasters.[77]

More explicitly, several authors have pointed to a comprehensive approach. Sandvik, for instance, describes how "the practice of [humanitarian actors] is increasingly taking place within a thickening framework of soft law […], host state regulations, and contractual agreements".[78] Cubie, building on Koh's theory of transnational legal process, describes the importance of a legal inquiry into humanitarian assistance being attentive to "binding and non-binding, formal and informal, humanitarian norms."[79] Zwitter, Lamont, Heintze and Herman's edited collection also provides case studies showcasing the interaction of international, regional, and domestic legal regimes.[80]

These implicit and explicit allusions to a comprehensive approach underscore the value of reconstructing the field of laws from the perspective of humanitarian practitioners. Attentiveness to a broader range of sources can highlight how other norms shape the everyday legal lives of humanitarians. These other sources can cover areas on humanitarian assistance upon which international law is silent, such as tax exemptions or domestic incorporation. They may also be more detailed or specific than more broadly worded international laws. Further, expanding our range of sources can expose clashes between different regimes—such as between foreign counterterrorism laws and international humanitarian law.

To that effect, the following sub-sections explore selected areas of law within such a comprehensive framework. It begins with domestic law—considering both *in situ* domestic laws and laws from foreign states other than those directly affected—before considering private law—in particular host country agreements and donor contracts—and finally self-governance—where humanitarians act as norm-makers. This section is not intended as an exhaustive treatment of all the laws influencing humanitarian assistance. For instance, the agreements and covenants of non-state

---

[75] Pasquetti et al. 2019; Mégret 2021; Mann 2020.

[76] Ferraro 2022.

[77] Fisher 2007.

[78] Bergtora Sandvik 2018, p. 361; see also Lohne and Bergtora Sandvik 2017, pp. 10–11.

[79] Cubie 2019, p. 128.

[80] Zwitter et al. 2015.

16 D. Matyas

armed groups are not discussed in-depth here.[81] Instead, it provides a survey of several prominent areas of law shaping the humanitarian space.

1.3.1 Domestic Public Laws

Beyond public international law, a first essential area to engage in a comprehensive understanding of the laws of humanitarian assistance is domestic law. Domestic laws implicate humanitarians in the territories in which they operate. They also often reach across borders from states other than these operational contexts, as with counterterrorism or immigration laws.

If "international law not only percolates down from the international to the domestic sphere, but ...also bubbles up",[82] then domestic laws are essential examples of state practice, contributing to custom and shaping the international law of humanitarian assistance.[83] Further, in humanitarian contexts, international treaty law is also translated into domestic law. As one respondent noted,

> IHL means nothing if there is no domestic law that acknowledged that. [With] the Kampala Convention, for instance, refugee law means nothing if there is no domestication law that basically makes it a law for the country itself. That's where we have to basically work, I think, on complementarities between these different dimensions and sets of laws.[84]

While such statement should be tempered by the relationship between public international law and domestic law on the issue of the reception of customary international law, domestic laws may importantly provide context and specificity not found in general provisions of the international treaty. Further, the absence of a domesticated law may be indicative of the limited reach of the international covenant[85]—especially so in "dualist" states where international treaty law must be incorporated into domestic law before it is applicable in that state.

Beyond state practice and domesticated international law, though, domestic law also shapes humanitarian assistance of its own right. Indeed, UN General Assembly

---

[81] For instance, peace agreements signed by non-state armed groups such as the Revitalised Agreement on the Resolution of the Conflict in the Republic of South Sudan (R-ARCSS) (12 September 2018) Access at: https://docs.pca-cpa.org/2016/02/South-Sudan-Peace-Agreement-Sep tember-2018.pdf [Last Accessed: 12/06/2023] and Jeddah Declaration of Commitment to Protect the Civilians of Sudan, Access at: https://www.state.gov/jeddah-declaration-of-commitment-to-pro tect-the-civilians-of-sudan/ [Last Accessed: 12/06/2023] as well as covenants made between non-state armed groups and international organizations (such as Operation Lifeline Sudan Agreement on Ground Rules—SPLM 1996).

[82] Roberts 2011, p. 69.

[83] International Law Commission (2018) Draft Conclusions on Identification of Customary International Law, with Commentaries, UN Doc. A/73/10, Conclusion 5. See also Schwartz 2015, p. 616; Provost 2008, p. 171.

[84] DON1.

[85] The Kampala Convention, for instance, contains a requirement to incorporate the Convention's obligations on assistance to IDPs into domestic law (Kampala Convention, above n 28, Article 2(a)). On the extent of the domestication of the Kampala Convention, see ICRC 2020, p. 19.

Resolution 46/182 states that international cooperation "should be provided in accordance with international and *national* laws",[86] underscoring the expectation that humanitarian actors are not solely governed by public international law. The Kampala Convention contains a similar provision.[87]

For humanitarian actors, attentiveness to domestic law sources helps situate the laws of humanitarian assistance. Pasquetti et al., for instance, note, although "the humanitarian machine is often thought of as a structure that acts on a global scale, local contexts [...] are increasingly recognized as equally important for the law and politics of [assistance]".[88] Far from emanating from a single sovereign command, at the domestic level, humanitarians can face laws steeped in a variety of normative imperatives.

Between different contexts, the domestic laws impacting humanitarians can vary considerably. Some may focus explicitly and exclusively on humanitarians, whereas others may have only limited or incidental impact. Humanitarians may, for instance, face existing statutory laws—such as criminal,[89] counterterrorism,[90] IDL,[91] or immigration laws—administrative laws or regulations—focussed on visas, customs, or organizational registration—or more temporary states of emergency or discretionary executive orders—addressing matters such as armed escorts, privacy, or the movement of money. Additionally, Lohne and Sandvik describe a "shift towards court-ordered humanitarian practice",[92] highlighting case law as an increasingly important domestic source of law relevant to humanitarians. Relevant public law cases cover

---

[86] UN General Assembly (1991) Resolution 46/182, UN Doc. A/RES/46/182, para 5 (my emphasis).

[87] Kampala Convention, above n 28, Article 6(1).

[88] Pasquetti et al. 2019, p. 293; see also the influence of domestic and regional laws on humanitarian actors in the context of civil society search and rescue at sea, Irrera 2019, p. 286.

[89] See e.g. *Criminal Code Act 1995* (Australia), Divisions, 71, 80.1AA, 101.2, 102(5), 102.6, 102.8, 119.3, 119.4.

[90] See e.g. *Terrorism Act 2000*, c. 11 (United Kingdom); *Counter-Terrorism and Border Security Act 2019*, c. 3 (United Kingdom); 18 U.S. Code § 2339A *Providing Material Support to Terrorists* (United States).

[91] See IFRC 2019, pp. 92–100.

[92] Lohne and Bergtora Sandvik 2017, p. 17; see also Bergtora Sandvik 2018.

topics such as material assistance by humanitarians to terrorists,[93] criminal liability when assisting irregular migrants,[94] and tax law.[95]

Across these different areas of domestic law, we discern two distinct jurisdictions with bearing on humanitarian assistance. The domestic laws of the country in which the humanitarian assistance is occurring (*in situ* domestic laws) and those of outside states whose laws nevertheless reach humanitarians in their operational contexts (laws of states other than those directly affected). These two jurisdictions are discussed in turn.

1.3.1.1 *In Situ* Domestic Law

Often, the domestic laws of the country in which humanitarians engage can determine their ability to provide relief. Those states in which humanitarians operate have, of course, the competence under international law to enact and enforce laws within their territories.[96] *In situ*, humanitarians can thus face existing laws that directly affect humanitarian assistance but whose purpose is actually *not* directly related to humanitarian assistance—such as immigration, employment, or banking laws. They may also face laws that *are* tailored to humanitarian situations—such as pro-active disaster laws. The International Federation of the Red Cross has been a trailblazer here—their Disaster Law programme works with vulnerable countries to develop and reinforce pro-active domestic disaster laws.[97] Humanitarians can be impacted by executive orders and states of emergency (such as the one in our thought experiment). Further,

---

[93] See e.g. VSC, *R v Aruran Vinayagamoorthy*, Judgment, 31 March [2010] VSC 148; USCA (2nd Circuit), *United States v Farhane*, Appeal, 4 February 2011, [2011] 634 F.3d 127; USCA (9th Circuit), *Humanitarian Law Project v Mukasey*, Appeal, 10 December 2007, [2007] 552 F.3d 916; USSC, *Holder v Humanitarian Law Project*, Appeal, 21 June 2010, [2010] 561 U.S. 1.; USCA (7th Circuit) *Boim v Holy Land Foundation for Relief and Development*, Appeal, 2 December 2008, [2008] 549 F.3d 685; FCC, *Toronto Coalition to Stop the War v Canada*, Judicial Review, 27 September 2010, [2012] 1 F.C.R. 413; USDC (SDNY) *United States of America ex rel. TZAC, INC., v Norwegian People's Aid a/k/a Norsk Folkehjelp*, Settlement and Dismissal Order, 30 March, 2018, 15 Civ. 4892(GHW), https://charityandsecurity.org/wp-content/uploads/2020/08/NPA-Settlement-Stipulation-Dismissal.pdf. Accessed 11 December 2023.

[94] EWCA *R v Kakaei*, Appeal, 8 April 2021 [2021] EWCA Crim 503; EWHC *Sternaj v Director of Public Prosecutions/Sternaj v Crown Prosecution Service*, Judgement, 12 April 2011, [2011] EWHC 1094 (Admin); EWCA, *R v Bina (Arya)*, Appeal, 11 June 2014, [2014] EWCA Crim 1444; EWCA, *R v Kapoor*, Appeal, 9 Mach 2012, [2012] EWCA Crim 435; SCC, *R v Appulonappa*, Appeal, 27 November 2015, [2015] 2015 SCC 59; ONSC, *R v Abdulle*, Judgment, 23 December 2014, [2014] 2014 ONSC 7455; BCCA, *R v Christhurajah*, Appeal, 18 June 2019, [2019] 2019 BCCA 210; BCCA, *R v Rajaratnam*, Appeal, 18 June 2019, [2019] 2019 BCCA 209; SCC, *B010 v Canada*, Appeal, 27 November 2015, [2015] 2015 SCC 58; CJEU (Grand Chamber), *European Commission v Hungary*, Judgment, 16 November 2021, [2021] Case C-821/19; CJEU (3rd Chamber) *Aulinger v Germany*, Judgment, 9 March 2006, [2006] Case C-371/03.

[95] See e.g. Emon and Hasan 2021, pp. 9–11; TCC, *Godin v The Queen*, Judgment, 12 March 1998, [1998] 2 CTC 2853; FCA, *Brown v Care Canada*, Appeal, 24 May 2000, [2000] 3 CTC 205.

[96] Crawford 2019, p. 440.

[97] See for instance IFRC 2013, 2019, and 2022.

1 Humanitarians and Their Law(s): A Comprehensive Inquiry

they may confront domestic regulatory laws related to legal status, the recognition of foreign medical qualifications, quality standards for imported supplies, coordination requirements, or security provisions.[98] As one respondent noted,

> I think the legal regime of the country where you are operating has the biggest impact on what you are able to do, where you are able to go, and how you are able to [operate]. I have seen that in various contexts and I'm seeing it right now in Ethiopia. For example, the legal regime in terms of the number of international staff you can bring in has an impact on what you are able to do. The legal regime on where your international surge capacity can go has impact on where you are able to work. And then the legal regime on the processes you need to follow for approval of projects has impact on what you are able to do.[99]

In a comprehensive law of humanitarian assistance, domestic law thus cannot be viewed as less important than international law. Often the opposite is true. The humanitarian worker in our thought experiment must thus navigate the Nigerien state of emergency, requiring the use of armed escorts in a designated area—despite its potential conflicts with internal and soft law provisions that prohibit humanitarians from using armed escorts.[100]

The impact of *in situ* domestic law on the provision of assistance, can vary by context and jurisdiction. In some contexts, domestic law can take complete precedence (for instance, one respondent noted how the domestic law regulating assistance "is the only legal regime we have"[101]) while elsewhere it provides specificity over more everyday issues of assistance and access. As another respondent noted "a lot of the actual day-to-day regimes that affect our work is regimes of the host countries in which we work [...] these local regulations, local laws."[102] This variation is understandable given that some countries maintain laws explicitly focussed on humanitarian relief which are complemented by administrative capacity to enforce those laws, while others present weak (or non-existent) laws alongside limited enforcement capacity. Beyond legislation and enforcement capacity, some contexts are also generally more "legalistic" than others, where legal arguments are held as relatively more persuasive. Describing such relative persuasiveness, one respondent noted "I found [Lebanon and Palestine] a lot more litigious. [...] [In interactions with governments, t]he law was discussed a lot more explicitly in the context of Lebanon and Palestine than it was, for example, in South Sudan."[103]

Within certain jurisdictions, the impact of domestic laws can also vary over the course of a humanitarian response. These changes can occur suddenly and repeatedly or involve slow, singular regime shifts. One respondent noted how "South Sudan was famous for this one because almost on a daily basis you would have a new local law that was produced which would somehow constrain access."[104] By contrast, in

---

[98] Fisher 2007, pp. 359–367.

[99] NGO7.

[100] IASC 2013.

[101] NGO5.

[102] NGO8.

[103] NGO2.

[104] NGO2.

Turkey, another respondent described a shift in domestic legal regime in response to an ever-long-term refugee response,

> there was no requirement to have permission [...] in the beginning. Everyone was here, all the INGO's, providing aid. There were not any restrictions, no collaborations with governmental authorities [were needed]. [... E]veryone was expecting that it was going to be a temporary situation and the crisis would be over, and all the organisations will go and will leave the country, but actually it didn't happen. [At last the authorities] told us, sometimes formally sometimes informally, they have to control what has been going on in the country, especially by the international organisations. And then they started to introduce such restrictions day by day.[105]

Beyond the entrenchment of a humanitarian crisis over time, and a state's desire to wield laws to re-assert control in managing that new normal, a domestic legal regime may also shift as the nature of the crisis shifts. For instance, humanitarians providing disaster response in one region of a country may face the onset of an armed conflict in that same locale, and subsequently face changed regulations or emergency laws. Such was the case in the Cabo Delgado province of Mozambique, for instance, where several respondents described a domestic regulatory environment amenable to humanitarians wishing to assist in cyclone responses that became increasingly restrictive in the face of an armed insurgency in that same province.[106]

The impact of domestic law on humanitarian assistance as compared to other types of laws can also vary within a country. There may be areas outside of the central government's control, for instance, where an armed group with effective territorial control views international law as more persuasive than the law of the central authority with whom they are in conflict or who they do not view as legitimate. Describing the familiarity and affinity of one South Sudanese opposition leader to IHL, one respondent noted a "lot of opposition groups rely more on IHL because it gives them a certain power that they don't have from national legislation."[107] Whereas such groups may have limited protections under domestic law, they have rights under IHL, for instance establishing judicial guarantees in penal prosecutions,[108] and protection and care.[109] In such contexts, the choice of which law to prioritize can also play an important role in legitimization—both self-legitimization (by demonstrating, for instance, adherence to international law) and de-legitimization of an opposition group (and discounting the authority of their laws).

Further, domestic laws in operational contexts regularly lead to tensions between the respective governments and humanitarians engaged in their territories. One government representative recalled,

> I had very tough discussion with [the head of an organization]. And [she was] trying to say that they are above domestic, national laws and all those things. I explained to her that you have come in an area where you would like to work in. For that reason, you have also the

---

[105] NGO5.

[106] NGO12, IGO1.

[107] NGO2.

[108] Additional Protocol II, above n 31, Article 6.

[109] Additional Protocol II, above n 31, Article 7.

1 Humanitarians and Their Law(s): A Comprehensive Inquiry

obligation in working together with the authority on the ground. [...] I do believe that I insisted that they should abide by the local laws, rules, and regulations because as actors who are in one area, we should have laws which are, you know, good for all of us.[110]

Whereas humanitarians might view themselves as being unduly constrained by non-humanitarian rules, governments may perceive that humanitarians believe they are "above" domestic law. While such tensions can arise over procedural issues like oversight and reporting, they can also emerge over deep-seated moral questions, with significant operational implications. For instance, in late 2022 and early 2023, the Taliban in Afghanistan imposed bans on Afghan women working for NGOs and the UN. The bans, which constrained the ability of humanitarians to reach women in Afghanistan, also led some organizations to suspend all operations in the country.[111] The UN for instance, at one point asked all 3300 of its Afghan staff (both male and female) to stay home from work over concerns that adhering to the ban would constitute a violation of "basic international humanitarian principles."[112]

In summary, *in situ* domestic laws in operational humanitarian contexts—whether focused on the humanitarians specifically or not—can significantly impact the provision of humanitarian assistance. While these effects vary between contexts, identifying and understanding them is essential if we are to successfully expand our perspective of the laws of humanitarian assistance. These *in situ* domestic laws are not, however, the only domestic laws which shape the provision of humanitarian assistance. As the following sub-section explores, domestic laws of states *other* than those directly affected can also impact the provision of assistance.

1.3.1.2 The Domestic Laws of States Other than Affected States

Humanitarians can be subject to the criminal laws, counterterrorism laws, business or employment laws, financial crime laws, or regulatory laws—just to name a few—of states other than those directly affected by a shock. Having headquarters in an external country, employing nationals of that country, employing residents of that country, or receiving public funds from that country, are all factors that might bring about the cross-border application of the laws of an "external" state, based on, for instance, the extraterritorial prescriptive jurisdiction of those states.[113] In our thought experiment, the fact that our Country Director is an Australian national means that she is potentially subject to the jurisdiction of Australian criminal law prohibitions on Australian citizens entering or remaining in designated areas.[114] The impact of external laws on the provision of assistance can thus be considerable.

---

[110] GOV1.

[111] Latifi 2023.

[112] Associated Press 2023.

[113] Due, for instance, to the nationality principle, protective principle, or passive personality principle. See Crawford 2019, pp. 440–447.

[114] *Criminal Code Act 1995*, above n 100, Division 119.2, which creates such an offence, though there is an exception at 119.2(3) for providing aid of a humanitarian nature.

Firstly, we can consider how humanitarian actors may be impacted in their operational contexts by the company laws, employment laws, and charity laws of their home jurisdictions. Many large humanitarian organizations are structured such that the operational offices are branches of a parent organization registered in another country. A UK headquartered humanitarian organization, for instance, might have a branch in Yemen that is part of the same legal entity. As a UK-incorporated charity, that organization's Yemen branch may be concerned about falling foul of provisions in the UK Charities Act,[115] UK Companies Act,[116] or UK Employment Act.[117] Misconduct in those instances can lead, for example, to loss of UK charitable status, loss of ability to bid for UK government funding, or statutory inquiries. For instance, the UK Charity Commission launched a statutory inquiry into Oxfam following safeguarding and sexual harassment allegations in several of their countries of operation.[118]

Humanitarian actors are also increasingly impacted by the reach of criminal laws, counter-terrorism laws, domestic sanction regimes, and export control regulations from states other than affected states. Humanitarians may be concerned about providing material assistance to designated terrorist organizations, breaching sanction regimes, or the diversion of aid more generally.[119] In the prominent US Supreme Court Case of Holder v Humanitarian Law Project, for instance, the Humanitarian Law Project sought to provide training in peaceful conflict resolution to the Kurdistan Workers' Party of Turkey and the Liberation Tigers of Tamil Eelam in Sri Lanka, both of whom were designated by the United States Government as terrorist organizations. Concerned that their training would be caught by a federal law prohibiting the provision of material assistance to a foreign terrorist organization, the plaintiffs sought to have the law ruled unconstitutional. Deciding against the plaintiffs, however, the majority held that the paragraph at issue was constitutional.[120] The impact of these laws and rulings can be significant. As one respondent noted "the US law against terrorist groups are making it very difficult for any agency to be able to operate in areas where they will have to interact with these groups. So that's very constraining. It's blocking."[121] Such laws can thus have direct impacts on humanitarians.

Such laws can have even further indirect impacts on humanitarian actors. Where there are legal ambiguities about the reach of such laws, humanitarians may self-select out of operating in certain contexts, leading to a *cooling* of assistance. For instance, the American designation of the Houthis as a terrorist organization risked

---

[115] Charities Act 2022 c.6 [UK] https://www.legislation.gov.uk/ukpga/2022/6/contents/enacted. Accessed 8 December 2023.

[116] Companies Act 2006 c. 46 [UK] https://www.legislation.gov.uk/ukpga/2006/46/contents. Accessed 8 December 2023.

[117] Employment Act 2002 c. 22 [UK] https://www.legislation.gov.uk/ukpga/2002/22/contents. Accessed 8 December 2023.

[118] Charity Commission for England and Wales 2019.

[119] NGO11.

[120] *Holder*, above n 104, p. 2.

[121] DON1.

1 Humanitarians and Their Law(s): A Comprehensive Inquiry 23

significantly impacting humanitarian assistance in Yemen despite the existence of exemptions.[122]

Often, the laws of external states will be compatible with *in situ* domestic legislation, allowing humanitarians to meet the requirements in both contexts as long as they follow the stricter state standard. Clashes can (and do) arise, however, between these jurisdictions. Different financial standards, for instance could be one area. One respondent provided the following account of a prospective grant in Ethiopia,

> in Ethiopia, we were trying to instigate a cash programming, and there's no mobile money infrastructure there, so we were going to facilitate community individuals to get bank accounts and then we were going to do bank transfers for people to access the cash. Again, British legislation, Charity Commission obligations and responsibilities, account-ability, meant that our initial response to the Ethiopian banking system was, 'you've got to become compliant with British law.' And they said 'fuck off'.[123]

Such clashes can put humanitarian actors in complicated situations of uncertainty regarding which laws to follow.

Overall, as this section has highlighted, a close look at a broader range of laws of humanitarian assistance challenges a predominant focus on public international law. The *in situ* and *external* laws of domestic jurisdictions can have wide-reaching effects on how humanitarian assistance unfolds. These laws, however, are not always challenged by humanitarians to the same degree. As one respondent said,

> as a humanitarian organisation we tend to look at [the laws] of host countries far more critically than the ones from where we are coming, either our headquarters or our donors. I think that the scrutiny of them is equally important, if not more, because they, and us, are coming from at times positions of far greater power than the host community and the country.[124]

As the following sub-section considers, a comprehensive view can also look beyond public law and scrutinize the *private* laws shaping humanitarian assistance.

1.3.2 Private Law

Beyond the international and domestic *public* laws described above, humanitarian assistance is further shaped by bi-lateral agreements, laws of contract, and extra-contractual obligations. Another essential element to acknowledge in a comprehensive view, accordingly, is that the laws of humanitarian assistance implicate *private* laws and not solely public ones. And, across different areas of private law, case law is

---

[122] Slemrod and Parker 2021.

[123] NGO12.

[124] NGO7.

emerging related to humanitarian obligations on themes such as donor contracting,[125] carriage of goods,[126] employee contracting[127] and negligence.[128]

This section considers the role of private law in shaping humanitarian assistance by considering two common forms of private humanitarian obligation; memoranda of understanding (MoUs)/host country agreements, and donor contracts. These obligations differ from statutory laws in several respects. For instance, being bi-lateral, there is privity involved in these relations, which can impact their publicity, transparency, and consistency across the sector. Further, there can be some negotiation between the parties depending on their relative levels of power, and so they are not simply contracts of adhesion. Moreover, these relationships present humanitarian organizations as private contract norm-makers. I turn first to the role of MoUs and host country agreements in shaping humanitarian assistance.

1.3.2.1 Memoranda of Understanding and Host Country Agreements

In establishing their operations in particular countries, humanitarians regularly create agreements with host governments. For NGOs, these are usually referred to as MoUs while for the ICRC and UN they are referred to as headquarters, status, or host country agreements. Indeed the humanitarian organization in our thought experiment had such an MoU with the Government of Niger.

Though, under the international law of treaties, MoUs are generally understood as instruments which are *not* intended to create legally binding obligations,[129] in the context of humanitarian assistance these agreements may well have binding effects. Much as in contracts, the bindingness of these agreements is less about their name, and more a function of whether the parties intended to be bound by the obligations contained therein, and of whether the contents of these agreements are sufficiently

---

[125] CJEU (3rd Chamber) *International Management Group v Commission*, Judgment, 31 January 2019, C-183/17 P; CJEU (5th Chamber) *Internationaler Hilfsfonds eV v Commission of the European Communities*, Order, 15 October 2003, T-372/02.

[126] USDC (Louisiana), *US v. Ocean Steamship (Nigeria)*, Judgment, 27 June 1995, [1995] 1995 WL 384494; USDC (Louisiana) *Antilles Lloyd v Save the Children Foundation*, Motion to Dismiss, 27 March 1991, [1991] 1991 WL 42572; USDC (SDT-Houston Division), *United States of America v Ocean Bulk Ships Inc.*, Judgment, 24 June 2003, [2003], 2003 AMC 1785; FCC, *Canadian Red Cross Society v Air Canada*, Judgment, 11 September 2001 [2001], 2001 FCT 1012.

[127] QCCQ, *Bro c Oxfam Quebec*, Judgment, 12 December 2013, [2013] 2013 QCCQ 15843; CJEU (5th Chamber) *Mauerhofer v Commission*, Order, 31 March 2011, C-433/10; CJEU (Third Chamber) *Domínguez González v Commission*, Order, 12 November 2008, Case F-88/07.

[128] UKHL, *Sutradhar (FC) v Natural Environment Research Council*, Judgment, 5 July 2006, [2006] UKHL 33; *Boim*, above n 104; USDC (Maryland), *Vance v CHF International*, Motion to Vacate, 18 October 2012 [2012], Civil Case No. RWT 11-3120 8; USDC (SDNY), *Wagner v. Samaritan's Purse*, Demand for Jury Trial, 17 May 2011, [2011] 11-cv-03375 (RJS/AJP); USCA (DC Circuit) *Workman v United Methodists Committee on Relief*, Appeal, 25 February 2003, [2003] 320 F. 3d 259; Oslo District Court, *Dennis v Stiftelsen Flyktninghjelpen*, District Court Judgment, 25 November 2015, 15-032886TVI-OTI R/05.

[129] Crawford 2019, p. 357.

clear to be binding. Thus, the influence of these agreements in conditioning humanitarian assistance can be considerable. One respondent described this significance as such,

> [MoUs are] sometimes taking a kind of precedence over the law. I used to work in Egypt before and there, you know, every three years I had to renew the MoU with the government and the law says 'yes, civil societies can be there', but it doesn't really specify any sectors at all. But the MoU would have a bearing on where you can work, what you can do, what you cannot do, which kind of groups you can work with, which kind of funding you can access and so on and so forth. So those MoUs have a very significant bearing because ultimately it is those MoUs which, of course should not contradict the law, but are there to interpret the law, and also act as a guiding framework within which you are expected to operate.[130]

With scope to provide specificity on the extent of assistance, as well as the rights and obligations of those assisting, these agreements can narrow and give precision to existing laws, as well as establish private obligations between the signatories of a quasi-contractual nature. Where these agreements are breached by humanitarians, it may offer pretext for a government to suspend or terminate those humanitarians' operations.

MoUs and headquarters agreements can be bilateral arrangements between a single humanitarian organization and a state, or multilateral agreements between numerous humanitarian organizations and the state. They can be specific or general.[131] They can have global or project-specific applicability.[132] As one respondent noted, "in Ethiopia I need to sign an MoU and then [have a separate] agreement for every project".[133] Further, they can be quite old and long established. As another respondent stated "some have been in application since 1970s, the oldest. There are even some headquarters agreements that still say that the [representative] of X is [from a particular nationality]. Which [was] certainly applicable 40 years ago, but which is not anymore".[134] MoUs and host country agreements vary in scope between different countries and can also vary in content within the same country.

The contents of these agreements also vary depending on the country and the actors involved (be they NGOs, UN actors, or the ICRC). As a threshold matter, the existence of an MoU or host country agreement can be an expression of state consent for a humanitarian actor to provide assistance. More particularly, they can outline the scope of assistance—the time-period for which the assistance is permitted, the areas of the country where the humanitarians are allowed to operate, or the types of assistance that humanitarians can provide.[135] They may also require that organizations "conduct operations in accordance with domestic law"[136] and may contain other standards (such as humanitarian principles) that humanitarian actors are

---

[130] NGO7.
[131] IGO7.
[132] NGO7.
[133] NGO7.
[134] IGO7.
[135] NGO9.
[136] NGO6.

expected to adhere to[137]—an instance where a soft law requirement can crystalize into a formal obligation. They can contain provisions on recruitment oversight, tax filing requirements, reporting obligations, termination conditions, and dispute resolution, amongst others.[138]

Some provisions in these agreements will also aid humanitarian actors in their work. They can, for instance, exempt a humanitarian organization from its obligations to pay customs duties, income tax, or entry visa fees.[139] They can authorize an organization to open bank accounts, to enter contracts with domestic parties, or to have designated vehicle registration plates with protections in the event of road traffic incidents.[140] They may contain provisions which permit engaging in media activities—which may be advantageous for awareness raising campaigns—or that establish safeguards against being shut down.[141] They can authorize communication (that would otherwise be prohibited) with non-state armed groups.[142] They may also include privileges for humanitarians—mostly in the case of the UN and ICRC—such as certain immunities against criminal or civil liability.[143]

While the privileges and protections provided by these agreements are far from iron-clad—despite provisions limiting organizational expulsion, for instance, a host country may still *de facto* halt a humanitarian organization's operations with individual *persona non grata* actions[144] or refusing to issue visas[145]—the precarity of not having a bi-lateral agreement can be far greater. One respondent noted,

> the federal [Ethiopian] government no longer signs agreements, MOUs, or you know approvals for programmatic operations in Tigray. It's almost like a no man's zone. As INGOs we also do not feel empowered to sign agreements with the Tigray authority because they're not recognised by the federal government. So that would be an example […] where we're definitely operating in a grey zone.[146]

Even beyond the lack of protection that operating without an MoU entails, such situations create ambiguity around basic legal questions, such as whether the humanitarian actors have consent to provide assistance.

While advantageous for individual humanitarians, it is notable that these agreements do not provide sector-wide protections. As bilateral or multilateral agreements, these arrangements create particular rights and obligations between the

---

[137] NGO10.

[138] NGO13.

[139] NGO10.

[140] NGO13.

[141] NGO10.

[142] IGO7.

[143] See for instance, Debuf 2016.

[144] The use of *persona non grata* on United Nations personnel is a controversial subject. While state practice provides ample examples of this doctrine being used to expel UN personnel, the UN holds that the doctrine "has no application with respect to United Nations Staff." See Bandyopadhyay and Iwata 2016, para 110.

[145] IGO5.

[146] NGO4.

1 Humanitarians and Their Law(s): A Comprehensive Inquiry

parties involved. Some organizations stress this limited protection when engaging in advocacy for broader humanitarian protections. As one respondent described,

> when we advocate for humanitarian exemptions [states tell] us, 'why do you need the humanitarian exemption? You have headquarter agreements operating'. [...But] what we are advocating [for...] is much broader than something that only concerns X. It concerns the whole humanitarian sector.[147]

Beyond the parochial protection of these agreements, an approach to regulating humanitarians based on MoUs and host country agreements can also lead to variation in the contents of agreements between different humanitarian actors and the state.[148]

Further, these agreements are also often confidential, only occasionally being published in official gazettes, for instance.[149] An implication of this confidentiality is that certain humanitarian actors will not know the rights and obligations of other humanitarian actors. Additionally, confidentiality may mean that local governments are not aware of the rights and obligations established for these humanitarians at the national level. One humanitarian actor with an MoU may be operating alongside another without an MoU, or alongside one with an agreement consisting of significantly different privileges or immunities. These agreements, in other words, are not necessarily consistent, even in the same operational contexts. As such, they may favour those more powerful international humanitarians capable of negotiating more favourable terms, or they may risk exploiting less powerful ones.

1.3.2.2 Donor Contracts

Moving from private agreements with the affected state, humanitarians also conclude private contracts with external parties. Most notably, in receiving grants from state donors, humanitarians sign on to a range of contractual obligations. These obligations can significantly impact how assistance occurs, and thus accounting for them is essential in a comprehensive view of the laws of humanitarian assistance.

To begin, these contracts may require adherence to the donor state's laws,[150] thus transplanting that country's public norms through private law into foreign contexts. Whereas the extraterritorial reach of a foreign state's statutes might only apply to humanitarians under certain circumstances (such as, as above, having a headquarters in that foreign state or employing staff from that state), these contracts can bring those laws to bear on actors for whom those conditions would not otherwise apply. The contract that the humanitarian organization has with the US donor in our thought experiment may, for instance, bring into effect US material support to terrorists law[151] (paying the transit fee being particularly suspect), provided that the contract specifies US law as the applicable law.

---

[147] IGO6.

[148] IGO7.

[149] IGO7.

[150] See for instance, DG-ECHO 2021; USAID 2022, p. 58.

[151] 18 U.S. Code § 2339A, above n 101.

As another example, the standard service contract from the UK's former Department for International Development (DFID) states, "the contract shall be governed and interpreted in accordance with English Law and shall be subject to the exclusive jurisdiction of the Courts of England and Wales".[152] Thus, a Japanese humanitarian organization working in Burkina Faso and employing exclusively Japanese and West African staff could have found itself bound by English domestic employment, anti-money laundering, or counter-terrorism laws where that organization has received a grant from the UK government containing such a clause. The UK Foreign, Commonwealth and Development Office's more recent Sample Accountable Grant Agreement does not contain such a general provision on adherence to the laws of England and Wales, but instead creates an obligation that grantees "comply with all applicable legislation, regulations and rules *both in the countries they are registered and operating in*".[153] Here, legal obligations attach to the country of registration, rather than necessarily the laws of England and Wales.

Beyond general provisions on adherence to the laws of the donor state, donor contracts also create purely private obligations. These include auditing and financial reporting requirements, regulations on procurement, rules regarding sub-contractors, regulations on eligible and ineligible costs, or norms related to data protection.[154] Donor contracts can, for example, limit how, what, and from whom humanitarian goods can be purchased with donor money. Describing how donor rules shape the procurement of humanitarian goods, one respondent explained,

> At the very basic level, [donor sanction lists] limit our options in procurement. [...] automatically people that you buy from can't be from blacklisted companies. [...] It also increases the burden on us from a bureaucratic point of view where you have to be a lot more careful on who you are involving, who you are not, what are the latest black-listed companies.[155]

Such rules thus not only limit from whom humanitarians can procure supplies, they also establish procedures which can be time and labour-intensive—potentially implicating the state obligation under certain areas of international law to allow and facilitate humanitarian assistance. Downstream, humanitarian actors might also be required to ensure that their sub-contractors and local partners adhere to the same procurement rules.

Similarly, donor rules can impact the type of assistance that humanitarians provide. One respondent gave the following example,

> we had a [...] problem in Iraq in which we [we]re providing cash assistance, and cash assistance was supported by [our] donors. [...] But now at some point [US Government Officials] came to us and said, 'but some of these beneficiaries are buying Iranian products'.

---

[152] DFID 2017, Article 49.1; Note: the Foreign, Commonwealth and Development Office (FCDO) is the UK government organ which has subsumed the work of DFID. Existing DFID contracts, however, remain valid (FCDO Procurement at FCDO).

[153] FCDO 2020, p. 4.

[154] See for instance, DG-ECHO 2021.

[155] NGO9.

1 Humanitarians and Their Law(s): A Comprehensive Inquiry

> It was a bit of a difficult situation because what do you do? [...] Are we as an organization in a position to tell the government to tell everybody what should be in the market? [...] What we could do is switch to vouchers where we do have some control, and [where] you can tell them not to buy Iranian products.[156]

Here, we see how the chosen type of assistance for the humanitarian actor and the donor was, initially, cash assistance. However, this type of assistance eventually became unacceptable to the donor due to the cash being used by program beneficiaries to purchase products on the open market which would have breached the donor's sanction rules.

Donor contracts can also include penalty clauses. A major risk for humanitarians—and reason they adhere so strictly to donor laws—is that the costs they claim from donors will be disallowed. As another respondent added, if "you don't follow procedures, [there are] penalty clauses that say you will need to pay back money from your own pocket."[157] While such clauses for disallowed costs in donor contracts often focus on adherence to the laws of the state where the donor is headquartered, they can also force compliance with the laws of the state where assistance is occurring. For instance, one respondent described strict provisions in a World Bank contract for Syria which required adherence to domestic laws, stating, "if what you're doing is seen as a violation of the domestic law of Syria, they also will say these costs are disallowed and we're not going to pay them."[158]

Ultimately, like MoUs and host country agreements, donor contracts can significantly influence how humanitarian assistance occurs. Humanitarians are bound by these norms and take these obligations very seriously. As the following sub-section explores, they also take quite seriously self-governing norms and regulations.

1.3.3 Self-governance: Humanitarians as Norm-Makers

Beyond international, domestic, public, and private law sources, there are other normative regimes—both hard and soft—where humanitarians themselves act as norm-makers. Thus, another essential element of a comprehensive understanding is that the laws of humanitarian assistance are not just hard, external laws, but also encompass self-regulation and soft laws.

While describing humanitarians as norm-making entities could refer to their capacity to contribute to the negotiations of international treaties[159] or how they enforce international law,[160]—both of which they do—here, I am referring to more operational forms of norm-making.

---

[156] NGO8.

[157] NGO6.

[158] NGO1.

[159] Mantilla 2020, pp. 62–64, 75–77, 108–112, 118–120.

[160] Eilstrup-Sangiovanni and Sharman 2022.

The founding documents of humanitarian organizations may impose conduct on those actors. Weller describes this as "a constitutional requirement" of some humanitarian organizations to adhere to rules like, for example, the humanitarian principles.[161] While adherence to the principles by humanitarian actors is often advanced as an obligation of international law—where authors have suggested, for instance, that the humanitarian principles may in time crystallise "as general rules of customary international law"[162]—this obligation is not clear as a matter of public international law. Neutrality, for instance, is not a requirement of Articles 3[163] or 9/9/9/10[164] common to the Geneva Conventions. Independence is also absent from UNGA 46/182—often described as the "blueprint"[165] of the international humanitarian system—which only lists humanity, neutrality, and impartiality.[166] Similarly, the ILC Draft Articles list humanity, neutrality, and impartiality, but not independence, as humanitarian principles.[167] However, adherence to these principles may become obligatory for humanitarians where "they operate within the framework of general or specific legal regulations imposing the principles upon them as a matter of law".[168] For instance, as private limited companies, UK-based non-state humanitarians are governed by their articles of association. Accordingly, while it is not clear that adherence to humanitarian principles is a public international law requirement,[169] for these organizations it becomes a requirement based on their founding documents.[170] The country director in our thought experiment may thus need to act in a certain way based on these internal, constitutive norms.

---

[161] Weller 1997, pp. 441–450.

[162] Cubie 2019, p. 17.

[163] ICRC 2021, para 835.

[164] ICRC 2021, para 1164.

[165] See for instance, ALNAP 2022, p. 3; Cubie 2019, p. 13.

[166] UN General Assembly (1991) Resolution 46/182, UN Doc. A/RES/46/182, para 2.

[167] International Law Commission (2016) Draft Articles on the Protection of Persons in the Event of Disasters, with Commentaries, UN Doc. A/71/10, Article 6; While several countries, regional bodies, and organizations—including the Czech Republic, Thailand, Ecuador, the European Union, and OCHA—supported the inclusion of independence in the Draft Articles, a position recommended by the Special Rapporteur, it was ultimately excluded from the final articles (Valencia-Ospina E (2010) Third Report on the Protection of Persons in the Event of Disasters, UN Doc. A/CN/4/629, paras 132, 133, 138, 140.).

[168] Weller 1997, p. 449.

[169] Weller 1997; Sharpe 2023.

[170] It is important to note that the founding documents of humanitarian organizations within the United Nations system are generally based in public international law—be they treaties or General Assembly resolutions (see for instance UN General Assembly (1965) Resolution 2095 (XX), UN Doc. A/RES/2095(XX) on the continuation of the World Food Programme). For these organizations, the "constitutional requirement" is still of utmost importance but is not an example of self-governance.

1 Humanitarians and Their Law(s): A Comprehensive Inquiry

A range of soft law instruments have also been collectively developed by humanitarian groups[171] that establish norms which are (or at least are perceived as being) incumbent on these actors. Further, the "constitutional requirements" of some humanitarians—the ICRC and its Code of Conduct in particular—have moved beyond the confines of that organization to become more general, sectoral, soft law norms.

It is valuable to study these sources as soft law, with the view that a traditional, state-centric doctrine of international law sources is insufficient to fully detail the legal matrix navigated by humanitarians. But it is also important to consider these soft law sources for their hard law implications. For instance, some domestic courts have relied on codes of conduct to define concepts like humanitarian "reasonableness" in domestic negligence law. In *Dennis v. Stiftelsen Flyktninghjelpen* before the Oslo District Court, for instance, Deputy Judge Rafoss determined that "it may be of relevance whether or not industry standards were violated" in assessing reasonable conduct.[172] This allusion to industry standards raises questions about the reasonableness standard to apply in negligence cases regarding humanitarians. Should humanitarian liability be assessed based on a reasonable person standard? Or, based on a reasonable international humanitarian organization standard? If the latter, soft law norms may be central to determining hard law liability.

Soft law and internal norms can also clash with other normative regimes, creating challenging choices for humanitarians. For instance, in our thought experiment, the Government's state of emergency required humanitarians to travel to designated areas with an armed escort. However, several internal norms and soft law requirements demand that humanitarians not use armed escorts. For the ICRC, for instance, the use of armed escorts is determined by internal resolutions. The 1995 Resolutions of the Council of Delegates, for instance "*reiterates* the basic principle that the components of the Movement do not use armed protection"[173] while the 2005 Council of Delegates Guidance on Relations between the Components of the Movement and Military Bodies notes in its Annex that "[t]he components of the Movement may not resort to armed protection."[174] Diverting from this general rule is acceptable only when accepting these escorts is the only way to save human lives and where a minimal set of conditions detailed in the Handbook of the ICRC Movement have been met.[175] Such internal resolutions create hard rules for the ICRC. As one respondent summarized, the ICRC has

> approved two specific resolutions on the use of armed escorts [… which] come to exactly the same conclusion: [the ICRC does not] use armed escorts, unless very exceptional exceptions [are met]. That was [the ICRC's] way to say, 'if it is contrary [to] the regulatory framework of [the ICRC] to have escorts in some areas [then they] don't go to those areas.' That's the conclusion. [They] don't go.[176]

---

[171] See e.g. Sphere Association 2018; ICRC 1994.

[172] *Dennis*, above n 139, p. 13.

[173] ICRC 1995, Resolution 9.

[174] ICRC 2005, Resolution 7.

[175] ICRC 2008, pp. 879–883.

[176] IGO7.

Here we see a clear internal rule on the use of armed escorts that is incumbent on ICRC humanitarians. For such organizations, an escort mandated by a state of emergency could thus preclude their ability to provide assistance.

Alternatively, from a soft law perspective, the UN's Inter-Agency Standing Committee (IASC) has non-binding guidelines on the use of armed escorts for humanitarian convoys.[177] These guidelines hold that "[a]s a general rule, humanitarian convoys will not use armed escorts. However, there may be exceptional circumstances in which the use of armed escorts is necessary as a "last resort" to enable humanitarian action."[178] While the IASC Guidelines are directed towards UN humanitarian actors, other humanitarian actors have embraced them in policy documents. Care International's policy, for instance, references the IASC Guidelines, including the same general rule as well as an extended list of exceptional criteria which builds on them.[179] The Norwegian Refugee Council's Civil-Military Policy does not mention the IASC Guidelines explicitly, but does note that "[i]nteraction between military and humanitarian actors in [...] last resort cases should happen according to international guidelines — including [...] the use of armed escorts".[180] The IASC Guidelines thus hold strong normative force for a range of humanitarians across diverse contexts.

1.4 Conclusion: Where Can A Comprehensive View Provide Insights?

From domestic public laws, to private laws, to self-governance, the previous section highlighted a humanitarian legal landscape which is far broader than can be captured by public international law alone. Accordingly, as this chapter has argued, there is great salience to moving beyond public international law to consider a comprehensive view of the laws of humanitarian assistance. Such an approach can provide critical insights into the tangled legal universe humanitarian actors confront in their everyday lives.

Beyond this descriptive exercise of laying out "what is the law" of humanitarian assistance, a comprehensive view can provide a critical foundation for engaging with conceptual and practical challenges at the heart of humanitarian assistance. Developing a comprehensive field of inquiry into the laws of humanitarian assistance, in other words, is just a first step in developing new understandings of the legal opportunities for, and constraints to, more effective humanitarian assistance.

For instance, whereas legal scholars have provided essential insights into cross-border access constraints derived from the consent requirement in public international law, domestic and private law access constraints have not been canvassed nearly as systematically. A comprehensive inquiry can help to better understand

---

[177] IASC 2013.

[178] IASC 2013, p. 3.

[179] Care International 2022, p. 6.

[180] Norwegian Refugee Council Civil-Military Policy, p. 1.

other, more general patterns of obstruction deriving from *in situ* domestic laws, foreign domestic laws, private laws, and forms of self-governance. For instance, are humanitarians experiencing general patterns of obstruction from *in situ* administrative movement regulations—such as internal travel permits or administrative movement requirements? Are humanitarians experiencing general patterns of obstruction from foreign criminal or counterterrorism laws with extraterritorial reach into the contexts where they are operational? Are there systemic and repeating constraints that bear on humanitarians deriving from donor contracts and MoUs? Understanding these general patterns of obstruction is essential for developing legal strategies for overcoming them, all to the end of better meeting the humanitarian needs of affected populations.

Further, beyond international law understandings of which actors qualify as humanitarians, norms from other areas of law can significantly constrain who counts as a humanitarian. Domestic statutes may specify which actors are eligible for humanitarian defences and donor requirements may narrow which humanitarians may contract with their government in the provision of assistance. Taking a comprehensive view is thus an important perspective for understanding how different areas of law define (and ultimately crowd out) certain types of humanitarians. In a field that has both promoted, and struggled to implement, processes like the localization of humanitarian assistance as an essential means of improving the effectiveness of relief,[181] it is essential to understand which actors different laws see as being worthy of being called humanitarians.

A comprehensive view can also help humanitarians to isolate which areas of law most constrain their access, to the end of identifying which legal strategies to rely on to confront those constraints. In recent years, for instance, humanitarian exemptions have been lauded as a promising strategy for overcoming certain types of humanitarian access constraints.[182] In theory, and optimistically, humanitarian exemptions are an approach that can preserve "both the legitimate right of States to take [sovereign decisions over matters of national concern ...] and the access of impartial humanitarian organizations."[183] UNSC Resolution 2664, for example—which has been described as a "watershed development for humanitarian assistance"[184]—exempts various forms of humanitarian assistance from the scope of asset freezes imposed by UN sanction regimes.[185] But while an invaluable legal strategy for addressing constraints deriving from certain areas of law, humanitarian exemptions are no panacea for confronting the diversity of constraints arising from all the areas of law discussed in this chapter.

---

[181] Green 2023.

[182] King et al. 2016, p. 7; Lewis 2016, p. 143.

[183] Ferraro 2022, p. 881.

[184] Lewis and Modirzadeh 2022.

[185] UN Security Council Resolution 2664 (2022), UN Doc. S/RES/2664, para 1.

Humanitarian exemptions insulate humanitarians from the adverse effects of specific legal regimes—asset freezes under UN sanction regimes, or material assistance prohibitions under a counter-terrorism law, for instance. But, taking a comprehensive view, it can emerge that the legal regimes most constraining of access are not those in which the exemptions are found. For instance, while UNSC Resolution 2664 is binding on UN member states in the context of asset freezes under UN sanction regimes, it does not require them to replicate the carve-out in their own independent asset-freeze regimes.[186] Humanitarians might be constrained by a domestic asset freeze that is independent of the UNSC asset freeze where the exemption is found. More broadly, humanitarians may be constrained by entirely separate areas of law. One respondent, for instance, shared the example of a resolution that was tabled to end a particular humanitarian exemption in East Africa. The respondent noted,

> It took weeks to try and understand the tangible implications of what this change would have meant. [...] And the net impact was nothing. [...] the exemptions that we are supposedly enjoying, actually, we don't exert those. [...] Our models of operating and our standard operating procedures for delivery in Somalia are designed around our legal obligations to the UK Charity Commission and so it sets our threshold here. And the exemptions would have fallen short of that.[187]

Whereas individuals at the headquarters level in this humanitarian organization understood this humanitarian exemption as the key bulwark against legal access constraints, a more detailed legal analysis revealed that it was not actually relied on by the humanitarian organization. A comprehensive view taken from the perspective of humanitarian practitioners can thus reveal areas of law which may contain greater constraints on humanitarian access than those in which humanitarian exemptions are found (or proposed).

Finally, a comprehensive view can bring to fore clashes between different legal regimes with bearing on humanitarian actors. In their everyday work humanitarians may find themselves caught between competing obligations—between *in situ* and foreign laws, for instance—and be unsure how to proceed. A comprehensive view can assist humanitarians to identify such clashes, to determine the nature of such clashes—be they discretionary or non-discretionary—and to decide how best to proceed.

Ultimately, as humanitarian needs continue to grow globally, and the demands put on those providing assistance continue to expand, the need for analytic frameworks which are finely tuned to the everyday experiences of humanitarians become more pressing. A comprehensive view of the laws of humanitarian assistance from the perspective of humanitarian practitioners offers one such avenue.

---

[186] Some states and regional unions (notably the European Union), however, have taken UNSC 2664 as an invitation to introduce broader humanitarian carve-outs in their own independent sanction regimes (see EU 2024).

[187] NGO12.

References

Articles, Books and Other Documents

Akande D, Gillard E-C (2016a) The Oxford Guidance on the Law Relating to Humanitarian Relief Operations in Situations of Armed Conflict. OCHA, Geneva

Akande D, Gillard E-C (2016b) Arbitrary Withholding of Consent to Humanitarian Relief Operations in Armed Conflict. International Law Studies 92(483): 483–511

ALNAP (2022) More than the Sum of the Parts? Collective Leadership vs Individual Agency in Humanitarian Action https://reliefweb.int/report/world/more-sum-parts-collective-leadership-vs-individual-agency-humanitarian-action. Accessed 2 December 2023

Associated Press (2023) UN to Review Presence in Afghanistan Following Taliban Ban https://apnews.com/article/afghanistan-un-taliban-women-banbc9bb23c51e80a7bd36bdd22c583cf8b. Accessed 21 March 2024

Bandyopadhyay R, Iwata T (2016) Immunities and Privileges, VII Officials, Officials (Article V Sections 17-21 General Convention). In: Reinisch A and Bachmayer P (eds) The Conventions on the Privileges and Immunities of the United Nations and its Specialized Agencies: A Commentary. Oxford University Press, Oxford

Barber R (2009) Facilitating Humanitarian Assistance in International Humanitarian and Human Rights Law. International Review of the Red Cross 91(874): 371–39

Barber R (2020) Does International Law Permit the Provision of Humanitarian Assistance Without Host State Consent? Territorial Integrity, Necessity and the Determinative Function of the General Assembly. Yearbook of International Humanitarian Law 23: 85–121

Bergtora Sandvik K (2018) Humanitarians in Court: How Duty to Care Travelled from Human Resources to Legal Liability. The Journal of Legal Pluralism and Unofficial Law 50(3): 358–374

Brauman R (1996) Humanitaire — le Dilemme: Entretien avec Philippe Petit. Les Editions Textuel, Paris

Care International (2022) Care International Policy on Interactions with Armed Actors. https://www.carenederland.org/content/uploads/2022/07/CARE-International-Policy-on-Interactions-with-Armed-Actors-1st-July-2022.pdf. Accessed: 4 August 2023

Charity Commission for England and Wales (2019) Statement of the Results of an Inquiry Oxfam: Registered Charity Number 202918 https://assets.publishing.service.gov.uk/government/uploads/system/uploads/attachment_data/file/807945/Statement_of_the_Results_of_an_Inquiry_Oxfam.pdf. Accessed 8 December 2023

Collinson S, Elhawary S (2012) Humanitarian Space: A Review of Trends and Issues https://cdn.odi.org/media/documents/7643 pdf. Accessed 29 November 2023

Crawford J (2019) Brownlie's Principles of Public International Law 9th Edition. Oxford University Press, Oxford

Creta A (2012) A (Human) Right to Humanitarian Assistance in Disaster Situations? Surveying Public International Law. In: De Guttry A, Gestri M and Venturini G (eds) International Disaster Response Law. T.M.C. Asser Press, The Hague

Cubie D (2019) The International Legal Protection of Persons in Humanitarian Crises: Exploring the Acquis Humanitaire. Hart Publishing, Oxford

Cubie D (2022) Sources of IDL. Yearbook of International Disaster Law 3(1): 637–641

Debuf E (2016) Tools to do the Job: The ICRC's Legal Status, Privileges and Immunities. International Review of the Red Cross 97(897/898), 319–344

DFID (2017) Standard Terms and Conditions — Service Contracts, v 1.1. https://assets.publishing.service.gov.uk/government/uploads/system/uploads/attachment_data/file/649883/DFID-Standard-Terms-Conditions-Services-Contracts-Oct17b.pdf. Accessed 7 December 2023

DG-ECHO (2021) Grant Agreement. https://www.dgecho-partners-helpdesk.eu/files/reference documentfile/2021/Humanitarian_Aid_General_Model_Grant_Agreement.pdf. Accessed 7 December 2023

Eilstrup-Sangiovanni M and Sharman J.C. (2022) Vigilantes Beyond Borders: NGOs as Enforcers of International Law. Princeton University Press, Princeton

EU (2024) Humanitarian Action: EU Introduces Further Exception to Sanctions https://www.consilium.europa.eu/en/press/press-releases/2024/02/19/humanitarian-action-eu-introduces-further-exception-to-sanctions/. Accessed 9 June 2024

Emon A and Hasan N (2021), Under Layered Suspicion: A Review of CRA Audits of Muslim-Led Charities. https://www.layeredsuspicion.ca/#Intro. Accessed 10 December 2023

Ferraro R (2022) Challenges to Implementation of Humanitarian Access Norms in the Sahel. International Review of the Red Cross 103(918): 859–882

FCDO Procurement at FCDO. https://www.gov.uk/government/organisations/foreign-commonwealth-development-office/about/procurement. Accessed 7 December 2023

FCDO (2020) Sample Accountable Grant Agreement V. 2.8. https://assets.publishing.service.gov.uk/media/5fa1329a8fa8f57f3e0e9307/template-accountable-grant.odt. Accessed 8 December 2023

Fisher D (2007) Domestic Regulation of International Humanitarian Relief in Disasters and Armed Conflict: A Comparative Analysis. International Review of the Red Cross 89/866: 345–372

Gal T (2017) Territorial Control by Armed Groups and the Regulation of Access to Humanitarian Assistance. Israel Law Review 50(1): 25–47

Gavshon D (2009) The Applicability of IHL in Mixed Situations of Disaster and Conflict. Journal of Conflict and Security Law 12(2): 243–263

Green A (2023) Why the 'Grand Bargain' Failed to Deliver its Promise of Local Funding. Devex https://www.devex.com/news/why-the-grand-bargain-failed-to-deliver-its-promise-of-local-funding-105848 Accessed 2 April 2024

Hammersley M and Atkinson P (2007) Ethnography: Principles in Practice 3rd ed. Routledge, New York

Helton AC (1992) The Legality of Providing Humanitarian Assistance Without the Consent of the Sovereign. International Journal of Refugee Law 4(3): 373–375

Herman J (2015), International Law and Humanitarian Space in the Twenty-First Century: Challenged Relationships. In: Zwitter A, Lamont C, Heintze H-J and Herman J (eds) Humanitarian Action: Global, Regional and Domestic Legal Responses. Cambridge University Press, Cambridge

Hesselman M (2018). A Right to International (Humanitarian) Assistance in Times of Disaster: Fresh Perspectives from International Human Rights Law. In: Bartolini G, Casolari F, Sommario E and Giustiniani F (eds). Routledge Handbook of Human Rights and Disasters. Routledge, Abingdon

Hilhorst D, Jansen B J (2010) Humanitarian Space as Arena: A Perspective on the Everyday Politics of Aid. Development and Change 41(6): 1117–1139

IASC (2011) IASC Operational Guidelines on the Protection of Persons in Situations of Natural Disasters https://www.ohchr.org/sites/default/files/Documents/Issues/IDPersons/OperationalGuidelinesIDP.pdf. Accessed 28 March 2024

IASC (2013) IASC Non-Binding Guidelines on the Use of Armed Escorts for Humanitarians Convoys. https://reliefweb.int/report/world/iasc-non-binding-guidelines-use-armed-escorts-humanitarian-convoys#:~:text=The%20overriding%20principle%20articulated%20in,criteria%20can%20be%20fully%20met. Accessed 21 November 2023

ICRC (1952) Convention (1) for the Amelioration of the Condition of the Wounded and Sick in Armed Forces in the Field. Geneva, 12 August 1949. Commentary of 1952. https://ihl-databases.icrc.org/en/ihl-treaties/gci-1949/article-9/commentary/1952?activeTab=undefined. Accessed 2 April 2024

ICRC (1987) Protocol II In: Sandoz Y, Swinarski C and Zimmermann B (eds) Commentary on the Additional Protocols of 8 June 1977 to the Geneva Conventions of 12 August 1949. Geneva, Martinus Nijhoff Publishers

ICRC (1994) Code of Conduct for the International Red Cross and Red Crescent Movement and Non-Governmental Organizations in Disaster Relief. ICRC, Geneva

ICRC (1995), Resolutions of the Council of Delegates: Geneva, 1–2 December 1995) https://international-review.icrc.org/sites/default/files/S002086040007340Xa.pdf. Accessed 10 December 2023

ICRC (2005) Relations Between the Components of the Movement and Military Bodies (Adopted by Red Cross Council of Delegates 2005), https://disasterlaw.ifrc.org/sites/default/files/media/disaster_law/2021-07/03_GuidanceDoc_MilitaryBodies_EN.pdf. Accessed 10 December 2023

ICRC (2008) Handbook of the International Red Cross and Red Crescent Movement, 14th Edition. https://shop.icrc.org/handbook-of-the-international-red-cross-and-red-crescent-movement-pdf-en.html. Accessed 4 August 2023

ICRC (2016a) Fundamental Principles of the Red Cross and Red Crescent Movement. https://www.icrc.org/en/document/fundamental-principles-red-cross-and-red-crescent. Accessed 29 November 2023

ICRC (2016b) Convention (1) for the Amelioration of the Condition of the Wounded and Sick in Armed Forces in the Field. Geneva, 12 August 1949. Commentary of 2019. https://ihl-databases.icrc.org/en/ihl-treaties/gci-1949/article-9/commentary/2016?activeTab=undefined#_Toc452042984 Accessed 2 April 2024

ICRC (2020) The Kampala Convention: Key Recommendations Ten Years On https://www.icrc.org/en/document/kampala-convention-key-recommendations-ten-years. Accessed 6 December 2023

ICRC (2021) Commentary on the Third Geneva Convention: Convention (III) Relative to the Treatment of Prisoners of War. In: Henckaerts J-M, Demeyere B, Hiemstra H, Issar Y, La Haye E and Niebergall-Lackner H (Project Team). Cambridge University Press, Cambridge

ICRC Rule 55: Access for Humanitarian Relief to Civilians in Need. Customary IHL Rules. https://ihl-databases.icrc.org/en/customary-ihl/v1/rule55. Accessed 07 December 2023

ICRC Rule 56: Freedom of Movement of Humanitarian Relief Personnel. Customary IHL Rules. https://ihl-databases.icrc.org/en/customary-ihl/v1/rule56#:~:text=conflictsInterpretationException-,Rule%2056.,their%20movements%20be%20temporarily%20restricted. Accessed 28 March 2024

ICRC IHL Databases: Protocol Additional to the Geneva Conventions of 12 August 1949, and relating to the Protection of Victims of Non-International Armed Conflicts (Protocol II), 8 June 1977. https://ihl-databases.icrc.org/en/ihl-treaties/apii-1977/state-parties. Accessed 28 March 2024

IFRC (2013) Model Act for the Facilitation and Regulation of International Disaster Relief and Initial Recovery Assistance (with commentary) https://disasterlaw.ifrc.org/sites/default/files/media/disasterlaw/2021-02/IDRL%20Model%20Act%20%28English%29.pdf. Accessed 21 March 2024

IFRC (2019) Law and Disaster Preparedness and Response: Multi-Country Synthesis Report.https://disasterlaw.ifrc.org/sites/default/files/media/disaster_law/2020-09/DPR_Synthesis-Report_EN_Screen.pdf. Accessed 2 December 2023

IFRC (2022) An Introduction to IFRC Disaster Law https://disasterlaw.ifrc.org/sites/default/files/media/disaster_law/2022-11/20221026_IntroductionDisasterLaw.pdf. Accessed 21 March 2024

International Law Commission (2016) Draft Articles on the Protection of Persons in the Event of Disasters, with Commentaries, UN Doc. A/71/10

International Law Commission (2018) Draft Conclusions on Identification of Customary International Law, with Commentaries, UN Doc. A/73/10

IPCC (2012) Managing the Risks of Extreme Events and Disasters to Advance Climate Change Adaptation. Cambridge University Press, Cambridge

Irrera D (2019) Non-Governmental Search and Rescue Operations in the Mediterranean: Challenge or Opportunity for the EU? European Foreign Affairs Review 24(3): 265–286

James M (2020) 'Who Can Sing the Song of MSF?' The Politics of 'Proximity' and Performing Humanitarianism in Easter DRC. Journal of Humanitarian Affairs 2(2), 31–39

King K, Modirzadeh N and Lewis D (2016) Understanding Humanitarian Exemptions: U.N. Security Council Sanctions and Principled Humanitarian Action. Harvard Law School

Program on International Law and Armed Conflict: Working Group Briefing Memorandum. https://dash.harvard.edu/bitstream/handle/1/29998395/Understanding_Humanitarian_Exemptions_April_2016.pdf?sequence=1&isAllowed=y Accessed 4 June 2024

Kirchherr J, Charles K (2018) Enhancing the Sample Diversity of Snowball Samples: Recommendations from a Research Project on Anti-Dam Movements in Southeast Asia. PloS one 13(8)

Kuijt E (2014) A Humanitarian Crisis: Reframing the Legal Framework on Humanitarian Assistance. In: Zwitter A, Lamont C, Heintze H-J and Herman J (eds) Humanitarian Action: Global, Regional and Domestic Legal Responses. Cambridge University Press, Cambridge

Kuijt E (2015) Humanitarian Assistance and State Sovereignty in International Law: Towards a Comprehensive Framework. Intersentia, Cambridge

Latifi A M (2023) After the Taliban Ban on Women NGO Work, Local and Foreign Aid Groups Take Different Approaches. The New Humanitarian. https://www.thenewhumanitarian.org/news-feature/2023/03/02/afghanistan-ingos-find-workarounds-taliban-ban-on-women-ngo-work. Accessed 21 March 2024

Lewis D (2016) Humanitarian Exemptions from Counter-Terrorism Measures: A Brief Introduction. Proceedings of the Bruges Colloquium: Terrorism, Counter-Terrorism and International Humanitarian Law

Lewis D, Modirzadeh N (2021) Taking into Account the Potential Effects of Counterterrorism Measures on Humanitarian and Medical Activities: Elements of an Analytical Framework for States Grounded in Respect for international Law. https://dash.harvard.edu/bitstream/handle/1/37373495/Taking-Into-Account.pdf?sequence=1&isAllowed=y. Accessed 27 November 2023

Lewis D, Modirzadeh N (2022) The U.N. Security Council Adopts a Standing Humanitarian "Carve-Out". *Lawfare* https://www.lawfaremedia.org/article/un-security-council-adopts-standing-humanitarian-carve-out. Accessed 16 March 2024

Lohne K, Bergtora Sandvik K (2017) Bringing Law into the Political Sociology of Humanitarianism. Oslo Law Review 4(1): 4–27

Mackintosh K (2011) Holder v. Humanitarian Law Project: Implications for Humanitarian Action: A View from Medecins Sans Frontieres. Suffolk Transnational Law Review 34(3): 507–518

Mann I (2020) The Right to Perform Rescue at Sea: Jurisprudence and Drowning. German Law Journal 21: 598–619

Mantilla G (2020) Lawmaking Under Pressure: International Humanitarian Law and Internal Armed Conflict. Cornell University Press, Ithaca

Mégret F (2021) Activists on the High Seas: Reinventing International Law from the Mare Liberum? International Community Law Review 1–36

Modirzadeh N, Lewis D and Bruderlein C (2011) Humanitarian Engagement under Counter-Terrorism: A Conflict of Norms and the Emerging Policy Landscape. International Review of the Red Cross 93(883): 623–647

Modirzadeh N and Lewis D (2021) Humanitarian Values in a Counterterrorism Era. International Review of the Red Cross 103(915–917): 403–413

Nakjavani Bookmiller K (2016) Closing 'the Yawning Gap'? International Disaster Response Law at Fifteen In: Breau S and Samual K (eds). Research Handbook on Disasters and International Law. Elgar, Cheltenham.

Nelson T (2010) Rejecting the Gift Horse: International Politics of Disaster Aid Refusal. Conflict, Security and Development 10(3): 379–402

Norwegian Refugee Council Civil-Military Policy. https://www.nrc.no/globalassets/pdf/policy-documents/nrc-civil-military-policy.pdf. Accessed 21 November 2023

OCHA (2012) What are Humanitarian Principles? https://www.unocha.org/sites/dms/Documents/OOM-humanitarianprinciples_eng_June12.pdf Accessed 29 November 2023

OCHA (2020) Global Humanitarian Overview 2021 https://reliefweb.int/report/world/global-humanitarian-overview-2021-enarfres?_gl=1*1ok04hj*_ga*NDIzODUzNjA1LjE3MDA1NjMw ODE.*_ga_E60ZNX2F68*MTcwMTIxNjYyOC4yLjEuMTcwMTIxNzEyMS42MC4wLjjA. Accessed 29 November 2023.

OCHA (2023) Global Humanitarian Overview 2024 https://www.unocha.org/publications/report/world/global-humanitarian-overview-2024-enarfres. Accessed 8 June 2023

Pasquetti S, Casati N and Sanyal R (2019) Law and Refugee Crises. Annual Review of Law and Social Science 15:289–310

Pictet J (1979) The Fundamental Principles of the Red Cross. International Review of the Red Cross Archive 19(210): 130–149

Provost R (2008) Judging in Splendid Isolation. The American Journal of Comparative Law 56(1): 125–172

Roberts A (2011) Comparative International Law? The Role of National Courts in Creating and Enforcing International Law. International and Comparative Law Quarterly. 60(1): 57–92

Ryngaert C (2013) Humanitarian Assistance and the Conundrum of Consent: A Legal Perspective. Amsterdam LF 5: 5

Schwartz O G (2015) International Law and National Courts: Between Mutual Empowerment and Mutual Weakening. Cardozo Journal of International and Comparative Law. 23(3): 587–626

Schwendimann F (2011) The Legal Framework of Humanitarian Access in Armed Conflict. International Review of the Red Cross. 93(884): 993–1008

Sharpe M (2023) It's All Relative: The Humanitarian Principles in Historical and Legal Perspective. https://blogs.icrc.org/law-and-policy/2023/03/16/humanitarian-principles-historical-legal/. Accessed 27 November 2023

Sivakumaran S (2015) Arbitrary Withholding of Consent to Humanitarian Assistance in Situations of Disaster. International and Comparative Law Quarterly 64(3): 501–531

Slemrod A, Parker B (2021) US 'Terror' Label on Yemen's Houthis Could Hit Peace Talks, Aid https://www.thenewhumanitarian.org/news/2020/01/11/yemen-houthi-terrorist-us-effects. Accessed 27 November 2023

Sphere (2018) The Sphere Handbook: Humanitarian Charter and Minimum Standards in Humanitarian Response. Sphere Association, Geneva

SPLM (1996) Operation Lifeline Sudan Agreement on Ground Rules http://theirwords.org/media/transfer/doc/sd_splm_a_united_1996_28-6c881b0b7d668d23291914fe28ecd2c2.pdf. Accessed 8 December 2023

Sutton R (2020) Enacting the 'Civilian Plus': International Humanitarian Actors and the Conceptualization of Distinction. Leiden Journal of International Law 33(2): 429–449

Sutton R (2021) The Humanitarian Civilian: How the Idea of Distinction Circulates Within and Beyond International Humanitarian Law. Oxford University Press, Oxford

Sutton R (2023) Read the Room: Legal and Emotional Literacy in Frontline Humanitarian Negotiations. Yearbook of International Humanitarian Law 24(2021): 103–139

Thürer D (2007) Dunant's Pyramid: Thoughts on the "Humanitarian Space". International Review of the Red Cross 89(865): 47–61

UN General Assembly (1965) Resolution 2095 (XX), UN Doc. A/RES/2095(XX)

UN General Assembly (1991) Resolution 46/182, UN Doc. A/RES/46/182

UN General Assembly (2020) Resolution 75/127, UN Doc. A/RES/75/127

UN General Assembly (2021) Agenda Item 75(a), UN Doc. A/76/L.23

UNHCR (2018) Niger becomes the First Country in Africa to Adopt a National Law for the Protection and Assistance of Internally Displaced Persons https://reliefweb.int/report/niger/niger-becomes-first-country-africa-adopt-national-law-protection-and-assistance#:~:text=On%20Monday%2C%20the%20National%20Assembly,ratified%20by%20Niger%20in%202012. Accessed 2 December 2023

USAID (2022) Standard Provisions for Non-U.S. Nongovernmental Organizations: A Mandatory Reference for ADS Chapter 303 https://www.usaid.gov/sites/default/agency-policy/303mab.pdf. Accessed 8 December 2023

Valencia-Ospina E (2010) Third Report on the Protection of Persons in the Event of Disasters, UN Doc. A/CN/4/629

Weller M (1997) The Relativity of Humanitarian Neutrality and Impartiality. ASIL Proceedings, 1997: 441–450

Williams S, Simm G (2018) Assistance to Disaster Victims in an Armed Conflict: The Role of International Humanitarian Law In: Bartolini G, Casolari F, Sommario E and Giustiniani F (eds). Routledge Handbook of Human Rights and Disasters. Routledge, Abingdon

Wynn-Pope P, Zegenhagen Y and Kurnadi F (2016) Legislating Against Humanitarian Principles: A Case Study on the Humanitarian Implications of Australian Counterterrorism Legislation. International Review of the Red Cross 97(897/898): 235–261

Zimmermann A (2017) Humanitarian Assistance and the Security Council. Israel Law Review 50(1): 3–23

Zwitter, A (2011). United Nations' Legal Framework of Humanitarian Assistance. In: Heintze H-J and Zwitter A (eds) International Law and Humanitarian Assistance: A Crosscut Through Legal Issues Pertaining to Humanitarianism. Springer, London, pp 51–69

Zwitter A, Lamont C, Heintze H-J and Herman J (2015) Introduction. In: Zwitter A, Lamont C, Heintze H-J and Herman J (eds) Humanitarian Action: Global, Regional and Domestic Legal Responses. Cambridge University Press, Cambridge

Cases

BCCA, *R v Christhurajah*, Appeal, 18 June 2019, [2019] 2019 BCCA 210

BCCA, *R v Rajaratnam*, Appeal, 18 June 2019, [2019] 2019 BCCA 209

CJEU (2nd Chamber) *CAS Succhi di Frutta SpA v Commission of the European Communities*, Judgment, 14 October 1999, Case T-191/96 and T-106/97

CJEU (3rd Chamber) *Aulinger v Germany*, Judgment, 9 March 2006, [2006] Case C-371/03

CJEU (3rd Chamber) *International Management Group v Commission*, Judgment, 31 January 2019, C-183/17 P

CJEU (4th Chamber) *Internationaler Hilfsfonds eV v Commission*, Order, 7 December 2004, C-521/03

CJEU (4th Chamber) *Camós Grau v Commission*, Judgment, 6 April 2006, T-309/03

CJEU (5th Chamber) *Italian Republic v Commission of the European Communities*, Judgment, 6 June 1996, C-198/94

CJEU (5th Chamber) *Internationaler Hilfsfonds eV v Commission of the European Communities*, Order, 15 October 2003, T-372/02

CJEU (5th Chamber) *Mauerhofer v Commission*, Order, 31 March 2011, C-433/10; CJEU (Third Chamber) *Domínguez González v Commission*, Order, 12 November 2008, Case F-88/07

CJEU (9th Chamber) *NC v Commission*, Judgment, 27 June 2017, T-151/16

CJEU (Grand Chamber), *European Commission v Hungary*, Judgment, 16 November 2021, [2021] Case C-821/19

EWHC *Sternaj v Director of Public Prosecution/Sternaj v Crown Prosecution Service*, Judgement, 12 April 2011, [2011] EWHC 1094 (Admin)

EWCA, *R v Kapoor*, Appeal, 9 Mach 2012, [2012] EWCA Crim 435

EWCA, *R v Bina (Arya)*, Appeal, 11 June 2014, [2014] EWCA Crim 1444

EWCA *R v Kakaei*, Appeal, 8 April 2021 [2021] EWCA Crim 503

FCC, *Canadian Red Cross Society v Air Canada*, Judgment, 11 September 2001 [2001], 2001 FCT 1012

FCC, *Toronto Coalition to Stop the War v Canada*, Judicial Review, 27 September 2010, [2012] 1 F.C.R. 413

ICJ, *Military and Paramilitary Activities in and against Nicaragua (Nicaragua v United States of America)*, Judgment, 27 June 1986, [1986], ICJ Rep 392

ICJ Legality of the Threat of Use of Nuclear Weapons, Advisory Opinion, 8 July 1996, [1996] ICJ Rep 226

ICJ Legal Consequences of the Constriction of a Wall in the Occupied Palestinian Territory, Advisory Opinion, 9 July 2004, [2004] ICJ Rep 136

1 Humanitarians and Their Law(s): A Comprehensive Inquiry

ICTY, *Prosecutor v Aleksoveski*, Judgment, 25 June 1999, Case No. IT-95-14/1-T, T.Ch

ONSC, *R v Abdulle*, Judgment, 23 December 2014, [2014] 2014 ONSC 7455

Oslo District Court, *Dennis v Stiftelsen Flyktninghjelpen*, District Court Judgment, 25 November 2015, 15-032886TVI-OTI R/05

QCCQ, *Bro c Oxfam Quebec*, Judgment, 12 December 2013, [2013] 2013 QCCQ 15843

SCC, *B010 v* Canada, Appeal, 27 November 2015, [2015] 2015 SCC 58

SCC, *R v Appulonappa*, Appeal, 27 November 2015, [2015] 2015 SCC 59

TCC, *Godin v The Queen*, Judgment, 12 March 1998, [1998] 2 CTC 2853; FCA, *Brown v Care Canada*, Appeal, 24 May 2000, [2000] 3 CTC 205

UKHL, *Sutradhar (FC) v Natural Environment Research Council*, Judgment, 5 July 2006, [2006] UKHL 33

USCA (2nd Circuit), *United States v Farhane*, Appeal, 4 February 2011, [2011] 634 F.3d 127

USCA (7th Circuit) *Boim v Holy Land Foundation for Relief and Development*, Appeal, 2 December 2008, [2008] 549 F.3d 685

USCA (9th Circuit), *Humanitarian Law Project v Mukasey*, Appeal, 10 December 2007, [2007] 552 F.3d 916

USCA (DC Circuit) *Workman v United Methodists Committee on* Relief, Appeal, 25 February 2003, [2003] 320 F. 3d 259

USCA (DC Circuit) *U.S. v Fahnbulleh*, Judgment, 13 June 2014, [2014] 752 F. 3d 470

USDC (Louisiana) *Antilles Lloyd v Save the Children Foundation*, Motion to Dismiss, 27 March 1991, [1991] 1991 WL 42572

USDC (Louisiana), *US v. Ocean Steamship (Nigeria*, Judgment, 27 June 1995, [1995] 1995 WL 384494

USDC (Maryland), *Vance v CHF International*, Motion to Vacate, 18 October 2012 [2012], Civil Case No. RWT 11-3120 8

USDC (SDNY), *Wagner v. Samaritan's Purse*, Demand for Jury Trial, 17 May 2011, [2011] 11-cv-03375 (RJS/AJP)

USDC (SDNY) *United States of America ex rel. TZAC, INC., v Norwegian People's Aid a/k/a Norsk Folkehjelp*, Settlement and Dismissal Order, 30 March, 2018, 15 Civ. 4892(GHW), https://charityandsecurity.org/wp-content/uploads/2020/08/NPA-Settlement-Stipulation-Dismissal.pdf. Accessed 11 December 2023

USDC (SDT-Houston Division), *United States of America v Ocean Bulk Ships Inc.*, Judgment, 24 June 2003, [2003], 2003 AMC 1785

USSC, *Holder v Humanitarian Law Project*, Appeal, 21 June 2010, [2010] 561 U.S. 1

VSC, *R v Aruran Vinayagamoorthy*, Judgment, 31 March [2010] VSC 148

Treaties

18 U.S. Code § 2339A *Providing Material Support to Terrorists* (United States)

African Charter on the Rights and Welfare of the Child, opened for signature 11 July 1990 CAB/LEG/24.9/49(entered into force 29 November 1999)

African Union Convention for the Protection and Assistance of Internally Displaced Persons in Africa, opened for signatures 23 October 2009, UNTS 3014 (entered into force 6 December 2012) (Kampala Convention)

Employment Act 2002 c. 22 [UK] https://www.legislation.gov.uk/ukpga/2002/22/contents. Accessed 8 December 2023

Charities Act 2022 c.6 [UK] https://www.legislation.gov.uk/ukpga/2022/6/contents/enacted. Accessed 8 December 2023

Companies Act 2006 c. 46 [UK] https://www.legislation.gov.uk/ukpga/2006/46/contents. Accessed 8 December 2023

Constitution of the World Health Organization, opened for signatures 22 July 1946, UNTS 14, 185 (entered into force 7 April 1948)

Convention on the Rights of the Child, opened for signature 20 November 1989, UNTS 1577 p 3 (entered into force 2 September 1990)

Convention on the Rights of Persons with Disabilities, opened for signature 13 December 2006, UNTS 2515 p 3 (entered into force 2 May 2008)

Counter-Terrorism and Border Security Act 2019, c. 3 (United Kingdom)

Criminal Code Act 1995 (Australia)

Geneva Convention Relative to the Protection of Civilians in Time of War, opened for signature 12 August 1949, 75 UNTS 287 (entered into force 21 October 1950) (Geneva Convention IV)

Intergovernmental Authority on Development (2018) Revitalised Agreement on the Resolution of the Conflict in the Republic of South Sudan (R-ARCSS). https://www.peaceagreements.org/viewmasterdocument/2112. Accessed 9 December 2023

International Covenant on Civil and Political Rights, opened for signature 16 December 1966, UNTS 999 p 171 (entered into force 23 March 1977) (ICCPR)

International Covenant on Economic, Social and Cultural Rights, opened for signature 16 December 1966, UNTS 993 p 3 (entered into force 3 January 1976) (ICESCR)

Protocol Additional to the Geneva Convention of 12 August 1949, and relating to the Protection of Victims of International Armed Conflicts, opened for signature 8 June 1977, 1125 UNTS 3 (entered into force December 1978 (Additional Protocol 1)

Protocol Additional to the Geneva Conventions of 12 August 1949, and relating to the Protection of Victims of Non-International Armed Conflicts, opened for signature 8 June 1977, 1125 UNTS 609 (entered into force December 1978 (Additional Protocol II)

Statute of the International Court of Justice, opened for signature 26 June 1945, 33 UNTS 993 (entered into force 18 April 1946)

Tampere Convention on the Provision of Telecommunication Resources for Disaster Mitigation and Relief Operations, opened for signature 18 June 1998, 2296 UNTS 5 (entered into force 8 January 2005)

Terrorism Act 2000, c. 11 (United Kingdom)

UN Security Council (2022) Resolution 2664 (2022), UN Doc. S/RES/2664

David Matyas is an Assistant Professor at the University of New Brunswick Faculty of Law and Ph.D. Candidate at the University of Cambridge Faculty of Law (King's College). The author is grateful to Eyal Benvenisti, Sandesh Sivakumaran, Marthe Achtnich, Ori Pomson, Fabian Eichberger, and Maria Panezi for their comments and conversations about earlier drafts of this work. This chapter is derived from David Matyas' doctoral dissertation on the laws of humanitarian assistance which has been funded by the Gates Cambridge Scholarship. Fieldwork for this research was supported by the University of Cambridge University Fieldwork Fund. Any errors that remain are the author's alone.

Chapter 2
The State as a Humanitarian Actor: Opportunities and Challenges in Decolonizing Humanitarianism

Oscar A. Gómez

Contents

2.1	Introduction	44
2.2	Anti-State Bias and Coloniality in Humanitarianism	48
2.3	The Background of Humanitarianism in Colombia	50
2.4	Humanitarian Discourse and the Colombian State	52
	2.4.1 The Pre-history of Humanitarian Discourse	52
	2.4.2 Internalization of the Humanitarian Language	54
2.5	State Humanitarian Practice	58
	2.5.1 Disasters	58
	2.5.2 Internal Displacement	60
	2.5.3 Humanitarian Demining	62
	2.5.4 Missing Persons	64
2.6	The State as a Humanitarian Actor	65
2.7	Conclusion: The State and Decolonizing Humanitarianism	68
References		69

Abstract There is a strong anti-State bias in the humanitarian community. Under the assumptions of the incapacity or unwillingness to cover humanitarian needs, humanitarian studies primarily focus on non-state actors. This is problematic because, among many other reasons, it perpetuates the colonial structure of humanitarianism, in which rich Western States are benefactors through (also Western) non-state humanitarian actors helping the weak and wicked rest. This chapter argues that any effort to salvage humanitarianism from its colonial past and present will require recognizing and scrutinizing the State's role as a humanitarian actor. Therefore, this chapter asks: What kind of humanitarian actor is the State? What are its characteristics? How does it change our understanding of humanitarian action? I use the case study of Colombia and its long-standing struggle against multiple humanitarian needs to answer these questions. The chapter follows two analytical tracks: first, it analyses the discourse of humanitarianism in the country, describing a long apathy from the nineteenth century until the nineteen nineties, when a transformation gradually started, resulting

O. A. Gómez (✉)
Ritsumeikan Asia Pacific University, Beppu, Japan
e-mail: oagomez@apu.ac.jp

© T.M.C. ASSER PRESS and the authors 2025
H. Krieger et al. (eds.), *Yearbook of International Humanitarian Law, Volume 26 (2023)*,
Yearbook of International Humanitarian Law 26,
https://doi.org/10.1007/978-94-6265-663-5_2

in multiple State offices declaring humanitarian mandates. Second, I turn to practices and how the State slowly and selectively internalizes humanitarian action and makes it part of its functions. Finally, I provide a profile of the State as a humanitarian actor, outlining its main features and the implications for the future of humanitarianism.

Keywords Humanitarianism · Decolonization · Localization · Non-western approaches · Historical institutionalism · Humanitarian governance

2.1 Introduction

There is a strong anti-State bias in the humanitarian community. The bias is evident in both academic literature and in humanitarian practice. Lists of humanitarian actors and descriptions of the humanitarian system rarely include the State among humanitarians. For instance, Mac Ginty and Peterson's companion on humanitarian action does not include States among its twelve chapters dedicated to humanitarian actors.[1] Instead, it includes a chapter on "Non-DAC Humanitarian actors"[2] in which the author, Emma Mawdsley, a renowned scholar on South-South cooperation, opens with a footnote clarifying that the chapter focuses on State actors.[3] Moreover, histories of humanitarianism are mainly about Western non-governmental organizations (NGOs) and the personalities behind them, starting with Henry Dunant and the Red Cross Movement and later enlarged to include the United Nations (UN) and its agencies.[4]

The humanitarian system, as described by the Active Learning Network for Accountability and Performance (ALNAP), includes governments as "Entities that play a critical role in humanitarian response, but humanitarian action is not their core function".[5] Following this logic, the 2016 World Humanitarian Summit in Istanbul

---

[1] Mac Ginty and Peterson 2015.

[2] DAC refers to the Development Assistance Committee of the Organization for Economic Co-operation and Development (OECD-DAC), where major donors coordinate their international development cooperation.

[3] Mawdsley 2015, p. 213.

[4] See, for example, Barnett 2011; Davey 2013; Salvatici 2019. Hilton et al. 2018 offer a discussion on recent trends.

[5] ALNAP 2022, p. 7. There is no universally agreed-upon definition of humanitarianism or humanitarian action. This article is informed by Slim's 2015 general description of humanitarian action as "a compassionate response to extreme and particular forms of suffering arising from organized human violence and natural (sic) disaster.", p. 1. As Slim does, I understand International Humanitarian Law as one early effort to standardize humanitarian practice in the specific context of armed conflict, which eventually became a master narrative "providing the ethical, operational and legal foundations for humanitarian activities"—Labbé and Daudin 2015, p. 186, following Davies 2012. Yet, given the multiple and interconnected nature of human suffering sources, humanitarian action covers different situations beyond armed conflict. Because being able to provide such relief is highly regarded by all societies, multiple actors associate themselves with humanitarian protection provisions. These characteristics result in multiple ambiguities hindering efforts to narrow any definition.

2 The State as a Humanitarian Actor: Opportunities and Challenges …   45

was not organized as an interstate meeting, so there were no negotiations toward a joint framework for action or any other binding commitment. Instead, the most important outcome was "The Grand Bargain," the product of a high-level panel appointed by the UN Secretary-General.[6] From the Grand Bargain recommendations, the one getting most of the attention was a commitment to "localization," urging more support to national first responders, who only received directly 0.2% of the international humanitarian assistance. Still, localization efforts and reports are almost exclusively about local NGOs[7] and are largely seen as a continuation of humanitarian coloniality.[8]

This anti-State bias has critical consequences in rethinking humanitarianism in general and beyond its colonial origins. As far as humanitarian action is concerned with protecting vulnerable populations, it is hard to believe that it is not a core function of the State. The bias glosses over the fact that no non-Sate humanitarian actor has the resources to cover ever-growing humanitarian needs. It disregards that most countries—even those receiving the largest share of international humanitarian aid—have much more resources than those they receive as assistance.[9] The anti-State bias brushes aside the central role that States have had in confronting humanitarian crises throughout history and how affected populations would like to have responsible States capable of confronting those crises.[10] Consequently, the anti-Sate bias perpetuates the colonial structure of humanitarianism, in which rich Western States are benefactors through (also Western) non-state humanitarian actors helping the weak and wicked rest. This chapter makes the case for recognizing the State as a major humanitarian actor.[11] The State can and does serve important humanitarian functions in a scale and scope unfeasible to any other actor. The argument is not about the State sensibilities—i.e., whether States can uphold humanitarian

---

Therefore, while I use this general understanding as the chapter's starting point, I analyze the discursive use of humanitarianism in the case study to accommodate local interpretations. Consequently, "humanitarian community" refers to the actors who see themselves as belonging to that community. It is worth adding that humanitarian protection for the ICRC refers to "the effort to protect the fundamental well-being of individuals caught up in certain conflicts or 'man-made' emergencies" Forsythe 2001, p. 675. In this article, protection covers all types of emergencies.

[6] High-Level Panel on Humanitarian Financing 2016. This is the model that failed in negotiating the agenda to replace the Millennium Development Goals, see Fukuda-Parr and Muchhala 2020.

[7] See Robillard et al. 2021, p. 16, for a review noting how "most of the localization literature typically refers to" NGOs. Barbelet et al. 2021 offer another perspective, more inclusive of governmental action.

[8] Robillard et al. 2021; Zadeh-Cummings 2022.

[9] Development Initiatives 2019.

[10] Gómez 2019b.

[11] This is not a new claim. The best argument I know in this direction can be found in Harvey 2009. It can also be found in critical assessments of what humanitarianism (and localization) is, such as DuBois 2018 and Slim 2021. It is also implicit in thinking about humanitarian action in middle-income countries or non-Western countries, such as Mawdsley 2015, Rohwerder 2016 or Scott 2015. The humanitarian literature is radically different in this respect from that on human rights, peace, or development, in which the centrality of the State is widely recognized.

ideals—although they are not unimportant.[12] State's humanitarian action can result from random, contingent historical and political processes rather than an inherent humanitarian role or interest. States don't necessarily want to be more humanitarian; circumstances push States to develop humanitarian capabilities, and this is relevant to discussions on humanitarianism, which should not so easily discard them.[13] Ultimately, recognizing the fundamental role of the State forces us to rethink humanitarianism as part of the enlargement and evolution of the welfare state, which is not a monolithic structure but malleable and perennially under construction. These activities go beyond compliance with International Humanitarian Law (IHL) during armed conflict, encompassing a comprehensive arrangement of institutions dealing with the consequences of conflict and other humanitarian emergencies affecting populations who may or may not be the State's citizens.[14] Even more, the future of humanitarian action is in State capacity. This is important not only for classic humanitarian needs but also for emerging concerns, such as those linked to climate change. It was also evident during the pandemic, when cross-border support became largely unfeasible. A more systematic and sustained engagement with States as humanitarian actors is overdue.

Arguing that to decolonize humanitarianism, we need to recognize the State as an actor may sound contradictory to those familiar with postcolonial and decolonial studies. Thus, I start my argument by clarifying the proximal and distal origins of the contemporary discussion on humanitarian colonialism in the next section. Contemporary concerns with power distribution and racism in humanitarian action have no direct relation with postcolonial theory.[15] They are a reaction to what happened and did not happen during the World Humanitarian Summit: instead of power redistribution, emphasis on the biased and paternalistic idea of localization. Therefore, decolonizing in this conversation is closely related to the classic issue of self-determination, as humanitarianism keeps fixated on assumptions of the non-Western State's incapacity and evil nature. Since my original intention is to contribute to the discussion

---

[12] As explained below, humanitarianism's coloniality includes the presumption of evil in some non-Western States, which is used to justify intervention and domination.

[13] I thank one of the reviewers for this observation.

[14] It could be argued that this view about humanitarianism overlaps with States commitment to human rights. Given human rights broad range, this is true to a certain extent, and, indeed, domestic legal action related to humanitarian needs usually resorts to human rights. I have argued elsewhere that the relative absence of a humanitarian identity in Latin America can be partially explained by the importance of human rights in the region's history, particularly during the Cold War, when the liberal humanitarian order was taking shape elsewhere. See Lucatello and Gómez 2022. Yet, the practices and institutions of human rights and humanitarianism are very different—see for instance the multiple chapters in Barnett 2020—so I believe there is added value in recognizing the State as a humanitarian actor. I appreciate the comment in this direction by one of the reviewers.

[15] Postcolonial theory has engaged very little with humanitarianism. For instance, no article in the 26 volumes of the Postcolonial Studies journal includes the term "humanitarian action"; "humanitarianism" only appears twice in abstracts.

in the humanitarian community, I do not engage in detail with the postcolonial literature, although I suggest some implications of my argument. Engaging with the State does not mean being uncritical about its role. Yet, legitimate concerns must be distinguished from the prejudice underlying anti-State bias.

Colombia's experience is used to substantiate the chapter's conceptual argument. Focusing on a single case makes the conclusions tentative. Still, the trajectory of humanitarianism in Colombia has multiple characteristics that make it an appealing case for understanding the State's agency in humanitarian action. The country combines the strengths of a middle-income country with continuous exposure to multiple humanitarian crises, including hosting the largest internally displaced population in the two-thousands. It has been considered an ideal environment for IHL implementation[16] and lauded for its response to other crises. If the future of humanitarianism is State capacity, as I argue, Colombia is a revealing case because it has advanced too much in that path. While it is difficult to determine how singular the Colombian experience is and to what extent its experience is comparable to that of other middle-income countries, it offers a referent for our understanding of the long-term evolution of humanitarian institutions, which can inform future explorations in this direction. In Sect. 2.3, I further discuss the case selection, offering an overview of the country's background and its advantages and limitations for studying decolonization and State humanitarian practice.

The case study is divided into two sections: one on the discourse of humanitarianism and the other on its practice. Section 2.4, about humanitarian discourse in Colombia, presents a chronological recount of the use of humanitarian language since the nineteenth century. I show a relative absence until the 1990's, when a transformation gradually started, after which multiple State offices claim to have humanitarian mandates. Then, Sect. 2.5 describes different institutionalization processes of humanitarian practices inside the Colombian State, following the chronological order in which they emerged. Practice shows how the State slowly and selectively internalizes humanitarian action, making it part of its functions pressed by various circumstances. Disasters and Venezuelan migration are included because, although they are beyond the IHL reach, national institutions that address all types of humanitarian emergencies are closely interlinked in the field, offering multiple examples of the shapes, strengths, and weaknesses of State humanitarianism. Finally, I provide an abstract profile of the State as a humanitarian actor, outlining its main characteristics and the implications for the future of humanitarian assistance and protection.[17]

---

[16] Bradley 2013.

[17] This research is based on a sabbatical semester spent in Colombia during the spring of 2023, building on my previous research. The fieldwork included 51 interviews with practitioners and scholars working on crisis management and archival research in local libraries, the National Planning Department (DNP in Spanish), and the National Unit for Disaster Risk Management (UNGRD). Most sources and acronyms are in Spanish; all translations are mine unless otherwise specified.

2.2 Anti-State Bias and Coloniality in Humanitarianism

Anti-State bias when talking about humanitarian action has multiple possible origins and has been reinforced multiple times throughout the evolution of humanitarian institutions. The bias is present in the foundational myth underlying the creation of the Red Cross and the development of IHL. The global spread of the Red Cross and the unique condition of the International Committee of the Red Cross (ICRC) as guardian of IHL, made humanitarianism the epitome of non-state action.[18] Besides, the close connection between religious activism and anti-slavery movements reinforced this original conception of humanitarian agency happening outside the State.[19]

These two initial humanitarian aspirations, the rules of war and anti-slavery, were central to the idea of a "standard of civilization" justifying Western colonialism in the nineteenth century.[20] Barbarians and savages were seen as lacking the capacity or will necessary to avoid uncivilized behaviours.[21] Since then, capacity and will have remained the core arguments of the anti-State bias, institutionalized through formal and informal principles and rules of humanitarian action. Red Cross societies were created in non-Western countries as part of their struggle to be recognized as members of the international society.[22] A characteristic idea of this age of imperial humanitarianism is that humanitarianism is about helping "distant strangers," still very much in use today, which is incompatible with how protection actually works outside the West.

The Cold War and the emergence of the UN transformed and deepened the anti-State bias. While the holocaust made empty any claims of a superior European civilization, bipolarity facilitated the stigmatization of other political systems. As Hong argues:

> The formation of the postwar humanitarian regime was facilitated by the Soviet boycott at the turn of the 1950s of many of the global organizations through which this regime operated. This created a space in which France, Belgium, Britain, and the United States were able to define humanitarian and development problems as matters of security, both domestic and global, and then to instrumentalize such aid to contain communism, delegitimate national liberation movements, and reproduce neocolonial rule.[23]

Humanitarian crises were thus used to evidence the moral bankruptcy of communism. This was aggravated by embattled countries' rejection of Western international

---

[18] This should not be misunderstood as claiming that IHL and ICRC themselves have been anti-State—they have not. My point here is about the origins of the humanitarian identity and who can call itself a humanitarian actor. I thank Pablo Kalmanovitz for this observation.

[19] Barnett 2011.

[20] Gong 1984; Koskenneiemi 2002.

[21] On the question of local capacities, see Barbelet 2018 as it shows how even today there is no agreed way to measure them.

[22] For East Asian examples, see Checkland 1994; Käser 2016; Reeves 2020; Van Dijk 2021. Colombia (and Latin America) is different, as explained below.

[23] Hong 2015, p. 4.

2 The State as a Humanitarian Actor: Opportunities and Challenges …

support, resulting in two of today's most fundamental tenets of liberal humanitarianism: the overriding preoccupation with access[24] and the rejection taboo.[25] Both tenets reflect apprehension about the State hosting crises, rooted in the assumption that embattled governments are unwilling to protect populations under threat. Such stigmatization of aid rejection requires that the offering side is not part of the conflict or has no vested interests. This is why Vietnamese intervention to stop the Cambodian genocide was not recognized as humanitarian action.[26] There was thus a need for a third party to play the humanitarian role. UN agencies, Western NGOs, and the Red Cross movement gradually took over this role until it was finally streamlined into the UN by creating the Department of Humanitarian Affairs in 1991.

The consolidation of the liberal humanitarian system finally entrenched the anti-State bias, leaving only two options for States. States could be part of the problem, or they could be donors. Efforts to entrench this view can be seen in the agreement of principles of Good Humanitarian Donorship, adopted by the OECD-DAC in 2003, partly in reaction to the menace of the bilateralization of humanitarianism.[27] These principles present States as donors and the traditional club of humanitarian organizations as actors. Consequently, when new States make incursions into humanitarianism, they are usually presented as donors, regardless of whether this frame appropriately describes their roles.[28]

A niche exception to the anti-State bias is the work on civil-military relations. This work recognizes not only the operative strengths of armies to undertake the basic tasks of humanitarian action but also the parallel ownership militaries have of humanitarian assistance and disaster relief (HADR), particularly after the end of the Cold War.[29] Although work on HADR started linked to the colonial nature of traditional humanitarianism—i.e., exploring the collaboration between the armies of old colonial powers and traditional humanitarians—it has shifted to recognize the interoperability of militaries everywhere.[30] However, while important in understanding change in the humanitarian sphere, I believe this is a very narrow view of the State and its humanitarian role, so it is not included in the following analysis.

In sum, humanitarianism's anti-State bias can be seen as a continuation of its colonial origins. It was born from claims of incapacity and unwillingness of non-Western societies to manage their problems and protect vulnerable populations.

---

[24] For a recent example see Cunningham 2024.

[25] Gómez 2021.

[26] Finnemore 1996.

[27] Macrae et al. 2002; Gómez and Kawaguchi 2018.

[28] On non-Western humanitarian donors, and uneasiness about this classification, see Binder et al. 2010; Smith 2011; Aneja 2014; Roepstorff 2016.

[29] See for instance, Capie 2015.

[30] Trias and Cook 2023.

These are common concerns of postcolonial and decolonial narratives and the background of anticolonial struggles. However, because States can, voluntarily or not,[31] continue colonial practices, including through internal colonization,[32] postcolonial and decolonial studies tend to have a negative view of the State. This view deserves further attention, particularly given the limited interaction between humanitarian, postcolonial, and decolonial studies. However, postcolonial and decolonial calls for emancipation usually result in the reinventions of the State. As Getachew observes, efforts to rethink sovereignty "culminated in projects that reinforced the nation-state."[33] I believe neither postcolonial nor decolonial studies would accommodate how UN agencies and international NGOs use assumptions of non-Western States' incapacity and evil to position themselves as the only humanitarians. The present discussion about colonialism in humanitarian action shows that discrimination and domination concerns are still relevant and that it would be premature to give up on the welfare state as part of the evolution of self-determination. As calls for decolonizing humanitarianism grow, this chapter aims to show how recognizing the State as a humanitarian actor can help debunk misleading assumptions and prejudices hindering the transformation of humanitarianism. I do this through the case study of Colombia, which I introduce next.

2.3 The Background of Humanitarianism in Colombia

Colombia is an illuminating case to understand what kind of humanitarian actor the State is. This is because of the long-standing co-existence of emergencies and local capacities. Colombia has been affected by different types of humanitarian crises throughout its history. It is in the Pacific Ring of Fire, regularly hit by earthquakes and volcano eruptions. The Armero tragedy in 1985 was particularly important in creating the State's emergency response institutions. Yet, climatic disasters of different scales are more common, continuously affecting most of the territory. Indeed, catastrophic floods in 2010–2011 triggered a major institutional reorganization, resulting in today's disaster management system.

For most of its history, Colombia has been affected by internal conflict, which has conditioned how the State's emergency response institutions developed. This history usually starts with the independence wars in the early nineteenth century, followed by multiple conflicts, including major events such as the Thousand Days War (1899–1902) and the assassination of a political leader in 1948, "the Bogotazo," giving way to a decade of violence between the two major political parties; the armed conflict involving insurgencies and counter-insurgencies has been ongoing

---

[31] For how international law conditions Global South States, see Eslava and Pahuja 2020. The discussion is not limited to ex-colonies. See for instance Hönke and Müller 2016 on global policing practices.

[32] Santos 2024; Gonzalez-Jacome 2011.

[33] Getachew 2019, p. 179.

since 1958.[34] Violence has been largely low intensity, with limited impacts for the first decades, but gradually became more impactful and bloody through the eighties and nineties until its peak in the two-thousands. The estimated impacts of the conflict are a total of about 800,000 killed between 1985 and 2016 and 7,752,694 displaced between 1985 and 2019; in the worst year, more than 50,000 persons were killed and 730,000 displaced.[35] The various consequences of the conflict are one of the primary pressures for the State's involvement in humanitarian action.

Different actors have been involved in armed conflict, including multiple left-leaning guerrilla groups, paramilitary forces, and drug-trafficking groups. The peak of internal violence was the product of the emergence of paramilitary actors in the nineties, which started demobilizing in 2005 through a peace process. It is also important to mention that the presence of international organizations was limited until the nineties, and it was facilitated during the presidency of Ernesto Samper (1994–1998) partly because of accusations about his campaign being funded by drug trafficking money. Legislation creating State institutions to comprehensively address the problem of forced displacement in 1997, and subsequent Constitutional Court orders and jurisprudence, formalized both discourse and practice of State's humanitarianism. Later, two other initiatives to end the conflict had crucial implications for State humanitarian action: the broader recognition of victims and the creation of the UARIV (Victims Unit) at the start of Juan Manuel Santos government (2010–2018) and the peace agreement with the FARC (Revolutionary Armed Forces of Colombia) signed in 2016.

On the side of capacities, Colombia is an upper-middle-income country, one of the largest economies in Latin America, and a member of the OECD since 2020. It was already a middle-income country in the nineties, one factor keeping it outside the international cooperation focus. It was also under the United States (US) umbrella, another factor historically preventing intervention from outside the Americas.[36] Since its independence, Colombia was not ruled by the left until 2022. It only had a short, *sui generis* military government in the fifties, different from what happened in the South Cone and Central America during the second half of the twentieth century. It is proud to be one of the most stable democracies in Latin America. Particularly regarding humanitarian capabilities, the ICRC considers Colombia a near-ideal working environment.[37] By the mid of the 2010s, it was considered one of the best disaster management systems in the region,[38] and its response to Venezuelan displacement has been highly praised. However, Colombia is highly unequal, so strong institutions and capacities co-exist with poverty and vulnerability.[39] In as much as we

---

[34] Comisión de la Verdad 2022a.

[35] Comisión de la Verdad 2022b.

[36] Lucatello and Gómez 2022.

[37] Bradley 2013.

[38] Inter-American Development Bank 2014.

[39] Gómez et al. 2024.

expect crisis-affected countries to keep engrossing the ranks of middle-income countries, Colombia illustrates how such States appropriate and develop humanitarian capabilities.

Colombia is also a revealing case for understanding the coloniality of humanitarianism. Colombia was a Spanish colony and, thus, shares a colonial past that resonates with global discussions of decoloniality.[40] The more than two centuries of independence suggest that the experience of the country (and the region) could be an example of the evolution of humanitarian institutions in the long run. However, Colombia's colonial and post-colonial trajectory differs from Asia and Africa's. Its early independence, the Monroe Doctrine, and the dominance of Catholicism kept it largely unaffected by imperial humanitarianism.[41] Two archetypical humanitarian crises have not affected the country recently: international war and famine.[42] This conflation of factors resulted in Cold War humanitarianism being framed differently in the country and region, such as human rights violations, liberation theology, and solidarity. More recently, the massive movement of more than seven million persons out of Venezuela is the first time the country has confronted such an emergency. While there is a certain tendency to conflate all the Global South experiences, Colombia shows only one possible trajectory for decolonization, and its relevance to other countries and regions must be carefully assessed.

2.4 Humanitarian Discourse and the Colombian State

2.4.1 *The Pre-history of Humanitarian Discourse*

Humanitarianism entered the official Colombian discourse in 1991. The new country's Constitution included in its chapter on states of emergency (*estados de excepción*) an article about the obligation to respect IHL.[43] The inclusion of IHL in the 1991 Constitution was not the result of a late engagement in humanitarian affairs. On the contrary, it updated a well-established concern about the humanization of war, which was included in the Constitution at least from 1863 as *derecho*

---

[40] Indeed, decoloniality is considered of Latin American origin, including foundational works of Anibal Quijano, Arturo Escobar, and Walter Mignolo.

[41] Or at least exposed to it differently, e.g., Stamatov 2013. Despite that, Latin America was not openly welcome in the international society. See Schulz 2014.

[42] About the rules of war, see Gurmendi Dunkelberg 2023; on famines, de Waal 2018 offers a general view, and Davis 2001 comments on the last Brazilian famine by the end of the nineteenth century.

[43] As far as I know, it was accidental that the discourse of humanitarianism entered to Colombia at the same time as it became institutionalized at the UN. Direct inherence of UN agencies and donors' offices with humanitarian mandates, mainly the European Commission Directorate-General for European Civil Protection and Humanitarian Aid Operations (ECHO), will not start until some years later.

2 The State as a Humanitarian Actor: Opportunities and Challenges … 53

de gentes or *ius gentium*.[44] Just like in vernaculars for the laws of war, other areas of crisis management developed in the country using local framings that did not emphasize humanitarian language. Two examples further illustrate this pre-history of humanitarian discourse in Colombia: the Colombian Red Cross (CRC) history and the country's engagement with international disaster response.

The CRC began as an initiative of local physicians to provide health care to wounded soldiers during the country's multiple internal conflicts, particularly the Thousand Days' War (1899–1902).[45] In 1922, in order to be incorporated into the League of Red Cross Societies, the State recognized the CRC as "auxiliary to the Army's sanitary service."[46] The decree describes the CRC as a "scientific center." In 1937, a new law further clarified the rights and duties of the CRC, adding public assistance and charity to its original mandate, covering a large spectrum of activities: "all types of accidents, calamities, catastrophes and epidemics… social campaigns for the protection of mother and child and the fight against venereal diseases, tuberculosis, leprosy and alcoholism."[47] The law mentions the "humanitarian attention program" of the CRC, but that is the only occurrence of the word.

Then, during the 1948 "Bogotazo", the CRC played a distinguished role in managing the situation. This resulted in the creation by law of the "Socorro Nacional en caso de Calamidad Pública" (National Relief in Case of Public Calamity), an organization inside the CRC supported by the Ministries of War and Hygiene. The National Relief was entrusted with managing emergencies "at every time and anywhere in the country."[48] It remained responsible for emergency response until the seventies and still is central to the CRC work on disasters, nowadays renamed "Disaster Risk Management." Throughout its history, the CRC only started to gradually use humanitarian language in the eighties, mainly concerning the worsening internal conflict and establishing a National Department for Diffusion (of IHL) in 1989.[49]

Colombia began creating its national disaster relief institutions in the seventies. An essential factor in their creation was the occurrence of major regional disasters, notably an earthquake in Guatemala (1976).[50] The motivation arising from this disaster was not only the possibility of similar destruction taking place in Colombia but also, as a Pan American Health Organization (PAHO) resolution puts it, "[B]eing anxious that the international assistance given to countries affected by natural disasters should be better coordinated, rational and more effective".[51] The Colombian Ministry of Health started working on disasters through its Office of International Organizations and Agreements, which later moved to an office for preparedness and

---

[44] Valencia Villa 1995.

[45] Restrepo 2006.

[46] Decree 313 of 1922.

[47] Law 142 of 1937.

[48] Law 49 of 1948.

[49] Sandoval Jaramillo 1992.

[50] Ministerio de Salud 1986.

[51] PAHO 1979.

attention to domestic disasters. The national system was aware of international relief cooperation[52] and worked with PAHO to rein in its uncoordinated and wasteful operation.[53] None of these works and activities uses humanitarian language.[54] PAHO's relevant division, the Emergency Preparedness and Disaster Relief Coordination Program, started using an explicit humanitarian frame only after the creation of the UN Department of Humanitarian Affairs in 1991, and mainly concerning "complex disasters"—i.e. armed conflicts.[55]

2.4.2 Internalization of the Humanitarian Language

The inclusion of IHL in the 1991 Constitution opened space for its mainstreaming in Colombia concerning the humanization of armed conflict. The CRC made in 1992 a "humanitarian proposal" for an agreement between the government and one of the guerrilla groups, which is considered the first of its kind.[56] From there on, humanitarian language has been used constantly regarding IHL violations, usually in tandem with human rights law.[57] This is the case of the Truth Commission created in the 2016 peace agreement. The over-thousand-page volume on human rights and IHL violations includes sections on homicides, indiscriminate attacks, forced disappearance, intimidation, kidnapping, arbitrary detentions, torture, sexual violence, child soldiers, forced labour, forced displacement, land grabbing, confinement, attacks to protected infrastructure, pillage and extortion.[58] Providing protection and recovering from each of these violations has been part of the conception of government action to overcome the conflict and, thus, channels through which old and new government offices use humanitarian language.

Of all these consequences of the domestic conflict, forced displacement was the first to engender the development of State humanitarian action. While displacement because of the conflict was discussed since the fifties, it was initially conflated with rural-to-urban migration proper of Colombia's development and urbanization.[59] However, the connection between conflict and displacement became undeniable by

---

[52] The Ministerio de Salud 1982 three-volume Emergency Response Plan includes a section on international response and a description of the relevant international organizations and INGOs.

[53] This work resulted in some guidelines for Colombian Diplomatic and Consular Missions in case of disaster—Presidencia de la República and Ministerio de Relaciones Exteriores 1991—and an Inter-American Convention to Facilitate Disaster Assistance—Organization of American States 1991—among other outputs.

[54] From this period publications, only one decree (Decree 3489 of 1982) includes the word humanitarian, in the definition of disaster as events "requiring special attention from State organs or others of humanitarian or social service character."

[55] For instance, see PAHO 1994.

[56] Villarraga Sarmiento 2005.

[57] See for instance Kalmanovitz 2018.

[58] Comisión de la Verdad 2022b.

[59] See for instance the comment by Augusto Ramírez Ocampo in Restrepo 2006, pp. 12–19.

the mid-nineties. Francis Deng, then the representative of the UN Secretary-General on Internally Displaced Persons, visited Colombia for the first time in 1994, and then a 1995 Catholic Church report systematically showed the dimension of the problem.[60] The Church requested the government to devise a policy to confront the situation, resulting in a policy proposal for the integral attention of internally displaced populations the same year and a law in 1997.[61]

Law 387 of 1997 is a watershed in internalizing humanitarian language within the Colombian State. While the 1995 policy proposal differentiated the State's emergency response—entrusted to the national disaster prevention and attention system—from humanitarian support by the Red Cross, the law blurred this distinction. The law recognized at the same time (1) the right to request and receive international humanitarian aid and (2) humanitarian attention as one of the components of the management of displacement. This was further emphasized in law 418 of 1997, the law of public order, which, on the one hand, recognizes humanitarian actors as independent from the State while, on the other hand, delegates the responsibility to provide humanitarian assistance to a specific office of the government—the Social Solidarity Network (RSS). From there on, governmental offices in charge of forced displacement include providing humanitarian assistance inside their goals.

Addressing the consequences of armed conflict is thus one of the main channels for the State internalization of humanitarian language. In one way or another, all the institutions addressing each of the IHL infractions described by the Truth Commission use humanitarian language and present some of their actions as humanitarian. A detailed analysis is beyond the scope of this chapter, but I would like to highlight two examples: national efforts on humanitarian demining, ongoing since 2000, and the Search Unit for Missing Persons, created in 2017 as an entity of humanitarian character, part of the peace agreement. The practice of these two offices offers precious insight into the kind of humanitarian actor the State is.

Humanitarian language was useful for successive governments in the 2000s, mainly during the presidency of Alvaro Uribe (2002–2010). The government included "Forced Displacement and Humanitarian Assistance" as one of the priorities of its International Cooperation Strategy, which allowed the country to attract large amounts of resources despite being a middle-income country.[62] At the same time, international cooperation was coordinated by the same office in charge of addressing the consequences of conflict, *Acción Social* (Social Action), which conditioned humanitarian access to following national guidelines: mainly not recognizing the occurrence of conflict inside the country and discouraging the use of humanitarian language.[63] During this period, there was a constant uneasiness between traditional humanitarian actors and the government, not only because of the language appropriation but also because of a famous case of perfidy, in which the Red Cross emblem was used by the Colombian military to mislead FARC members in a rescue operation.

---

[60] Aparicio Cuervo 2012; Conferencia Episcopal de Colombia 1995.

[61] Departamento Nacional de Planeación 1995; Law 387 of 1997.

[62] Presidencia de la República 2003.

[63] Borda Guzmán 2014.

The head of the ICRC expressed concern about how "the expression humanitarian has been used to qualify or embellish acts or gestures with a different character" and emphasized the Committee's position that States should abstain from incorporating humanitarian action in their response to crises.[64]

A radical change occurred during the Juan Manuel Santos government (2010–2018). It openly recognized the occurrence of armed conflict and pushed through a peace process. This decision involved the continuation of work on the consequences of the conflict and the creation in 2011 of a Unit dedicated to the integral support and reparation of victims (UARIV). The change from forcedly displaced to victims more broadly was a meaningful expansion of State action, although humanitarian operations remained basically the same. By including reparation, the emphasis moved from a developmental logic of action to that of transitional justice (see next section).

The Santos government also opened a second major channel for internalizing humanitarian language in the country through the State's work in disasters. Colombia was heavily affected by floods between 2010 and 2011. The existing system for disaster management was overwhelmed by the magnitude of the disaster, so the government decided to create the strategy *Colombia Humanitaria* to respond to and recover from the emergency. The humanitarian framing of the strategy had two goals: to indicate it covered the emergency response to the crisis and to advocate for national and international solidarity.[65] The second goal had limited success, as the country did not make an international appeal, apparently following opposition by the Ministry of Foreign Affairs.[66] Final reports of the strategy describe the role of the UN as mainly executing national resources. The solidarity component was primarily domestic, contributing US$104 million to the US$2150 million allocated by the government.[67]

The flood emergency led to the structural reform of the national disaster management system, which had languished inside the Ministry of Interior. The National Unit of Disaster Risk Management (UNGRD) was created, again at the President's Office level,[68] and the disaster management system from the eighties was fully renovated.[69] Among multiple tasks, the Unit pushed for the standardization of humanitarian assistance in the country[70] and the coordination of non-state actors to avoid unrequested assistance—just as 40 years before, but now under the humanitarian umbrella.[71] Thus, the UNGRD covers humanitarian assistance as part of disaster management,

---

[64] ICRC 2009.

[65] Zapata Báez 2014.

[66] Colombia Humanitaria n.d. Observe that most of the expenses correspond to major reconstruction infrastructure projects. According to one interviewee, the government leadership expected the international community to support these expenditures, but the Ministry of Foreign Affairs was aware that humanitarian aid does not cover such projects.

[67] Colombia Humanitaria 2013.

[68] Decree 4147 of 2011.

[69] Law 1523 of 2012.

[70] UNGRD 2013.

[71] Gómez 2019a.

similar to the UARIV in the case of conflict.[72] The UNGRD has even expanded its management of emergencies to conflict situations, particularly supporting the starting phase of the FARC guerrilla demobilization after the peace agreement, and displacement, following instability in the Venezuelan border.

The massive migration of Venezuelans since 2016 adds a layer of complexity to the use of the humanitarian language in Colombia. Initially, the national government planned for an "integral policy for humanitarian response" to be led by the UNGRD[73] and focused on protection through access to health and education using the same services covering nationals.[74] The humanitarian framing helps justify the use of public resources for foreigners. The UNGRD and the UARIV were called to support this population with their capacities in humanitarian response. However, as the situation became protracted, the national government started with ad-hoc coordination through a "gerencia" (management office) inside the President's Office, eventually resulting in two significant changes in the discourse. The national government changed the focus to the long-term, developing a system for regularizing migrants so they could work and support themselves.[75] Besides, it allowed international organizations to lead humanitarian response inside the country, helping channel important financial resources from the international community. This somehow reverted the humanitarian language to its traditional use, although even then, the financial contribution of the Colombian State was the most significant.[76]

Paradoxically, reverting to traditional humanitarian discourse allowed the use of humanitarian assistance in Cold War fashion. In February 2019, with the support of the US, Paraguay, and Chile, the government tried to force humanitarian assistance into Venezuela while attempting to promote regime change.[77] The new government of Gustavo Petro (2022–2026) has drastically changed the approach to Venezuela, so migration has lost visibility, and the management office has been disbanded. This has also resulted in a drastic decrease in international cooperation money for Venezuelans.

---

[72] Indeed, interviewees mentioned efforts for joint deployment and the possibility of both units merging in the future.

[73] Law 1873 of 2017.

[74] Departamento Nacional de Planeación 2018.

[75] Departamento Nacional de Planeación 2022. This resulted in the internationally praised creation of a Temporal Protection Status (TPS) that concedes ten years of stay in the country to all Venezuelans who arrived irregularly until January 31, 2021, and those entering regularly until March 2023.

[76] Colombia has appeared as a major humanitarian donor in the region between 2020 and 2022, according to the Office for the Coordination of Humanitarian Affairs' Financial Tracking Service.

[77] See BBC (2019) Venezuela crisis: Border clashes as aid row intensifies. https://www.bbc.com/news/world-latin-america-47329806. Accessed 11 June 2024.

2.5 State Humanitarian Practice

The history of the Colombian State's adoption of the humanitarian discourse describes a gradual institutionalization of emergency response tasks understood as humanitarian. This process started with calamities, armed conflict, and forced displacement but gradually expanded to other government offices involved in crisis response. While this adoption allowed the government to manipulate international humanitarian assistance, the change primarily resulted from taking over its responsibilities in protecting Colombians. State practices in dealing with the consequences of disasters and conflicts are the best candidates to understand better what kind of humanitarian actor the State is, which I explore next.

2.5.1 Disasters

Colombia's first national disaster management office was created after the 1985 Armero tragedy. Following a volcanic eruption, a lahar buried the town of Armero on its path, killing most of its 29,000 inhabitants. Until then, several actors were involved in emergency response without a solid organization. The CRC had overseen calamities since 1945 and played a central role in the response. Civil defence groups were created in the sixties in Colombia as part of the Cold War dynamics to address the Communist menace and gradually got involved in responding to disasters; they were officially in charge, yet the magnitude of the disaster overwhelmed their capacities.[78] Besides, the Ministry of Health had a division working in disasters since the early eighties, which still supports the health sector's action after disasters today, but at that moment, it was only a work in progress. The Office was created as the National Office for Disaster Response (ONAD), although its work comprised response and prevention as soon as it started to work beyond the Armero tragedy.[79] It was located under the President's Office, the "highest possible level",[80] which conferred a direct connection to the top of the executive. The office started with only one national staff member, the director, while the team was subcontracted by international cooperation and national resources. The office concentrated on organizing the response and pushing local governments to start prevention and mitigation activities, trying to shift the attention from the former to the latter. Moreover, reconstruction activities occurred independently through ad-hoc initiatives, which have been the standard procedure since then.[81]

---

[78] Ramirez Gómez and Cardona Arboleda 1996; Saavedra 1996.

[79] Ramirez Gómez and Cardona Arboleda 1996 argue that this reflected a tension between the State and the opinions of individual actors.

[80] ONAD 1990.

[81] The reconstruction of an earthquake in the city of Popayán in 1983 is the first referent. Incorporating reconstruction into the system has been a major topic in recent years—e.g., OECD 2019—but that discussion is outside the scope of this chapter.

2 The State as a Humanitarian Actor: Opportunities and Challenges …

Some of the main characteristics of the first version of the system offer insights into the institutionalization challenges[82]:

- The law creates a system encompassing multiple line ministries, national, regional, and local offices, and includes participation from the private sector and civil society. A system was considered necessary because of the prevention goal since only emergency response did not require such a system.[83] The emphasis was thus on prevention.
- The system was expected to advance decentralization—and, thus, guided by the subsidiarity principle. Local offices were responsible for response, rehabilitation, and prevention, while regional and national offices supported only when local capabilities were exhausted.
- The system was expected to be bureaucratically small and focused on coordination. It was also expected to be less money-intensive and more organization-intensive.
- The system avoided concentrating resources on a single entity, which could result in clientelism and corruption. Local governments should appropriate resources for emergencies, while the national government aims to supplement these efforts.
- The system aimed to avoid the "congestion and avalanche of unnecessary assistance," including to "circumscribe the request and acceptance of international assistance to the strictly necessary." This was mainly about goods and services scarce or unavailable in the country.

In 1992, a new government moved the ONAD from the President's Office to the Ministry of Interior. This change was seen as a dangerous downgrading by the director, who had been in charge since 1986, so he quit. Another highly qualified person replaced him, but by 1995, leadership was lost to political postings. As a result, the response to the following major disaster in the country, the 1999 earthquake in Armenia, was primarily undertaken by the CRC, which also coordinated international support, and the RSS, employing its humanitarian assistance capacities developed for attending to internally displaced populations' needs.

From the middle of the nineties until *Colombia Humanitaria*, the national system for disaster management remained weak, although city and regional level offices kept developing their capabilities, displaying the importance of the decentralized model. *Colombia Humanitaria* and the new Unit draw from these more than two decades of experience to recreate the system. The UNGRD was located again under the President's office. The selected director came from a long trajectory at the CRC, through which he was involved in response since Armero and managed the 2010 CRC deployment in Haiti.

The initial leadership of the UNGRD placed great emphasis on the balanced development of response, prevention, and knowledge management capabilities—the three main sections of the Unit. As mentioned above, it aimed to standardize and rein in humanitarian assistance from domestic and international sources, as informed by

---

[82] ONAD 1990.

[83] Ramirez Gómez and Cardona Arboleda 1996.

the director's long experience in humanitarian action. The UNGRD has remained in its place under the President after two changes of government, has around 200 career workers, and contractors can reach 3 or 4 times that number, depending on the needs. This does not include the local and regional committee members. It works mainly with its budget. The possibility of corruption is usually mentioned concerning State emergency response at the UNGRD.[84]

2.5.2 Internal Displacement

The State's response to the needs of internally displaced populations was originally planned through a whole-of-government approach. Law 387 of 1997 created the "National System for the Integral Attention of the Displaced Population," composed of the relevant "public, private, and community" entities. Local and regional governments were required to create committees to support the system, including the army, the police, the health secretaries, the office in charge of children's welfare (ICBF), the CRC, the Civil Defence, the Church, and representatives of the displaced population. This lineup of actors suggests an orientation towards response.

However, the initial conception of the State's action included comprehensive displacement management. It started with the collection of information to identify and diagnose the problem. The other components were prevention, emergency humanitarian attention, return, and socioeconomic consolidation and stabilization. Institutions at the national level included line ministries and offices related to land rights, agriculture, education, and job creation. The law also created a fund to finance the system's work inside the Ministry of Interior.

The law did not include a visible head of the system, but eventually, it was entrusted to the RSS and continued by *Acción Social* from 2005 until 2011, when the UARIV was created. The leadership of the RSS and *Acción Social* meant that this first period of State humanitarian assistance was subsumed inside long-standing peacebuilding-as-poverty-reduction efforts in the country's more remote areas. This was the original spirit of the RSS, following up the work of the National Plan for Rehabilitation from the nineteen eighties, blurring the lines between humanitarian action and social policy.[85] This suggests the system had an ingrained vocation toward development while, at the same time, pushing for the quick creation of emergency response capabilities. During this period, the international humanitarian community parachuted into the country and took root, supported by generous US and European Union support.

---

[84] Regular State procurement requires a lengthy process to ensure fairness and avoid corruption. Given the situation's urgency, emergency relief and reconstruction activities usually have a different regime. Thus, these activities are carefully surveilled by the Comptroller's Office. For instance, during *Colombia Humanitaria*, the Office prevented the diversion of 30,000 million Colombian pesos (over US$16 million dollars) of humanitarian assistance; see Morelli 2011.

[85] Aparicio Cuervo 2022.

2 The State as a Humanitarian Actor: Opportunities and Challenges ...

Yet, different Colombian actors remained cautious about expanding international humanitarian support. There was an aversion to charity (*asistencialismo*) and the direct provision of goods or money because of its political use. Similarly, the Catholic Church also preferred transformative solutions emanating from Latin Americans' reaction to the Second Vatican Council and the Liberation Theology tradition. The RSS also incorporated ideas of capabilities, human development, and human capital while questioning *asistencialismo* and seeing people as passive recipients of government support.[86] It is interesting how even the CRC questioned emergency support that could create dependency on the population.[87] Moreover, as soon as 2002, situations of harm resulting from external cooperation were already occurring in the country, adding reasons of concern.[88]

A critical change in the system's dynamics occurred in 2004 when the Constitutional Court sentenced that there was an "unconstitutional state of affairs" concerning the State's protection of the displaced populations. This legal tool pressures the government to act, requiring periodic reports to the Court until a certain threshold has been passed and the situation is again considered under control. From there on, it is possible to follow in detail the evolution of the State's action through government reports, reviews from civil society to the reports, and new requests by the Court to the government.[89]

By 2011, just before the UARIV was created, the issue of registering and characterizing displaced populations remained a central, open issue.[90] Recognition as forcibly displaced is necessary to access all protection mechanisms, including humanitarian assistance. Colombia's Attorney General's Office observed that structural discrimination against the displaced at all government levels was a significant barrier to access support. The displaced were seen by State officials as "bleeding the State".[91] The budget allocation was also an issue of concern because, despite commitments from the central level, distribution at the local level was compromised by other expenditures and other budget execution difficulties.[92]

Regarding humanitarian assistance provision, local distribution faced a double challenge. First, the registration assessment was centralized in Bogota so that the disbursement of national resources could be approved. This slowed down the reaction

---

[86] On the RSS see Casasbuenas 2001 presentation about going beyond *asistencialismo* and promoting the full development of all human capabilities. Also, see Partridge and Mejía 2000.

[87] Restrepo 2006.

[88] Nubia Bello and Millán 2005. This paper resulted in the creation of a graduate program on *Acción sin Daño* (Doing no-harm), especially oriented to humanitarian workers that still exists at the National University of Colombia.

[89] Rodríguez Garavito and Rodríguez Franco 2010. CODHES, a Colombian civil society organization, has been publishing follow up reports since 2008, at least 22 by March, 2024. They are available at https://codhes.org/category/publicaciones/el-reto-ante-la-tragedia-humanitaria-del-desplazamiento-forzado/. Accessed 11 June 2024.

[90] Procuraduría General de la Nación 2011.

[91] Ibid., p. 120.

[92] Ibid, pp. 121–126.

to the emergency. Second, local offices took advantage of the availability of international cooperation support, delegating a large amount of their fiscal, administrative, and operational responsibilities, thus resulting in little to no capacity building.[93]

The creation of the UARIV was a paradigm change in institutionalizing humanitarian functions inside the government. It enlarged the population eligible for State support, from displaced to all types of victims. Reparation was added to the ongoing tasks, offering a lump payment to those affected by the conflict, besides land restitution efforts. In this sense, the creation of the UARIV separated the problem of displaced populations from poverty reduction. This is very significant from conceptual and institutional points of view because poverty reduction is an expansion of the welfare state while reparation as transitional justice is only temporary. The office in charge of poverty reduction strategies, particularly cash transfers, became a department, i.e., almost a ministry. Conversely, the UARIV, located under this new office, was given a finite mandate of ten years, which was extended for another ten years in 2021.[94] A consequence of this time limit is that, at some point, UARIV humanitarian capabilities may pass to the UNGRD.

This new phase of work on displacement resulted in progress at different levels, including allocating up to 1.5% of the country's gross domestic product.[95] Humanitarian attention has mainly been standardized, with clear protocols for different types of displacement, the contents of the support, and the responsibilities of different offices. Massive displacement keeps challenging national capacities, though, while the government highlights that humanitarian support should be temporal, giving way to opportunities for self-support.[96] The unconstitutional state of affairs has been only partially resolved.[97]

2.5.3 Humanitarian Demining

While all IHL and human rights violations require a response by the State, not all are presented as humanitarian action. For instance, changes in the protocols on the use of force by the army relate to abiding by IHL but not, of course, becoming a humanitarian actor. Land restitution, a critical component of the peace process, is also not framed as humanitarian. At an early stage, the Ministry of Defence presented support to demobilized guerrillas as "humanitarian attention", the first step towards

---

[93] An interviewee at the UARIV mentioned this is still the case in some regions.

[94] Law 2078 of 2021.

[95] DNP 2021. Civil society comments to the figures point out that they include general allocations covering education and health, so the budget exclusive for victims is less than half the one reported— Comisión de Seguimiento a la Política Pública sobre Desplazamiento Forzado 2022.

[96] DNP 2021.

[97] Comisión de Seguimiento a la Política Pública sobre Desplazamiento Forzado 2022.

2 The State as a Humanitarian Actor: Opportunities and Challenges … 63

full reintegration.[98] This program resembles the support to displaced populations while adding emphasis on child guerrillas, yet reincorporation is not considered humanitarian anymore.

Humanitarian demining is another action that started as part of the army's actions and gradually expanded. The Colombian government was an early adopter of the 1997 Ottawa Convention on the anti-personnel mine prohibition, which it stopped domestically producing in 1996.[99] Through law 759 of 2002, the government created a commission to follow up on the demining commitments, comprised of the Vice-president, Defence, Interior, Foreign Affairs, and Health Ministries, the DNP, and the President's office in charge of IHL, as well as invitees from other offices of the State, armed forces and civil society. It included "National humanitarian missions" led by the ombudsman's office, responsible for fact-finding and providing recommendations.

The law also created the Land-mine Observatory inside the President's Office to gather and systematize information about the demining process—location of mines, incidents, and demining activities. In the end, this office has been coordinating the de-mining actions since then, with different degrees of authority as governments prioritize this task differently. In 2007, it became a program,[100] followed by a national policy in 2009 around four objectives: provide centralized coordination, increase national capacities, educate the population about mine risk, and support mine victims.[101] In 2014, it became a "dirección" (office),[102] gaining prominence towards the 2016 peace agreement, but in 2019, it was subsumed into the Office of the High Commissioner for Peace[103] and presented as a "group".

It should also be noted that demining was expected to be a finite task, namely ending "not later than ten years after the entry into force" of the Convention.[104] For Colombia, the deadline was 2010, when the government asked for an extension, which happened again in 2020, so the present deadline is 2025. The peace agreement resulted in a drastic decrease in mine incidents, but given that armed conflict persists and illegal groups keep using mines, finishing the task is extremely challenging.

Compared to other State humanitarian practices, there are two facts to highlight. First, while the system benefits from decentralized local support, the core of its work depends on specialized technical capabilities concentrated on specific battalions. The impossibility of covering all the needs with the existing capabilities gave way in 2011 to authorize humanitarian demining by civilians, both domestic and international

---

[98] Ministerio de Defensa 2002.

[99] Comisión de la Verdad 2022b, p. 159.

[100] Decree 2150 of 2007.

[101] Departamento Nacional de Planeación 2009.

[102] Decree 1649 of 2014.

[103] Decree 179 of 2019.

[104] Convention on the Prohibition of the Use, Stockpiling, Production and Transfer of Anti-Personnel Mines and on their Destruction, opened for signature December 3, 1997, entered into force 1 March 1999, Article 5.

organizations.[105] Given the risks associated with demining, authorization requires a strict accreditation process. Even in this case, organizations such as the CRC still only participate in risk education activities, as the inherent closeness of demining with the army is seen as a menace to its neutrality.

Second, demining is exceptional because it is a State humanitarian action that financially depends not insignificantly on international cooperation. The 2009 policy expected 14% of the costs to be covered by donors, and the opening to civilian demining also sought to tap into international funding—external sources fully pay for it.[106] Full institutionalization of this humanitarian practice has not been achieved.

2.5.4 Missing Persons

Another State humanitarian practice associated with armed conflict that deserves to be mentioned is finding persons missing due to the armed conflict. Finding missing persons[107] offers an illuminating contrast with demining because it is a humanitarian action long under the umbrella of the ICRC. However, given that around 121,768 persons went missing because of the armed conflict between 1985 and 2016,[108] the task of finding them is beyond what any NGO can do. The State has had identification capacities inside the Office of the Attorney General. These are not presented as humanitarian mainly because identification is not disconnected from the criminal investigation. It is also worth noting that the disappearances were part of the counterinsurgency strategy, inherited later by paramilitary forces—but not exclusive of them. Forced disappearance was not banned until 2000,[109] and the practice remained common until 2013, still happening today.

Finding missing persons was included in the 2016 peace agreement, resulting in the creation of a specific Unit to this end inside the new transitional justice system.[110] The Unit is extrajudicial, as it does not aim to establish responsibility behind disappearances but mainly to find and identify the remains of disappeared persons and return them to their families. The ICRC and Switzerland have supported the Unit and UNDP for contracting staff. Yet, by 2018, it already had its own national staff

---

[105] Decree 3750 of 2011.

[106] A US philanthropic foundation has provided more than US$ 40 million dollars for demining, including through the army. See: La Silla Vacía (2021) Howard Buffet, El Nuevo Gran Colombiano. https://www.lasillavacia.com/silla-nacional/howard-buffett-el-nuevo-gran-colombiano/. Accessed 11 June 2024.

[107] Missing persons is the term used by the ICRC, included in the official name of the Unit.

[108] Comisión de la Verdad 2022b, p. 169.

[109] Law 589 of 2000.

[110] Legislative act 1 of 2017.

and growing financial independence.[111] Resources from international cooperation are available, and the Unit has a section in charge, but it is not always keen on taking advantage of them.

Given the size of the task, a significant issue has been planning for action. The creation of the Unit raises expectations that it cannot fulfil in the short run. Capacities are limited—e.g., there is a shortage of forensic physicians in the country—and the work is physically and psychologically demanding. Decentralizing action is not necessarily easy for multiple reasons, including stretching limited resources and implications in terms of access. Indeed, staff working for the Unit have been killed doing their job.

The Unit was also conceived with a finite mission, initially 20 years, which has conditioned its institutionalization. Particularly problematic has been creating forensic capabilities, as it is unclear if using resources for physical infrastructure is desirable and what will happen to it once the unit stops existing. The assigned time will probably be insufficient, so strategies for becoming permanent require consideration.

2.6   The State as a Humanitarian Actor

The Colombian State became involved in humanitarian language and practices because of international trends that started in the nineties. This was not because humanitarian issues were unimportant before this. Indeed, Colombian institutions had embraced humanitarian law even before it was created. A humanitarian framing was not common or significant before the nineties, at least in the country, so other frameworks were used instead.

The gradual appropriation of the humanitarian language to describe some of the State's actions was not the result of a co-option strategy—although manipulation existed. On the contrary, it started to permeate State institutions as the country welcomed international humanitarian action, and emergency response was included among the components of crisis management. Response to internally displaced populations was pivotal in this transformation, as it combined the characteristics of a traditional humanitarian crisis with the indisputable responsibility of the State to offer protection to the affected populations. Initial legislation to address forced displacement recognized a right to receive humanitarian assistance and the responsibility to offer it as part of the integral attention to the problem. Thereon, the State started generating capacities to fulfil this responsibility.

Thus, the history of the State's humanitarian practice in Colombia is primarily about the enlargement of the welfare state. It has resulted from emergencies hitting Colombian society to a degree that national institutions cannot ignore. Attending

---

[111] According to two interviewees, the State pays better than the international cooperation.

to these crises demands articulating solutions that reach different degrees of institutionalization, depending on multiple factors. Understanding these processes and their contribution to protecting vulnerable populations is the aim of recognizing the State as a humanitarian actor.

The institutionalization process starts with deciding whether to create an office in charge. As crises are expected to be temporal, it may be enough to outsource support, as calamities to the CRC in the 1940s, to create ad-hoc initiatives, as for reconstructions after disasters, or to create "systems" that distribute responsibilities across different existing offices—initially the case for internal displacement. When offices are created, they can also receive a finite mandate for a fixed number of years. This is common in efforts linked to transitional justice, which always include a deadline for the transition.

Interestingly, except for the case of missing persons, all these offices are created as part of the President's Office. This position, the highest level possible, allows these offices to access resources and attain cooperation from other branches of the government. These offices also gain visibility nationally and internationally as crises gather the public's attention and motivate concern among donors, neighbouring countries, NGOs, and philanthropic organizations. State humanitarian offices tend to be dynamic and creative, usually supported by the inspiring leadership of their first heads.

On the other hand, being so close to the top of the executive makes their work vulnerable to the politics of the presidential system. Every four years, these offices and units are subject to the new government reconsideration, which can go from disbanding (Venezuelan migration) to moving to a ministry (disasters in 1992), merging into another office (landmines), or becoming part of an administrative department—i.e., close to a ministry (victims). Through these different outcomes, humanitarian action becomes (or not) part of the State, more than a government initiative. They gain permanent staff, a fixed budget, and recognition among other State branches. Policies become official, procedures become standardized, and the goal of protection starts to take shape and reach those in need. This is not a fast or linear process but benefits from the State's overall capacities, contributing to its consolidation and legitimacy. It must be stressed that understanding this transition from the government to the State is essential to studying the State's humanitarianism and the politics of protection.

The present review of State humanitarianism in Colombia describes multiple challenges in consolidating the different offices' efforts. Still, at least three deserve attention in the future exploration of the State as a humanitarian actor in other settings: decentralization, the local interplay of checks and balances, and the aversion to *asistencialismo*. Starting at the top of the government, humanitarian offices are also far from the field. Their initial compact nature and central location challenge their capacity to reach those in need, usually in the country's more remote areas. For this, partnering with local governments is crucial but difficult, as those have different dynamics, capacities, and priorities that may or may not align with those devised in Bogota. Some technical knowledge, such as demining and forensics, can hinder decentralization efforts, while local governments can use international humanitarianism to avoid their responsibilities—as mentioned about internal displacement. This challenge resonates with the decolonial query on the State, while focusing on the practical problem of provision. How State humanitarianism achieves functional decentralization is basic to understanding its reach.

Domestic checks and balances are critical to the evolution of State humanitarian institutions. Typical actors, such as NGOs and civil society, play well-understood roles. Still, State humanitarianism grows to an important extent through the interaction of bureaucracies,[112] the pressure of Courts, and the surveillance of the control institutions—i.e., the Comptroller's Office, the Attorney's Office, and the Office of the Ombudsman. Crises require extraordinary faculties, which may not be covered by the Constitution or by procurement regulation. Emergency declarations are ex-post validated by the judicial system, and State humanitarian offices have special regimes for contracting and project execution. This makes them appealing and vulnerable to political use and corruption. Consequently, their work is zealously audited by the public offices and by mass media. Interaction with the Comptroller's Office is frequently mentioned as central to the considerations in responding to all types of crises, especially if they need to execute actions that have not been done before—a multi-million reconstruction or attending to Venezuelan migrants. International humanitarianism plays a role in bypassing regulations or overcoming restrictions, which can help in the short run but can negatively affect institutionalization. Indeed, sometimes it is better to encourage affected populations to use the judicial system so structural solutions are incorporated legally into State humanitarianism rather than the immediate momentary support from external actors. This trial-and-error construction of the institutions is also essential to understanding the State's humanitarianism.[113]

Finally, practically none of these offices are exclusively humanitarian or limited to providing assistance. They all incorporate a disaster management cycle way of thinking, articulating relief, recovery, and prevention. Even the Unit in charge of missing persons includes actions in participation and work with the affected communities and is part of a larger system of justice and reparation. The so called nexus[114] is inherent to them, a central preoccupation from their conception. This is so mainly because, despite their different time limits and institutional configurations, protecting populations is the *raison d'être* of the State, and all the State's humanitarian efforts are interlocked with its welfare functions. At the same time, all actors have a general aversion to generating dependency. Indeed, this has to do with the reluctance by some of these offices to be seen as "humanitarian", as this is still associated with charity—a view shared even by traditional humanitarian actors, such as the CRC and the Catholic Church. Such a vision gave way to the internationally praised solution

---

[112] Sierra and Ibarra 2019; Vera Lugo 2022.

[113] This point largely overlaps with the humanitarian community discussion about accountability.

[114] Gómez and Kawaguchi 2018.

for Venezuelan migrants that, while far from perfect, is close to the humanitarian ideal. Understanding how State humanitarianism embodies the nexus and provides solutions that reflect this preoccupation with both short and long-term is another critical part of acknowledging it as an actor.

2.7 Conclusion: The State and Decolonizing Humanitarianism

The challenge of decentralization, local checks and balances, and addressing the aversion to *asistencialismo* make for an appealing research agenda in understanding States' humanitarian agency. Still, they do not directly answer how this perspective addresses colonialism concerns and the assumptions underlying the anti-State bias. For this, it is necessary to go back to the roots of the problem.

First, State humanitarianism maintains our shared concern for human suffering but cannot present it in terms of "distant strangers". The subjects of State humanitarianism are neither distant nor strangers. They are, to a large extent, its citizens and, when not, as in the case of Venezuelans, they are neighbours linked by a shared history, directly present in the territory, and an opportunity for development. This is not, of course, the only perception of Venezuelans in Colombia, as xenophobia will always be a concern, but that is part of what State humanitarianism must deal with.

Understanding how engaging in humanitarian action enlarges the welfare state rescues the question of capacities that make traditional humanitarianism colonial and puts it at the centre. It recognizes that States are the only sustained, durable, nexus-inclusive, accountable solution to humanitarian problems. The history of Colombia shows first how this enlargement of the welfare state occurs organically through domestic struggles for protection, the creation of institutions for its provision, and their evolution. As international humanitarianism enters the scene, traditional humanitarian actors also help create these institutions, and only from that perspective does their colonial breath fade out. Focusing on how capacities are engendered and the challenges of making them up to the task in the long run is a more constructive approach to understanding how human societies develop protective structures. It also better reflects the second or third-best nature of traditional humanitarian solutions.

Acknowledging the State as a humanitarian actor is not "the end of history". There is no perfect way to protect humans against multiple crises with humanitarian consequences. State humanitarian offices are not silver bullets or models easily replicable in different contexts. Nurturing State capabilities is a slow, non-linear process. The classic concerns that make liberal humanitarianism overly sensitive about access and diplomacy will not disappear or become irrelevant. The possibility of extreme cases making distrust of the State necessary cannot be discarded, but making such a worldview central to humanitarianism negates the possibility of progress, reproduces the conditions for distrust, and fails to build toward a more resilient future. Humanitarianism is too important be left to traditional humanitarians.

Acknowledgments This research was possible thanks to an academic development leave granted by my home institution, Ritsumeikan Asia Pacific University, and the support of the Research Office. I am grateful to Sandra Borda and the Department of Political Science and Global Studies, Universidad de los Andes, for hosting me in Bogotá. My deepest gratitude goes to all the people who generously opened time in their busy agendas, gave me access to resources, or provided precious comments. This includes the Latin American Humanitarian Observatory, as well as many friends, such as Roberto Angulo, Juan Ricardo Aparicio, Al Cook, Ana María Cruz, Pablo Kalmanovitz, Rodrigo Mena, Juliana Poveda, Gloria Restrepo, Maria Camila Suarez Pava, Juan Pablo Vera, among many others that I cannot mention. I presented this research at the 2023 International Humanitarian Studies Association Conference in Dhaka, Bangladesh, where the audience offered encouraging feedback. Appreciations to the panel organizers—Jessica Hawkins, Maria Kett, James Smith—and my fellow panellists. I greatly benefitted from the continuous support of the YIHL editors and the extremely useful comments from two anonymous reviewers. The usual disclaimers apply.

References

ALNAP (2022) The State of the Humanitarian System. Report, London: ALNAP/ODI

Aneja U (2014) South-South Humanitarianism. Report, Haryana: Jindal School of International Affairs

Aparicio Cuervo JR (2012) Rumores, residuos y Estado en "la mejor esquina de Sudamérica": Una cartografía de lo "humanitario" en Colombia. Bogotá D.C.: Universidad de los Andes

Aparicio Cuervo JR (2022) Relaciones sociales, infraestructuras y manejo del riesgo en los sistemas de protección social en Colombia: hacia una etnografía de la política pública. In: Aparicio Cuervo JR and Fernández Pinto M (eds) Neoliberalismo en Colombia: Contextos, Complejidad y Política Pública. Bogotá: Universdad de los Andes, pp 135–163

Barbelet V (2018) As local as possible, as international as necessary: Understanding capacity and complementarity in humanitarian action. Report, London: ODI

Barbelet V, Davies G, Flint J, et al. (2021) Interrogating the evidence base on humanitarian localisation: a literature study. Report, London: ODI

Barnett M (2011) Empire of humanity: A history of humanitarianism. Ithaca: Cornell University Press

Barnett M (2020) Humanitarianism and Human Rights: A World of Differences? Cambridge: Cambridge University Press

Binder A, Steets J and Meier C (2010) Humanitarian assistance: truly universal? A Mapping Study of Non-Western Donors. *GPPi Research Paper No. 12.* Berlin: Global Public Policy Institute

Borda Guzmán S (2014) Providing Relief in Times of War: The Role of the ICRC in the Colombian Conflict During the Uribe Administration (2002-2010). In: Zwitter A, Lamont CK, Heintze H-J, et al. (eds) Humanitarian Action: Global, Regional and Domestic Legal Responses. Cambridge: Cambridge University Press

Bradley M (2013) International humanitarian law, non-state armed groups and the International Committee of the Red Cross in Colombia. Journal of International Humanitarian Legal Studies 4(1): 108–134

Capie D (2015) The United States and Humanitarian Assistance and Disaster Relief (HADR) in East Asia: Connecting Coercive and Non-Coercive Uses of Military Power. Journal of Strategic Studies 38(3): 309–331

Casasbuenas G (2001) Colombia: La Red de Solidaridad Social. Washington D.C.: IADB

Checkland O (1994) Humanitarianism and the Emperor's Japan. New York: St. Martin's Press

Colombia Humanitaria (2013) Modelo Integrado de Intervención para la Atención y la Rehabilitación. Report, Bogotá: Colombia Humanitaria

Colombia Humanitaria (n.d.) Estudio de Caso. Report, Bogota: Colombia Humanitaria

Comisión de la Verdad (2022a) No matarás: relato histórico del conflicto armado interno en Colombia. Bogotá: Comisión de la Verdad

Comisión de la Verdad (2022b) Hasta la guerra tiene limites: violaciones de los derechos humanos, infracciones al derecho internacional humanitario y responsabilidades colectivas. Bogotá: Comisión de la Verdad

Comisión de Seguimiento a la Política Pública sobre Desplazamiento Forzado (2022) Estado de los derechos de los desplazados anted de la prórroga de la Ley de Víctimas. Bogotá: CODHES

Conferencia Episcopal de Colombia (1995) Derechos Humanos. Desplazados por Violencia en Colombia. Santafé de Bogotá D.C.: Conferencia Episcopal de Colombia

Cunningham AJ (2024) Authoritarian Practices and Humanitarian Negotiations. Abingdon: Routledge

Davey E (2013) A history of the humanitarian system: Western origins and foundations. Report, London: ODI

Davies K (2012) Continuity, change and contest: Meanings of humanitarian' from the 'Religion of Humanity' to the Kosovo war. Report, London: ODI

Davis M (2001) Late Victorian holocausts: El Niño famines and the making of the third world. London: Verso de Waal A (2018) Mass Starvation: The History and Future of Famine. Cambridge: Polity

Departamento Nacional de Planeación (1995) Programa Nacional de Atención Integral a la Población Desplazada por la Violencia. Santafé de Bogotá, D.C.: DNP

Departamento Nacional de Planeación (2009) Política Nacional de Acción Integral contra Minas Antipersona (MAP), Municiones sin Explotar (MUSE) y Artefactos Explosivos Improvisados (AEI). Bogotá: DNP

Departamento Nacional de Planeación (2018) Estrategia para la Atención de la Migración desde Venezuela. Bogotá: DNP

Departamento Nacional de Planeación (2022) Estrategia para la Integración de la Población Migrante Venezolana como Factor de Desarrollo para el País. Bogotá: DNP

Development Initiatives (2019) Global Humanitarian Assistance Report 2019. Bristol

DNP (2021) Política Nacional de Atención y Reparación Integral a las Víctimas. Bogotá: DNP

DuBois M (2018) The new humanitarian basics. Report, London: ODI

Eslava L and Pahuja S (2020) The State and International Law: A Reading from the Global South. Humanity 11(1): 118–138

Finnemore M (1996) Constructing Norms of Humanitarian Intervention. In: Katzenstein PJ (ed) The Culture of National Security: Norms and Identity in World Politics. New York: Columbia University Press, pp 153–185

Forsythe DP (2001) Humanitarian protection: The International Committee of the Red Cross and the United Nations High Commissioner for Refugees. Revue Internationale de la Croix-Rouge/International Review of the Red Cross 83(843): 675–698

Fukuda-Parr S and Muchhala B (2020) The Southern origins of sustainable development goals: Ideas, actors, aspirations. World development 126: 104–706

Getachew A (2019) Worldmaking after Emprire: The Rise and Fall of Self-Determination. Princeton: Princeton University Press

Gómez OA (2019a) Humanitarian Crises and the Rise of the Rest: The future of humanitarianism from four Latin American emerging countries perspective. Report, Tokyo: JICA-RI

Gómez OA (2019b) What Is at Stake in Localizing Human Security Norms in the ASEAN+3?: A Comparative Analysis of 11 Qualitative Regional Review Surveys. In: Mine Y, Gómez OA and Muto A (eds) Human Security Norms in East Asia. Cham: Palgrave Macmillan, pp 273–294

Gómez OA (2021) Localisation or deglobalisation? East Asia and the dismantling of liberal humanitarianism. Third World Quarterly 42(6): 1347–1364

Gómez OA and Kawaguchi C (2018) A theory for the continuum: multiple approaches to humanitarian crisis management. In: Hanatani A, Gómez OA and Kawaguchi C (eds) Crisis Management Beyond the Humanitarian-Development Nexus. Abingdon: Routledge, pp 15–36

Gómez OA, Lucatello S and Mena R (2024) The Latin American experience: inequality's role in shaping humanitarianism. In: Roth S, Purkayastha B and Denskus T (eds) Handbook on Humanitarianism and Inequality. Cheltenham: Edward Elgar Publishing Inc., pp 458–473

Gong GW (1984) The Standard of 'Civilization' in International Society. New York: Oxford University Press

Gonzalez-Jacome J (2011) Emergency Powers and the Feeling of Backwardness in Latin American State Formation. American University International Law Review 26(4): 1073–1106

Gurmendi Dunkelberg A (2023) Des-Encanto: Latin America and International Humanitarian Law. In: Krieger H, Kalmanovitz P, Lieblich E, et al. (eds) Yearbook of International Humanitarian Law, Volume 24 (2021): Cultures of International Humanitarian Law. The Hague: T.M.C. Asser Press, pp 3–31

Harvey P (2009) Towards good humanitarian government: The role of the affected state in disaster response. Report, London: Overseas Development Institute

High-Level Panel on Humanitarian Financing (2016) Too important to fail—addressubg the humanitarian financing gap. Report

Hilton M, Baughan E, Davey E, et al. (2018) History and Humanitarianism: A Conversation. Past & Present 241(1): e1–e38

Hong Y-S (2015) Cold War Germany, the Third World, and the Global Humanitarian Regime. New York: Cambridge University Press

Hönke J and Müller M-M (2016) The Global Making of Policing: Postcolonial Perspectives. Abingdon: Routledge

ICRC (2009) Informe 2008 Colombia. Report, Bogotá: ICRC

Inter-American Development Bank (2014) Informe iGOPP Regional. Report, Washington D.C.: IABD

Jaramillo Sierra IC and Buchely Ibarra LF (2019) Etnografías Burocráticas: Una Nueva Mirada aa la Construcción del Estado en Colombia. Bogotá, D.C.: Universidad de los Andes

Kalmanovitz P (2018) Entre el deber de protección y la necesidad militar: oscilaciones del discurso humanitario en Colombia, 1991–2016. Latin American Law Review 1: 33–60

Käser F (2016) A civilized nation: Japan and the Red Cross 1877–1900. European Review of History: Revue européenne d'histoire 23(1–2): 16–32

Koskenneiemi M (2002) The Gentle Civilizer of Nations: The Rise and Fall of International Law 1870–1960. Cambridge: Cambridge University Press

Labbé J and Daudin P (2015) Applying the humanitarian principles: Reflecting on the experience of the International Committee of the Red Cross. International Review of the Red Cross 97(897–898): 183–210

Lucatello S and Gómez OA (2022) Understanding humanitarian localization in Latin America—as local as possible, but how necessary? Journal of International Humanitarian Action 7(1)

Mac Ginty R and Peterson JH (2015) The Routledge Companion to Humanitarian Action. Abingdon: Routledge

Macrae J, Collinson S, Buchanan-Smith M, et al. (2002) Uncertain power: The changing role of official donors in humanitarian action. HPG Report. London: ODI, 91

Mawdsley E (2015) The Routledge Companion to Humanitarian Action. In: Mac Ginty R and Peterson JH (eds) The Routledge Companion to Humanitarian Action. Abingdon: Routledge, pp 204–214

Ministerio de Defensa (2002) Programa para la Atención Humanitaria al Desmovilizado. Bogotá: Ministerio de Defensa

Ministerio de Salud (1982) Atención de Emergencias en el Sector Salud. Report, Bogotá: Ministerio de Salud

Ministerio de Salud (1986) Programa de Preparativos para Emergencias y Desastres. Report, Bogotá: Ministerio de Salud

Morelli S (2011) Presentación. Economía Colombiana 331: 2

Nubia Bello M and Millán C (2005) La intervención institucional en contextos culturales distintos: lógicas en tensión y contradicción. Palimpsestvs 5: 250–260

OECD (2019) Evaluación de la gobernanza del riesgo en Colombia. Paris: OECD Publishing

ONAD (1990) Prevención de Desastres y Gestión Municipal: Compendio de documentos de trabajo. Report, Bogotá, D.E.: ONAD

Organization of American States (1991) Inter-American Convention to Facilitate Disaster Assistance. Santiago: OAE

PAHO (1979) Emergency Preparedness and Disaster Relief Coordination Program in the Americas. Report, Washington, D.C.: PAHO

PAHO (1994) Emergency Preparedness and Disaster Relief Coordination Program (PED), with Emphasis on PAHO's Experience in Humanitarian Assistance. Report, Washington, D.C.: PAHO

Partridge WL and Mejía MC (2000) La Respuesta Institucional al Desplazamiento Forzado en Colombia. In: Partridge WL (ed) Reasentamiento en Colombia. pp 233–243

Presidencia de la República (2003) International cooperation strategy. Bogotá: Presidencia de la República, Agencia Colombiana de Cooperacifon Internacional, Ministerio de Relaciones Exteriores

Presidencia de la República and Ministerio de Relaciones Exteriores (1991) Guidelines for Colombian Diplomatic and Consular Missions in Case of Disaster. Report, Bogotá D.E.: Presidencia de la República

Procuraduría General de la Nación (2011) Superación o Persistencia del Estado de Cosas Inconstitucional. Bogotá: Procuraduría General de la Nación

Ramirez Gómez F and Cardona Arboleda OD (1996) El Sistema Nacional para la Prevención y Atención de Desastres en Colombia. Estado, Sociedad y Gestión de los Desastres en América Latina: En Busca del Paradigma Perdido. Lima: ITDG, pp 255–307

Reeves C (2020) The early history of the Red Cross Society of China and its relation to the Red Cross Movement. In: Wylie N, Oppenheimer M and Crossland J (eds) The Red Cross Movement: Myths, practices and turning points. Manchester: Manchester University Press, pp 81–96

Restrepo JD (2006) La Cruz Roja en la historia de Colombia: 1915–2005. Bogotá: Cruz Roja Colombiana

Robillard S, Atim T and Maxwell T (2021) Localization: A "Landscape" Report. Report, Boston: Feinstein International Center

Rodríguez Garavito C and Rodríguez Franco D (2010) Cortes y cambio social: Cómo la Corte Constitucional transformó el desplazamiento forzado en Colombia. Bogotá D.C.: Dejusticia

Roepstorff K (2016) India as Humanitarian Actor: Convergences and Divergences with DAC Donor Principles and Practices. In: Sezgin Z and Dijkzeul D (eds) The New Humanitarians in International Practice: Emerging actors and contested principles. Abingdon: Routledge, pp 45–63

Rohwerder B (2016) Humanitarian response in middle-income countries. Report, Birmingham: GSRDC

Saavedra A. MdR (1996) Desastre y Riesgo: Actores Sociales en la reconstrucción de Armero y Chinchiná. Santafé de Bogotá D.C.: CINEP

Salvatici S (2019) A history of humanitarianism, 1755–1989: In the name of others. Manchester: Manchester University Press

Sandoval Jaramillo C (1992) *La Difusión del Derecho Internacional Humanitario en Colombia y la Cruz Roja*. Universidad Externado de Colombia, Bogotá

Santos BdS (2024) The Law of the Excluded: Indigenous Justice, Plurinationality and Interculturality in Bolivia and Ecuador. In: Santos BdS, Araújo S and Aragón Andrade O (eds) Decolonizing Constitutionalism: Beyond False or Impossible Promises. Abingdon: Routledge, pp 288–322

Schulz C-A (2014) Civilisation, Barbarism and the Making of Latin America's Place in 19th-Century International Society. Millennium 42(3): 837–859

Scott R (2015) Financing in Crisis? Making humanitarian finance fit for the future. Report, Paris: OECD

Slim H (2015) Humanitarian Ethics: A Guide to the Morality of Aid in War and Disaster. Oxford: Oxford University Press

Slim H (2021) Localization is Self-Determination. Frontiers in Political Science 3

Smith K (2011) Non-DAC Donors and Humanitarian Aid: Shifting structures, changing trends. Report, Wells: Development Initiatives

Stamatov P (2013) The Origins of Global Humanitarianism: Religion, Empires, and Advocacy. Cambridge: Cambridge University Press

Trias APL and Cook ADB (2023) Military humanitarian and disaster governance networks in Southeast Asia: framework and analysis. Disasters 47(1): 205–241

UNGRD (2013) Estandarización de Ayuda Humanitaria de Colombia. Report, Bogotá: UNGRD

Valencia Villa A (1995) Derecho Humanitario para Colombia. Santafé de Bogotá, D.C.: Defensoría del Pueblo

Van Dijk B (2021) Internationalizing Colonial War: on the Unintended Consequences of the Interventions of the International Committee of the Red Cross in South-East Asia, 1945–1949*. Past & Present 250(1): 243–283

Vera Lugo JP (2022) Burocracias humanitarias en Colombia: conocimiento técnico y disputas políticas en la implementación de la Ley de Víctimas y Restitución de Tierras. Revista de Estudios Sociales 81: 21–37

Villarraga Sarmiento A (2005) Exigencias Humanitarias de la Población Civil: Hacia el logro de compromisos y acuerdos humanitarios. Bogotá D.C.: Fundación Cultura Democrática

Zadeh-Cummings N (2022) Through the looking glass: Coloniality and mirroring in localisation. Report, Burwood: Deakin University

Zapata Báez RA (2014) 90 lecciones aprendidas para la atención humanitaria y la rehabilitación de desastres identificadas a partir de la experiencia de atención de la emergencia a generada por el fenómeno de la Niña 2010–2011 en Colombia. Bogotá: Colombia Humanitaria

Part II
Other Articles

Chapter 3
Nerve Agents by Another Name: The Thirty-Year Effort to Close a Loophole on Chemical Weapons

Neil Davison

Contents

3.1   Introduction 78
3.2   Origins 79
3.3   A Trigger for Action 82
3.4   Reframing the Narrative: The Role of the ICRC 84
3.5   Expanding Multilateral Initiatives and Unforeseen Events 87
3.6   Multilateral Decision-Time 90
3.7   An Important Clarification of International Law 92
3.8   Ambiguities Revisited? 93
3.9   A "Riot Control Agents-Only" Approach 95
3.10 Lessons for Other Multilateral Efforts 96
3.11 Conclusion 99
References 100

Abstract   A political compromise during the negotiation of the 1993 Chemical Weapons Convention created ambiguity at the heart of the treaty. The question of whether the use of toxic chemicals as weapons for law enforcement must be limited to riot control agents ("tear gas") only, or whether other highly toxic chemicals could also be used, was left open to interpretation. This chapter traces the thirty-year struggle to close that loophole. These efforts eventually resulted in a legal clarification in 1 December 2021 confirming that the use of aerosolized central nervous system-acting chemicals is prohibited for law enforcement. The chapter explores key developments that led to this decision, with particular attention to the efforts of the ICRC and experts in academia, civil society organizations, and the scientific and medical communities, to highlight and reframe the problem. The loophole may have shrunk, but has it closed? The chapter highlights remaining ambiguities and draws lessons for broader disarmament and arms control efforts.

Keywords   Chemical weapons · International law · Chemical Weapons Convention (CWC) · Law enforcement · Organisation for the Prohibition of Chemical Weapons (OPCW) · Disarmament · Arms control · Toxic chemicals ·

N. Davison (✉)
Geneva, Switzerland

© T.M.C. ASSER PRESS and the authors 2025
H. Krieger et al. (eds.), *Yearbook of International Humanitarian Law, Volume 26 (2023)*,
Yearbook of International Humanitarian Law 26,
https://doi.org/10.1007/978-94-6265-663-5_3

Riot control agents · Fentanyl · Central nervous system · International Committee of the Red Cross (ICRC)

This chapter is dedicated to the memory of Julian Perry Robinson (1941–2020)[1]

3.1 Introduction

After a decade of disarmament negotiations, the 1993 Chemical Weapons Convention (CWC) was an extraordinary achievement in establishing a comprehensive ban on chemical weapons. It is now almost universal, with 193 States party to it and only four yet to join.[2] Today the prohibition of the use of chemical weapons is part of customary international humanitarian law binding on all parties to all armed conflicts.[3] The CWC was a significant leap forward following prior attempts to codify a taboo against poisoning by prohibiting the use in armed conflict of "asphyxiating or deleterious gases" in the 1899 Hague Declaration[4] and of "asphyxiating, poisonous or other gases" in the 1925 Geneva Protocol.[5] Neither of these treaties prohibited their development, production, stockpiling and transfer, nor prevented extensive use of chemical weapons during the First World War and several other conflicts, including the Iran–Iraq War during the 1980s.

For the most part the word "comprehensive" is justified. However, the CWC provisions permitting the use of some toxic chemicals—namely riot control agents (e.g. "tear gas")—as weapons for law enforcement purposes, created ambiguity, for some at least, about whether such permitted use extended to other toxic chemicals. This ambiguity risked the continued pursuit of chemical weapons by another name and, for nearly three decades, remained unfinished business for the Convention. It was finally addressed, to a significant extent, in a 1 December 2021 decision by the CWC Conference of States Parties stating "… that the aerosolised use of CNS [central nervous system]-acting chemicals is understood to be inconsistent with law

---

[1] McLeish 2020.

[2] Organisation for the Prohibition of Chemical Weapons (OPCW), "Member States", available at: www.opcw.org/about-us/member-states. Non-Member States: Egypt, Israel, the Democratic People's Republic of Korea and South Sudan.

[3] See ICRC 2005.

[4] Declaration (IV.2) concerning Asphyxiating Gases, The Hague, opened for signature 29 July 1899 (entered into force 4 September 1900).

[5] Protocol for the Prohibition of the Use of Asphyxiating, Poisonous or Other Gases, and of Bacteriological Methods of Warfare, opened for signature 17 June 1925 (entered into force 8 February 1928).

enforcement purposes as a 'purpose not prohibited' under the Convention".[6] In other words, the decision clarifies that their use is prohibited.

The story of this important legal clarification is a long and twisting tale of military and law enforcement pressures, technological claims, inconsistent and contradictory terminology, unexpected events, breaks with consensus and ultimately a compromise that is both a successful multilateral achievement and an imperfect solution that leaves some questions unresolved. One contributing factor (among others) to the 2021 decision, which this chapter draws attention to, was the successful attempt to reframe the narrative around the use of toxic chemicals in law enforcement to focus on the actual or foreseeable impact on victims, notably through the work of the International Committee of the Red Cross (ICRC) and experts in academia, civil society organisations, and the scientific and medical communities. This approach remains relevant for continued efforts to ensure that any perceived loophole remains completely closed, and the experience holds lessons for other multilateral initiatives to uphold and strengthen constraints on weapons and methods of warfare.

3.2 Origins

During the latter stages of negotiations to adopt the CWC, provisions and definitions related to the use of toxic chemicals for law enforcement purposes were a point of debate.[7] Despite an absolute prohibition in the Convention of chemical weapons, including on the use of riot control agents as a "method of warfare",[8] governments wanted to retain the ability to use certain toxic chemicals as weapons in law enforcement and civil disturbances. The CWC defined toxic chemicals broadly as "[a]ny chemical which through its chemical action on life processes can cause death, temporary incapacitation or permanent harm to humans or animals",[9] established "law enforcement including domestic riot control purposes" as a purpose not prohibited under the Convention[10] and specifically defined riot control agents, a sub-category of toxic chemicals, as "[a]ny chemical not listed in a Schedule, which can produce rapidly in humans sensory irritation or disabling physical effects which disappear

---

[6] OPCW 2021a.

[7] Robinson 2007.

[8] Convention on the Prohibition of the Development, Production, Stockpiling and Use of Chemical Weapons and on their Destruction, opened for signature 13 January 1993, 1975 UNTS 45 (entered into force 29 April 1997) (Chemical Weapons Convention) Art. I.5.

[9] Ibid., Article II.2.

[10] Ibid., Article II.9(d).

within a short time following termination of exposure".[11] These toxic chemicals are permitted for law enforcement provided the "types and quantities are consistent with such purposes".[12]

Leaving aside the questionable merits of normalising the use of toxicity as a weapon for law enforcement in a treaty intended to prohibit this practice in general,[13] the compromise text on law enforcement purposes hid more disturbing disagreements. Firstly, a minority of States wanted to retain the ability to execute their citizens with toxic chemicals, including by lethal injection.[14] Secondly, and significantly, while most States saw "law enforcement purposes" as synonymous with the domestic use of riot control agents, some wanted room to develop other toxic chemicals as weapons, whether for use domestically or in military operations abroad.[15] In fact, the law enforcement provision in the Convention also left open disagreements as to which types of situations constitute "law enforcement purposes" where the use of certain toxic chemicals is permitted, in particular related to extra-territorial law enforcement activities carried out by militaries and UN peacekeeping forces.[16]

So-called "incapacitating agents" or "incapacitating chemical agents" were developed as part of military chemical weapons programmes as early as the 1950s[17] and were generally considered as chemical agents producing "… a temporary disabling condition that persists for hours to days after exposure to the agent (unlike that produced by riot control agents)".[18] These included "off the rocker" agents, such as LSD (lysergic acid diethylamide), PCP (phencyclidine) and BZ (3-quinuclidinyl benzilate) (the latter weaponised by the United States in various munitions including cluster bombs during the 1960s), that cause psychotropic effects such as hallucinations; and "on the floor" agents, such as morphine-like opioid analgesics and benzodiazepines, that have anaesthetic and sedative effects. The focus was on chemicals altering or impairing the functioning of the central nervous system, (unlike riot

---

[11] Ibid., Article II.7. Toxic chemicals listed on the CWC schedules are subject to specific verification measures and include those weaponized in the past and their precursor chemicals. BZ, a chemical previously weaponized as a military "incapacitating agent", is listed on Schedule 2. See OPCW, Annex on Chemicals.

[12] Chemical Weapons Convention, above n 8, Article II.1(a). See also ICRC 2020, p. 11.

[13] Davison 2015. On concerns about the contemporary (mis)use of riot control agents, see Crowley 2016.

[14] "Extraneous factors often cited as having influenced the final outcome [of the CWC text] include: … The continued existence of the death penalty in the criminal codes of some countries. When executed with lethal chemicals, the death-penalty procedure may perhaps be regarded as a law-enforcement application of toxic chemicals, and was so regarded by a number of individuals engaged in the CWC negotiation. However, such an association between capital punishment and law enforcement is nowhere referred to in the formal papers of the CWC negotiation." Robinson 2007, p. 13.

[15] Ibid., p. 13; Davison 2009a, pp. 105–42.; Krutzsch and Trapp 2014.

[16] For a discussion of this inter-related ambiguity (which is not explored in detail in the present article) see Dunworth 2012. See also Fry 2010.

[17] Robinson 2003a, b; Dando and Furmanski 2006; Robinson 2013.

[18] Cooper and Rice 2001, pp. 388–391. See also, Stockholm International Peace Research Institute (SIPRI) 1973; US Army 1996, para 601.

control agents which cause sensory irritation and injury to the eyes, skin, respiratory tract), but there was also consideration of weaponising chemicals that could incapacitate people by interfering with other physiological processes, such as through chemically induced impairment of blood pressure and temperature regulation, and through causing muscle paralysis, temporary blindness or vomiting.[19]

As the CWC negotiations were nearing completion in the early 1990s there was particular attention among weapons developers to the opioid fentanyl and related "derivative" chemicals, whose effects are many orders of magnitude stronger than morphine. Various legal and terminological ruses were attempted at the time (during and following the negotiation of the CWC) to justify the continued development of these toxic chemicals for use for law enforcement purposes and even for certain military or peacekeeping operations that would not be considered law enforcement activities. Chemical weapons were marketed as "non-lethal capabilities", and "incapacitating agents" were advertised as "advanced riot control agents" with a view to pushing them into the bounds of purposes not prohibited under the CWC, a strategy that continued well into the 2000s.[20]

The compromise solution in the CWC treaty text of 1992[21] left enough ambiguity for drastically different views. As the Convention entered into force in 1997, it was left open to interpretation whether the legitimate use of toxic chemicals as weapons for law enforcement was limited to riot control agents only, as was the prevailing view during the negotiations, or whether other types of toxic chemicals could also be used.[22]

The dangers of a perceived loophole were known at the time. In March 1994, leading scholars of chemical and biological weapons—Mathew Meselson and Julian Perry Robinson of the Harvard–Sussex Program warned "… the language used to exempt other law-enforcement purposes has created an ambiguity in the heart of the Convention".[23] Robinson later observed that this left behind "… a treaty text that is, in several respects, confusing to its interpreters …" and "… lends cover to interpretations of the treaty that are not conducted in good faith, done without proper regard to the object and purpose of the Convention", and thereby risked a "creeping legitimization" of chemical weapons.[24]

This intentional ambiguity resulting from political compromise set the stage for a thirty year battle to ensure a protective interpretation in keeping both with the object

---

[19] Robinson 1967, pp. 33–40; SIPRI 1973, pp. 298–306; Dando 1996; Davison 2009a, pp. 105–142. Other outlandish methods of incapacitation were suggested, for example, a military proposal to explore chemicals that have an aphrodisiac effect or those making people very sensitive to sunlight. See US Air Force 1994; The Guardian (2007) Air Force Looked at Spray to Turn Enemy Gay. www.theguardian.com/world/2007/jun/13/usa.danglaister. Accessed on 7 April 2024.

[20] Davison 2009a, pp. 105–42; Davison 2009b.

[21] The CWC was agreed in August 1992 and the treaty opened for signature in January 1993.

[22] For an especially informative account of the CWC negotiations on this issue, see Robinson 2007.

[23] Meselson and Robinson 1994. The authors asked: "Is the Convention really to be read as allowing any non-Schedule-1 toxic chemical or precursor to be developed, produced, weaponized, stockpiled or traded, so long as it is said to be for 'law enforcement purposes'?"

[24] Robinson 2007, pp. 2 and 13.

and purpose of the CWC to prohibit the use of toxicity as a weapon and both with the commitment of States parties "… to exclude completely the possibility of the use of chemical weapons".[25]

3.3 A Trigger for Action

Any sense of this being an academic discussion was shattered on 26 October 2002 when Russian special forces pumped "a compound based on derivatives of fentanyl" through the air conditioning system during a hostage rescue attempt at the Dubrovka theatre in Moscow.[26] In this awful situation over 900 people were taken hostage by forty armed attackers demanding an end to the war in Chechnya and withdrawal of Russian troops, while threatening to set off explosives inside the theatre. While the majority of hostages were freed, 129 died during the rescue operation, mostly due to the effects of the chemicals, which impaired breathing and caused vomiting and unconsciousness leading to suffocation. Some survivors also suffered permanent disabilities. Many of the hostage takers were shot and killed while unconscious.[27] By one assessment a year later, it was "the first time that a therapeutic agent ha[d] been used as a weapon in a tactical situation".[28] There was never official acknowledgement of the specific chemical(s) used, but one subsequent analysis of clothing and urine samples[29] assessed it to be a mixture of carfentanil, used as a tranquilizer for large animals such as elephants, and remifentanil, used in medical anaesthesia. These

---

[25] Chemical Weapons Convention, above n 8, Preamble. "Determined for the sake of all mankind, to exclude completely the possibility of the use of chemical weapons."

[26] Russian News Agency (ITAR-TASS) 2002a; ITAR-TASS 2002b.

[27] Details of the incident are summarized in: European Court of Human Rights (ECtHR), *Finogenov and Others v Russia*, Judgement, 20 December 2011, Application Nos. 18299/03 and 27311/03 (*Finogenov and Others v. Russia*), paras 22–29. The Russian Judge at the ECtHR, Anatoly Kovler, did not submit a separate opinion. See also Wines 2002; BBC News (2002) How Special Forces Ended Siege.http://news.bbc.co.uk/2/hi/europe/2363601.stm. Accessed on 7 April 2024; BBC News (2012) Moscow Theatre Siege: Questions Remain Unanswered. www.bbc.com/news/world-europe-20067384. Accessed on 7 April 2024; РИА Новости (2012), Ветеран 'Альфы': применение газа при штурме 'Норд-Оста' было оправдано [Alpha veteran: the use of gas during the assault on Nord-Ost was justified]. https://ria.ru/20121026/906935884.html. Accessed on 7 April 2024; INTERFAX.RU (2018) Патрушев рассказал о неоднократном применении использованного на Дубровке газа [Patrushev spoke about the repeated use of gas used at Dubrovka]. www.interfax.ru/russia/603690. Accessed on 7 April 2024.

[28] Coupland 2003, p. 1346. Fentanyl compounds were considered (but not used) by the United States during the Vietnam War. Fentanyl was reportedly used by Israel in an attack on an individual in 1997 and, in 2011, the Israeli Defence Forces were reported to possess aerosolized "sleeping gas". There were further reports of deployment of such chemicals by Russia during the Beslan school siege (2004) and fighting in Nalchik (2005). Robinson 2003a, b; Chemical and Biological Weapons Nonproliferation Program 2002; The CBW Conventions Bulletin 2005, p. 60; Robinson 2007, p. 6.

[29] Riches et al. 2012.

3 Nerve Agents by Another Name: The Thirty-Year Effort to Close …

drugs are, respectively, 10,000 and 100–200 times stronger than morphine.[30] For comparison,[31] a lethal dose of the nerve agent (and well-known chemical warfare agent) VX ranges from 5 to 30 mg (depending on the route of exposure).[32] The lethal dose of fentanyl—which is 100 times less potent than carfentanil—can be as little as 2 mg.[33] Suddenly so-called "non-lethal" weapons seemed fairly lethal. In fact, the "lethality" of around 15% of those exposed killed during the Moscow hostage situation, and as might be expected based on scientific modelling, was comparable with the effects of some conventional weapons in armed conflict and twice as "lethal" (in percentage terms) as chemical warfare during the First World War.[34]

The Moscow incident brought the CWC's ambiguities to the fore[35] and spurred paradoxical reactions. Defenders of the attempt to resolve an extremely difficult situation by using highly toxic chemicals to incapacitate both hostage takers and hostages included political leaders in the United States and Europe.[36] Some observers limited their criticism to the way the operation was carried out,[37] and, among them, some scientists encouraged "greater collaboration between clinicians and military

---

[30] National Center for Biotechnology Information 2017; Vardanyan 2017.

[31] This type of comparison was made shortly after the Moscow incident by Meselson and Robinson, and would later prove important in policy discussions; see Meselson and Robinson 2003. "Some toxic substances that have been considered for use as disabling chemical weapons are even more toxic than the chemicals developed for lethal purposes, in the sense that extremely small amounts are sufficient to cause an effect. Lofentanil, for example, which is a derivative of fentanyl, is far more toxic than nerve agent. It will cause anaesthesia at a dose of 0.025 micrograms per kilogram body weight, which is hundreds of times smaller than the estimated lethal dose of VX."

[32] National Research Council Committee on Toxicology 1997; Chai et al. 2017.

[33] National Center for Biotechnology Information 2017.

[34] Klotz et al. 2003, p. 8. "We have shown, at least within the approximations of our simple (but generous) two-receptor equilibrium model, that even with a therapeutic index [TI] of 1,000 (above any known anaesthetic or sedative agent), a chemical agent used as an incapacitating weapon can be expected to cause about 10% fatalities. Even with an astronomical TI of 10,000, under actual conditions of use in the field, fatalities could easily reach the same level. This is comparable to the effects of traditional 'lethal' technologies. For instance, in military combat, firearms typically cause about 35% of deaths among total casualties, shells about 20%, and grenades about 10%. 'Lethal' chemical weapons are comparable; in World War I the lethality of gas was about 7%."

[35] Legal interpretations varied from the permissive—Fidler 2005—to the non-permissive—e.g. Krutzsch and Trapp 2014. Robinson observed: "The fact that state practice prior to the Moscow theatre siege of October 2002 seemed not to conflict with either interpretation [of the CWC] perhaps explains why OPCW member states had made no attempt to resolve the ambiguity that the two contrasting interpretations created." Robinson 2007, p. 4.

[36] In the midst of the so-called "global war on terror" and the run-up to the invasion of Iraq in March 2003, this included public support for the rescue attempt at the highest political levels, including from US President George Bush, UK Prime Minister Tony Blair, and Denmark's Prime Minister, Anders Fogh Rasmussen. See Walsh 2002; BBC News Online (2022) Putin: Foreign support but also concern. http://news.bbc.co.uk/2/hi/europe/2367735.stm. Accessed on 7 April 2024; Associated Press (2022) Russians tally dead hostages. https://eu.gainesville.com/story/news/2002/10/27/russians-tally-dead-hostages/31617922007/. Accessed on 7 April 2024; The CBW Conventions Bulletin 2003; Robinson 2007, p. 23; Crowley 2009, pp. 68–74.

[37] NATO Research and Technology Organization (RTO) 2006; Fenton 2007.

planners" in related weapons development efforts.[38] They would have done it differently and, indeed, the incident seemingly spurred a resurgence of interest among a number of countries in developing similar weapons, often driven by the promise of (mis)applying new drug discovery and delivery technologies from the medical sector.[39]

Almost ten years later, in December 2011, a judgment by the European Court of Human Rights, in a case brought against Russia by some of the victims from the Dubrovka theatre, found a violation of the right to life due to inadequate planning and implementation of the rescue operation.[40] The fact that the Court did not find a violation simply for the use of these toxic chemicals raises more questions than answers, since the Court was not informed which specific fentanyl-related compounds were used, and the consequences were evident. Furthermore, it is highly doubtful whether it would ever be feasible to provide adequate medical care to protect life following the use of such toxic chemicals as weapons in a tactical situation.[41]

For those who had heeded the warning about this eventuality a decade earlier, the incident presented a different opportunity: to clarify the meaning of the CWC's law enforcement provision in a way that would rule out the use of such highly toxic chemicals as weapons for law enforcement. The aim being to prevent future incidents with serious consequences for the life and health of those exposed, and to avoid wider risks to the integrity of the "comprehensive" prohibition of chemical weapons.

3.4 Reframing the Narrative: The Role of the ICRC

The ICRC had been worried about this area of weapons development for some time and it would have an opportunity to voice its concerns six months after the Moscow incident at the First Review Conference of the CWC in April 2003. At that time, interrelated concerns had been raised about the United States' authorisation of the use of riot control agents during the armed conflict in Iraq in situations that raised questions given the CWC's prohibition of using them as a "method of warfare".[42]

---

[38] Wax et al. 2003; see also Stanley 2003.

[39] For a summary of such interest drawn from limited publicly available information, see Davison 2009a, pp. 105–42; Crowley 2009, pp. 74–84.

[40] *Finogenov and Others v. Russia* 2011, above n 27. The judgment did not mention the Chemical Weapons Convention, nor did it tackle the question of whether the theatre incident could have been seen as part of a non-international armed conflict between Russia and Chechen armed groups rather than a law enforcement operation. See Dunworth 2012.

[41] Davison 2013, pp. 304–305. For scientific and medical rebuttal of the notion of the "safe" use of these toxic chemicals as weapons, see Klotz et al. 2003; Nathanson 2007; Nixdorf and Melling 2007; Coupland 2012; The Royal Society 2012; OPCW 2012, paras 12–14 and 83–86.

[42] Chemical Weapons Convention, above n 8, Article I.5; Lean and Carrell 2003; The Guardian (2003) Out of the Straitjacket. https://www.theguardian.com/world/2003/mar/12/usa.iraq. Accessed on 7 April 2024; New York Times (2003) A Nation at War: Weapons; U.S. Use of Tear Gas Could Violate Treaty, Critics Say. https://www.nytimes.com/2003/04/05/us/a-nation-at-war-weapons-us-use-of-tear-gas-could-violate-treaty-critics-say.html. Accessed on 7 April 2024; See also United States, Executive Order 1975, p. 980.

3 Nerve Agents by Another Name: The Thirty-Year Effort to Close ...

In the Hague the ICRC "express[ed] its alarm at the increasing interest among police, security and armed forces in the use of incapacitating chemicals and the lack of expressions of concern about the implications of such developments by States parties". It noted that the clear intent of the CWC negotiators was "only to permit the use of domestic riot control agents and the use of lethal chemicals for executions – where permitted by national law" stressing that "it is illusory to believe that rapid incapacitation can be achieved without a certain level of mortality". The ICRC urged States to "begin a process ... which would aim to clarify the meaning of the Convention's law enforcement provisions and so address the risks ...".[43]

Somehow reinforcing the ICRC's alarm was the unusual, and successful, effort by the United States delegation to prevent the organisation from delivering its statement after initial approval had been given by the Conference[44] and the fact that only a few States shared similar concerns publicly about these weapons developments, including Switzerland, New Zealand and Norway.[45] Such was the strong opposition by some States, and the apparent lack of concern publicly among many others, that it took another decade before multilateral initiatives started to take shape, despite the concerted efforts by Switzerland to keep the issue high on the CWC agenda.[46]

Meanwhile, much ink was spilled in the literature both by those developing these weapons[47] and those seeking policy solutions to constrain them.[48] Attention to the issue also exposed disagreements within governments, notably differing legal interpretations of the CWC held by the United States Department Defense and the Department of State.[49]

One influential report published by the British Medical Association successfully exposed the myth of the "harmless" knockout gas while highlighting the serious

---

[43] ICRC 2003.

[44] Ruppe 2023; The Washington Times (2003) Red Cross concerned by U.S. use of tear gas. https://www.washingtontimes.com/news/2003/aug/17/20030817-105448-8897r/. Accessed on 7 April 2024.

[45] The CBW Conventions Bulletin 2003; Kelle 2003.

[46] OPCW 2008.

[47] For example, Lakoski et al. 2000 (Some of the information on US weapons research, including this report, only became publicly available following Freedom of Information Requests made by The Sunshine Project, a non-governmental organisation working on chemical and biological arms control issues); US National Research Council (NRC) 2003; Klochikhin et al. 2003; Barriot and Bismuth 2003; Bismuth et al. 2004; Klochikhin et al. 2005; Hess et al. 2005; Shreiberova et al. 2005; NATO RTO 2006.

[48] For example, see Coupland 2003; Dando 2003; Klotz et al. 2003; Meselson and Robinson 2003; Dando 2004; Wheelis and Dando 2005; Robinson 2007; Davison 2007; Pearson et al. 2007; Crowley 2009; The Royal Society 2012.

[49] NRC 2003. In its report in 2003 the NRC recommended prioritising work on so-called "calmatives" but noted: "Following completion of the security review a prepublication copy of the report was released to the public on November 4, 2002. Subsequent to that release, it became apparent that the Department of Defense and the Department of State have differing legal interpretations of the Chemical Weapons Convention as it pertains to the development of chemical non-lethal weapons for military purposes."

medical ethics concerns with using therapeutic drugs as weapons.[50] The Organisation for the Prohibition of Chemical Weapons (OPCW) Scientific Advisory Board also examined the problem and, with support from the International Union of Pure and Applied Chemistry (IUPAC), provided advice to States at successive five-yearly Review Conferences of the CWC.[51]

It was a series of meetings held in Switzerland between 2010 and 2012 that eventually contributed to breaking the conceptual and political deadlock, two of which were convened by the ICRC[52] and two others were held at the Swiss government's Spiez Laboratory.[53] Three of the meetings brought together military, legal, scientific and policy experts from government, academia, civil society and international organisations to examine the problem and discuss potential policy solutions. The report of the other scientific meeting, convened by the OPCW and IUPAC at Spiez, formed the basis of the OPCW's Scientific Advisory Board's recommendations to the Third Review Conference of the CWC in February 2013 on technical aspects of the issue.[54]

The ICRC's expert meetings served at least two purposes: to highlight and build support for its concerns among States; and to inform its own legal assessment and policy positioning. In addition to the reports of proceedings, the ICRC published a short document outlining the implications of different policy choices by States.[55] In February 2013, in advance of the Third Review Conference of the CWC, the ICRC published and promoted its position that "… the use of toxic chemicals as weapons for law enforcement purposes should be limited exclusively to riot control agents …" as defined in the CWC. The organisation had also reached the conclusion that the applicable legal framework "leaves little room, if any, for the legitimate use of toxic chemicals as weapons for law enforcement other than the use of riot control agents" taking into account the CWC, international narcotics Conventions and international human rights law.[56]

---

[50] Nathanson 2007.

[51] For a detailed analysis of the role played by the OPCW Scientific Advisory Board and IUPAC, see Mathews 2018.

[52] ICRC 2010; ICRC 2013a , above note 17. States that participated in one or both ICRC meetings were: Australia, China, Czech Republic, Finland, France, Germany, India, Norway, Pakistan, Russia, South Africa, Switzerland, United Kingdom and the United States.

[53] Mogl 2012; Smallwood et al. 2013.

[54] Ibid., pp. 854–855. Notably the observation that: "Certain classes of chemicals effect biological organisms through action on the central nervous system (CNS) in a manner commonly referred to as incapacitating (e.g. fentanyl derivatives and other opioids). These chemicals are highly toxic (some with LD_{50} values comparable to VX)." Mathews describes the findings as significant as they "subsequently became the basis of recommendations of the SAB [Scientific Advisory Board] to the 3rd RevCon [Review Conference], as well as the 'Joint Initiative' [by Australia and Switzerland] … and the SAB report to the 4th RevCon." Mathews 2018. Ten years later the SAB reiterated: "The Board has assessed that certain CNS-acting chemicals are extremely toxic, with some as lethal as nerve agents." OPCW 2023, para 9.

[55] ICRC 2012.

[56] ICRC 2013b.

3 Nerve Agents by Another Name: The Thirty-Year Effort to Close …

During these meetings, and related analyses, several important contradictions were further exposed: semantic, medical, scientific and legal. The marketing terminology of "non-lethal weapons" or "less lethal capabilities", "advanced riot control agents" and "calmatives" was replaced with the reality of "drugs as weapons" and "toxic chemicals as weapons for law enforcement".[57] Claims—or rather hopes— about "safe" incapacitation with these chemicals were confronted with the medical realities of inevitable deaths and permanent disabilities among those exposed in a tactical situation.[58] Perhaps most strikingly, it was more widely recognised that some toxic chemicals—such as fentanyl and its derivatives—promoted as so-called "non-lethal" weapons have comparable toxicity and potency to chemical warfare agents, such as nerve agents.[59] From a legal perspective, it was no longer sufficient to hide behind the (de)constructive ambiguity in the CWC's provisions on law enforcement purposes. States had to acknowledge a range of legal constraints, including the object and purpose of the Convention to prevent the use of toxicity as a weapon as well as obligations under the near universal international treaties on the control of narcotic drugs permitting their use only for "medical and scientific purposes"[60] and the strict rules of international human rights law constraining the use of force in law enforcement situations.[61] This reflected a wide-ranging approach to weapons regulation that goes beyond traditional disarmament and international humanitarian law frameworks, and has been described as "holistic arms control".[62]

3.5 Expanding Multilateral Initiatives and Unforeseen Events

As the Third Review Conference of the CWC approached in spring 2013 it seemed the time might be right to shift up a gear in multilateral efforts to clarify the CWC's law enforcement provisions. However, there is no accounting for unforeseen events. In

---

[57] Nathanson 2007; ICRC 2012; The Royal Society 2012.

[58] Nathanson 2007; The Royal Society 2012. Koplow observed a few years after Moscow theatre incident: "In these agonizing scenarios, we earnestly wish for some magic calmative potion that would instantly, safely, and totally incapacitate the combatants, a lightning strike that could free the hostages, defuse the explosives, seize the firearms, and incarcerate the malefactors. But that sort of anesthetic pixie dust is currently unavailable; in fact, it may never be achievable." Koplow 2005.

[59] Mogl 2012, p. 46: "ICAs [Incapacitating Chemical Agents] are toxic chemicals, some are more potent than Nerve Agents – in that less of the substance will be required to cause the anticipated effect – and these effects could be irreversible. The term 'ICA' is a sugar coating to help make the concept – of using once again the toxic properties of chemicals as weapons – somehow more acceptable." See also above notes 31 and 53.

[60] Single Convention on Narcotic Drugs, opened for signature 30 March 1961, 520 UNTS 151 (entered into force 13 December 1964); Convention on Psychotropic Substances, opened for signature 21 February 1971, 1019 UNTS 175 (entered into force 16 August 1976).

[61] ICRC 2020.

[62] Crowley 2016, pp. 4–7.

late 2012 and early 2013 the first allegations of the use of chemical weapons in Syria started to emerge, and political attention rightly shifted to these (since confirmed) violations of international humanitarian law prohibitions on the use of chemical weapons.[63] On 21 August, just as United Nations (UN) investigations were beginning, chemical weapons (the nerve agent, sarin) were used on a large scale in the Ghouta area of rural Damascus, killing and injuring many civilians including children.[64] Subsequent "death toll estimates range[d] from 281 to more than 1,400".[65] The Ghouta attacks were the worst chemical attacks seen in twenty-five years.[66] The last time the world had witnessed such an attack was during the extensive chemical warfare of the Iran–Iraq War; notably the Iraqi attack with nerve agents in Halabja in 1988,[67] which preceded the agreement of the CWC by some five years and added urgency to its adoption.

Reports of the use of chemical weapons (nerve agents, chlorine and mustard gas) in Syria persisted until 2019. Many of these attacks were attributed by subsequent OPCW-UN[68] and OPCW[69] investigations to the Syrian government (despite Syria's accession to the CWC in September 2013 and their denial of responsibility) and several were attributed to the Islamic State.[70] (Chemical weapons were also used in Iraq during the same period and nerve agents were used to poison individuals in Malaysia, the UK and Russia).[71] Some States nevertheless managed to keep attention focused in parallel on concerns about the development and use of highly toxic chemicals as weapons for law enforcement, and related military interest.

---

[63] Naqvi 2017. Syria was not a party to the CWC at the time of the Ghouta attacks but the use of chemical weapons in international and non-international armed conflicts is, in any case, prohibited by customary international humanitarian law. See also ICRC 2005.

[64] UN General Assembly and Security Council (2013), Report of the United Nations Mission to Investigate Allegations of the Use of Chemical Weapons in the Syrian Arab Republic on the Alleged Use of Chemical Weapons in the Ghouta Area of Damascus on 21 August 2013, UN Doc. A/67/997–S/2013/553; UN General Assembly and Security Council (2013), United Nations Mission to Investigate Allegations of the Use of Chemical Weapons in the Syrian Arab Republic: Final Report, UN Doc. A/68/663–S/2013/735, p. 21.

[65] Naqvi 2017, p. 965.

[66] OPCW 2013; See also UN Secretary General (2013) Secretary-General's Briefing to the General Assembly on the Report of the United Nations Mission to Investigate Allegations of the Use of Chemical Weapons in the Syrian Arab Republic: Report on the Incident of 21 August 2013 in the Ghouta Area of Damascus, Statement of 17 September 2013 "This is the most significant confirmed use of chemical weapons against civilians since Saddam Hussein used them in Halabja in 1988."

[67] Tucker 2006, pp. 280–284; Kaszeta 2020, pp. 174–178.

[68] See, for example, on the use of sarin at Khan Shaykhun on 4 April 2017: UN Security Council (2017) Seventh Report of the Organisation for the Prohibition of Chemical Weapons–United Nations Joint Investigative Mechanism, UN Doc. S/2017/904, p. 33.

[69] See, for example, on the use of sarin and chlorine at Ltamenah in March 2017 and the use of chlorine at Saraqib on 4 February 2018: OPCW 2020g; OPCW 2021f.

[70] For a detailed discussion of the use of chemical weapons in Syria and associated UN and OPCW investigations between 2012 and 2017, see Naqvi 2017.

[71] ICRC 2017; Hart 2016, pp. 523–525; OPCW 2017, 2018a, 2020a.

3 Nerve Agents by Another Name: The Thirty-Year Effort to Close ...

Significantly, in 2014, Australia introduced a paper at the annual Conference of the States Parties to the CWC, which characterised its concerns about the weaponisation of "central nervous system (CNS)-acting chemicals", in particular the dangers of their "aerial dispersion".[72] This approach to describing, and narrowing, the toxic chemicals of concern and the method of delivery—as compared to the vague terminology of "incapacitating chemical agents"—proved important for common understandings among States and political progress.[73] But it was an approach that would ultimately lead to weaknesses in the eventual legal clarification agreed upon in 2021. The ICRC, for its part, had urged States to keep their attention on the risks posed by using any toxic chemicals other than riot control agents as weapons for law enforcement.[74]

In 2015 Australia and Switzerland joined forces, submitting a paper to the Conference of the States Parties on CNS-acting chemicals, which was supported by twenty other States, most notably including the United States.[75] In 2014 the United States, for the first time, supported the "call for an active dialogue on this issue"[76] and by 2015 stressed the "need to address the issue of CNS-acting chemicals to help prevent the re-emergence of chemical weapons".[77]

It is hard to say what precise combination of factors triggered this policy reversal by the United States, but it has increasingly expressed its concerns about military research and development of "pharmaceutical-based agents" in China, Iran and Russia.[78] One additional factor, though unrelated to chemical weapons, appears to have been the mounting number of deaths in the United States among drug users caused by synthetic opioids, primarily fentanyl. The illicit production and distribution of fentanyl started increasing in 2013 and such deaths increased dramatically year on year from 3,105 in 2013 to 5,544 in 2014 (a 79% increase)[79] and to over 70,000 in 2021.[80]

---

[72] OPCW 2014a.

[73] Mathews 2018.

[74] ICRC 2012, 2013.

[75] OPCW 2015.

[76] OPCW 2014b.

[77] United States, Statement by Deputy Assistant Secretary Mallory Stewart to the Twentieth Session of the Conference of the State Parties Organisations for the Prohibition of Chemical Weapons 2015.

[78] United States, Bureau of Arms Control, Verification and Compliance 2021, pp. 10–17.

[79] "During 2013–2014, fentanyl submissions in the United States increased by 426%, from 1,015 in 2013 to 5,343 in 2014, and synthetic opioid deaths increased by 79%, from 3,105 in 2013 to 5,544 in 2014" Gladden et al. 2016.

[80] "Deaths involving synthetic opioids other than methadone (primarily fentanyl) continued to rise with 70,601 overdose deaths reported in 2021." National Institute on Drug Abuse 2023.

3.6 Multilateral Decision-Time

By the time of the Fourth CWC Review Conference in late 2018 the joint initiative was being spearheaded by Australia, Switzerland and the United States. A joint paper arguing that CNS-acting chemicals pose a serious challenge to the Convention and calling for development of concrete recommendations to address the problem garnered support among a large cross-regional group of forty-two States.[81] No doubt this was enabled by sustained bilateral, regional and multilateral outreach by the three States at the forefront of the initiative. The ICRC, welcomed the initiative but continued to advocate for states to adopt strict "riot control agents-only" approach with respect to the use of toxic chemicals as weapons for law enforcement, including its public interventions in The Hague.[82]

However, the initiative had faced strong opposition from Russia, as well as China, Iran and Syria.[83] Ultimately, any calls for a clarification of the CWC's law enforcement provisions could be blocked in the decision-making bodies of the OPCW Executive Council, where a two-thirds majority is needed for decisions on substantive issues, or the annual Conference of the States Parties, where consensus decision-making is prioritised, which are together responsible for the implementation of the Convention.[84]

In October 2019 a draft decision was introduced at the OPCW Executive Council[85] and at the Conference of the States Parties in late 2020 a group of States urged the Executive Council and the Conference to take action during 2021.[86] Finally, at a meeting of the Executive Council on 11 March 2021 a draft "Understanding Regarding the Aerosolised Use of Central Nervous System-Acting Chemicals for Law Enforcement Purposes", introduced by the United States with thirty-one other

---

[81] OPCW 2018a "This joint paper is issued on behalf of Albania, Argentina, Australia, Austria, Belgium, Brazil, Bulgaria, Canada, Chile, Colombia, Croatia, Cyprus, Czech Republic, Ecuador, Estonia, Finland, Germany, Greece, Ireland, Japan, Latvia, Lithuania, Luxembourg, Malta, the Netherlands, New Zealand, Norway, Panama, Philippines, Poland, Portugal, Republic of Korea, Romania, Senegal, Slovenia, Spain, Sweden, Switzerland, Turkey, United Kingdom of Great Britain and Northern Ireland, United States of America, and Uruguay."

[82] See, for example, OPCW 2018c. See also ICRC 2013b.

[83] See, for example, OPCW 2016, 2020b, c, d, 2021b.

[84] Chemical Weapons Convention, above n 8, Article VIII.18 ("Decisions [at the Conference] on matters of substance should be taken as far as possible by consensus. [...] If consensus is not possible [...] the Conference shall take the decision by a two-thirds majority of members present and voting [...]") and Article VIII.29 ("[...] the Executive Council shall take decisions on matters of substance by a two-thirds majority of all its members.").

[85] OPCW 2020e: "A revised proposal entitled 'Understanding Regarding the Aerosolised Use of Central Nervous System-Acting Chemicals for Law Enforcement Purposes', co-sponsored by Albania, Australia, Austria, Bulgaria, Canada, Colombia, Croatia, Cyprus, the Czech Republic, Estonia, Finland, Greece, Japan, Latvia, Lithuania, Luxembourg, Malta, the Netherlands, Norway, Poland, the Republic of Korea, Romania, Slovenia, Spain, Sweden, Switzerland, Turkey, Ukraine, and the United States of America, was issued and circulated to States Parties."

[86] OPCW 2020f.

3 Nerve Agents by Another Name: The Thirty-Year Effort to Close … 91

States, was adopted by a vote with just over two-thirds (twenty-eight out of forty-one) of Executive Council members in favour.[87]

The final hurdle would be the Conference of the States Parties in late 2021 where the Executive Council decision would be adopted by States Parties to the CWC provided, according to the rules of procedure, it was supported by a two-thirds majority. The decision was adopted on 1 December 2021 by a vote with a large majority of eighty-five of voting States Parties in favour, thirty-three abstentions, and ten voting against.[88] Four of the States that voted against the decision (China, Iran, Russia and Syria) released a joint statement in which they "categorically reject the decision", arguing that it "… could not have any legal effect(s) on the States Parties' rights and obligations under the Convention".[89]

It is unusual for decisions of such significance to be put to a vote given the strong preference for consensus decision-making at Conference of the States Parties. However, the limits of consensus have been tested in recent years, especially in efforts to address the repeated use of chemical weapons attributed to Syria by UN-OPCW and OPCW investigations. These pressures led several significant decisions to be adopted by a vote at the Executive Council and the Conference of States Parties since 2016, including at a "special session" of the Conference in 2018, which granted the OPCW Technical Secretariat with new investigatory powers to attribute responsibility for the use of chemical weapons.[90]

---

[87] OPCW 2021c; OPCW 2021d: "28 in favour (Argentina, Australia, Austria, Belgium, Brazil, Bulgaria, Chile, El Salvador, France, Germany, Ghana, Guatemala, Italy, Japan, Lithuania, Mexico, Morocco, Norway, Peru, Poland, the Republic of Korea, Romania, Saudi Arabia, Senegal, Spain, the United Arab Emirates, the United Kingdom of Great Britain and Northern Ireland, and the United States of America); three against (China, Iran (Islamic Republic of), and the Russian Federation); and 10 abstentions (Algeria, Bangladesh, Cameroon, India, Kenya, Nigeria, Pakistan, the Philippines, South Africa, and the Sudan)."

[88] CWC Coalition 2021. "No" votes: Belarus, Bolivia, Cambodia, China, Iran, Laos, Nicaragua, Russia, Tajikistan and Zimbabwe. "Abstentions": Afghanistan, Algeria, Angola, Armenia, Bangladesh, Botswana, Burkina Faso, Burundi, Cameroon, Congo, Côte d'Ivoire, Eswatini, Holy See, India, Indonesia, Kazakhstan, Kenya, Kyrgyzstan, Lebanon, Madagascar, Mali, Mongolia, Nepal, Pakistan, Rwanda, South Africa, Sri Lanka, State of Palestine, Sudan, Togo, Uganda, United Republic of Tanzania, and Vietnam.

[89] OPCW 2021e Decision: Understanding Regarding the Aerosolised Use of Central Nervous System-Acting Chemicals for Law Enforcement Purposes, Conference of the States Parties, Twenty-Sixth Session, Doc. C-26/DEC.10.

[90] Thereby expanding part of the OPCW's prior mandate to determine, through investigations, whether chemical weapons were used without attributing responsibility for their use. See OPCW 2018b; Caves et al. 2022.

3.7 An Important Clarification of International Law

In clarifying the existing provisions of the CWC (as opposed to introducing new ones) through a voting majority States Parties decided "… that the aerosolised use of CNS-acting chemicals is understood to be inconsistent with law enforcement purposes as a 'purpose not prohibited' under the Convention".[91] Further the decision noted "… that munitions and devices specifically designed to cause death or other harm through the toxic properties of those toxic chemicals specified in subparagraph 1(a) of Article II of the Convention, including aerosolised CNS-acting chemicals … would constitute a 'chemical weapon'".[92]

In other words, it is prohibited to use aerosolised CNS-acting chemicals for law enforcement purposes, and munitions or devices designed to disperse these chemicals to cause harm also constitute prohibited chemical weapons.

The December 2021 decision marks the success of a thirty-year-long effort by civil society, international organisations and governments to close the perceived loophole in the CWC's law enforcement provisions. There will be implementation challenges ahead, practical and political[93]: not least the presumed responsibilities of those CWC States Parties in possession of these weapons to declare them and ensure their destruction under supervision by the OPCW,[94] and the challenges of ensuring that those who opposed the decision or abstained during the clarification process, some of whom explicitly questioned the legality of the decision, will abide by this understanding.

Normatively speaking, however, the decision largely addresses the serious concerns about the development and use of highly toxic anaesthetic and sedative drugs as weapons (by both military and law enforcement actors), which persisted in a number of countries as a legacy of past military chemical weapons programmes, posing a serious threat to the integrity of the Convention and its prohibition of chemical weapons. The decision clearly covers the toxic chemicals that were of primary interest to weapons developers and the primary method of their delivery (aerosolization). It sends a signal that the use of other highly toxic chemicals as weapons for law enforcement would be similarly incompatible with the treaty.

---

[91] OPCW 2021a.

[92] Ibid.

[93] Crowley and Dando 2022.

[94] Declaration requirements are specified in the Chemical Weapons Convention, Chemical Weapons Convention, above n 8, Article III.

3.8 Ambiguities Revisited?

And yet, the understanding may not be a comprehensive solution to underlying concerns about the stability of the CWC's prohibition of chemical weapons. In other words, the loophole may have shrunk, but has it closed? There are several questions and remaining ambiguities.

First, and perhaps most significantly, the new understanding does not clearly specify whether the use of toxic chemicals that neither fit the definition of riot control agents nor are considered CNS-acting chemicals, including those that cause death or other harm through effects on bodily processes other than the CNS, are also considered inconsistent with law enforcement purposes under the CWC. There are many reasons that this should be made explicit, not least because military and law enforcement actors who long sought to develop "incapacitating agent" weapons also pursued chemically-induced incapacitation by impairing bodily systems other than the CNS.[95] More broadly, a clarification offering a different understanding of the CWC would leave the remarkably dangerous question of whether it is legitimate to use other toxic chemicals as weapons for law enforcement, be it a known chemical or a yet to be discovered new compound.[96] In a world where common toxic industrial chemicals, such as chlorine, have been used as weapons,[97] where some parties to armed conflicts claim they are carrying out law enforcement operations, and where the capacity for the discovery of novel drugs and toxic chemicals has been amplified by emerging technologies, such as artificial intelligence (AI),[98] serious risks would remain for the CWC and the prohibition of chemical weapons, and serious dangers for those who might be exposed to such toxic chemicals. The simple fact remains that, if the use of highly toxic chemicals (other than aerosolised CNS-acting chemicals) as weapons for law enforcement is considered permissible by some States, then the risk of chemical weapons development by another name persists.

Second, and relatedly, the new understanding does not clearly specify whether the use of CNS-acting chemicals (or other toxic chemicals not fitting the definition of riot control agents) delivered by means other than aerosolisation (including other airborne formulations) is also considered inconsistent with law enforcement purposes under the CWC.[99] Again, there are strong arguments for making this explicit

---

[95] See above note 19.

[96] As already highlighted by Meselson and Robinson in March 1994: "Is the Convention really to be read as allowing any non-Schedule-1 toxic chemical or precursor to be developed, produced, weaponized, stockpiled or traded, so long as it is said to be for 'law enforcement purposes'?" Meselson and Robinson 1994. See also Robinson 2007, p. 13.

[97] See, for example Naqvi 2017; New York Times (2007) Iraq Insurgents Employ Chlorine in Bomb Attacks. https://www.nytimes.com/2007/02/22/world/middleeast/22iraq.html#:~:text=BAG HDAD%2C%20Feb.,by%20insurgents%20against%20Iraqi%20civilians. Accessed on 7 April 2024.

[98] Urbina et al. 2022.

[99] "When CNS-acting chemicals are disseminated in an airborne form, the delivered dose cannot be controlled. ... The SAB notes that the term "aerosolised" specifically refers to small solid particles or liquid droplets dispersed in a gas. The term does not, however, cover gases or vapours, and wording

given that military and law enforcement weaponisation of CNS-acting chemicals included prototype weapons that deliver these chemicals via a felt-pad or paintball-type capsule for absorption through the skin,[100] as well as dart-guns to inject people at a distance.[101] The narrow focus on aerosolisation is perhaps, in part, due to the fact that, among the minority of countries that still retain the death penalty in their national criminal law, most are party to the CWC, and some carry out executions by lethal injection with CNS-acting chemicals.[102] There have also been worrying reports about the forcible injection of individuals with CNS-acting chemicals by military, police and intelligence actors during arrest and detention.[103]

Third, and perhaps the most disappointing indication that even some States supporting this legal clarification have yet to truly draw a line under this area of weapons development, is that the new understanding "… is based upon the current state of scientific and technological progress" and the decision instructs the OPCW's Scientific Advisory Board "to continue to review relevant developments in science and technology related to CNS-acting chemicals and provide updates to the Conference".[104] This could be read as a signal to those in laboratories tasked with weapons development that they can continue their more than seventy-year research and development efforts in the hope they will eventually discover an aerosolised drug (or drug–antidote combination) that can rapidly incapacitate people without significant risk of death or permanent disability in a tactical situation; the "harmless" knockout gas of fictional portrayals. Sadly, this is exactly the type of wishful thinking and technological solutionism that has sustained this legacy from military chemical weapons programmes in the face of scientific evidence, real-world consequences, legal obligations and ethical considerations to the contrary.[105] It also could put the OPCW's Scientific Advisory Board in a difficult position in future, by indicating that scientific developments could reverse a policy decision on an issue that is not merely technical in nature, and could even engage the Board itself in the search for new chemicals to be used as weapons.

This apparent caveat in the understanding shows the limits of the political compromise reached in the new decision (as in the original CWC text) and indicates an unwillingness among some states to internalize one of the main lessons of the past

---

would need to be revised to extend the understanding to cover all possible airborne formulations." OPCW 2023, paras 8 and 12.

[100] Davison 2009a, pp. 118, 128 and 130. Skin absorption is a known exposure route and risk; see Dalton et al. 2021.

[101] Robinson 2007, p. 6; Crowley 2009, p. 82.

[102] Council of Europe 2021, pp. 44–46.

[103] See, for example, The Guardian (2021) 'Weaponization of Medicine': Police Use of Ketamine Draws Scrutiny after Elijah McClain's Death. www.theguardian.com/us-news/2021/dec/17/ket amine-law-enforcement-deaths-custody-elijah-mcclain. Accessed on 7 April 2024. For a history of such practice in the United States, see Calkins 2010.

[104] OPCW 2021a.

[105] Davison 2009a, pp. 105–142.

thirty years. That is, poisoning—or involuntarily drugging—people for law enforcement purposes[106] is not a technical problem to be solved by scientific "progress", but a humanitarian necessity, ethical responsibility and security imperative to prevent, in order to uphold the centuries-old taboo against using toxicity as a weapon and the object and purpose of the CWC.[107]

More broadly, the 2021 decision leaves open other clarifications around the use of toxic chemicals as weapons for law enforcement purposes that may yet be necessary. Notably the question of which types of situations permitted chemicals, namely riot control agents, can be used in? i.e. which situations constitute law enforcement purposes?[108] and which types and quantities of riot control agents, and their delivery systems, are consistent with those purposes.[109]

3.9 A "Riot Control Agents-Only" Approach

The ICRC argued that the new understanding should *not* be interpreted as meaning that non-CNS-acting, non-aerosol-delivered toxic chemicals are therefore acceptable as weapons in law enforcement. The organisation has also stressed that the use of CNS-acting chemicals delivered by other means and/or the use of toxic chemicals to poison other parts of the human body would raise the same humanitarian and legal concerns.[110]

The ICRC will no doubt continue to advocate for a "riot control agents-only" approach to the use of toxic chemicals as weapons for law enforcement, urging States to adopt both national policies and legislation to this effect, while clarifying this understanding in international forums. This is especially the case given its legal assessment that there is "little room, if any, for the legitimate use of toxic chemicals as weapons for law enforcement other than the use of riot control agents".[111]

Not only would such an approach be more effective in addressing the attendant risks, but it is also the logical conclusion for those who realize that you cannot reliably "exclude completely the possibility of the use of chemical weapons", as in the CWC's

---

[106] Coupland 2003, pp. 49–50. Coupland argues that "[a]s 'tactical anaesthesia' by definition is carried out without the consent of those given the drug(s), and without the continuous medical care provided in a clinical setting, it amounts to poisoning people.", p. 49; and that "[t]he real issue for the ICRC, however, is whether States should employ poison as a weapon in any context, and the profound implications of doing so for various fields of law including international humanitarian law, international human rights law, the CWC, and the Biological Weapons Convention (BWC)." p. 50.

[107] Chemical Weapons Convention, above n 8, Preamble.

[108] See above note 16.

[109] Crowley 2016, pp. 270–271.

[110] ICRC 2021a.

[111] ICRC 2013b.

preamble, while at the same time refusing to rule out the use of comparably toxic chemicals as weapons for law enforcement.[112]

A "riot control agents-only" approach would be more effective at a practical implementation level, allowing a clear delineation between permitted and non-permitted law enforcement chemicals. Riot control agents are the only sub-category of toxic chemicals specifically defined in the CWC and clearly permitted for law enforcement purposes. They must be declared by States Parties to the OPCW, and the OPCW's Scientific Advisory Board has assembled a list of toxic chemicals that fall under the CWC's definition of riot control agents.[113]

3.10   Lessons for Other Multilateral Efforts

There are, no doubt, many lessons to be learned from this sustained effort by States, civil society, the scientific and medical communities, and the ICRC to push for a clarification of certain provisions in a near-universal international Convention in order to protect its integrity and strengthen its implementation. There are at least five lessons that are relevant to other multilateral efforts to uphold and strengthen international constraints on weapons.

First, the experience shows that concerned actors should rigorously examine military and law enforcement claims made about the potential for scientific and technology developments to offer weapon capabilities that present fewer risks to civilians and/or greater compatibility with international law. This is essential to avoid policy choices based on unsupported claims about weapon technologies rather than the foreseeable or actual consequences of their use in practice. The perceived loophole in the CWC at its origin, the 2021 decision that shrunk that loophole, and objections by some States to that decision, all suffer from a desire among some actors to seek normative exceptions based on scientific claims that turn out to be unfounded; in this case the idea of a "harmless" knockout gas. Claims that the development and use of other weapons technologies will lead to reduced risks for civilians and/or will enable greater compliance with international law—as heard in debates around armed (remote controlled) drones, autonomous weapon systems, cyber operations, directed energy weapons, and applications of AI in military decision-making—should be treated

---

[112] Still, more humane would be a clarification that also specifically prevents the use of toxic chemicals for executions, many of which entail lethal injection with anaesthetic and sedative drugs. However, the universal abolition of the death penalty is something that will have to be solved at the national level and through international human rights mechanisms. See UN Office of the High Commissioner for Human Rights, *Reports to the Human Rights Council: Death Penalty*, available at: www.ohchr.org/en/death-penalty/reports-human-rights-council. In the meantime, some pharmaceutical companies have taken initiatives to avoid supplying drugs for executions, and the European Union has taken measures to prevent transfer of drugs for such purposes. See Council of Europe 2021, pp. 44–46.

[113] OPCW 2014c.

with similar scepticism and subjected to a reality-based scientific and operational assessment to inform international policy making.

Second, concerned actors should be wary of terminology that is used to conceal technical realities and evidence of harm, as part of efforts to seek exemption from normative constraints. Perhaps the most effective refutation of the concept of so-called "non-lethal" weapons was the simple fact that some of the toxic chemicals presented as such have comparable toxicity to nerve agents developed and used for chemical warfare. The ICRC countered with the more accurate terminology of "toxic chemicals as weapons for law enforcement" in making its recommendations to policymakers. Claims about the "non-lethality" of any weapon should always be treated with caution, as should other terminology that seeks to present a weapon as intrinsically less harmful (i.e. by virtue of technical design alone rather than the combination of design and the context of use), and these types of claims should not be used as a basis for excluding a weapon from regulatory discussion, as was also attempted (unsuccessfully) in efforts to resist the prohibition of blinding laser weapons.[114] Third, the experience with this legal clarification process under the CWC illustrates the importance of evidence—on specific weapons development activities and on the adverse human impact of their use—in triggering political action. In this case, efforts by academics, scientists and civil society organisations to publicly document and raise awareness of weapons developments of concern provided critical information that could be used by concerned actors, including the ICRC, to inform their policy development as well as private and public advocacy. The evidence of real-world adverse consequences, based on from pharmacological and physiological realities and observed following the first known use of such chemicals in a tactical situation in Moscow, added considerable impetus to long-term efforts to clarify international law. It remains difficult to generate the political energy to shift from a reactive to a preventive posture in addressing concerns raised by weapons and methods of warfare in the absence of evidence of real-world adverse consequences. Although, it can be done, as illustrated by the successful adoption of Convention on Certain Conventional Weapons (CCW) Protocol IV on Blinding Laser Weapons in 1995, which prohibited these weapons before they were use in armed conflict. In that case, the blinding effects were well understood from a scientific and medical perspective, and reports of imminent deployment provided impetus for political action.[115] This is a shift that concerned actors must attempt if they are to genuinely prevent rather than respond to the unacceptable harms caused by the use of new weapons in armed conflict and peacetime.

---

[114] Davison 2009a, pp. 147–148.

[115] However, it can be done, as illustrated by the successful adoption of CCW Protocol IV on Blinding Laser Weapons, which prohibited them before they were deployed. In that case, the blinding effects were well understood from a scientific and medical perspective, and reports of imminent deployment provided impetus for political action. See ICRC 1993; Human Rights Watch 1995.

These three lessons are, for instance, relevant to current international discussions on autonomous weapon systems. At the CCW in Geneva some States have claimed so-called "humanitarian benefits" associated with the development and use of weapons that select and apply force to targets without human intervention, while others insist that any agreements reached should only be applicable to "lethal" weapons. Although some autonomous weapon systems are already used in highly constrained circumstances, current political efforts to adopt new legally binding rules with specific prohibitions and restrictions are focused on preventing the harm that would accompany their expanded, less constrained, development and use.[116] These lessons may also have relevance to multilateral discussions on other weapons technologies and practices, such as efforts to constrain, and prevent the adverse impact, of cyber and information operations,[117] military operations in outer space,[118] and military applications of AI, such as in weapons and high consequence military decision-making.[119]

Fourth, this story is an illustration of the limits of a consensus-based approach in multilateral efforts to regulate weapons and methods of warfare, and in the implementation of associated international agreements, as well as the benefits and risks that accompany a non-consensus-based approach. The 2021 CWC understanding on CNS-acting chemicals would not have been possible, even after thirty years, without the resort to majority votes, both in the OPCW's Executive Council and the annual Conference of the States Parties. Consensus often protects the status quo, and, at worst, it can give a single State a veto against progress. The long-term adverse effects can be seen in various disarmament forums—from the Conference on Disarmament (CD), which has not produced a treaty since the CWC (the Comprehensive Nuclear Test Ban Treaty was negotiated in the CD but had to be adopted by the UN General Assembly in 1996 due to issues of consensus, and is yet to enter into force),[120] to the Biological Weapons Convention (BWC), which has only been able to agree modest additional measures to strengthen the Convention since the collapse of negotiations on a verification Protocol in 2001[121] and the Nuclear Non-Proliferation Treaty, where States have not agreed on any plans to implement their disarmament (or other) obligations since 2010.[122] The CCW has not produced a new Protocol since 2003 (Protocol V on Explosive Remnants of War). Its rules on landmines proved

---

[116] ICRC 2021b.

[117] UN, *Open-Ended Working Group on Security of and in the Use of Information and Communication Technologies*, available at: www.un.org/disarmament/open-ended-working-group/. See also ICRC 2022a.

[118] UN, *Open-Ended Working Group on Reducing Space Threats*, available at: https://meetings.unoda.org/meeting/oewg-space-2022/. See also ICRC 2022b.

[119] Netherlands, Ministry of foreign affairs 2023; United States, Bureau of Arms Control, Deterrence, and Stability 2023. See also ICRC 2021c.

[120] Comprehensive Nuclear-Test-Ban Treaty, opened for signature 10 September 1996, not yet in force (CTBT); Meyer 2021.

[121] Butler 2001; Revill et al. 2022, p. 22. "For all the BWC's normative success, its lack of machinery for monitoring compliance and for dealing with non-compliance concerns remains a problem in the eyes of many of its States parties."

[122] Jaramillo 2022.

3 Nerve Agents by Another Name: The Thirty-Year Effort to Close …

insufficient, its protections against incendiary weapons have not yet been strengthened, it failed to address humanitarian concerns about cluster munitions, and it has not yet started negotiations of new legally binding rules on autonomous weapon systems after a decade of discussions.[123] Meanwhile, initiatives pursued independently, or through the vote-led UN General Assembly, supported by a critical mass of States have produced agreements with significant normative and protective humanitarian impact, even influencing the policies of States that have yet to join: the Anti-Personnel Mine Ban Convention (1997), the Convention on Cluster Munitions (2008), the Arms Trade Treaty (2013) and the Treaty on the Prohibition of Nuclear Weapons (2017). And yet, a non-consensus-based approach can bring certain risks, not least uneven legal obligations among states, and also challenges for the implementation of near-universal treaties, as seen in the strong objections by some States party to the CWC to the vote establishing the new understanding on toxic chemicals as weapons for law enforcement.

A fifth lesson is that humanitarian organisations, civil society organisations and concerned States have an opportunity—and one could argue a responsibility—to take a strong protective stance when addressing the adverse impacts of weapons and methods of warfare. This is especially so in situations where there is perceived legal ambiguity or uncertainty. Even the existence of such multilateral efforts, whether preventive or reactive, can arguably have some protective effect before they come to fruition; for example, there have been only a few other alleged uses of CNS-acting chemicals as weapons in the thirty years since the CWC was adopted.[124] Other multilateral initiatives on weapons can have a constraining effect in advance of States clarifying the international law or adopting new rules with prohibitions and/or restrictions, as has been the influence of UN discussions on autonomous weapon systems. In contrast, a repetitive discussion of differing interpretations of existing legal obligations can be less constructive. A narrow debate among States and other actors over many years about differing legal interpretations of the CWC's law enforcement provisions ultimately led nowhere in terms of addressing the risks posed by using highly toxic chemicals as weapons for law enforcement and even allowed dangerous legal interpretations and weapons programmes to proliferate.

3.11 Conclusion

While the December 2021 understanding on aerosolised CNS-acting chemicals leaves some questions that should be clarified, it constitutes a significant multilateral achievement; a concrete reinforcement of the CWC's prohibition of chemical weapons in all circumstances. If properly implemented by all States Parties, it will have a protective impact for those who may find themselves subject to the use of force

---

[123] Prokosch 2021; Reuters (2021) U.N. Talks Adjourn Without Deal to Regulate 'Killer Robots'. www.reuters.com/article/us-un-disarmament-idAFKBN2IW1UJ. Accessed on 7 April 2024.

[124] See above note 28.

in law enforcement operations (whether carried out by law enforcement, military or peacekeeping forces) as well as a protective effect on the integrity of the CWC. The time taken to reach this understanding is an illustration of the persistence, patience and ultimately imperfect compromise that often underpins international disarmament and arms control agreements.

Although there are many factors that contributed to this outcome, the ICRC's approach, starting with an assessment of the actual or potential adverse impact of a particular weapon on its victims, and the organisations' engagement with policy debates was significant.[125] Careful examination of scientific and medical realities, and operational practices led the ICRC to challenge military and law enforcement claims—and terminology—to the contrary. Other key elements of the ICRC's approach were to stress the constraints of all applicable international law, while highlighting the risks for the norm prohibiting chemical weapons found in the CWC and in customary international humanitarian law, and to incorporate ethical concerns, in this case from the medical community about the use of drugs as weapons. Ultimately the ICRC distilled the key message to its core, for the purposes of influencing decision-makers, which remains that "poisoning is not a legitimate means of warfare and it cannot be a legitimate means of law enforcement".[126]

There is no accounting for external events, of course, which can always draw political attention elsewhere or, conversely, help galvanise positive political action to address a problem. Ultimately, successful humanitarian-driven disarmament and arms control initiatives are a question of helping create opportunities for change and of persistence in contributing to bringing those changes to fruition.

Acknowledgements Thank you to the following friends and colleagues for their useful comments on earlier drafts of this chapter: Robin M. Coupland, Peter Herby, Dominique Loye, Robert J. Mathews and Beat Schmidt. Thanks also to the two anonymous reviewers for their thoughtful comments. The views expressed in this chapte are those of the author alone.

References

Articles, Books and Other Documents

Barriot P, Bismuth C (2003) De destruction massive ou conventionnelles, les armes tuent les civils. Le Monde Diplomatique. https://www.mondediplomatique.fr/2003/05/BARRIOT/1016
Bismuth C, Borron SW, Baud FJ, Barriot P (2004) Chemical Weapons: Documented Use and Compounds on the Horizon. Toxicology Letters 149:1–3

---

[125] Herby, "Protecting and Reinforcing Humanitarian Norms: The Way Forward", in Pearson et al. 2007, pp. 285–289. "In conclusion, protecting and reinforcing humanitarian norms in this field requires an approach based not only on knowledge of tactical objectives and technological possibilities, but also on the real effects on people of biological and chemical weapons."
[126] ICRC 2021a.

Butler D (2001) Bioweapons Treaty in Disarray as US Blocks Plans for Verification. Nature 414, p 675

Calkins L (2010) Detained and Drugged: A Brief Overview of the Use of Pharmaceuticals for the Interrogation of Suspects, Prisoners, Patients, and POWS in the US. Bioethics 24

Caves JP, Carus S (2022) Controlling Chemical Weapons in the New International Order CSWMD Proceedings. https://wmdcenter.ndu.edu/Portals/97/CSWMD%20Proceed ings%20Aug%202022%20Final%20for%20Web.pdf. Accessed on 7 April 2024

Chai PR, Boyer EW, Al-Nahhas H, Erickson TB (2017) Toxic Chemical Weapons of Assassination and Warfare: Nerve Agents VX and Sarin. Toxicology Communications 1, pp 21–23

Chemical and Biological Weapons Nonproliferation Program (2002) The Moscow Theater Hostage Crisis: Incapacitants and Chemical Warfare. https://nonproliferation.org/the-moscow-theater-hostage-crisis-incapacitants-and-chemical-warfare/. Accessed on 7 April 2024

Cooper G, Rice P (2001) Special Issue – Chemical Casualties: Centrally Acting Incapacitants. Journal of the Royal Army Medical Corps 148:388–391

Council of Europe (2021) Measures Against the Trade in Goods Used for the Death Penalty, Torture and other Cruel, Inhuman or Degrading Treatment or Punishment, SPDP, Strasbourg. https://rm.coe.int/publication-measures-against-the-trade-in-goods-used-for-the-death-pen/1680a2cb8b. Accessed on 7 April 2024

Coupland RM (2003) Incapacitating Chemical Weapons: A Year After the Moscow Theatre Siege. The Lancet 362, p 1346

Coupland RM (2012) Incapacitating Chemical Agents. In: Mogl S (ed) Technical Workshop on Incapacitating Chemical Agents. Spiez, Switzerland, 8–9 September 2011. Spiez Laboratory, Swiss Federal Office for Civil Protection FOCP, pp 49–52

Crowley M (2009) Dangerous Ambiguities: Regulation of Riot Control Agents and Incapacitants under the Chemical Weapons Convention, Bradford Non-lethal Weapons Research Project, University of Bradford. https://omegaresearchfoundation.org/sites/default/files/uploads/Public ations/BNLWRPDangerous1.pdf. Accessed on 7 April 2024

Crowley M (2016) Chemical Control: Regulation of Incapacitating Chemical Agent Weapons, Riot Control Agents and their Means of Delivery. Palgrave Macmillan, Basingstoke

Crowley M, Dando M (2022) Central Nervous System Weapons Dealt a Blow. Science 375

CWC Coalition (undated), Summary Report: 26th Session of the Conference of the States Parties (CSP-26). www.cwccoalition.org/csp26-summary. Accessed on 7 April 2024

Dalton C, Watkins R, Pritchard S, Graham S (2021) Percutaneous Absorption of Carfentanil In Vitro. Toxicology in Vitro 72

Dan Kaszeta (2020) Toxic: A History of Nerve Agents, From Nazi Germany to Putin's Russia, Oxford University Press, Oxford

Dando M (1996) A New Form of Warfare: The Rise of Non-Lethal Weapons Brassey's (UK) Limited, London, 1996, pp 136–168

Dando M (2003) The Danger to the Chemical Weapons Convention from Incapacitating Chemicals, First CWC Review Conference. University of Bradford

Dando M (2004) Non-Lethal Weapons: More Realistic Scenarios. Biotechnology, Weapons and Humanity II. Board of Science and Education, British Medical Association. London

Dando M, Furmanski M (2006) Midspectrum Incapacitant Programs. In: Wheelis M, Lajos R, Malcolm D (eds), Deadly Cultures: Biological Weapons since 1945. Harvard University Press, Cambridge, MA, pp 236–251

Davison N (2007), "Off the Rocker" and "On the Floor": The Continued Development of Biochemical Incapacitating Weapons. Bradford Non-Lethal Weapons Research Project Report No. 8. http://www.statewatch.org/news/2007/aug/bradford-biological%20weapons-report.pdf. Accessed on 7 April 2024

Davison N (2009a) "Non-Lethal" Weapons, Palgrave Macmillan Limited, London

Davison N (2009b) Marketing New Chemical Weapons. Bulletin of the Atomic Scientists. https://thebulletin.org/2009/06/marketing-new-chemical-weapons. Accessed on 7 April 2024

Davison N (2013) New Weapons: Legal and Policy Issues Associated with Weapons Described as 'Non-Lethal'. In: Dan Saxon (ed.), International Humanitarian Law and the Changing Technology of War. Brill, Leiden, pp 281–313

Davison N (2015) Book Review: Chemical Control: Regulation of Incapacitating Chemical Agent Weapons, Riot Control Agents and their Means of Delivery, by Michael Crowley. International Review of the Red Cross 97, 923–928

Dragffy N (2003) News Chronology – November 2002 through January 2003. The CBW Conventions Bulletin 59:9–29

Dragffy N (2005) News Chronology - May through October 2005. The CBW Conventions Bulletin 69:27–63

Dunworth T (2012) The Silent Killer: Toxic Chemicals for Law Enforcement and the Chemical Weapons Convention. New Zealand Yearbook of International Law 10

Fenton GP (2007) Current and Prospective Military and Law Enforcement Use of Chemical Agents for Incapacitation. In: Pearson AM, Chevrier MI, Wheelis M (eds) Incapacitating Biochemical Weapons: Promise or Peril? Lexington Books, Lanham, MD, pp 103–121

Fidler DP (2005), The Meaning of Moscow: 'Non-Lethal' Weapons and International Law in the Early 21st Century. International Review of the Red Cross 87, pp 525–552

Fry JD (2010) Gas Smalls Awful: U.N. Forces, Riot-Control Agents, and the Chemical Weapons Convention. Michigan Journal of International Law 31:475–558

Gladden RM, Martinez P, Seth P (2016) Fentanyl Law Enforcement Submissions and Increases in Synthetic Opioid-Involved Overdose Deaths – 27 States, 2013–2014. Morbidity and Mortality Weekly Report 65:837–844

Hart J (2016) Allegations of Use of Chemical Weapons in Iraq. In: SIPRI Yearbook 2017, Oxford University Press, Oxford, pp 523–525

Harvard Sussex Program on CBW Armament and Arms Litigation (2003) 'Non-Lethal' Weapons, the CWC and the BWC. The CBW Conventions Bulletin 61:1–2

Herby P (2007) Protecting and Reinforcing Humanitarian Norms: The Way Forward. In: AM Pearson AM, Chevrier MI, Wheelis M (eds) Incapacitating Biochemical Weapons: Promise or Peril? Lexington Books, Lanham, MD, pp 285–289

Hess L, Schreiberova J, Fusek J (2005) Pharmacological Non-Lethal Weapons. Proceedings of the 3rd European Symposium on Non-Lethal Weapons. Ettlingen

Human Rights Watch (1995) Blinding Laser Weapons: The Need to Ban a Cruel and Inhumane Weapon 7 1. www.hrw.org/reports/1995/General1.htm. Accessed on 7 April 2024

ICRC (1993) Blinding Weapons: Reports of the Meetings of Experts Convened by the International Committee of the Red Cross on Battlefield Laser Weapons, 1989–1991, Geneva

ICRC (2003) First Special Session of the Conference of the States Parties to Review the Operation of the Chemical Weapons Convention (First Review Conference), The Hague. www.icrc.org/en/doc/resources/documents/news-release/2009-and-earlier/5m5dah.htm. Accessed on 7 April 2024

ICRC (2010) "Incapacitating Chemical Agents": Implications for International Law. www.icrc.org/en/doc/assets/files/publications/icrc-002-4051.pdf. Accessed on 7 April 2024

ICRC (2012) Toxic Chemicals as Weapons for Law Enforcement: A Threat to Life and International Law? www.icrc.org/en/download/file/7781/toxic-chemicals-for-law-enforcement-synthesis-icrc-09-2012.pdf. Accessed on 7 April 2024

ICRC (2013a) "Incapacitating Chemical Agents": Law Enforcement, Human Rights Law and Policy Perspectives. www.icrc.org/en/doc/assets/files/publications/icrc-002-4121.pdf. Accessed 7 April 2024

ICRC (2013b) ICRC Position on the Use of Toxic Chemicals as Weapons for Law Enforcement. www.icrc.org/en/doc/resources/documents/legal-fact-sheet/2013-02-06-toxic-chemicals-weapons-law-enforcement.htm. Accessed 7 April 2024

ICRC (2017) Iraq: ICRC Strongly Condemns Use of Chemical Weapons Around Mosul. www.icrc.org/en/document/iraq-icrc-strongly-condemns-use-chemical-weapons-around-mosul. Accessed on 7 April 2024

ICRC (2020) The Use of Weapons and Equipment in Law Enforcement Operations. www.icrc. org/en/download/file/121972/qa-use_of_force_in_law_enforcement_operations_en-web.pdf. Accessed on 7 April 2024

ICRC (2021a) ICRC Emphasizes the Prohibition of Chemical Weapons at 26th Conference of the States Parties to the Chemical Weapons Convention: Twenty-Sixth Session of the Conference of the States Parties to the Chemical Weapons Convention 29 November–3 December 2021, The Hague. www.icrc.org/en/document/prohibition-chemical-weapons-26th-conference. Accessed on 7 April 2024

ICRC (2021b) ICRC Position on Autonomous Weapon Systems, Position and Background Paper. www.icrc.org/en/document/icrc-position-autonomous-weapon-systems. Accessed on 7 April 2024

ICRC (2021c) ICRC Position Paper: Artificial intelligence and machine learning in armed conflict: A human-centred approach. International Review of The Red Cross 913:463–479

ICRC (2022a) ICRC Statement on International Law in the Second Session of the OEWG on Security of and in the Use of Information and Communications Technologies. https://documents.unoda.org/wp-content/uploads/2022/03/OEWG_Second-session_Statement-on-International-Law.pdf. Accessed on 7 April 2024

ICRC (2022b) Constraints under International Law on Military Operations in Outer Space During Armed Conflicts. Working paper submitted by the International Committee of the Red Cross to the open-ended working group on reducing space threats through norms, rules and principles of responsible behaviours, as convened under United Nations General Assembly Resolution 76/231, and to the Secretary-General of the United Nations in reply to General Assembly Resolution 76/230 on "Further practical measures for the prevention of an arms race in outer space". https://www.icrc.org/en/download/file/241858/icrc_working_paper_on_the_con straints_under_international_law_on_military_space_operations_final_en.pdf. Accessed on 7 April 2024

ICRC (undated) Customary IHL Database, Rule 74. Chemical Weapons. https://ihl-databases.icrc. org/customary-ihl/eng/docs/v1_rul_rule74. Accessed on 7 April 2024

Jaramillo C (2022) Death by a Thousand Red Lines: The Colossal Failure of the 10th NPT Review Conference. Ploughshares

Kelle A (2003) The CWC After Its First Review Conference: Is the Glass Half Full or Half Empty? Disarmament Diplomacy 71, pp 31–40

Klochikhin V, Lushnikov A, Zagaynov V, Putilov A, Selivanov V, Zatevakhin M (2005) Principles of Modelling of the Scenario of Calmative Application in a Building with Deterred Hostages. Proceedings of the 3rd European Symposium on Non-Lethal Weapons, Ettlingen

Klochikhin V, Pirumov V, Putilov A, Selivanov V (2003) The Complex Forecast of Perspectives of NLW for European Application. Proceedings of the 2nd European Symposium on Non-Lethal Weapons, Ettlingen

Klotz L, Furmanski M, Wheelis M (2003) Beware the Siren's Song: Why "Non-Lethal" Incapacitating Chemical Agents are Lethal. Federation of American Scientists Working Group on Biological Weapons. https://armscontrolcenter.org/wp-content/uploads/2016/02/Beware-the-Sirens-Song.pdf. Accessed on 7 April 2024

Koplow DA (2005) Tangled up in Khaki and Blue: Lethal and Non-Lethal Weapons in Recent Confrontations. Georgetown Journal of International Law:703–808

Krutzsch W, Trapp R (2014) Article II: Definitions and Criteria. In: Krutzsch W, Myjer E, Trapp R (eds), The Chemical Weapons Convention: A Commentary. Oxford University Press, Oxford, pp 73–105

Lakoski JM, Bosseau Murray W, Kenny JM (2000) The Advantages and Limitations of Calmatives for Use as a Non-Lethal Technique, College of Medicine, Applied Research Laboratory, Pennsylvania State University

Lean G and Carrell S (2003) US Prepares to Use Toxic Gases in Iraq", The Independent on Sunday, 2 March 2003.

Mathews RJ (2018) Central Nervous System-Acting Chemicals and the Chemical Weapons Convention: A Former Scientific Adviser's Perspective. Pure and Applied Chemistry 90

McLeish (2020) Julian Perry Robinson (1941–2020). Obituary, Nature, 21 May 2020. www.nature.com/articles/d41586-020-01450-1. Accessed 7 April 2024

Meselson M, Robinson J (1994) New Technologies and the Loophole in the Convention. Chemical Weapons Convention Bulletin 23. www.sussex.ac.uk/Units/spru/hsp/documents/CWCB23.PDF. Accessed on 7 April 2024

Meselson M, Robinson J (2003) 'Non Lethal' Weapons and Implementation of the Chemical and Biological Weapons Conventions. 20th Pugwash Workshop Study Group on the Implementation of the CBW Conventions, Geneva, Switzerland, 8–9 November 2003. www.sussex.ac.uk/Units/spru/hsp/documents/Non%20Lethal.pdf. Accessed 7 April 2024.

Meyer P (2021) Does the Conference of Disarmament Have a Future? Journal for Peace and Nuclear Disarmament 4:287–294

Mogl S (ed) (2012) Technical Workshop on Incapacitating Chemical Agents. Spiez, Switzerland, 8–9 September 2011. Spiez Laboratory, Swiss Federal Office for Civil Protection FOCP.

Naqvi Y (2017) Crossing the Red Line: The Use of Chemical Weapons in Syria and What Should Happen Now. International Review of the Red Cross 99:959–993

Nathanson V (2007) The Use of Drugs as Weapons: The Concerns and Responsibilities of Healthcare Professionals. British Medical Association, London

National Center for Biotechnology Information (undated) PubChem Compound Summary for CID 62156, Carfentanil. https://pubchem.ncbi.nlm.nih.gov/compound/Carfentanil. Accessed on 7 April 2024

National Research Council Committee on Toxicology (1997) Chapter 6: Review of Acute Human-Toxicity Estimates for VX. Review of Acute Human-Toxicity Estimates for Selected Chemical-Warfare Agents. National Academies Press, Washington, DC. www.ncbi.nlm.nih.gov/books/NBK233724/. Accessed on 7 April 2024

National Institute on Drug Abuse (2023) Overdose Death Rates. https://nida.nih.gov/drug-topics/trends-statistics/overdose-death-rates. Accessed on 7 April 2024

NATO Research and Technology Organization (2006) The Human Effects of Non-Lethal Technologies, RTO-TR-HFM-073, Human Factors and Medicine Panel, Annex M, Brussels. https://www.sto.nato.int/publications/STO%20Technical%20Reports/RTO-TR-HFM-073/$$TR-HFM-073-ALL.pdf. Accessed on 7 April 2024

Netherlands (2023) REAIM Call to Action. Responsible AI in the Military Domain Summit, Ministry of Foreign Affairs

Nixdorf K, Melling J (2007) Potential Long-Term Physiological Consequences of Exposure to Incapacitating Biochemicals. In: Pearson AM, Chevrier MI, Wheelis M (eds) Incapacitating Biochemical Weapons: Promise or Peril? Lexington Books, Lanham, MD, pp 149–169

OPCW (2008) Switzerland: Riot Control and Incapacitating Agents under the Chemical Weapons Convention, Doc. RC-2/NAT.12

OPCW (2013) Statement by the International Committee of the Red Cross, Conference of the States Parties, Doc C-18, NAT.25

OPCW (2014a) Australia: Weaponisation of Central Nervous System Acting Chemicals, Conference of the States Parties, Nineteenth Session, Doc. C-19/NAT.1

OPCW (2014b) United States of America: Statement by Rose E. Gottemoeller Under Secretary of State of the United States of America at the Nineteenth Session of the Conference of States Parties, Conference of the States Parties, Doc. C-19/NAT.40

OPCW (2014c) Declaration of Riot Control Agents: Advice from the Scientific Advisory Board, Doc. S/1177/2014

OPCW (2015) Aerosolisation of Central Nervous System-Acting Chemicals for Law Enforcement Purposes. Joint Statement, Twentieth Session, Doc. C-20/NAT.2/Rev.2

OPCW (2016) Russian Federation: Statement by the Delegation of the Russian Federation at the Twenty-First Session of the Conference of the States Parties (On the Matter of Incapacitants), Doc. C-21/NAT.32

OPCW (2017) OPCW Executive Council Condemns Chemical Weapons Use in Fatal Incident in Malaysia. https://www.opcw.org/media-centre/news/2017/03/opcw-executive-council-condemns-chemical-weapons-use-fatal-incident. Accessed on 7 April 2024

OPCW (2018a) Note by the Technical Secretariat. Summary of the Report on Activities Carried Out in Support of a Request for Technical Assistance by the United Kingdom of Great Britain and Northern Ireland (Technical Assistance Visit – TAV/02.18). Doc. S/1612/2018. https://www.opcw.org/sites/default/files/documents/S_series/2018/en/s-1612-2018_e___1_.pdf. Accessed on 7 April 2024

OPCW (2018b) Aerosolisation of Central Nervous System-Acting Chemicals for Law Enforcement Purposes, Conference of the States Parties, Twentieth Session, Doc. RC-4/NAT.26

OPCW (2018c) Statement by the International Committee of the Red Cross at the Fourth Special Session of the Conference of the States Parties to Review the Operation of the Chemical Weapons Convention, Doc. RC-4/NAT.21

OPCW (2020a) Note by the Technical Secretariat. Summary of the Report on Activities Carried Out in Support of a Request for Technical Assistance by Germany (Technical Assistance Visit – TAV/01/20). S/1906/2020. https://www.opcw.org/sites/default/files/documents/2020/10/s-1906-2020%28e%29.pdf. Accessed on 7 April 2024

OPCW (2020b) Russian Federation: On an Understanding Regarding the Aerosolized Use of Central Nervous System-Acting Chemicals for Law Enforcement Purposes, Doc. EC-93/NAT.6

OPCW (2020c) Russian Federation: Statement by the Delegation of the Russian Federation to the OPCW at the Ninety-Fourth Session of the Executive Council Under Agenda Item 16, Doc. EC-94/NAT.69

OPCW (2020d) China, the Islamic Republic of Iran, and the Syrian Arab Republic: Technical Ambiguity and Legal Uncertainty on the Proposed Draft Decision Entitled "Understanding Regarding the Aerosolised Use of Central Nervous System-Acting Chemicals for Law Enforcement Purposes, Doc. EC-95/WP.1

OPCW (2020e) Report by the Director-General: Financial, Administrative and Programme and Budget Implications of the Proposal for an Understanding Regarding the Aerosolised Use of Central Nervous System-Acting Chemicals for Law Enforcement Purposes, Executive Council, Doc. EC-93/DG.2/Rev.1

OPCW (2020f) Joint Statement of States Parties on the Aerosolised Use of Central Nervous System-Acting Chemicals for Law Enforcement, Conference of the States Parties, Twenty-Fifth Session, Doc. C-25/NAT.71

OPCW (2020g) First Report by the OPCW Investigation and Identification Team pursuant to Paragraph 10 of Decision C-SS-4/Dec.3 "Addressing the Threat From Chemical Weapons Use" Ltamenah (Syrian Arab Republic) 24, 25, and 30 March 2017, Doc. S/1867/2020

OPCW (2021a) Decision. Understanding Regarding the Aerosolised Use of Central Nervous System-Acting Chemicals for Law Enforcement Purposes, Conference of the States Parties, Twenty-Sixth Session, Doc. C-26/DEC.10

OPCW (2021b) Russian Federation: Questions and Answers Regarding the Proposal to Prohibit the Aerosolized Use of Central Nervous System-Acting Chemicals for Law Enforcement Purposes, Doc. EC-96/NAT.6

OPCW (2021c) Draft Decision: Understanding Regarding the Aerosolised Use of Central Nervous System-Acting Chemicals for Law Enforcement Purposes, Executive Council, Ninety-Sixth Session, Doc. EC-92/DEC/CRP.9/Rev.6*

OPCW (2021d) Report of the Ninety-Sixth Session of the Executive Council, Executive Council, Ninety-Sixth Session, Doc. EC-96/2

OPCW (2021e) Joint Statement on behalf of 4 Delegations Delivered by the Delegation of the Islamic Republic of Iran at the 26th Session of the Conference of States Parties of the OPCW under the Subitem 26.1 "Any Other Business" on the Draft Decision entitled "Understanding Regarding the Aerosolized Use of Central Nervous System-Acting Chemicals for Law Enforcement Purposes", Conference of the States Parties

OPCW (2021f) Second Report by the OPCW Investigation and Identification Team Pursuant to Paragraph 10 of Decision C-SS-4/DEC.3 "Addressing the Threat from Chemical Weapons Use" Saraqib (Syrian Arab Republic) 4 February 2018, Doc. S/1943/2021

OPCW (2023) Report by the Director-General. Report of the Scientific Advisory Board on Developments in Science and Technology to the Fifth Special Session of the Conference of the States Parties to Review the Operation of the Chemical Weapons Convention, Doc. RC-5/DG.1. https://www.opcw.org/sites/default/files/documents/2023/02/rc5dg01%28e%29.pdf. Accessed on 7 April 2024

OPCW (undated) Annex on Chemicals. https://www.opcw.org/chemical-weapons-convention/ann exes/annex-chemicals/annex-chemicals Accessed on 7 April 2024

Pearson AM, Chevrier MI, Wheelis M (eds) (2007) Incapacitating Biochemical 705 Weapons: Promise or Peril?, Lexington Books, Lanham, MD.

Prokosch E (2021) The Development of the Convention on Conventional Weapons 1971–2003. Article 36, https://article36.org/wp-content/uploads/2021/12/The-Development-of-the-CCW.pdf. Accessed on 7 April 2024

Robinson JP (1967) Chemical Warfare. Science Journal III 4

Robinson JP (2003a) Disabling Chemical Weapons: A Documented Chronology of Events, 1945–2003. Harvard Sussex Program, University of Sussex, unpublished

Robinson JP (2003b) 'Non Lethal' Weapons and Implementation of the Chemical and Biological Weapons Conventions. 20th Pugwash Workshop Study Group on the Implementation of the CBW Conventions, Geneva. http://www.sussex.ac.uk/Units/spru/hsp/documents/Non%20L ethal.pdf. Accessed on 7 April 2024

Robinson JP (2007) Non Lethal Warfare and the Chemical Weapons Convention. Harvard Sussex Program SPRU – Science & Technology Policy Research, University of Sussex. http://hsp.sussex.ac.uk/new/_uploads/publications/2007_Robinson_Non_Lethal_War fare_and_the_Chemical_Weapons_Convention.pdf. Accessed on 7 April 2024

Robinson JP (2013) 'Incapacitating Chemical Agents' in Context: An Historical Overview of States' Policy. In: ICRC, "Incapacitating Chemical Agents": Law Enforcement, Human Rights Law and Policy Perspectives. pp 89–96

Revill J, Borrie J, Lennane R (2022) Back to the Future for Verification in the Biological Disarmament Regime? WMD Compliance Enforcement Series 14, UNIDR, Geneva

Riches JR, Read RW, Robin MB, Cooper NJ, Timperley CM (2012) Analysis of Clothing and Urine from Moscow Theatre Siege Casualties Reveals Carfentanil and Remifentanil Use. Journal of Analytical Toxicology 36

Ruppe D (2023) CWC: Red Cross Says It Was Muzzled Over Stand on Incapacitating Weapons, Global Security Newswire, 30 April 2003.

Shreiberova J, Hess L, Marcus M, Joostens E (2005) A Search for Safe and Rapid Method of Immobilization. A Study in Macaque Monkeys. European Journal of Anaesthesiology 22

Smallwood K, Trapp R, Mathews R, Schmidt B, Sydnes LK (2013) Impact of Scientific Developments on the Chemical Weapons Convention. Pure and Applied Chemistry 85: 2323–2352

Stanley T (2003) Human Immobilization: Is the Experience in Moscow Just the Beginning? European Journal of Anaesthesiology 20: 427-428

Stockholm International Peace Research Institute (1973) The Problem of Chemical and Biological Warfare Volume II: CB Weapons Today. Almqvist & Wiksell, Stockholm, pp 298–306

Royal Society (2012) Brain Waves Module 3: Neuroscience, Conflict and Security. London. https://royalsociety.org/-/media/Royal_Society_Content/policy/projects/brain-waves/2012-02-06-BW3.pdf

Tucker JB (2006) War of Nerves: Chemical Warfare from World War I to Al-Qaeda, Ebury Press, London

UN General Assembly and Security Council (2013), Report of the United Nations Mission to Investigate Allegations of the Use of Chemical Weapons in the Syrian Arab Republic on the Alleged Use of Chemical Weapons in the Ghouta Area of Damascus on 21 August 2013, UN Doc. A/67/997–S/2013/553

UN General Assembly and Security Council (2013), United Nations Mission to Investigate Allegations of the Use of Chemical Weapons in the Syrian Arab Republic: Final Report, UN Doc. A/68/663–S/2013/735

UN Office of the High Commissioner for Human Rights, Reports to the Human Rights Council: Death Penalty, available at: www.ohchr.org/en/death-penalty/reports-human-rights-council.

UN Security Council (2017) Seventh Report of the Organisation for the Prohibition of Chemical Weapons–United Nations Joint Investigative Mechanism, UN Doc. S/2017/904

UN, Open-Ended Working Group on Reducing Space Threats, available at: https://meetings.unoda.org/meeting/oewg-space-2022/. Accessed on 7 April 2024

UN, Open-Ended Working Group on Security of and in the Use of Information and Communication Technologies, available at: www.un.org/disarmament/open-ended-working-group/. Accessed on 7 April 2024

United States (1975) Executive Order 11850 – Renunciation of Certain Uses in War of Chemical Herbicides and Riot Control Agents. Doc 40 FR 16187, 3 CFR1971-1975 Comp., p 980

United States (2015) Statement by Deputy Assistant Secretary Mallory Stewart to the Twentieth Session of the Conference of the States Parties Organization for the Prohibition of Chemical Weapons, The Hague. https://www.opcw.org/sites/default/files/documents/CSP/C-20/national_statemements/USA.pdf

United States (2021) Compliance with the Convention on the Prohibition of the Development, Production, Stockpiling and Use of Chemical Weapons and on their Destruction. https://www.state.gov/wp-content/uploads/2021/04/2021-Condition-10-c-Report.pdf. Accessed on 7 April 2024

United States (2023) Political Declaration on Responsible Military Use of Artificial Intelligence and Autonomy, Department of State. https://www.state.gov/wp-content/uploads/2023/10/Latest-Version-Political-Declaration-on-Responsible-Military-Use-of-AI-and-Autonomy.pdf. Accessed on 7 April 2024

Urbina F, Lentzos F, Invernizzi C, Ekins S (2022) Dual Use of Artificial-Intelligence-Powered Drug Discovery, Nature Machine Intelligence 4

US Air Force (1994) Harassing, Annoying, and "Bad Guy" Identifying Chemicals (redacted), US Air Force Wright Laboratory, Wright-Patterson Air Force Base. https://web.archive.org/web/20060502201217/; http://www.sunshine-project.org/incapacitants/jnlwdpdf/wpafbchem.pdf

US Army (1996) Incapacitants. In: Department of the Army, the Navy, and the Air Force (ed) NATO Handbook on the Medical Aspects of NBC Defensive Operations. Washington, DC, pp 337–344

US National Research Council (2003) An Assessment of Non-Lethal Weapons Science and Technology, Committee for an Assessment of Non-Lethal Weapons Science and Technology, Naval Studies Board, Division on Engineering and Physical Sciences. National Academies Press, Washington, DC

Vardanyan R (2017) 4-Substituted and 1,4-Disubstituted Piperidines. In: Piperidine-Based Drug Discovery. Elsevier, Cambridge, MA, pp 147–221

Wax PM, Becker CE, Curry SC (2003) Unexpected 'Gas' Casualties in Moscow: A Medical Toxicology Perspective. Annals of Emergency Medicine 41 5: 700–705

Wheelis M, Dando M (2005) Neurobiology: A Case Study of the Imminent Militarization of Biology. International Review of the Red Cross 87 859

Wines M (2002) The Aftermath in Moscow: Post-Mortem in Moscow; Russia Names Drug in Raid, Defending Use", New York Times, 31 October 2002. www.nytimes.com/2002/10/31/world/aftermath-moscow-post-mortem-moscow-russia-names-drug-raid-defending-use.html. Accessed 7 April 2024.

Cases

European Court of Human Rights, Finogenov and Others v. Russia, Judgment, 20 December 2011, Application Nos. 18299/03 and 27311/03

Treaties

Comprehensive Nuclear-Test-Ban Treaty, opened for signature 10 September 1996, not yet in force

Convention on Psychotropic Substances, opened for signature 21 February 1971, 1019 UNTS 175 (entered into force 16 August 1976)

Convention on the Prohibition of the Development, Production, Stockpiling and Use of Chemical Weapons and on their Destruction, opened for signature 13 January 1993, 1975 UNTS 45 (entered into force 29 April 1997)

Declaration (IV.2) concerning Asphyxiating Gases, The Hague, opened for signature 29 July 1899 (entered into force 4 September 1900)

Protocol for the Prohibition of the Use of Asphyxiating, Poisonous or Other Gases, and of Bacteriological Methods of Warfare, Geneva, 17 June 1925 (entered into force 8 February 1928)

Single Convention on Narcotic Drugs, opened for signature 30 March 1961, 520 UNTS 151 (entered into force 13 December 1964)

Chapter 4
On the Sideline or on the Pitch? *The Classification of Third States Supporting Active Belligerents in an International Armed Conflict with Satellite Imagery*

Robin Sebastiaan David Sinnige

Contents

4.1	Introduction	110
4.2	Becoming a Co-party—*Lex Lata*	112
	4.2.1 Terminology: Co-belligerency Versus Co-party Status	113
	4.2.2 The Effects of Being a Co-party	114
	4.2.3 Direct and Indirect Intervention and the Ambiguity of the Latter	115
	4.2.4 The Desirability of the Legal Uncertainty Surrounding Indirect Intervention	119
4.3	Discussion of Possible Thresholds for Becoming a Co-party Through Indirect Intervention	120
	4.3.1 Systematic or Significant Violation of Neutrality Law	120
	4.3.2 Systematic or Substantial Supply of Support	123
	4.3.3 Significant Participation in Hostilities Through (Indirect) Support that Has a Direct Nexus with Belligerent of Hostile Activities	124
	4.3.4 The ICRC's 'Direct Participation in Hostilities' Test	125
	4.3.5 An Analogy with NIACs	127
4.4	Proposal for a Threshold that Fits Best Within IHL	131
	4.4.1 State Practice	131
	4.4.2 The Threshold for Becoming a Co-party Through Indirect Intervention	133
4.5	Application of the Threshold to States Supporting Active Belligerents with Processed Satellite Imagery	137
	4.5.1 The Purpose and Use of Satellite Imagery	137
	4.5.2 The Practice of Supporting a Belligerent with Satellite Imagery	138
	4.5.3 The Systematic Supply of Tactical Intelligence	140
	4.5.4 The Role of Private Space Companies and Consequences of Co-party Status for Those Companies	144
4.6	Conclusion	146
	References	147

This chapter was written in a personal capacity, before the author started in his current position. The views expressed in this chapter are those of the author and do not represent the views of the Dutch government.

R. S. D. Sinnige (✉)
Dutch Ministry of Infrastructure and Water Management, The Hague, The Netherlands
e-mail: robin.sinnige@minienw.nl

© T.M.C. ASSER PRESS and the authors 2025
H. Krieger et al. (eds.), *Yearbook of International Humanitarian Law, Volume 26 (2023)*,
Yearbook of International Humanitarian Law 26,
https://doi.org/10.1007/978-94-6265-663-5_4

Abstract The most common support by third States for Ukraine, in the context of the international armed conflict between Russia and Ukraine, is the provision of goods and services, or indirect support. This indirect support includes processed satellite imagery, also called intelligence. With the content of third States' support to Ukraine intensifying over the course of the armed conflict, this situation has highlighted the legal question whether a third State will become a co-party to a pre-existing international armed conflict, by providing one of the active belligerent parties to that conflict with processed satellite imagery. This legal question requires clarification for it has led to legal uncertainty, corresponding potential unwanted exploitation, and a tense situation in which Russia claims the "collective West" has become a party to the conflict in Ukraine, with third States denying. Focusing on the *lex lata*, international humanitarian law does not provide a conclusive answer to this legal question. Still, it is accepted that a third State can become a co-party by intervening directly or indirectly. While indirect intervention may encompass intelligence support to a belligerent, it lacks a clear threshold. After discussing several possible thresholds for co-party status through indirect intervention, this chapter introduces its own threshold. Accordingly, a third State can be qualified as a co-party when the following criteria are met:

1. The extent of the support: a third State must support a belligerent State to such an extent that the support is systematic in nature and makes a material and integral tactical contribution to military operations related to specific hostilities;
2. Causal link: there must be a direct causal link between the support and the specific hostilities;
3. Intent: the supporting State must have intended to contribute to specific hostilities engaged in by the supported belligerent.

Applying this newly introduced threshold to States supplying belligerents with processed satellite imagery, there are certainly instances in which tactical intelligence support will cross the threshold, resulting in co-party status of the supporting State.

Keywords Armed conflict · Satellite imagery · Intelligence support · Tactical intelligence · Indirect intervention · Co-party status

4.1 Introduction

Although it has been common practice for some States to support active belligerents in pre-existing armed conflicts in the past, the Russo–Ukrainian war has shown us this is still a matter of great controversy. Since the beginning of the Russian invasion of Ukraine in February 2022, a large number of third States has shown their full support to Ukraine by sending it military, financial, and humanitarian support.[1] Importantly though, while mainly Western States are supporting Ukraine to

---

[1] Kiel Institute for the World Economy 2023.

an increasingly significant extent, they do not view themselves as becoming co-parties to the conflict.[2]

International humanitarian law (hereinafter IHL), as a part of public international law, aims to regulate and control something, i.e. armed conflicts, which is not easily regulated or controlled. The present situation, in which third States support a belligerent but maintain they are not co-parties, is no exception to this. Indeed, it has brought the international community to a very grey, but pivotal, part of international law regarding the classification of supporting States, since IHL does not sufficiently explain to what extent third States can become co-parties to a pre-existing armed conflict.[3] Although this issue has been dealt with, to some extent, with respect to non-international armed conflicts (hereinafter NIACs), the legal effects of supporting a belligerent in a pre-existing international armed conflict (hereinafter IAC) remain virtually unexplored. Metaphorically speaking, it is unclear to what extent the support by a third State, to one of the teams engaged in a game, changes the legal status of the supporting State from a mere supporter on the sideline, cheering on one of the teams, to an actual participant in the game on the pitch itself.

This legal uncertainty is especially striking in situations where third States support a belligerent with detailed processed satellite imagery. In contrast to conventional military support, the supply of satellite images is rather complex because of the different entities involved, the potential difference between the purpose and the ultimate use of those images, and the game changing effects they can have in an armed conflict. To illustrate, the interplay between States and private space companies is highlighted by a statement made by a government official from the United States of America (hereinafter U.S.) in which it was acknowledged that the U.S. has been providing Ukraine with an unprecedented amount of satellite images obtained from private space companies.[4] When it comes to the use and the significance of these satellite images in the context of the IAC in Ukraine, it is important to stress that satellite images not only contribute to documenting the war, but they might also significantly contribute to the planning and execution of Ukraine's military operations. Hence, satellite imagery could actually be used in hostilities, just like conventional military materiel support, like battle tanks.

Amidst the IAC in Ukraine, the international community finds itself confronted with the legal question what the threshold is for third States to become a co-party to a pre-existing IAC due to their support to an active belligerent. Even though there are important legal consequences attached to becoming a co-party, third States are still providing Ukraine with increasingly significant support, without there being any certainty regarding their classification in the armed conflict. In the meantime, while legal uncertainty is already undesirable, it could also be (mis)used by States to exploit international law. It is for these reasons that this legal uncertainty needs to be addressed as soon as possible, for only then can international law be further developed, improved, and applied consistently.

---

[2] NATO 2022b.

[3] Wentker 2023, p. 647.

[4] Universe Magazine 2022.

This chapter therefore focuses on the question whether a third State will become a co-party to a pre-existing IAC, by providing one of the active belligerent parties to that conflict with processed satellite imagery. This chapter aims to contribute to the legal debate and the further development and improvement of IHL by providing new insights. To this end, sect. 4.2 focuses on the *lex lata* as it stands at the time of writing. After a brief discussion on terminology and turning to the legal effects of becoming a co-party, this section describes how third States can become a co-party to a pre-existing armed conflict by way of direct or indirect intervention. Afterwards, an evaluative analysis will follow regarding the desirability of the legal uncertainty surrounding the latter method of intervention. Given that supplying a belligerent with satellite imagery could qualify as a form of indirect intervention, sect. 4.3 discusses multiple possible thresholds for a State to become co-party through indirect intervention, that are put forward by case law and scholars. This discussion illustrates how fragmented the academic literature is on the matter and why all potential thresholds fall short of providing a fitting threshold. Section 4.4, however, will prove valuable for the legal debate because, on the basis of the discussion in the previous section, it introduces a threshold for indirect intervention in a pre-existing IAC that fits best within the system of IHL as a whole. Lastly, sect. 4.5 applies this newly introduced threshold to situations in which a third State supports a belligerent by providing it with processed satellite imagery. This section starts by describing the possible functions of satellite imagery and third State's practice of supporting belligerents with such imagery. Apart from merely applying the threshold to a static situation, this section takes into consideration the varying circumstances which could be relevant, such as the intent of the supporting State, the eventual use of the images, and the original source of the images.

4.2 Becoming a Co-party—*Lex Lata*

Given that third State's support to Ukraine is intensifying as the IAC between Russia and Ukraine drags on, the urgency of the legal question when a third State becomes a co-party due to its support to an active belligerent is becoming quite apparent. Poland and Slovakia, for instance, promised Ukraine to send it a significant number of Soviet-era MiG-29 fighter jets.[5] Also, the Netherlands and Denmark jointly decided to provide Ukraine with fourteen modern Leopard 2A4 tanks.[6] This illustrates an important upward trend in the military support to Ukraine, since third States have

---

[5] Dahiya N, Schmitz R (2023) Slovakia joins fellow NATO member Poland in sending fighter jets to Ukraine. https://www.npr.org/2023/03/16/1163895110/poland-will-send-fighter-jets-to-ukraine-the-first-nato-country-to-do-so#:~:text=Slovakia%20announced%20it%20would%20send,parts%20for%20Ukraine%27s%20existing%20fleet. Accessed 28 November 2023.

[6] Dutch Ministry of Defence 2023.

4 On the Sideline or on the Pitch? *The Classification of Third States ...*   113

been reluctant in the past to supply Ukraine with such heavy weaponry.[7] Indeed, until recently third States saw the supply of battle tanks as a red line leading to co-party status if crossed.[8] Evidently, there is no definitive threshold for becoming a co-party. Perhaps some States are even trying to push the boundary increasingly further by providing Ukraine with significantly more heavy weaponry. After some notes on terminology and the effects of co-party status, this chapter discusses how current IHL determines when a third State becomes a co-party.

4.2.1 Terminology: Co-belligerency Versus Co-party Status

Under the concept of co-belligerency, a third State could enter a pre-existing IAC alongside an active belligerent, fighting a common enemy, and therefore becoming a fully-fledged belligerent and a party to the conflict itself.[9] It is further explained that the concept of co-belligerency applies to IACs, and concerns the situation in which a third State becomes a co-belligerent through formal or informal processes.[10] While formal processes could concern a treaty of alliance, an informal process encompasses a third State's assistance to a common cause with belligerent forces.[11] The terms 'co-belligerent' and 'co-belligerency' have become widely used over the last year in the context of third States' support to Ukraine.[12] However, for terminology reasons, this chapter will not use these terms. This chapter aims to analyse whether a third State will become a co-party to a pre-existing IAC by providing one of the active belligerents in that conflict with processed satellite imagery. Crucially, this concerns a situation of indirect involvement, without the direct resort to armed force. To potentially qualify such a third State as a 'co-belligerent' intrinsically implies that it is directly engaged in the hostilities. Moreover, IHL refers to "Party to the conflict" regarding party status, and not to terms like 'co-belligerent'. Therefore, this chapter continues to use the terms 'co-party' and 'co-party status' with regard to indirect support, which, in essence, bear the same meaning and effects as the concept of 'co-belligerency' set out above, but have the terminological advantage of being more neutral, less escalatory in

---

[7] Financial Times (2023) Why Olaf Scholz is reluctant to send battle tanks to Ukraine. https://www.ft.com/content/9e0e5ed8-a924-469d-bea7-dc0de81f2c82. Accessed 28 November 2023; Seitz-Wald A (2022) Why did the U.S. reject Poland's plan to give Ukraine its Soviet-era fighter jets? https://www.nbcnews.com/politics/national-security/us-reject-polands-plan-give-ukraine-soviet-era-fighter-jets-rcna19396#. Accessed 28 November 2023 and Politico (2022) EU countries won't send Ukraine fighter jets after all. https://www.politico.eu/article/eu-promise-to-supply-fighter-jets-to-ukraine-gets-grounded/. Accessed 28 November 2023.

[8] NOS (2023) Tanks en Oekraïne: een rode lijn die steeds verder opschuift [Tanks and Ukraine: a red line that continues to shift forward]. https://nos.nl/artikel/2459492-tanks-en-oekraine-een-rode-lijn-die-steeds-verder-opschuift. Accessed 28 November 2023.

[9] Ingber 2011, p. 90; Bradley and Goldsmith 2005, p. 2112.

[10] Weizmann 2015.

[11] Ibid.

[12] E.g. Schmitt 2022a; Konchak 2022.

nature, and providing a better fit in the context of third States supporting a belligerent with satellite imagery.

4.2.2 The Effects of Being a Co-party

Although Russia regularly claims that States supporting Ukraine are party to "the conflict in Ukraine",[13] these claims can mostly be regarded as sable-rattling, given that Russia is not yet acting on these claims. In the meantime, there are important international legal consequences attached to being a co-party. While co-party status has significant implications on the operation of general international law, the most important consequence of co-party status is the application of IHL.[14]

The question whether a third State becomes a co-party due to its support to a belligerent is a "threshold question that determines whether IHL applies between the State providing the aid and the enemy of the State to whom it is delivered".[15] If it can be established that a third State qualifies as a co-party, IHL dictates that the co-party will be bound by IHL, for it binds all parties to an armed conflict, for the duration of the armed conflict. Consequently, the supporting State's co-party status will shift that State's legal paradigm applicable to actions against its adversaries from the law enforcement paradigm to the conduct of hostilities paradigm.[16] Amongst other things, the conduct of hostilities paradigm imposes special restrictions on the use of several means and methods of warfare, like riot control agents and undercover operations, which are normally used for law enforcement in peacetime.[17] IHL is the body of law that governs the conduct of hostilities paradigm by, *inter alia*, regulating the conduct of hostilities and offering special protection to particular persons and objects.[18] This, in combination with the rule that IHL applies on the entire territories of the parties to the conflict, including that of the co-party,[19] results in the fact that military objectives and combatants within the territory of the co-party might be lawfully targeted under IHL, while other persons and objects, like civilians and civilian objects, enjoy protection. Hence, by becoming a co-party to a pre-existing IAC, the supporting State exposes the military objectives, but also its civilians and civilian objects, on its entire territory to the risk of hostilities.[20] It is therefore crucial to discuss the threshold for becoming a co-party. It must be stressed, however, that the application of IHL does not provide a legal basis under international law for

---

[13] TASS (2023) Involvement of US, collective West in conflict in Ukraine grows — Kremlin. https://tass.com/politics/1567315. Accessed 28 November 2023.

[14] ILA Committee on the Use of Force 2010, p. 1; Verlinden 2019, p. 70.

[15] Schmitt 2022a.

[16] Verlinden 2019, p. 71.

[17] Melzer and Gaggioli Gasteyger 2017, p. 87.

[18] Ibid., p. 74.

[19] Vermeer et al. 2017, pp. 92–93.

[20] Verlinden 2019, p. 74.

the use of force. Indeed, it is understood that the *ius ad bellum* not only applies to the initial resort to force, but also to each subsequent act involving the use of force occurring in the course of hostilities.[21] Accordingly, this chapter agrees with the position that even if IHL applies due to co-party status, the supported belligerent's adversary still needs a legal basis under the *ius ad bellum* to conduct attacks on the co-party's military objectives.[22]

Additionally, there is a large number of obligations binding upon all parties to an IAC, regardless of the actions they undertake. These obligations are relevant for co-parties that do not engage in hostilities themselves. For example, all parties to the conflict are under the obligation to treat foreign nationals in their territory, including nationals of the adversary party, as protected persons to whom certain rights are granted under the Fourth Geneva Convention.[23]

4.2.3 Direct and Indirect Intervention and the Ambiguity of the Latter

The material scope of IHL prescribes that it applies in times of 'armed conflict'. IHL distinguishes between two types of armed conflict: IACs, which occur between two or more States, and NIACs, occurring between one or more States and one or more armed groups, or between such groups. It follows from case law, State practice, and academic literature that an IAC is initiated whenever there is resort to armed force between States, regardless of the reasons for and the intensity of the force used.[24] This last aspect, concerning the intensity, is still debated though, for some argue that a certain level of intensity is required for hostilities to qualify as an armed conflict.[25] Assuming that no certain level of intensity is required, the threshold at which an IAC is triggered sits relatively low.[26] This is the *lex lata* as it exists today. Clearly,

---

[21] Ibid., pp. 74–75; Wentker 2023, pp. 645–646; Greenwood 1983, pp. 222–223; Moussa 2008, p. 968; Sloane 2009, pp. 67 68; Protocol Additional to the Geneva Conventions of 12 August 1949, and relating to the Protection of Victims of International Armed Conflicts, opened for signature 8 June 1977, 1125 UNTS 3 (entered into force 7 December 1978) (API), Preamble ("[…] nothing in this Protocol or in the Geneva Conventions of 12 August 1949 can be construed as legitimizing or authorizing any act of aggression or any other use of force inconsistent with the Charter of the United Nations.").

[22] Kreß 2022, p. 14; Wentker 2023, p. 645; Wentker et al. 2024, pp. 25–26.

[23] Fourth Geneva Convention relative to the Protection of Civilian Persons in Time of War, opened for signature 12 August 1949, 75 UNTS 287 (entered into force 21 October 1950) (Fourth Geneva Convention).

[24] ICTY, *Prosecutor v. Dusko Tadić a/k/a "Dule"*, Tadić Decision on the Defence Motion for Interlocutory Appeal on Jurisdiction, 2 October 1995, Case. No. IT-94-1 (*Tadić Jurisdiction* 1995), para 70; ICRC Commentary on the Third Geneva Convention 2020, Article 2, para 251; Crawford and Pert 2020, p. 56.

[25] ILA Committee on the Use of Force 2010, p. 2; UK Ministry of Defence 2004, p. 29; Dinstein 2017, p. 10.

[26] Schmitt 2022b.

supplying a belligerent with weapons, ammunition, and processed satellite imagery, for instance, will not trigger an IAC out of itself.[27] But apart from determining when an IAC is initiated, current IHL remains silent about the circumstances under which a third State becomes a co-party to such a conflict.[28] Nevertheless, there are two recognized ways through which a third State's co-party status to an IAC is established: direct and indirect intervention.

Firstly, a third State can become a co-party through direct intervention, which concerns the provision of direct military support to a belligerent. When a third State intervenes directly in a pre-existing IAC, through the use of force by its own armed forces against a belligerent State, resulting in a loss of life, injury, damage, or destruction to persons or objects, the direct involvement in the pre-existing IAC is established, resulting in co-party status for the supporting State.[29] This line of reasoning is in conformity with the definition of an IAC, which requires a resort to armed force between States. Hence, similar to the relatively easy initiation of an IAC due to its low threshold, the threshold for direct intervention also sits relatively low.[30] Put differently, a third State becomes a co-party in the same manner as an IAC is initiated: by resorting to the use of force against another State, which is a belligerent in a pre-existing IAC. Noteworthy in this regard, and perhaps to clarify the point made in the previous paragraph, is that the concept of direct intervention covers situations in which the intervening State would qualify as a co-belligerent. Indeed, in this case the intervening State directly participates in the hostilities, thus actually taking on the role of belligerent.

Although direct intervention is relatively straightforward, it does not cover situations in which a third State assists a belligerent with indirect support, including military materiel or processed satellite imagery (also called intelligence[31]).[32] As previously mentioned, this type of support will not reach the threshold to initiate an IAC. Accordingly, a gray area in IHL is highlighted. Nevertheless, there seems to be consensus that States can also become a co-party by way of their indirect intervention in a pre-existing IAC.[33] It should be noted, though, that this second method of becoming a co-party is much more ambiguous than the first one and leaves many questions unresolved. Indirect intervention encompasses situations which are radically different from those where a State resorts to the traditional use of armed force. A third State intervenes indirectly in an IAC by supplying a belligerent with goods and services, like military materiel and intelligence. In contrast to 'resort to the use of armed force', which provides a relatively clear threshold, indirect intervention is

---

[27] Verlinden 2019, pp. 118, 174.

[28] Grignon 2022.

[29] Ibid., Upcher 2020, p. 63; Heller and Trabucco 2022, p. 264; Boddens Hosang 2023, p. 19.

[30] Boddens Hosang 2023, p. 19.

[31] This chapter defines intelligence as the product that results from the collection, processing, integration, evaluation, analysis, and interpretation of - in this case - satellite imagery concerning foreign countries or areas, that is done for strategic, operational, or tactical purposes.

[32] See note 27.

[33] Grignon 2022; Konchak 2022; Schmitt 2022b.

harder to grasp. Indeed, the most important question that arises is of what nature and extent the indirect support must be for it to qualify as an indirect intervention.[34] In other words, what is the threshold for indirect intervention?

The only guidance we seem to have in this regard is provided by the *Nicaragua* judgment of the International Court of Justice (hereinafter ICJ) and by traditional neutrality law. Starting with the former, in the *Nicaragua* case the ICJ was confronted with the question whether the acts of the 'contras', an armed opposition group operating in and against Nicaragua, were attributable to the U.S. for the latter to incur State responsibility.[35] After concluding that the contras could not be equated with a *de facto* U.S. State organ,[36] the ICJ turned to the question whether the specific wrongful conduct of the contras was attributable to the U.S.[37] The ICJ then introduced the 'effective control test': for the internationally wrongful conduct of an entity to be attributed to the intervening power, it must be shown that the *de jure* organs of the intervening power exercised effective control over the particular operation or activity in the course of which the wrongful conduct has been committed.[38] This means that the intervening State was involved in planning the operation, choosing the targets, giving specific directives and instructions, and the provision of operational support.[39] Accordingly, the intervening State must have been able to control the beginning of the military operation, the way it was carried out, and its end.[40] If this is the case, and the specific acts of the supported entity are attributable to the supporting State because of the latter's effective control, perhaps the supporting State can be qualified as a co-party.[41] A question that remains is whether providing aid and support for a belligerent, that crosses the threshold of (indirect) use of force, would not also be sufficient to make the supporting State a co-party. This is a valid question, warranting three short remarks. Firstly, while the ICJ concluded in its *Nicaragua* case that the provision of weapons or other support to the contras can certainly be said to involve a threat or use of force,[42] it is generally unsettled whether, and if so to what extent, aid or assistance to a belligerent will constitute a use of force.[43] Secondly, if the provision of aid or assistance to a belligerent does qualify as a use of force, its wrongfulness

---

[34] Schmitt 2022a.

[35] ICJ, *Military and Paramilitary Activities in and against Nicaragua (Nicaragua v. United States of America)*, Judgment, 27 June 1986, ICJ Rep. 14 (*Nicaragua* 1986) and ILC Draft articles on Responsibility of States for Internationally Wrongful Acts (2001) (ARSIWA), Article 4.

[36] *Nicaragua* 1986, above n 34, para 110.

[37] ARSIWA, above n 34, Article 8.

[38] *Nicaragua* 1986, above n 34, para 115.

[39] Ibid., para 112; Talmon 2009, p. 503.

[40] Talmon 2009, p. 503.

[41] Boddens Hosang 2023, p. 20.

[42] *Nicaragua* 1986, above n 34, para 195 and 228.

[43] Green 2023, pp. 8–11; Schmitt and Biggerstaff 2023, pp. 204, 227–228; Kreß 2022, p. 16.

could be precluded provided that the aid or assistance qualifies as collective self-defence.[44] Lastly, and most important, there are no indications in State practice and scholarship of a connection between the (indirect) use of force and co-party status.[45] Hence, an alleged (indirect) use of force in and of itself would not provide clear answers regarding co-party status.

Traditional neutrality law, in turn, applies a binary approach by dictating that a State is either neutral or a co-party.[46] Consequently, if a third State supports only one belligerent in an IAC, to the detriment of the other, it acts in violation of traditional neutrality law, thus becoming a co-party to that IAC.[47] This chapter assesses neutrality law in more detail in Sect. 4.3.1.

Some sidenotes are in order regarding this guidance. To start, the effective control test was developed within the context of a NIAC, which is why it might not be easy to apply it by analogy to IACs.[48] Secondly, we do not know whether the effective control test provides a suitable threshold to determine whether a State becomes a co-party, for it is predominantly concerned with the question of attribution of State responsibility.[49] Besides, times have changed significantly since the 1940s after the United Nations (hereinafter UN) framework was introduced which prohibits the use of force except in cases of self-defence, consent, or an authorization by the UN. This has caused many to believe traditional neutrality law has become obsolete, or at least should be interpreted differently.[50] Moreover, modern military technology has come a long way over the years. Nowadays, intelligence plays an important role in modern warfare, thanks to sophisticated technologies gathering high-resolution satellite images.[51] In fact, (near) real-time intelligence can point out military objectives for a belligerent, thus providing a significant military advantage. This chapter therefore argues that both the effective control test and traditional neutrality law are inadequate and outdated to determine whether a third State becomes a co-party to an IAC through its indirect support to a belligerent party to that conflict.

---

[44] ARSIWA, above n 34, Article 21; Schmitt 2022a; Heller and Trabucco 2022, pp. 254–255; *Nicaragua* 1986, above n 34, para 229.

[45] Wentker et al. 2024, pp. 15–16.

[46] Dinstein 2011, p. 25; Boddens Hosang 2023, p. 15.

[47] Von Heinegg 2022.

[48] Boddens Hosang 2023, p. 21.

[49] Ibid.

[50] See Sect. 3.1.

[51] Dutch Ministry of Defence 2022.

4.2.4 The Desirability of the Legal Uncertainty Surrounding Indirect Intervention

Whether the ambiguity regarding the threshold for indirect intervention is desirable, can be analysed from both an internal perspective—from within the law—and an external perspective—from outside the law.

Starting with the latter, it is first and foremost the case that legal uncertainty often results in unwanted exploitation by States that seek to flirt with legal boundaries, or even circumvent legal obligations.[52] So, one could argue that some States find this legal uncertainty desirable to further their own political interests. Fact of the matter is that indirect intervention in an armed conflict is still an important tool for powerful States to influence foreign affairs. Take the U.S.' intervention in the NIAC in Nicaragua in the 1980s, for instance, where it supplied the contras with training, equipment, and intelligence.[53] Although the U.S. was found to have violated, *inter alia*, the principle of non-intervention and the prohibition of the use of force, the question whether the U.S. had become a co-party through its indirect intervention remained unresolved. This likely played right into the hands of some of the most powerful States. Obviously, those States would be perfectly fine with an ambiguous threshold so they can continue to influence foreign affairs by indirectly intervening in armed conflicts, without becoming a co-party and bearing the duties IHL imposes upon the parties to a conflict.

There is also another side to the same coin. For example, several States are advocating indirect intervention as a method to respond to foreign humanitarian crises and promote the rule of law.[54] Furthermore, thanks to modern space technologies and the media, populations across the globe witness the hostilities on Ukrainian soil on a very detailed and personal level. This results in a common feeling of compassion for Ukraine, which is why third States want to show their support to Ukraine by sending it indirect support. By virtue of the legal uncertainty surrounding indirect intervention, third States are able to do this to a certain extent.

From an internal, legal, perspective this uncertainty is undesirable. If the international rule of law is to function properly, it requires predictability and consistency, which both add to legal certainty.[55] Although legal certainty is a concept which must always be pursued, it most certainly must be pursued with regard to the legal ambiguity set out above. Again, the Russo—Ukrainian war illustrates this urgency. Indeed, third States, mostly Western, are providing Ukraine with unprecedented levels of support, without fully knowing the legal implications of this support. While this is a problem out of itself, it is exacerbated by the fact that the legal consequences of becoming a co-party are far-reaching. Moreover, the matter has become largely politicized, leading to diverging *opinio iuris*. This legal uncertainty has climaxed

---

[52] Nasu 2022.

[53] *Nicaragua* 1986, above n 34.

[54] Frowe and Matheson 2020; White 2012.

[55] Arajärvi 2021, pp. 185–186.

into a standoff between Russia and, most notably, the West, amidst a war which is claiming the lives of thousands of people, resulting in a stagnation of the development of international law.

4.3 Discussion of Possible Thresholds for Becoming a Co-party Through Indirect Intervention

The previous section established that indirect intervention, as a method to become co-party, features an ambiguous threshold resulting in legal uncertainty. Considering that third State's indirect support is currently the most common type of assistance in the context of the Russo—Ukrainian IAC, it must be analysed what possible threshold exists for a State to become co-party through indirect intervention. This section discusses potential thresholds that are put forward by case law and scholars, in a specific order from low to high thresholds, thus showing the most important differences between them. These thresholds can be roughly divided into two sets: support amounting to control and support not amounting to control.

4.3.1 Systematic or Significant Violation of Neutrality Law

The core rules that neutrality law imposes upon neutral States are the prohibition of participation and the duty to remain strictly impartial and take measures to sustain their neutral status.[56] This latter duty of impartiality entails a prohibition to discriminate, which, as the International Committee of the Red Cross (hereinafter ICRC) further explains, means that differential treatment of the belligerents in an IAC is not justified.[57] Indeed, neutrality as an attitude of impartiality prohibits neutral States to support one belligerent, as is detrimental to the other.[58] The rationale behind this fundamental duty of impartiality is to protect belligerents against interference by a neutral State to the benefit of only one belligerent.[59] Though not explicitly mentioned, Hague Convention V[60] therefore prohibits the transfer of supplies, like military materiel, from a neutral State to one belligerent.[61] In contrast, article 6 of

---

[56] Antonopoulos 2022, p. 9; Von Heinegg 2017, p. 381.

[57] ICRC 2002, p. 5; U.S. Department of Defense 2023, para 15.3.2.

[58] Oppenheim and Lauterpacht 1952, pp. 362–363.

[59] Von Heinegg 2017, p. 381.

[60] Hague Convention V Respecting the Rights and Duties of Neutral Powers and Persons in Case of War on Land, opened for signature 18 October 1907 (entered into force 26 January 1910) (Hague V).

[61] Von Heinegg 2022; Schmitt 2022a; Boddens Hosang 2023, p. 12.

Hague Convention XIII[62] explicitly prohibits neutral States to transfer warships, ammunition, or war materiel to an active belligerent with regard to naval warfare. Some argue that a State can become a co-party by 'systematically or significantly violating its duties under neutrality law'—either through direct intervention or by flagrantly violating the fundamental duty of impartiality.[63] Accordingly, a neutral State will become a co-party by systematically or significantly transferring goods and services to one beneficiary belligerent, but to the detriment of the other.[64] To test the validity of this argument, it must first be established whether neutral States violate neutrality law by providing indirect support to a belligerent.

If one were to follow traditional neutrality law, States violate their neutrality by indirectly supporting a belligerent in an IAC.[65] As a consequence, traditional neutrality law would qualify those supporting States as co-parties to that IAC.[66] On that account, traditional neutrality law applies a binary approach, in which a State is either neutral or a co-party.[67] However, the practical application of traditional neutrality law, including this binary approach, significantly changed during the first half of the twentieth century.[68] This change started in 1928 when war was renounced by the Kellogg-Briand Pact. Later, the UN mechanism, adopted in 1945, introduced a peremptory norm of international law that prohibits the use of force.[69] As a consequence, belligerent States were no longer equal in the eyes of the law, for one of them would have violated international law, and the other was the victim of that violation.[70] With this development of international law, a new concept emerged, called 'qualified neutrality'. Although this concept remains controversial and lacks a legal basis, several States assert that qualified neutrality covers scenarios in which a third State is neither neutral according to traditional neutrality law, nor a co-party.[71] Qualified neutrality therefore covers the middle-ground between party status and neutral status. To illustrate, the UN Security Council (hereinafter UNSC) could, acting under Chapter VII of the UN Charter, authorize UN member States to supply a victim belligerent with military materiel. This should not result in a violation of neutrality law because UNSC resolutions are binding and obligations under the UN Charter trump conflicting international obligations.[72] However, it remains unclear whether qualified neutrality still applies when the UNSC is stymied, like it currently

---

[62] Hague Convention XIII Concerning the rights and Duties of Neutral Powers in Naval War, opened for signature 18 October 1907 (entered into force 26 January 1910) (Hague Convention XIII).

[63] Bradley and Goldsmith 2005, p. 2112; Weizmann 2015; Bridgeman 2010, p. 1200.

[64] Bradley and Goldsmith 2005, pp. 2112–2113.

[65] Von Heinegg 2022; Schmitt 2023.

[66] Boddens Hosang 2023, p. 15.

[67] Dinstein 2011, p. 25; Schmitt 2023.

[68] Dinstein 2011, p. 12.

[69] Charter of the United Nations, opened for signature 26 June 1945 (entered into force 24 October 1945) (UN Charter), Article 2(4).

[70] Schmitt 2022a.

[71] Boddens Hosang 2023, p. 16; Von Heinegg 2022.

[72] UN Charter, above n 68, Article 25 and 103 respectively.

is in the context of the Russo—Ukrainian IAC.[73] An important nuance regarding qualified neutrality is in order, since State practice with respect to third States' support for Ukraine in the context of the Russo—Ukrainian IAC is devoid of any reference to qualified neutrality.[74] Instead of drawing upon qualified neutrality as a possible justification for their supportive acts, third States assert they assist Ukraine's right of individual self-defence to uphold the principles of the UN Charter.[75] Consequently, it is argued that qualified neutrality lacks the required *opinio juris* to speak of a customary right of qualified neutrality.[76] Leaving the question whether qualified neutrality applies or not aside, it is generally unclear whether States supporting Ukraine in its IAC with Russia violate their duties under neutrality law. Von Heinegg, for instance, argues that third States' indirect support to Ukraine is not violating neutrality law, because Russia's invasion is an apparent act of aggression, the majority of the international community labels Russia as the aggressor,[77] and the UNSC is unable to act under Chapter VII of the UN Charter due to the aggressor.[78] Moreover, it is held that with the end of traditional neutrality law, strict impartiality also came to an end.[79] This allows States to support victims of aggression, because it no longer results in a violation of the duty of impartiality. Like Attorney General Jackson mentioned in his speech in 1941 regarding the U.S.' support to the Allies in their war against Nazi-Germany, the decision to outlaw war conferred upon neutral States the right to act in a discriminatory manner against the aggressor.[80] This legal reasoning, in combination with recent States' practice of claiming to assist Ukraine as a victim of aggression in the exercise of its individual right of self-defence, is reminiscent of qualified neutrality, but the argument is ultimately made in the context of collective security.[81] Thus, there seems general consensus that under the current international legal order, States would not violate neutrality law by supporting a victim belligerent.[82]

More generally, a majority argues that co-party status as a consequence of violating neutrality law is severely overstated, which is why systematically or significantly violating neutrality law will not establish co-party status.[83] State practice and scholarship confirm this position, for they show no connection between the violation of neutrality law and co-party status.[84] In this respect, this chapter agrees with Wentker's

---

[73] Schmitt 2022a; Boddens Hosang 2023, p. 16; Nasu 2022.

[74] Antonopoulos 2023.

[75] See Sect. 4.4.1.

[76] Antonopoulos 2023.

[77] UN General Assembly (2022) Aggression against Ukraine, UN Doc. A/RES/ES-11/1.

[78] Von Heinegg 2022; Schmitt 2022a.

[79] Hathaway and Shapiro 2022.

[80] Ibid.

[81] Antonopoulos 2023.

[82] Kreß 2022, pp. 17–18.

[83] Ingber 2017, p. 93; Vermeer 2023, p. 103; Wentker 2022; Upcher 2020, pp. 61–63; Wentker et al. 2024, p. 14.

[84] Upcher 2020, pp. 61–63; Wentker et al. 2024, p. 14.

and Schmitt's position that it is best to distinguish between neutrality law violations and the termination of neutral status.[85] Wentker argues, *inter alia*, that the availability of traditional enforcement measures for the State that is the victim of neutrality law violations suggests that a neutral State retains its neutral status after violating neutrality law.[86] Therefore, the question whether a third State becomes a co-party must be determined by IHL and its hostile actions in an IAC, not by its potential violations of the law of neutrality.[87] The US Department of Defence Law of War Manual reiterates in this regard that "[v]iolations of neutrality by belligerent or neutral States should be distinguished from the end of a State's neutral status [...]" and "[a]cts that are incompatible with the relationship between the neutral State and a belligerent State under the law of neutrality need not end the neutral State's neutrality and bring that State into the conflict as a belligerent."[88] Certainly, if neutrality law is violated there may be legal implications for the delinquent State, but these are limited to the consequences the international law of State responsibility attaches to such a violation.[89] A violation of the law of neutrality will not result in the loss of neutral status and the acquisition of co-party status.[90] Especially given that the application and contents of contemporary neutrality law are so unsettled. It is argued that this line of reasoning is consistent with the object and purpose of neutrality law, which is to contain hostilities.[91]

4.3.2 Systematic or Substantial Supply of Support

There are some scholars who argue that the systematic or substantial supply of military materiel, armed forces, or financial support to an active belligerent in an IAC will result in co-party status for the supporting State.[92] Although this threshold shows similarities with the aforementioned one, this is a distinct threshold, not related to neutrality law, for the systematic or substantial support itself would result in co-party status, not possible neutrality law violations.

It seems, however, that this threshold is only supported by a minority, for most believe that the mere supply of military materiel or financial support lacks a required direct operational connection with the hostilities.[93] Indeed, there is a strong argument

---

[85] Wentker 2023, p. 648; Schmitt 2022a.

[86] Wentker 2023, p 648.

[87] Schmitt 2022a; Wentker 2023, p. 648; Vermeer 2023, p. 103; Krajewski 2022; Heller and Trabucco 2022, p. 264; Oppenheim and Lauterpacht 1952, p. 753.

[88] U.S. Department of Defense 2023, para 15.4.1.

[89] Heller and Trabucco 2022, p. 260; Wentker et al. 2024, p. 14.

[90] Wentker et al. 2024, p. 15.

[91] Ibid.

[92] Weizmann 2015.

[93] Wentker 2022; Heller and Trabucco 2022, p. 265.

that merely equipping or financing a belligerent will not result in co-party status.[94] The systematic or substantial nature of the supply of military materiel or financial support does not change this argument, for the required direct operational connection with the hostilities is still missing. Moreover, since 'support' is not specified by this threshold, it does not differentiate between different types of support. Hence, it attaches the same consequence to, for instance, the systematic or substantial supply of military medical supplies, and the systematic or substantial supply of fighter jets. Accordingly, if a State systematically or substantially supports a belligerent with medical supplies, it will become a co-party. This threshold is therefore too generic, which is not desirable.

4.3.3 Significant Participation in Hostilities Through (Indirect) Support that Has a Direct Nexus with Belligerent of Hostile Activities

Yet another threshold is proposed by Konchak.[95] He asserts that a third State becomes a co-party when it participates in the hostilities of an active belligerent "to a significant extent". He goes on to argue that a State can do this in two ways: (i) it can intervene directly in the armed conflict by providing a belligerent "direct military support" or (ii) it could intervene indirectly by providing a belligerent with support that has a "direct nexus with belligerent or hostile activities". This latter way of participating to a significant extent, in turn, may take two forms. The first form of indirect participation is when a third State carries out logistical, operational, and/or intelligence functions which are integrated into a specific military operation by the beneficiary belligerent. Within this category would therefore fall intelligence support that is immediately used by the beneficiary belligerent to conduct military operations. The second form concerns the supply of a belligerent with logistical, operational, and/or intelligence support that directly contributes to the beneficiary belligerent's "overall military effort in the conflict". Consequently, supplying a belligerent with the means to conduct military operations, such as weapons, ammunition, or intelligence, contributes to the beneficiary State's war fighting capabilities, thus amounting to an act of war, and rendering the supporting State a co-party.[96]

This proposed threshold is not desirable, for the scope of the second form of indirect participation is too wide. Let us think of a situation in which a State supplies an active belligerent in an IAC with car fuel. The beneficiary belligerent, in turn, might use this fuel to keep medical cars operable, to take care of its wounded armed forces. This way, it is arguable that the fuel is used to contribute to the belligerent's overall military effort. Would it be right to say this type of indirect support has a direct

---

[94] Schmitt 2022a; Heller and Trabucco 2022, p. 265; ICTY, *Prosecutor v. Dusko Tadić*, Appeals Chamber judgment, 15 July 1999, Case No. IT-94-1-A (*Tadić* 1999), para 145.

[95] Konchak 2022.

[96] Ibid.; Moore 1933, p. 625.

nexus with belligerent or hostile actions? While the term 'overall military effort' is wide in scope, Judge Moore already argued in 1933 that "the supply of such articles [weapons and ammunition] to a fighting force is a direct contribution to its *military resources*, and as such is a participation in the war [...]."[97] To be fair, a contribution to a belligerent's military resources could include almost anything, ranging from arms and ammunition, to flak jackets and medical supplies. Evidently, this threshold is far too wide, and it leaves too many questions unresolved, hence falling short of providing a fitting threshold for indirect intervention.

The first form of indirect participation—support integrated into a specific military operation—is a step into the right direction. Rather than focusing on support that contributes to the overall military effort of a belligerent, we need to focus on support that directly contributes to specific hostilities. Only this way will indirect support have a truly direct nexus with belligerent or hostile actions. This view is commonly shared by other proposed thresholds, as will be discussed below.

4.3.4 The ICRC's 'Direct Participation in Hostilities' Test

The ICJ has recognized that the principle of distinction is one of the "cardinal" principles of IHL, according to which the parties to an armed conflict must always distinguish between civilians and combatants on the one hand, and between civilian objects and military objectives on the other.[98] Accordingly, civilians and civilian objects may never be the object of attack, neither in IACs nor in NIACs.[99] However, civilians lose this protection for as long as they take direct part in hostilities (hereinafter DPH).[100] The ICRC further explained the notion of DPH in its Interpretative Guidance on the notion of DPH, and formulated three cumulative criteria for an act to qualify as DPH[101]:

(1) the act must likely adversely affect the military operations or capacity of a party to the armed conflict [...] (threshold of harm);
(2) there must be a direct causal link between the act and the harm likely to result from that act or from a coordinated military operation of which the act forms an integral part (direct causal link);

---

[97] Moore 1933, p. 625.

[98] ICJ, *Legality of the Threat or Use of Nuclear Weapons*, Advisory Opinion, 8 July 1996, ICJ Rep. 226 (*Nuclear Weapons*), para 78; API, above n 21, Article 48.

[99] API, above n 21, Article 51(2) and 52; Protocol Additional to the Geneva Conventions of 12 August 1949, and relating to the Protection of Victims of Non-International Armed Conflicts, opened for signature 8 June 1977, 1125 UNTS 609 (entered into force 7 December 1978) (APII), Article 13(2).

[100] API, above n 21 Article 51(3); AP II, above n 98, Article 13(3).

[101] ICRC Interpretative Guidance on the notion of direct participation in hostilities 2009, p. 46.

(3) the act must be intended to directly cause the required threshold of harm in support of one party to the armed conflict and to the detriment of the other (belligerent nexus).

The notion of DPH shows strong similarities with a State becoming a co-party to a pre-existing IAC. In both situations, the entity concerned, a civilian or a State, initially enjoys protection from the harmful effects of an armed conflict,[102] but loses it due to its support to one belligerent and to the detriment of the other. The notion of DPH could therefore be a relevant source of inspiration for developing a threshold for indirect intervention. In fact, some scholars claim that the logic behind the notion of DPH is similar to that of foreign intervention in a pre-existing NIAC resulting in co-party status, which is why all, or most, of the DPH criteria could also be relevant with respect to such an intervention.[103] Although this proposition was made within the context of a NIAC, the DPH criteria might also be useful for developing a threshold for indirect intervention in a pre-existing IAC. What matters is whether a supporting State becomes a co-party and whether a civilian becomes targetable—or the classification of an entity in an armed conflict—not the classification of the armed conflict.

It should be noted, however, that although the logic behind the notion of DPH seems similar to that of becoming a co-party through indirect intervention in a pre-existing IAC, the notion of DPH is still very different. DPH is concerned with the participation of civilians in hostilities, on the micro-level, while indirect intervention concerns the participation of third States in a pre-existing IAC, on the macro-level. The effects of both notions are very different from each other as well. While civilians are no longer immune from attack due to their DPH, a State becomes a co-party due to its indirect intervention. Moreover, a civilian loses its protection for the duration of his or her DPH. Would a similar rule apply to the notion of indirect intervention, resulting in the end of co-party status as soon as a co-party ceases to indirectly support a belligerent? These important differences warrant some alterations of the notion of DPH to be applicable to foreign indirect intervention.[104] Also, the definition of DPH provided by the ICRC does not reflect current State practice, resulting in a disparity of approaches maintained by States and the ICRC regarding the notion of DPH.[105]

Even though the notion of DPH is different from foreign indirect intervention, it features interesting criteria which could be relevant when thinking about a threshold for co-party status through indirect intervention. As a matter of fact, the three DPH criteria formulated by the ICRC are very similar to the criteria of the ICRC's support-based approach, which will be discussed below.[106]

---

[102] API, above n 21, Article 51(2); AP II, above n 98, Article 13(2) and neutrality law respectively.

[103] Van Steenberghe and Lesaffre 2019, pp. 19–20.

[104] Ibid.

[105] Verlinden 2019, p. 136.

[106] Ferraro 2013, p. 585.

4.3.5 An Analogy with NIACs

The characteristics of support or control that would render a supporting or controlling State a co-party are still a debated issue, and, as we have seen so far, there is no accepted threshold. Nevertheless, this issue has been dealt with, to some extent, within in the context of NIACs.[107] These dealings with the issue in the context of NIACs could be a source of inspiration in addressing the issue with respect to IACs.

4.3.5.1 Support-Based Approach

Greenwood claims that a third State's support to a belligerent will qualify as an act of war if the support is "directly related [...] to measures harmful to the adversary."[108] However, Greenwood notes that intelligence, financial, and political support cannot be directly related, thus never qualifying as an act of war. In his article, Schmitt disagrees with this last part, and argues that intelligence support might qualify as an act of war, resulting in co-party status.[109] To determine when intelligence support qualifies as such, Schmitt turns to the somewhat controversial support-based approach.[110]

The support-based approach was initially adopted by the ICRC to determine when a third State, supporting a belligerent in a NIAC, becomes a co-party to that NIAC. The ICRC held that the contribution made by the third State "to the collective conduct of hostilities" of the beneficiary belligerent is the decisive element.[111] A third State's support will amount to such a contribution when it has "a direct impact on the enemy's ability to carry out military operations."[112] Indeed, the ICRC explicitly dismisses the hypothesis that a third State's indirect support, that contributes to a belligerent's overall war fighting capabilities, renders it a co-party.[113] In other words, support must constitute something more than the mere provision of training or equipment.[114] Hence, the ICRC rejects both the threshold proposed by Konchak, in part, and the systematic or substantial supply of support threshold. The ICRC established four criteria which, if fulfilled, would demonstrate a genuine belligerent intent on the part of the supporting State, and its effective involvement in hostilities aimed to harm the adversary[115]:

(1) a pre-existing NIAC;

---

[107] Schmitt 2022a, b.

[108] Greenwood 2008, p. 214.

[109] Schmitt 2022b.

[110] Boddens Hosang 2023, p. 22; Van Steenberghe and Lesaffre 2019.

[111] ICRC 32nd International Conference 2015, p. 22.

[112] Ibid.

[113] Ibid., pp. 22–23; Ferraro 2013, p. 585.

[114] Droege and Tuck 2017.

[115] ICRC 32nd International Conference 2015, p. 23.

(2) support that is related to the conduct of hostilities in that pre-existing conflict;

(3) the support must benefit a party to that pre-existing conflict, and;

(4) the supporting State must officially have decided to support a belligerent.

Even though this support-based approach was developed in the context of NIACs, it is suggested that the approach could also be applied, by analogy, in the context of IACs.[116] Indeed, the support-based approach revolves around a supporting State's contribution to the collective conduct of hostilities, not the type of armed conflict. Schmitt agrees with this proposition, and, after reviewing the support-based approach, proposes to look at four factors in determining whether a supporting State becomes a co-party to an IAC[117]:

(1) the supporting State must have intended to contribute to specific conduct of hostilities operations by the supported State or frustrate those of the adversary.

(2) the extent to which the support benefits specific conduct of hostilities operations of the supported belligerent, or frustrates those by its adversary;

(3) the degree to which the support is integral to specific conduct of hostilities operations of the supported State or defensive action against its enemy;

(4) the degree of immediacy between the provision of intelligence and its use;

Schmitt clearly wants us to assess how support has contributed to specific hostilities by the beneficiary State. Thus, applying the support-based approach to intelligence support, Schmitt admits that the supply of general information, or operational intelligence, will not meet the threshold. However, the intentional supply of tactical, or *actionable*, intelligence, upon which the beneficiary belligerent can immediately act by, for instance, avoiding or conducting an attack, could cross the threshold, resulting in co-party status for the supporting State. Evidently, what matters is whether the intelligence support makes a material and integral contribution to specific hostilities, whether in offense or defence.[118]

This somewhat altered support-based approach might provide a workable and solid threshold for indirect intervention in IACs. However, it leaves a considerable number of questions unresolved. Schmitt's factors use ambiguous phrases like "the extent to which" and "the degree of". Of course, developing a coherent threshold for indirect intervention requires it to be relatively flexible if it is to be applied to a vast number of scenarios in the future. But this chapter argues that the factors provided by Schmitt are too vague and do not provide a clear legal framework. This is exacerbated by the fact that the factors are based on the support-based approach, which remains somewhat controversial, and arguably lacks a legal basis and supportive State practice.[119]

---

[116] Droege and Tuck 2017.

[117] Schmitt 2022b.

[118] Ibid.

[119] Boddens Hosang 2023, p. 22; Van Steenberghe and Lesaffre 2019, p. 18; Verlinden 2019, p. 162.

4.3.5.2 Overall Control Test

This threshold constitutes support by control out of which co-party status is born. It should be noted, though, that it is still debated which degree of control is required to trigger co-party status[120]: effective control as proposed by the ICJ, or overall control, which will be discussed here.

In 1995 the International Criminal Tribunal for the former Yugoslavia (hereinafter ICTY) was, *inter alia*, faced with the question whether the accused, Mr. Tadic, was guilty of grave violations of the Geneva Conventions committed during the armed conflict in Bosnia and Herzegovina in 1992. Whether the accused was to be found guilty depended on whether the conduct of the armed forces of the Bosnian Serb secessionist entity, Republika Srpska, fighting the recognized Government of Bosnia and Herzegovina, could be attributed to the Federal Republic of Yugoslavia (hereinafter FRY), the outside power. If this was the case, the *prima facie* NIAC in Bosnia and Herzegovina would be internationalized.[121] On the basis of the "overall control" test, the ICTY ultimately held that the armed forces of the Republika Srpska could be equated with *de facto* organs of the FRY, thus transforming the initial NIAC into an IAC.[122] To establish overall control, the ICTY held that the support from the outside power must go beyond the mere financing and equipping of the secessionist entity in question. In fact, the outside power must also participate in the organization, coordination, planning, and supervision of military operations, not necessarily including "the issuance of specific orders or instructions relating to single military actions."[123]

The overall control test has been widely accepted as the appropriate tool to classify armed conflicts.[124] For instance, this test was recently applied by the Dutch Criminal Court in The Hague in the *MH17* case. Here the Court found itself confronted with the question whether flight MH17 was downed within the context of an ongoing IAC between Ukraine and the Donetsk People's Republic (DPR) under Russia's overall control.[125] It was found that Russia not only supplied the DPR with manpower, military equipment, and military training, but Russia also took on a coordinating role, instructed the DPR, and played a prominent role in planning and supervising specific military operations.[126] Hence, establishing overall control.

The elements from the overall control test were developed, and are applied, in the context of a *prima facie* NIAC, as a tool for conflict classification. Nevertheless,

---

[120] Verlinden 2019, p. 173.

[121] Talmon 2009, p. 504.

[122] *Tadić* 1999, above n 93, para 167.

[123] Ibid., para 137, 145.

[124] ICRC Commentary on the First Geneva Convention 2016, Article 2, para 271; ICC, *Prosecutor v Thomas Lubanga Dyilo*, Judgment Pursuant to Article 74 of the Statute, 14 March 2012, Case No. ICC-01/04-01/06-2842 (*Lubanga* 2012), para 541; Verlinden 2019, p. 110.

[125] The District Court of The Hague, *MH17 criminal case*, Judgment, 17 November 2022, ECLI:NL:RBDHA:2022:12218 (*MH17*), para 4.4.3.1.

[126] Ibid., para 4.4.3.1.3.

according to Grignon, we can deduce elements from the overall control test to develop a threshold for indirect intervention in a pre-existing IAC.[127] Grignon argues that merely financing, equipping, or providing intelligence or training would not suffice to consider a supporting State a co-party. A third State would only become a co-party if it (i) directly engages in the hostilities, (ii) if it engages indirectly by "taking part in the planning and supervision of military operations of another State", or (iii) if it would make available its own military bases for the use by one of the parties.[128]

Although the overall control test potentially provides a coherent threshold for indirect intervention, there are some important drawbacks. For a start, the ICTY's overall control test is criticized for being too flexible and misinterpreting international law. This is because the ICTY allegedly misunderstood the ICJ's *Nicaragua* judgment and mistakenly replaced the ICJ's 'strict control test'—featuring an exceptionally high threshold[129]—with its more flexible overall control test.[130] Secondly, it is argued that the sharing of intelligence would fall within the scope of the overall control test if it contributes to the planning of a military operation.[131] This means that one single act of intelligence sharing is enough for a supporting State to become co-party. It might therefore be more logical that a "more elaborate involvement in the general planning of the operations" is required.[132]

As mentioned earlier, it is debated what degree of control is best to assess the relationship between a supporting entity and a supported entity. Although this dispute between the overall control test and the effective control test falls beyond the scope of this chapter, it argues that the overall control test provides the better fitting potential threshold with respect to indirect intervention. While the outcomes of both tests have important implications on State responsibility and the classification of armed conflicts, the effective control test was introduced as a tool of attribution of State responsibility. The overall control test, in contrast, is used to classify armed conflicts. The classification of armed conflicts by the overall control test has an explicit bearing on the classification of the parties involved, which is why the overall control test fits better within the system of IHL as a whole. The overall control test also features a lower threshold than the effective control test, which proves to be more helpful in dealing with widespread current State practice, like the support to secessionist entities or terrorist groups abroad.[133]

---

[127] Grignon 2022.

[128] Ibid.

[129] ICJ, *Case Concerning Application of the Convention on the Prevention and Punishment of the Crime of Genocide (Bosnia and Herzegovina v Serbia and Montenegro)*, Judgment, 26 February 2007, ICJ Rep. 43 (*Bosnian Genocide*), paras 391–393.

[130] Ibid., para 406; Milanovic 2006, p. 581; Talmon 2009, p. 507.

[131] Verlinden 2019, p. 111.

[132] Ibid.

[133] Cassese 2007, pp. 665–667.

4.4 Proposal for a Threshold that Fits Best Within IHL

So far, this chapter has established that a State can become a co-party by intervening directly or indirectly. However, indirect intervention is surrounded by legal uncertainty. The previous section therefore analysed several possible thresholds for indirect intervention. The present section will draw on these thresholds to introduce a proposal for a threshold that fits best within IHL. But first, current State practice warrants some remarks.

4.4.1 State Practice

Working with State practice in the context of this legal issue is crucial, yet also challenging. The position taken by, most notably, the West[134] regarding the red line of support, before becoming a co-party, has shifted considerably over the course of the IAC in Ukraine. Every time the West was faced with the question whether or not to support Ukraine with modern military materiel, it was initially quite hesitant because it feared to cross a red line that would provoke Russia.[135] Nevertheless, the West continuously seemed to shake off this hesitation, and supplied Ukraine with modern military materiel as the war dragged on.[136] Something similar happened with regard to the supply of intelligence. At first, the U.S. acknowledged the existence of a fine line between sharing intelligence and providing direct targeting support: "We're not doing that [intelligence for real-time targeting], because that steps over the line to making us participating in the war."[137] However, eventually all U.S. legal and policy constraints on the sharing of intelligence were removed, including constraints on the sharing of near real-time intelligence for targeting.[138] Growing evidence now shows that the U.S., along with other North Atlantic Treaty Organization (hereinafter

---

[134] Parsi T (2023) Why Non-Western Countries Tend to See Russia's War Very, Very Differently. https://iaffairscanada.com/why-non-western-countries-tend-to-see-russias-war-very-very-differently-2/. Accessed 28 November 2023 Financial Times (2023) 'We are for peace': Latin America rejects pleas to send weapons to Ukraine. https://www.ft.com/content/fc8d51c8-5202-4862-a653-87d1603deded. Accessed 28 November 2023.

[135] Politico (2022) 'These are not rental cars': As Ukraine pleads for tanks, the West holds back. https://www.politico.com/news/2022/09/22/ukraine-requests-american-tanks-counte roffensive-00058303. Accessed 28 November 2023.

[136] Ibid.; NOS (2023) Tanks en Oekraïne: een rode lijn die steeds verder opschuift [Tanks and Ukraine: a red line that continues to shift forward]. https://nos.nl/artikel/2459492-tanks-en-oek raine-een-rode-lijn-die-steeds-verder-opschuift. Accessed 28 November 2023.

[137] Dilanian K (2022) Biden administration walks fine line on intelligence-sharing with Ukraine. https://www.nbcnews.com/news/investigations/biden-administration-walks-fine-line-int elligence-sharing-ukraine-rcna18542. Accessed 28 November 2023.

[138] Dilanian K, Kube C, Lee CE, De Luce D (2022) U.S. intel helped Ukraine protect air defenses, shoot down Russian plane carrying hundreds of troops. https://www.nbcnews.com/politics/nat ional-security/us-intel-helped-ukraine-protect-air-defenses-shoot-russian-plane-carry-rcna26015. Accessed 28 November 2023.

NATO) allies, is supplying Ukraine with (near) real-time tactical intelligence[139] used for Ukrainian military operations, as will be discussed in more detail in Sect. 4.5.3. Although the levels of third States' support to Ukraine have grown to unprecedented proportions over time,[140] they emphasize that their supportive acts do not render them co-parties.[141] In fact, States supporting Ukraine justify their support by explicitly arguing that they assist Ukraine in the exercise of its right of individual self-defence, which does not make them co-parties.[142] Importantly, third States do not invoke collective self-defence regarding their support to Ukraine, for this would enable the lawful use of force, resulting in co-party status.[143] Moreover, rather than drawing on the law of neutrality in any shape, way, or form, States supporting Ukraine emphasize Russia's unlawful and aggressive use of force and the importance of upholding the principles of the UN Charter through Ukraine's individual self-defence.[144] Russia, on the other hand, claims States supporting Ukraine are directly or indirectly involved in the conflict in Ukraine,[145] with Russian President Vladimir Putin recently stating: "They [NATO] are sending tens of billions of dollars in weapons to Ukraine. This really is participation [...]. This means that they are taking part, albeit indirectly, in the crimes being carried out by the Kyiv regime."[146] Russia bases these claims, *inter alia*, on the law of neutrality. Indeed, it has argued before the UN Security Council that States supporting Ukraine violate international law, including the Hague Convention XIII,[147] by providing Ukraine with military materiel and intelligence, approving strikes conducted with Western weapons, and training Ukrainian forces on their own territories.[148] As a consequence, Russia asserts that those third States must

---

[139] This chapter defines tactical intelligence as the intelligende required for the planning and execution of operations on the tactical level of warfare, which concerns specific engagements to achieve particular military goals.

[140] NATO 2023.

[141] Deutsche Welle (2023) Germany says it is not a warring party in Ukraine. https://www.dw.com/en/germany-says-it-is-not-a-warring-party-in-ukraine/a-64541484. Accessed 28 November 2023; NATO 2023.

[142] UN Security Council (2023) 9325th meeting, UN Doc. S/PV.9325, pp. 8, 10, and 13; UN Security Council (2023) 9364th meeting, UN Doc. S/PV.9364, p. 18; UK Parliament 2023; Deutscher Bundestag 2022, p. 39; Reuters (2023) NATO says F-16 training doesn't make it party to Ukraine conflict. https://www.reuters.com/world/europe/nato-says-f-16-training-ukrainians-does-not-make-it-party-conflict-2023-05-23/. Accessed 14 March 2024.

[143] Antonopoulos 2023; Schaller 2023, p. 177.

[144] UN Security Council (2023) 9325th meeting, UN Doc. S/PV.9325, p. 10; Antonopoulos 2023.

[145] TASS (2023) Russia certain US, NATO involved in conflict in Ukraine — Kremlin spokesman. https://tass.com/politics/1601459?utm_source=google.com&utm_medium=organic&utm_campaign=google.com&utm_referrer=google.com. Accessed 28 November 2023.

[146] BARRON'S (2023) NATO Taking Part In Ukraine Conflict With Arms Supplies: Putin. https://www.barrons.com/news/nato-taking-part-in-ukraine-conflict-with-arms-supplies-putin-60886649. Accessed 28 November 2023.

[147] Hague Convention XIII, above n 54.

[148] UN Security Council (2023) 9325th meeting, UN Doc. S/PV.9325, p. 3; UN Security Council (2023) 9364th meeting, UN Doc. S/PV.9364, p. 12.

4 On the Sideline or on the Pitch? *The Classification of Third States ...*   133

lose their neutral status, thus becoming co-parties to the Russo—Ukrainian IAC.[149] Nevertheless, Russia has not acted on this claim.

This State practice may help in an indicative manner to establish a threshold for indirect intervention. However, this chapter argues that current practice by States supporting Ukraine stretches the limits of the legal vacuum which IHL leaves third States for supporting belligerents in pre-existing IACs, to a dangerous point. Surely, at some point must this escalatory ladder of indirect support to Ukraine lead to co-party status.

4.4.2   The Threshold for Becoming a Co-party Through Indirect Intervention

The first two discussed thresholds—'systematic or significant violations of neutrality law' and 'systematic or significant supply of support'—are not fit to function as threshold. The former attaches a consequence to the violation of neutrality law that is too far-reaching under the contemporary UN framework. More generally, it is unclear whether States violate current neutrality law by transferring indirect support to one belligerent, to the detriment of the other. Moreover, the question of co-party status should be dealt with by IHL, and not be influenced by arguments stemming from the *ius ad bellum*. The latter threshold is too generic to function as a clear 'red line' threshold. Plus, it is accepted that merely financing and/or equipping a belligerent with military materiel will not lead to co-party status.[150] Indeed, it follows from the discussion of possible thresholds that support must have a direct connection with the hostilities. Regarding intelligence support, for example, it is widely endorsed in academic literature that intelligence support must have a direct connection to harm to the adversary, through its material and integral tactical contribution to specific hostilities.[151]

Accordingly, while the third and fourth thresholds—'significant participation in hostilities through (indirect) support that has a direct nexus with belligerent or hostile activities' and 'DPH'—take a step into the right direction, the last two thresholds—Schmitt's take on the 'support-based approach' and 'the overall control test'—are especially centred around the requirement of a direct operational link between the support and specific hostilities. These last two thresholds have in common that support must facilitate specific hostilities on the tactical level for the supporting State to become a co-party. But there is a slight difference between these two thresholds. Whereas the support-based approach states that tactical intelligence crosses the threshold if it makes a material and integral contribution to specific hostilities, the overall control test requires that the third State takes part in the planning and

---

[149] Ibid.

[150] Schmitt 2022a; Heller and Trabucco 2022; *Tadić* 1999, n 93, para 145; Wentker 2023, p. 653; *Nicaragua* 1986, above n 34, para 115.

[151] Wentker 2022; Heller and Trabucco 2022, p. 265; Schmitt 2022b.

supervision of military operations of another State. So, one focuses on support and the other on control. In his article, Milanovic demonstrates the fine line between supplying intelligence and being involved in the targeting decisions.[152] He argues that, in contrast to supplying a belligerent with mere information, "actually making decisions or specific suggestions on what targets should be struck" would likely render the supporting State a co-party.[153] Making decisions in the targeting process would then relate to the requirement set by the overall control test. Making specific suggestions, on the other hand, would fall within the scope of the support-based approach. As such, Milanovic harmonizes support amounting to control and support not amounting to control.

Taking into account the State practice and the thresholds proposed, this chapter introduces the following threshold for a third State to become a co-party to a pre-existing IAC through indirect intervention.

A third State can be qualified as a co-party when the following criteria are met:

1. The extent of the support: a third State must support a belligerent State to such an extent that the support is systematic in nature and makes a material and integral tactical contribution to military operations related to specific hostilities;
2. Causal link: there must be a direct causal link between the support and the specific hostilities;
3. Intent: the supporting State must have intended to contribute to specific hostilities engaged in by the supported belligerent.

It must be kept in mind that an IAC is initiated by the use of force between States. Accordingly, for a third State to become a co-party due to its indirect intervention, it needs to do something more than merely supplying a belligerent with goods and services. In fact, to potentially qualify as indirect intervention, the support must have made a material and integral tactical contribution to specific hostilities, and thus showcase a direct nexus to those hostilities. Because of this contribution, the supporting State enables military operations related to specific hostilities and should therefore be bound by IHL. Furthermore, the indirect support must be systematic in nature and, as such, constitute an elaborate, or systematic, involvement in the hostilities. If this were not the case, one single tactical supportive act that crosses the threshold would potentially lead to co-party status. This consequence is too severe, for the rationale behind this threshold is to contain IACs, while fostering legal certainty. In addition, regarding intelligence support specifically, this chapter asserts that the support may either be decisive or suggestive in nature with regard to the targeting decision-making process.

Furthermore, the threshold requires a direct causal link between the material and integral support and the specific hostilities. Only with the establishment of such a direct causal link can a third State be said to have a necessary direct nexus with the

---

[152] Milanovic 2022.

[153] Ibid.

4 On the Sideline or on the Pitch? *The Classification of Third States ...*   135

hostilities.[154] To establish a causal link between the support and the specific hostilities, the support must have been indispensable for the hostilities to be conducted. This indispensable nature of the support illustrates the reliance on the supporting State by the supported belligerent, and therefore also the required causal link.

The term 'hostilities' in the sense of this threshold entails "physical, armed clashes between conflict parties".[155] As such, hostilities are characterized as means or methods intended to directly injure the adversary.[156] Importantly, the notion of hostilities includes non-violent activities in support of a belligerent by directly harming the other, such as providing tactical intelligence.[157] In this sense, if a third State provides a material, integral, and indispensable contribution to specific hostilities, it will have a direct nexus to harm caused to the adversary. This chapter is of the view that harm includes physical harm, but also the inability of the adversary to achieve certain military goals. The term 'tactical support' encompasses support required for the planning and execution of operations on the tactical level of warfare, which concerns specific engagements to achieve particular military goals.

Lastly, this chapter regards belligerent intent on the part of the supporting State necessary for co-party status. This is because belligerent intent provides clear evidence of a State's effective involvement in specific hostilities.[158] Moreover, as Wentker argues, the requirements for co-party status cannot be considered fulfilled when the supporting State is not aware of its actions, as the result of being misled or an error.[159] If, for instance, Ukraine draws upon third States' support to attack Belarus, we cannot conclude that third States intended their support to be used in such a way.[160] Also Schmitt, drawing on the support-based approach, views belligerent intent as an important requirement for co-party status.[161] Of course, the question whether IHL applies due to co-party status cannot solely rest upon a subjective criterium.[162] This chapter stresses, however, that intent must be distinguished from motive. While motive denotes a subjective quality, intent concerns the foreseeable ramifications of a third State's support, irrespective of its underlying motives.[163] Hence, the supporting State's intent ought to be objectivized by all facts ruling at the time.[164] In more practical terms, belligerent intent can be established when the supporting State's actions are "purposely and consciously designed" to contribute

---

[154] Melzer and Gaggioli Gasteyger 2017, pp. 72–73

[155] ICRC 'Hostilities'.

[156] ICRC Interpretative Guidance on the notion of direct participation in hostilities 2009, p. 43; ICRC Commentary on the Additional Protocols of 8 June 1977 to the Geneva Conventions 1987, Article 51, para 1942; Wentker 2023, p. 649; Melzer and Gaggioli Gasteyger 2017, p. 72.

[157] Melzer and Gaggioli Gasteyger 2017, p. 74; Dinstein 2016, p. 2; Wentker 2023, p. 649.

[158] ICRC 32nd International Conference 2015, p. 8.

[159] Wentker 2023, p. 651.

[160] Schmitt and Biggerstaff 2023, p. 207.

[161] Schmitt 2022b.

[162] Van Steenberghe and Lesaffre 2019, p. 14; Wentker et al. 2024, p. 20.

[163] Schmitt and Biggerstaff 2023, p. 207.

[164] Van Steenberghe and Lesaffre 2019, p. 14.

to the supported State's specific hostilities.[165] Based upon an objective assessment, taking into account the circumstances ruling at the time, one could infer intent from factual patterns, such as the systematic supply of tactical support that crosses the threshold.[166]

This chapter's threshold corresponds, for a large part, with Wentker's recently proposed threshold.[167] Importantly, however, this chapter's threshold places emphasis on the extent of the support, as a degree of the 'directness' to harm to the adversary. At the same time, while Wentker requires that the contribution is closely coordinated with one or more other co-parties,[168] this coordination element is implicit in this chapter's threshold for it requires that the support makes a tactical contribution to specific hostilities. Additionally, Wentker requires that co-parties are involved in the strategic, operational, and/or tactical decision-making process relating to military operations. Conversely, this chapter argues that only contributions to the tactical level of warfare will have a necessary direct nexus to specific hostilities.[169]

This newly introduced threshold draws inspiration from several important notions of IHL like the support-based approach, the overall control test, and the notion of DPH. Also, it is drawn up while keeping the ideology of IHL in mind: the regulation of armed conflict. We do not live in an ideal world. At some point we must face the fact that a third State is engaged in a pre-existing IAC because of its indirect support to a belligerent. Intentionally and systematically providing a belligerent with indispensable tactical support, which materially and integrally contributes to specific hostilities, is such an indirect intervention. IHL must regulate this. If a third State were to locate a possible target with the use of satellite imagery, and share this tactical intelligence with a belligerent, the third State must ascertain that it located a true military objective within the meaning of IHL.[170] The beneficiary belligerent, like Ukraine, might not have the capabilities to process satellite imagery, let alone gather satellite imagery itself. The supporting State should therefore be bound by IHL when it pinpoints Russian targets and instructs or suggests Ukraine to attack them. Furthermore, this threshold provides clear criteria that require a factual assessment, which adds to the assurance that maximum protection for those who need it during an armed conflict is realized.[171] For these reasons, this threshold fits within the system of IHL as a whole.

---

[165] Schmitt and Biggerstaff 2023, p. 206.

[166] Wentker 2023, p. 651.

[167] Wentker 2023.

[168] Ibid., pp. 650–651.

[169] U.S. Department of Defence 2021, p. 210.

[170] API, above n 21, Article 52.

[171] Schmitt 2022b.

4.5 Application of the Threshold to States Supporting Active Belligerents with Processed Satellite Imagery

This section examines whether supplying a belligerent with processed satellite imagery, also called intelligence, crosses the threshold for indirect intervention introduced in the previous chapter. To do this, the two functions of intelligence will be set out first. In addition, the practice of States to supply a belligerent with intelligence will be analysed. Afterwards, this section explains what type of intelligence supply crosses the threshold, leading to co-party status. Lastly, the important role of private space companies necessitates this section to take the consequences of a State's co-party status for those companies into account.

4.5.1 The Purpose and Use of Satellite Imagery

Satellite imagery has become an important asset for militaries around the world. It helps armed forces to conduct their operations, both in times of peace and in times of armed conflict, while being well-informed of the overall situation at hand.[172] The European Union indeed acknowledges in its 'Space Strategy for Security and Defence' that Earth Observation, thus including satellite imagery, is essential for militaries' autonomous assessment and decision-making.[173] Satellite imagery assists militaries in a myriad of applications, such as maintaining overall situational awareness, locating and observing other States and armed groups, and conducting targeting operations.[174]

Additionally, satellite imagery has important functions for the general public. At the outset, by piercing through the fog of war and documenting armed conflicts, satellite imagery ensures that populations across the globe remain well-informed of the developments of those conflicts.[175] Importantly, satellite imagery also plays a vital role in uncovering the truth and countering falsities. Modern conventional military operations are oftentimes carried out alongside 'psychological and influence operations', which are closely related to 'information operations'.[176] Both operations are designed to shape and influence the emotions, perceptions, reasoning, motives, and behaviour of foreign governments, groups, and/or populations, by conveying to those recipients selected information.[177] Russia provides an example in this context, for in its current IAC with Ukraine it invests a lot in information operations. Russia does this to push false narratives and blame 'Nazi-Ukraine' to justify its actions, to spread

---

[172] Volynskaya 2015.

[173] European Commission 2023, p. 11.

[174] Klinkenberg 2015, pp. 84–85.

[175] Beale J (2022) Space, the unseen frontier in the war in Ukraine. https://www.bbc.com/news/technology-63109532. Accessed 28 November 2023.

[176] Cathcart 2017, pp. 450–451.

[177] Ibid.; Pijpers and Ducheine 2020.

confusion across the general public, and, most importantly perhaps, undermine third States' sympathy for and support to Ukraine.[178] Russian disinformation schemes include the allegation that Ukraine planned to use a 'dirty-bomb' on its own territory with the aid of the U.S.[179] and the claim that the massacre of Ukrainian civilians in Bucha, Ukraine, was staged.[180] Satellite imagery is an important tool to counter these Russian psychological and influence operations.[181] With regard to Russia's disinformation scheme concerning the events in Bucha, for instance, recent reports have used satellite images as evidence to counter Russia's false claims, by establishing that the massacres of Ukrainian civilians by the Russian armed forces did take place.[182] Hence, satellite imagery denies Russia's attempts to isolate Ukraine from the rest of the world.

4.5.2 The Practice of Supporting a Belligerent with Satellite Imagery

States have invested a lot in space capabilities gathering satellite imagery.[183] While satellite images prove to be important for civil and academic purposes, they have also become a valuable asset for militaries. This is why satellite imagery provides a belligerent an unrivalled military advantage as opposed to a belligerent who does not have satellite imaging capabilities.[184] The lack of said capabilities on the part of a belligerent creates the urgent dependency on third States for their supply of satellite imagery. It could therefore be the case that in future armed conflicts third States' support to a belligerent will shift from predominantly conventional military materiel to intelligence. As a matter of fact, we can already witness this in the context of the IAC between Russia and Ukraine. After the war broke out in January 2022, third States assisted Ukraine not only by supplying it with conventional military materiel,

---

[178] Bond S (2023) How Russia is losing — and winning — the information war in Ukraine. https://www.npr.org/2023/02/28/1159712623/how-russia-is-losing-and-winning-the-information-war-in-ukraine. Accessed 28 November 2023.

[179] The Guardian (2022) UN nuclear inspectors shut down Russian 'dirty bomb' claim against Ukraine. https://www.theguardian.com/world/2022/nov/04/un-nuclear-inspectors-shut-down-russian-dirty-bomb-claim-against-ukraine. Accessed 28 November 2023.

[180] OECD 2022.

[181] See n 173.

[182] Strick 2022; BBC (2022) Bucha killings: Satellite image of bodies site contradicts Russian claims. https://www.bbc.com/news/60981238. Accessed 28 November 2023.

[183] European Space Agency 2021; Dutch Ministry of Defence 2022, p. 16.

[184] Siegel 2022.

but also by providing tactical intelligence support.[185] Crucially, satellite imagery has been, and will be, key for Ukraine to be able to withstand Russia's aggression.[186]

The lawfulness of gathering satellite imagery is dependent on its compatibility with international law, the Outer Space Treaty[187] (hereinafter OST) in particular. Article I of the OST stipulates that outer space shall be free for exploration and use by any State, on the basis of equality and in accordance with international law. Furthermore, Principle IV of the UN Resolution on Remote Sensing,[188] which is not legally binding, specifically emphasizes that remote sensing activities ought to be carried out in accordance with article I of the OST. This implies that gathering satellite imagery is legal, provided it is done in compliance with article I OST. The OST also underlines in its preamble and article IV that the exploration and use of outer space is reserved for peaceful purposes. Since satellite imagery is widely used by States for military purposes, States seem to agree on the position that the term 'peaceful purposes' entails 'non-aggressive' conduct rather than 'non-military' conduct.[189] Still, some States are of the opinion that the acquisition of data concerning them, like satellite images, violates their sovereignty when this is done without their prior consent.[190] The majority of the States swiftly brushed aside this argument by claiming that the legality of information gathering is dependent on the medium which is used to gather information. In this case the medium is outer space, which is free for peaceful exploration and use to all States, meaning that gathering satellite imagery is lawful.[191] Consequently, States have proceeded to increase their space capabilities to gather satellite images from the territories of other States, resulting in an alleged customary international law rule allowing this practice.[192] Hence, it is generally accepted that gathering satellite imagery is lawful under international law.[193]

---

[185] Milanovic 2022; Boddens Hosang 2023, p. 22; Harris S, Lamothe D (2022) Intelligence-sharing with Ukraine designed to prevent wider war. https://www.washingtonpost.com/national-security/2022/05/11/ukraine-us-intelligence-sharing-war/. Accessed 28 November 2023; Dilanian K, Kube C, Lee CE, De Luce D (2022) U.S. intel helped Ukraine protect air defenses, shoot down Russian plane carrying hundreds of troops. https://www.nbcnews.com/politics/national-security/us-intel-helped-ukraine-protect-air-defenses-shoot-russian-plane-carry-rcna26015. Accessed 28 November 2023; Barnes JE, Cooper H, Schmitt E (2022) U.S. Intelligence Is Helping Ukraine Kill Russian Generals, Officials Say. https://www.nytimes.com/2022/05/04/us/politics/russia-generals-killed-ukraine.html#:~:text=WASHINGTON%20—%20The%20United%20States%20has,according%20to%20senior%20American%20officials. Accessed 28 November 2023.

[186] European Commission 2023, p. 11.

[187] Treaty on Principles Governing the Activities of States in the Exploration and Use of Outer Space, including the Moon and Other Celestial Bodies, opened for signature 27 January 1967, 610 UNTS 205 (entered into force 10 October 1967) (Outer Space Treaty).

[188] Principles Relating to Remote Sensing of the Earth from Outer Space, UNGA Res. 41/65, 3 December 1986.

[189] Schmitt and Tinkler 2020; Vermeer 2023, p. 99; Nirmal 2012, p. 476.

[190] Nirmal 2012, pp. 471–472.

[191] Ibid., p. 472.

[192] Ibid.

[193] Vermeer 2023, p. 100.

4.5.3 The Systematic Supply of Tactical Intelligence

Intelligence support with a public function will not fall within the scope of the threshold provided in Sect. 4.4.2. The supply of intelligence with a military function, in contrast, could cross this threshold, thus potentially leading to co-party status. This paragraph will use the U.S.' supply of tactical intelligence [194] to Ukraine as a case study to determine which intelligence support potentially crosses the newly introduced threshold for indirect intervention.

Since the run up to the IAC between Russia and Ukraine, the U.S. has deployed its intelligence, surveillance, and reconnaissance (ISR) assets to monitor the developments of the conflict.[195] Apart from this relatively passive act, the U.S. is acting actively on its received intelligence in cooperation with Ukraine. There is a great number of reports that show the U.S., along with other NATO allies, is engaged in the sharing of tactical intelligence, based on satellite imagery, with a "decisive" impact on the battlefield, with Ukraine.[196] Although the Pentagon tried to push back on the allegations,[197] U.S. officials earlier stated that "there has been a lot of real-time intelligence shared in terms of things that could be used for specific targeting of Russian forces".[198] This is confirmed by a Ukrainian official who was cited saying that "the [U.S.] intelligence is very good. It tells us where the Russians are so that we can hit them."[199] Even more so, leaked Pentagon documents show satellite images portraying damaged targets from Ukrainian strikes, carried out with the help of U.S. intelligence.[200]

---

[194] See footnote 140.

[195] Klippenstein K, Sirota S (2022) U.S. Quietly Assists Ukraine With Intelligence, Avoiding Direct Confrontation With Russia. https://theintercept.com/2022/03/17/us-intelligence-ukraine-russia/. Accessed 28 November 2023.

[196] See n 183; Barnes JE, Cooper H, Schmitt E (2022) U.S. Intelligence Is Helping Ukraine Kill Russian Generals, Officials Say. https://www.nytimes.com/2022/05/04/us/politics/russia-generals-killed-ukraine.html#:~:text=WASHINGTON%20—%20The%20United%20States%20has,according%20to%20senior%20American%20officials. Accessed 28 November 2023; Hitchens T (2022) How US intel worked with commercial satellite firms to reveal Ukraine info. https://breakingdefense.com/2022/04/how-us-intel-worked-with-commercial-satellite-firms-to-reveal-ukraine-info/. Accessed 28 November 2023.

[197] BBC (2022) Moskva sinking: US gave intelligence that helped Ukraine sink Russian cruiser – reports. https://www.bbc.com/news/world-us-canada-61343044. Accessed 28 November 2023.

[198] Dilanian K, Kube C, Lee CE, De Luce D (2022) U.S. intel helped Ukraine protect air defenses, shoot down Russian plane carrying hundreds of troops. https://www.nbcnews.com/politics/national-security/us-intel-helped-ukraine-protect-air-defenses-shoot-russian-plane-carry-rcna26015. Accessed 28 November 2023.

[199] Harris S, Lamothe D (2022) Intelligence-sharing with Ukraine designed to prevent wider war. https://www.washingtonpost.com/national-security/2022/05/11/ukraine-us-intelligence-sharing-war/. Accessed 28 November 2023.

[200] Toler A (2023) Anatomy of Three Leaked US Intelligence Documents. https://www.bellingcat.com/news/2023/04/28/anatomy-of-three-leaked-us-intelligence-documents/. Accessed 28 November 2023.

In practical terms, while being denied by the Pentagon,[201] U.S. intelligence likely paved an important way for Ukraine to target, *inter alia*, Russian generals, a Russian plane carrying Russian forces, and Russia's flagship the Moskva.[202] This situation is acknowledged by Ukrainian officials, who claim that Ukraine requires coordinates provided or confirmed by the U.S. "for the vast majority" of its targeting operations carried out with HIMARS rocket launchers.[203] Apart from allegedly assisting in Ukrainian targeting operations, leaked Pentagon documents also show that U.S. intelligence support, potentially including processed satellite imagery, warns Ukraine when and where Russian strikes will hit, allowing Ukraine to conduct defensive military operations.[204] Pentagon spokespersons confirm that the U.S. is sharing intelligence with Ukraine. But they also emphasize that Ukraine is responsible for locating Russian targets and making their own targeting decisions.[205] At the same time, disclosed classified reports reveal Washington persuaded Ukraine to postpone its intended strikes on Moscow on the 24th of February 2023. This shows the U.S. is seemingly involved in Ukraine's targeting decision-making process after all.[206]

Let us assume that the U.S. is providing Ukraine with tactical intelligence, based on satellite imagery, showcasing Russian targets and threats, which Ukraine can immediately act on by engaging in specific hostilities, both in offense and defence.

In the first place, regarding the extent of the support, U.S. intelligence makes a material and integral contribution to Ukrainian targeting operations, because the intelligence is integrated, and plays a vital role, in those hostilities. As such, the intelligence is tactical, or *actionable*, in the sense that Ukraine can immediately act on the received intelligence by conducting those operations. Additionally, evidence shows U.S. tactical intelligence also contributes materially and integrally to Ukrainian

---

[201] Basu Z (2022) Pentagon denies U.S. is providing Ukraine intel to kill Russian generals, https://www.axios.com/2022/05/05/ukraine-us-intelligence-russian-generals. Accessed 28 November 2023.

[202] See n 193, n 194, and n 195; Matisek et al. 2023.

[203] Khurshudyan I, Lamothe D, Harris S, Sonne P (2023) Ukraine's rocket campaign relies on U.S. military personnel providing precision targeting, officials say. https://www.washingtonpost.com/world/2023/02/09/ukraine-himars-rocket-artillery-russia/. Accessed 28 November 2023.

[204] Barnes JE, Cooper H, Gibbons-Neff T, Schwirtz M, Schmitt E (2023) Leaked Documents Reveal Depth of U.S. Spy Efforts and Russia's Military Struggles. https://www.nytimes.com/2023/04/08/us/politics/leaked-documents-russia-ukraine-war.html. Accessed 28 November 2023.

[205] Milanovic 2022; Khurshudyan I, Lamothe D, Harris S, Sonne P (2023) Ukraine's rocket campaign relies on U.S. military personnel providing precision targeting, officials say. https://www.washingtonpost.com/world/2023/02/09/ukraine-himars-rocket-artillery-russia/. Accessed 28 November 2023.

[206] Harris S, Khurshudyan I (2023) At U.S. behest, Ukraine held off anniversary attacks on Russia. https://www.washingtonpost.com/world/2023/04/24/discord-leaks-moscow-strikes-ukraine/. Accessed 28 November 2023.

defensive military operations, including evasive actions.[207] These supported operations significantly hinder Russia from achieving certain military goals, thus falling within the scope of hostilities. Furthermore, considering that reports show the U.S. is actively engaged in transferring tactical intelligence to Ukraine on a regular basis, this support is not incidental, but rather systematic in nature. The fact that the Pentagon claims that Ukraine makes its own targeting decisions does not alter the fact that the intelligence support is of such an extent to potentially qualify as an indirect intervention. Indeed, the support may have a suggestive function, as long as its contribution forms a systematic, material, and integral part of military operations related to specific hostilities. So, U.S. intelligence showing in great detail the location of the Moskva would suffice, even if it is Ukraine that decides to act on the intelligence and target the Moskva.

Next, a direct causal link must be established between the material and integral tactical intelligence support and the specific hostilities, which entail harm caused to the adversary.[208] Indeed, if it can be shown that the U.S. tactical intelligence support was indispensable for military operations related to specific hostilities, the required causal link can be established relatively easily. Examples of harm to the adversary in this context include the killings of Russian generals, the downing of the Russian transport plane, and the sinking of the Moskva. Additionally, Russia's overall inability to achieve certain military goals due to effective Ukrainian offensive or defensive military operations related to specific hostilities, to which U.S. tactical intelligence contributed, also amounts to harm to the adversary. Evidence shows in this regard that U.S. tactical intelligence is indispensable for Ukraine to conduct precision targeting operations. Indeed, two U.S. intelligence officers were cited saying that their intelligence was "instrumental" for Ukraine to target Russian generals and the Moskva.[209] Moreover, if it is truly a precondition for Ukraine to continuously receive coordinates from the U.S. before it can carry out attacks with HIMARS rocket launchers, it can certainly be concluded that the U.S. intelligence is indispensable to Ukraine. This establishes a necessary causal link between the support and the specific hostilities.

Lastly, the U.S. must have intended to contribute to Ukrainian military operations related to specific hostilities. This subjective criterium might be more difficult to meet. Regarding the targeting of Russian generals, for example, the White House stressed the U.S. had no intention to kill those generals when it shared intelligence with Ukraine.[210] A similar statement was issued by a Pentagon spokesperson about the sinking of the Moskva: "We were not involved in the Ukrainians' decision to strike

---

[207] Dilanian K, Kube C, Lee CE, De Luce D (2022) U.S. intel helped Ukraine protect air defenses, shoot down Russian plane carrying hundreds of troops. https://www.nbcnews.com/politics/national-security/us-intel-helped-ukraine-protect-air-defenses-shoot-russian-plane-carry-rcna26015. Accessed 28 November 2023.

[208] Wentker 2023, p. 643.

[209] Borger J (2022) US intelligence told to keep quiet over role in Ukraine military triumphs. https://www.theguardian.com/us-news/2022/may/07/us-spies-ukraine-russia-military-intelligence. Accessed 28 November 2023.

[210] Ibid.

the ship or in the operation they carried out. We had no prior knowledge of Ukraine's intent to target the ship."[211] However, intent can be inferred from the scenario in which the U.S. systematically supplies Ukraine with tactical intelligence, while it knows that this intelligence is vital for Ukraine to carry out military operations related to specific hostilities. Indeed, it is widely acknowledged that third States, including the U.S., are systematically providing Ukraine with tactical intelligence support. A strong argument can therefore be made that U.S. tactical intelligence support is purposely and consciously designed to contribute to Ukrainian hostilities.

It follows from this case study that the requirements for co-party status are challenging to meet with regard to intelligence support, since this type of support is oftentimes classified. U.S. officials also seem to contradict each other on a regular basis, and we cannot rule out the possibility that these contradictions are part of information operations. Evidently, we do not know for certain whether the reports showing the significance of U.S. intelligence support are true. Nevertheless, assuming the reports are right, the U.S. can arguably be qualified as a co-party to the IAC between Russia and Ukraine because the U.S. tactical intelligence support to Ukraine (i) makes a material and integral tactical contribution to Ukrainian military operations related to specific hostilities, and forms part of a systematic chain of support with a similar extent, (ii) the Ukrainian military operations related to specific hostilities could not have been conducted but for the U.S. support, thus illustrating the indispensable nature of the U.S. support, and (iii) the U.S. intended to contribute to those specific hostilities.

An important question remains, however, regarding the temporal scope of co-party status. Wentker proposes that a State's co-party status should end once its supportive activities no longer meet the criteria for classifying it as a co-party in the first place.[212] Consequently, a State would no longer be a co-party if there is an "externally discernible manifestation of a significant change of the contribution or its cessation", meaning that a co-party should not have to fully disengage from supporting a belligerent in an IAC.[213] A "changed pattern over a prolonged period" could serve as evidence in this respect.[214] According to Wentker, such an approach would prevent legal uncertainty resulting from, *inter alia*, a revolving door problem. Although this chapter agrees that the temporal scope of co-party status should focus on avoiding legal uncertainty, it does not agree with Wentker's proposed temporal scope. The first issue with this temporal scope revolves around the significant change of the contribution, which has to be detectable by other States. Clearly, classifying a third State as a co-party in the first place, because of its supply of tactical intelligence, is difficult since the contours of intelligence are less clear and detectible than the contours of conventional military support. Hence, determining whether there is a

---

[211] Dilanian K, Kube C, Lee CE (2022) U.S. intel helped Ukraine sink Russian flagship Moskva, officials say. https://www.nbcnews.com/politics/national-security/us-intel-helped-ukraine-sink-russian-flagship-moskva-officials-say-rcna27559#. Accessed 28 November 2023.

[212] Wentker 2023, p. 652.

[213] Ibid.

[214] Ibid.

significant change of a co-party's supply of tactical intelligence is a time-consuming task. Moreover, Wentker's proposed scope requires a continuous analysis, likely to be made by the international community, of whether specific co-parties demonstrate a significant change of the contribution. In the hypothetical situation that a third State provides a belligerent with tactical intelligence support, then stops doing so for a couple of months, and subsequently decides to continue its tactical intelligence support, three individual legal analyses are required: (i) whether the threshold for co-party status through indirect intervention is met regarding the initial intelligence support, (ii) if so, whether there is a significant change of the contribution, thus terminating the co-party status, and (iii), again, whether the threshold for indirect intervention is met regarding the continued intelligence support. Wentker's proposed scope would leave the termination of co-party status to the discretion of other States. Naturally, this would only result in uncertainty regarding the classification of co-parties, for it would be almost impossible to unanimously agree on all legal analyses regarding all co-parties. This chapter therefore argues that such an approach would, conversely, result in, endless discussions regarding the classification of co-parties, a revolving door problem, and legal uncertainty. Instead, this chapter asserts that the temporal scope of IHL should apply by analogy to co-parties. Hence, a State loses its co-party status, *inter alia*, upon the general close of military operations.[215] Not only will this scope fit best within the system of IHL as a whole, but it will also prevent the revolving door problem. If a less strict temporal scope is applied, it is left to the discretion of third States when they want to become co-party and subsequently lose that status. Such a scenario would undermine the deterrent effect of intentionally providing material, integral, and indispensable indirect support and becoming a co-party.

4.5.4 The Role of Private Space Companies and Consequences of Co-party Status for Those Companies

The war in Ukraine shows the important role private space companies played leading up to, and during, the IAC.[216] In their intelligence support to Ukraine, it has become common practice for States to rely on private space companies for the gathering of satellite imagery.[217] The U.S., for instance, has a big fleet of satellites of its own,

---

[215] Fourth Geneva Convention, above n 23, Article 6; Crawford and Pert 2020, p. 36; Milanovic 2014, p. 174.

[216] Vermeer 2023, p. 96; Borowitz 2022; Siegel 2022.

[217] Vermeer 2023, pp. 96, 102; Siegel 2022; Baraniuk C (2022) How access to satellite images shifts the view of war. https://www.bbc.com/news/business-60762772. Accessed 28 November 2023; Hitchens T (2022) How US intel worked with commercial satellite firms to reveal Ukraine info. https://breakingdefense.com/2022/04/how-us-intel-worked-with-commercial-satellite-firms-to-reveal-ukraine-info/. Accessed 28 November 2023.

yet it has doubled its purchase and use of commercial satellite images since the war in Ukraine.[218] A reason for a State to do this is to hide the capabilities of its own satellites,[219] or to benefit from sophisticated equipment, like synthetic aperture radar (SAR), with which some commercial satellites are equipped.[220] Russia already claimed that the use by the U.S., and other NATO allies, of private space companies for military purposes constitutes an indirect involvement in military conflicts.[221]

Importantly, if a State becomes a co-party, IHL becomes applicable, with the result that military objectives within its territory may be targeted under IHL. So, if ground-based infrastructure located on that territory, operated by a private space company that directly[222] or indirectly provides Ukraine with tactical intelligence, qualifies as a military objective, it might be attacked. Additionally, during a UN Open-Ended Working Group session, Russia warned that *dual-use* satellites could also become a target for retaliation if they are used by States for military purposes.[223] This raises multiple thorny questions: what is the legal basis for IHL to apply to *dual-use* satellites? If a *dual use* satellite qualifies as a military objective, how must the residual civilian use of that satellite be factored into the proportionality assessment as a necessary part of the targeting planning phase? Are the people operating the *dual-use* satellite targetable due to their DPH?[224] While these questions go beyond the scope of this chapter, it is noteworthy that it is generally accepted that IHL also applies to armed conflicts in space.[225] Consequently, although the specific nature of *dual-use* satellites and outer space undoubtedly influence the way military operations are conducted in space, the rules and principles of IHL will still apply.[226] Thus, a *dual-use* satellite must qualify as a military objective,[227] all foreseeable incidental harm to civilians or damage to civilian objects, as a result from the attack, must not outweigh the expected military advantage,[228] and both the attacking State and the defending State must take precautions.[229]

---

[210] Albon 2022; Universe Magazine 2022.

[219] Borowitz 2022.

[220] Erwin 2022.

[221] UN Open-Ended Working Group 2022.

[222] ICEYE 2022.

[223] See n 218.

[224] Blount 2012.

[225] Vermeer 2023, p. 104; Schmitt and Tinkler 2020; Steer and Stephens 2020, p. 34.

[226] Vermeer 2023, p. 104.

[227] API, above n 21, Articles 48 and 52.

[228] API, above n 21, Articles 51(5)(b) and 57(2)(b).

[229] API, above n 21, Articles 57 and 58.

4.6 Conclusion

While IHL remains silent on the topic, there are two recognized ways for a third State to become co-party to a pre-existing IAC. Clearly, a third State becomes co-party when it intervenes directly by deploying its armed forces and resorting to the use of force against one of the belligerents. Secondly, a third State can become co-party by intervening indirectly, which concerns the transfer of goods and services to one of the belligerents, to the detriment of the other. This latter way of becoming a co-party remains ambiguous, however, for there is no established threshold for indirect intervention. This legal ambiguity is undesirable from both an internal and external perspective because it creates legal uncertainty, the consequences of co-party status are severe, and it potentially leads to unwanted exploitation. This, in addition to the fact that satellite imagery plays an increasingly important role for militaries, is why this chapter sought to answer the following question:

Will a third State become a co-party to a pre-existing IAC, by providing one of the active belligerent parties to that conflict with processed satellite imagery?

Several potential thresholds for indirect intervention that are proposed by scholars and case law were discussed. All proposed thresholds feature interesting aspects. Importantly, it follows from this discussion that a majority argues that a direct connection with the hostilities is required. This chapter shares this view. Co-party status as a consequence of the supply of goods or services with no such link, like arms or medicines, is too far-reaching. The discussion also showed, however, that no proposed threshold seems sufficiently adequate, since they all lack important aspects. Therefore, this chapter drew important inspiration from the discussed thresholds and IHL as a whole to introduce a threshold for co-party status through indirect intervention of its own. As such, this chapter sought to develop a threshold that fits neatly within the system of IHL and adds to the legal debate and the development of IHL.

The supply of processed satellite imagery with a military function has the potential to cross this newly introduced threshold, thus rendering a third State supplying the imagery a co-party. Indeed, it is possible to gather high-resolution satellite imagery of virtually anything on earth, including military objectives or threats. If a State does this, processes the imagery, thus turning it into intelligence, and sends it to a belligerent, it might cross the threshold for co-party status through indirect intervention. In fact, looking at the U.S.' practice of sending Ukraine tactical intelligence, evidence shows the U.S. is systematically supporting Ukraine with processed (near) real-time tactical intelligence which integrally, materially, and indispensably contributes to Ukrainian military operations related to specific hostilities. Accordingly, provided the reports are right, the threshold is likely crossed, rendering the U.S. a co-party to the IAC between Russia and Ukraine. This conclusion could have significant consequences for private space companies that are involved in the gathering and distribution of satellite images that are sent to Ukraine. For a start, their ground-based infrastructure, located on the territory of a co-party, could be lawfully targeted under IHL if it qualifies as a military objective. Secondly, perhaps their

4 On the Sideline or on the Pitch? *The Classification of Third States ...* 147

space-based assets could also be targeted for similar reasons. These last points raise important questions which call for further extensive examination.

One nuance to my findings is in order. Insufficient evidence of State practice is available, for now, to support the threshold this chapter introduces and its application to tactical intelligence support. Certainly, State practice is indicative of the way in which international law is moving. However, current practice by most States supporting Ukraine is stretching IHL's vacuum regarding third States' support to an active belligerent in a pre-existing IAC to an almost untenable position. Indeed, at some point third States will become co-parties due to their indirect support to a belligerent, whether they like it or not. States cannot exclusively bear the fruits of exploiting legal ambiguity, there must be a legal turning point. States must be wary of this.

References

Articles, Books, and Other Documents

Albon C (2022) Intelligence agencies accelerate use of commercial space imagery to support Ukraine. C4ISRNET. https://www.c4isrnet.com/battlefield-tech/space/2022/04/06/intelligence-agencies-accelerate-use-of-commercial-space-imagery-to-support-ukraine/. Accessed 26 November 2023

Antonopoulos C (2022) Non-Participation in Armed Conflict. Cambridge University Press, Cambridge

Antonopoulos C (2023) Russia's Lawfare Against the West in the UN Security Council and the Law of Neutrality. Opinio Juris. http://opiniojuris.org/2023/11/21/russias-lawfare-against-the-west-in-the-un-security-council-and-the-law-of-neutrality/. Accessed 14 March 2024

Arajärvi N (2021) The core requirements of the International Rule of Law in the Practice of States. Hague Journal on the Rule of Law:173–193

Blount PJ (2012) Targeting in Outer Space: Legal Aspects of Operational Military Actions in Space. National Security Journal. https://harvardnsj.org/2012/11/25/targeting-in-outer-space-legal-aspects-of-operational-military-actions-in-space/. Accessed 20 November 2023

Buddens Hosang JFR (2023) Militaire steun aan Oekraïne: neutraliteit, gekwalificeerde neutraliteit en co-belligerente status in het internationaal recht. Militair Rechtelijk Tijdschrift 116:11–23 [Military support to Ukraine: neutrality, qualified neutrality, and co-belligerent status under international law]

Borchard E (1941) War, Neutrality and Non-Belligerency. The American Journal of International Law 35:618–625

Borowitz M (2022) War in Ukraine highlights the growing strategic importance of private satellite companies – especially in times of conflict. The Conversation https://theconversation.com/war-in-ukraine-highlights-the-growing-strategic-importance-of-private-satellite-companies-especially-in-times-of-conflict-188425. Accessed 20 November 2023

Bradley CA, Goldsmith JL (2005) Congressional Authorization and the War on Terrorism. Harvard Law Review 118:2047–2133

Bridgeman T (2010) The Law of Neutrality and the Conflict with Al Qaeda. New York University Law Review:1186–1224

Cassese A (2007) The Nicaragua and Tadić Tests Revisited in Light of the ICJ Judgment on Genocide in Bosnia. The European Journal of International Law 18,4: 649–668

Cathcart B (2017) Legal Dimensions of Special Operations and Information Operations. In: Gill TD and Fleck D (eds.) The Handbook of the International Law of Military Operations. Oxford University Press, Oxford, pp 444–455

Congressional Research Service (2023) U.S. Security Assistance to Ukraine https://crsreports.con gress.gov/product/pdf/IF/IF12040. Accessed 22 November 2023

Crawford E, Pert A (2020) International Humanitarian Law. Cambridge University Press, New York

Deutscher Bundestag (2022) Schriftliche Fragen mit den in der Woche vom 16. Mai 2022 einge-gangenen Antworten der Bundesregierung. https://dserver.bundestag.de/btd/20/019/2001918. pdf. Accessed 17 March 2024

Dinstein Y (2011) War, Aggression and Self-Defence. Cambridge University Press, Cambridge

Dinstein Y (2016) The Conduct of Hostilities under the Law of International Armed Conflict. Cambridge University Press, Cambridge

Dinstein Y (2017) War, Aggression and Self-Defence, Cambridge University Press, Cambridge

Droege C, Tuck D (2017) Fighting together and international humanitarian law: Setting the legal framework (1/2). Humanitarian Law and Policy. https://blogs.icrc.org/law-and-policy/2017/10/12/fighting-together-international-humanitarian-law-setting-legal-framework-1-2/. Accessed 20 November 2023

Dutch Ministry of Defence (2022) Defence Space Agenda. https://www.defensie.nl/downloads/pub licaties/2022/11/25/defensie-ruimte-agenda. Accessed 22 November 2023

Dutch Ministry of Defence (2023) Netherlands to purchase Leopard 1 tanks for Ukraine. https://english.defensie.nl/latest/news/2023/02/07/netherlands-to-purchase-leopard-1-tanks-for-ukraine. Accessed 22 November 2023

DW (2023) Germany says it is not a warring party in Ukraine. Deutsche Welle. https://www.dw.com/en/germany-says-it-is-not-a-warring-party-in-ukraine/a-64541484. Accessed 20 November 2023

Erwin S (2022) Drawing lessons from the first 'commercial space war'. Space-news. https://spacenews.com/on-national-security-drawing-lessons-from-the-first-commercial-space-war/. Accessed 25 May 2024

European Commission (2021) Knowledge Centre on Earth Observation. https://knowledge4policy.ec.europa.eu/earthobservation_en. Accessed 22 November 2023

European Commission (2023) European Union Space Strategy for Security and Defence. https://ec.europa.eu/transparency/documents-register/detail?ref=JOIN(2023)9&lang=en. Accessed 22 November 2023

European Union External Action (2023) European Space Conference: Opening speech by High Representative/Vice-President Josep Borrell. https://www.eeas.europa.eu/eeas/european-space-conference-opening-speech-high-representativevice-president-josep-borrell_en. Accessed 22 November 2023

European Space Agency (2021) Putting Earth observation into 'the market perspec-tive'. https://www.esa.int/Applications/Observing_the_Earth/Putting_Earth_observation_into_the_market_perspective. Accessed 22 November 2023

Ferraro T (2013) The applicability and application of international humanitarian law to multinational forces. International Review of the Red Cross: 561–612

Frowe H, Matheson B (2020) Symposium on The Ethics of Indirect Intervention. Journal of Applied Philosophy 39

Green JA (2023) The provision of weapons and logistical support to Ukraine and the jus ad bellum. Journal on the Use of Force and International Law 10: 3–16

Greenwood C (1983) The Relationship between Ius ad Bellum and Ius in Bello. Review of International Studies 9: 221–234

Greenwood C (2008) Scope of Application of Humanitarian Law. In: Fleck D (ed) The Handbook of International Humanitarian Law. Oxford University Press, New York

Grignon J (2022) Co-belligerency » or when does a State become a party to an armed conflict?. Institut de Recherche Stratégique de l'École Militaire 10 May 2022, https://www.irsem.fr/pub lications-de-l-irsem/breves-strategiques/strategic-brief-no-39-2022-co-belligerency-or-when-does-a-state-become-a-party-to-an-armed-conflict.html. Accessed 20 November 2023

Hathaway OA, Shapiro S (2022) Supplying Arms to Ukraine is Not an Act of War. Just Security. https://www.justsecurity.org/80661/supplying-arms-to-ukraine-is-not-an-act-of-war/. Accessed 20 November 2023

Heller KJ, Trabucco L (2022) The Legality of Weapons Transfers to Ukraine Under International Law. Journal of International Humanitarian Legal Studies 13,2: 251–274

ICEYE (2022) ICEYE Signs Contract to Provide Government of Ukraine with Access to Its SAR Satellite Constellation. https://www.iceye.com/press/press-releases/iceye-signs-contract-to-provide-government-of-ukraine-with-access-to-its-sar-satellite-constellation. Accessed 22 November 2023

ICRC (1987) ICRC Commentary on the Additional Protocols of 8 June 1977 to the Geneva Conventions of 12 August 1949. https://ihl-databases.icrc.org/en/ihl-treaties/api-1977/article-51/commentary/1987?activeTab=undefined

ICRC (2002) The Law of Armed Conflict, Neutrality. https://www.icrc.org/en/doc/assets/files/other/law8_final.pdf. Accessed 22 November 2023

ICRC (2009) Interpretative Guidance on the notion of direct participation in hostilities under international humanitarian law. https://www.icrc.org/en/doc/assets/files/other/icrc-002-0990.pdf. Accessed 22 November 2023

ICRC (2015) 32nd International Conference of the Red Cross and Red Crescent, International humanitarian law and the challenges of contemporary armed conflicts. https://www.icrc.org/en/document/international-humanitarian-law-and-challenges-contemporary-armed-conflicts. Accessed 22 November 2023

ICRC (2016) ICRC Commentary on the First Geneva Convention. https://ihl-databases.icrc.org/en/ihl-treaties/gci-1949. Accessed 22 November 2023

ICRC (2020) ICRC Commentary on the Third Geneva Convention. https://ihl-databases.icrc.org/en/ihl-treaties/gciii-1949/toc/commentary/2020?activeTab=undefined. Accessed 22 November 2023

ICRC 'Hostilities'. https://casebook.icrc.org/a_to_z/glossary/hostilities. Accessed 22 November 2023

ILA Committee on the Use of Force (2010) ILA Committee on the Use of Force. https://www.rulac.org/assets/downloads/ILA_report_armed_conflict_2010.pdf. Accessed 24 November 2023

ILC (2001) Draft articles on Responsibility of States for Internationally Wrongful Acts. https://legal.un.org/ilc/texts/instruments/english/commentaries/9_6_2001.pdf. Accessed 24 November 2023

Ingber R (2011) Untangling Belligerency from Neutrality in the Conflict with Al-Qaeda. Texas International Law Journal 47: 75–114

Ingber R (2017) Co-Belligerency. Yale Journal of International Law 67: 67–120

Kiel Institute for the World Economy (2023) Ukraine Support Tracker. https://www.ifw-kiel.de/topics/war-against-ukraine/ukraine-support-tracker/. Accessed 22 November 2023

Klinkenberg JC (2015) Space: de logische stap naar het ruimtedomein. Militaire Spectator 184,2: 83–93 [Space: the logical step to the space domain]

Kleffner JK (2014) Scope of Application of International Humanitarian Law. In: Fleck D (ed) The Handbook of International Humanitarian Law. Oxford University Press, Oxford

Konchak PS (2022) U.S. and Allied Involvement in the Russo-Ukrainian War: The Belligerent Status of NATO States and Its Implications. OpinioJuris. http://opiniojuris.org/2022/07/20/u-s-and-allied-involvement-in-the-russo-ukrainian-war-the-belligerent-status-of-nato-states-and-its-implications/. Accessed 20 November 2023

Krajewski M (2022) Neither Neutral nor Party to the Conflict? On the Legal Assessment of Arms Supplies to Ukraine. Völkerrechtsblog. https://voelkerrechtsblog.org/neither-neutral-nor-party-to-the-conflict/. Accessed 20 November 2023

Kreß C (2022) The Ukraine War and the Prohibition of the Use of Force in International Law. TOAEP Occasional Paper Series

Lee RJ, Steele SL (2014) Military Use of Satellite Communications, Remote Sensing, and Global Positioning Systems in the War on Terror. Journal of Air Law and Commerce 79: 69–112

Lyons J (2012), Documenting violations of international humanitarian law from space: a critical review of geospatial analysis of satellite imagery during armed conflicts in Gaza (2009), Georgia (2008), and Sri Lanka. International Review of the Red Cross 94: 739–763

Masters J, Merrow W (2023) How Much Aid Has the U.S. Sent Ukraine? Here Are Six Charts. Council on Foreign Relations. https://www.cfr.org/article/how-much-aid-has-us-sent-ukraine-here-are-six-charts. Accessed 22 November 2023

Matisek J, Reno W, Rosenberg S (2023) The Good, the Bad and the Ugly: Assessing a Year of Military Aid to Ukraine. Royal United Services Institute. https://www.rusi.org/explore-our-research/publications/commentary/good-bad-and-ugly-assessing-year-military-aid-ukraine. Accessed 28 November 2023

Melzer N, Gaggioli Gasteyger G (2017) Conceptual Distinction and Overlaps Between Law Enforcement and the Conduct of Hostilities. In: Gill TD, Fleck D (ed) The Handbook of the International Law of Military Operations. Oxford University Press, Oxford, pp 63–94

Milanovic M (2006) State Responsibility for Genocide. European Journal of International Law 17:553–604

Milanovic M (2014) The end of application of international humanitarian law. International Review of the Red Cross 96:163–188

Milanovic M (2022) The United States and Allies Sharing Intelligence with Ukraine. EJIL:Talk!

Moore JB (1933) The New Isolation. The American Journal of International Law 27:607–629

Moussa J (2008) Can jus ad bellum override jus in bello? Reaffirming the separation of the two bodies of law. International Review of the Red Cross 90:963–990

Nasu H (2022) The Future Law of Neutrality. Articles of War. https://lieber.westpoint.edu/future-law-of-neutrality/. Accessed 20 November 2023

NATO (2022a) Press conference by NATO Secretary General Jens Stoltenberg following the meetings of NATO Defence Ministers. https://www.nato.int/cps/en/natohq/opinions_208063.htm. Accessed 22 November 2023

NATO (2022b) Press point with NATO Secretary General Jens Stoltenberg. https://www.nato.int/cps/en/natohq/opinions_207788.htm. Accessed 22 November 2023

NATO (2023) Doorstep statement by NATO Secretary General Jens Stoltenberg ahead of the meetings of NATO Defence Ministers in Brussels. https://www.nato.int/cps/en/natohq/opinions_211698.htm. Accessed 16 March 2024

NATO (2024) NATO's response to Russia's invasion of Ukraine. https://www.nato.int/cps/en/natohq/topics_192648.htm. Accessed 22 November 2023

Nirmal BC (2012) Legal Regulation of Remote Sensing: Some Critical Issues. Journal of the Indian Law Institute 54:451–479

OECD (2022) Disinformation and Russia's war of aggression against Ukraine, Threats and governance responses. https://www.oecd.org/ukraine-hub/policy-responses/disinformation-and-russia-s-war-of-aggression-against-ukraine-37186bde/. Accessed 22 November 2023

Oppenheim L, Lauterpacht H (1952) International law: a treatise. Vol. II, Disputes, war and neutrality. Longmans, Green and Co, London

Pijpers BMJ, Ducheine PAL (2020) Influence Operations in Cyberspace – How They Really work. Amsterdam Center for International Law 31:1–27

Potter M (2015) Cybersecurity in the Space Age. Proceedings of the International Institute of Space Law:267–283

RULAC Geneva Academy (2023) International armed conflict in Ukraine. https://www.rulac.org/browse/conflicts/international-armed-conflict-in-ukraine. Accessed 20 November 2023

Russell M (1984) Military activities in outer space: soviet legal views. Harvard International Law Journal 25:153–194

Schaller C (2023) When aid or assistance in the use of force turns into an indirect use of force. Journal on the Use of Force and International Law 10:173–200

Schmitt MN, Tinkler K (2020) War in Space: How International Humanitarian Law Might Apply. Just Security. https://www.justsecurity.org/68906/war-in-space-how-international-humanitarian-law-might-apply/. Accessed 20 November 2023

4 On the Sideline or on the Pitch? *The Classification of Third States ...* 151

Schmitt MN (2022a) Providing Arms and Materiel to Ukraine: Neutrality, Co-belligerency, and the Use of Force. Articles of War. https://lieber.westpoint.edu/ukraine-neutrality-co-belligerency-use-of-force/. Accessed 20 November 2023

Schmitt MN (2022b) Ukraine Symposium – Are We at War?. Articles of War. https://lieber.westpoint.edu/are-we-at-war/. Accessed 28 November 2023

Schmitt MN (2023) "Strict" versus "Qualified" Neutrality. Articles of War. https://lieber.westpoint.edu/strict-versus-qualified-neutrality/. Accessed 20 November 2023

Schmitt MN, Biggerstaff WC (2023) Aid and Assistance as a "Use of Force" Under the Jus Ad Bellum. International Law Studies 100:186–228

Siegel J (2022) Commercial satellites are on the front lines of war today. Here's what this means for the future of warfare. Atlantic Council. https://www.atlanticcouncil.org/content-series/airpower-after-ukraine/commercial-satellites-are-on-the-front-lines-of-war-today-heres-what-this-means-for-the-future-of-warfare/. Accessed 20 November 2023

Sloane RD (2009) The Cost of Conflation: Preserving the Dualism of *Jus ad Bellum* and *Jus in Bello* in the Contemporary Law of War. The Yale Journal of International Law 34:48–112

Steer C, Stephens D (2020) International Humanitarian Law and Its Application in Outer Space in: War and Peace in Outer Space: Law, Policy, and Ethics (eds. Steer C, Hersch M). Oxford University Press, Oxford

Strick B (2022) Disinformation & Denial: Russia's attempts to discredit open source evidence of Bucha. Centre for Information Resilience

Talmon S (2009) The Responsibility of outside Powers for Acts of Secessionist Entities. The International and Comparative Law Quarterly 58:493–517

UK Ministry of Defence (2004) The joint service manual of the law of armed conflict. UK Ministry of Defence. Oxford University Press, Oxford

UK Parliament (2023) Military Support to Ukraine. https://hansard.parliament.uk/Commons/2023-07-20/debates/23072054000018/MilitarySupportToUkraine#contribution-B352B3AF-0A0F-4AA7-99F1-57A1B1F98317. Accessed 14 March 2024

Universe Magazine (2022) USA constantly provides Ukraine with satellite images. https://universemagazine.com/en/usa-constantly-provides-ukraine-with-satellite-images/. Accessed 22 November 2023

UN General Assembly (1986) Principles Relating to Remote Sensing of the Earth from Outer Space, UN Doc. A/RES/41/65

UN Open-Ended Working Group (2022) Statement by the Head of the Russian Delegation K.V. Vorontsov at the second session of the Open-Ended Working Group established pursuant to UNGA resolution 76/231. https://documents.unoda.org/wp-content/uploads/2022/09/Unofficial-translation-in-English.pdf. Accessed 22 November 2023

UN Security Council (2023) 9325th meeting, UN Doc. S/PV.9325

UN Security Council (2023) 9364th meeting, UN Doc. S/PV.9364

Upcher J (2020) Neutrality in Contemporary International Law. Oxford University Press, Oxford

U.S. Department of Defense (2016) Law of War Manual. https://dod.defense.gov/Portals//Documents/pubs/DoD%20Law%20of%20War%20Manual%20-%20June%202%20Updated%20Dec%202016.pdf. Accessed 24 November 2023

U.S. Department of Defense (2021) Dictionary of Military and Associated Terms. https://irp.fas.org/doddir/dod/dictionary.pdf

U.S. Department of Defense (2023) Law of War Manual. https://media.defense.gov/2023/Jul/2003271432/-1/-1/0/DOD-LAW-OF-WAR-MANUAL-JUNE-2015-UPDATED-JULY%202023.PDF. Accessed 26 March 2024

U.S. Department of State (2023) U.S. Security Cooperation with Ukraine. https://www.state.gov/u-s-security-cooperation-with-ukraine/#:~:text=To%20date%2C%20we%20have%20provided,invasion%20of%20Ukraine%20in%202014. Accessed 22 November 2023

Van Steenberghe R, Lesaffre P, 'The ICRC's 'support-based approach': A suitable but incomplete theory. Questions of International Law 2019:5–23

Verlinden N (2019) "Are we at war?" State support to parties in armed conflict: consequences under jus in bello, jus ad bellum and neutrality law. PhD thesis Leuven

Vermeer A (2023) Het eerste commerciële gewapende conflict in de ruimte en het internationaal recht. Militair Rechtelijk Tijdschrift 116:95–110 [The first commercial armed conflict in space and international law]

Vermeer A, Pieters B, De Bruin M (2017) Inleiding Humanitair Oorlogsrecht. T.M.C. Asser Press, Den Haag [Introduction to international humanitarian law]

Volynskaya OA (2015) The Applicability of the Right to Self-Defence to the Area of Exploration and Exploitation of Outer Space. Proceedings of the International Institute of Space Law:257–266

Von Heinegg WF (2017) The Law of Military Operations at Sea. In: Gill TD, Fleck D (ed) The Handbook of the International Law of Military Operations. Oxford University Press, Oxford, pp 375–421

Von Heinegg WF (2022) Neutrality in the War Against Ukraine. Articles of War. https://lieber.wes tpoint.edu/neutrality-in-the-war-against-ukraine/. Accessed 20 November 2023

Wentker A (2022) At War: When Do States Supporting Ukraine or Russia become Parties to the Conflict and What Would that Mean?. EJIL:Talk!. https://www.ejiltalk.org/at-war-when-do-sta tes-supporting-ukraine-or-russia-become-parties-to-the-conflict-and-what-would-that-mean/. Accessed 20 November 2023

Wentker A (2023) At war? Party status and the war in Ukraine. Leiden Journal of International Law 36:643–656

Wentker A, Jackson M, Hill-Cawthorne L (2024) Identifying co-parties to armed conflict in international law, How states, international organizations and armed groups become parties to war. Chatham House International Law Programme

Weizmann N (2015) Associated Forces and Co-belligerency. Just Security. https://www.justsecur ity.org/20344/isil-aumf-forces-co-belligerency/. Accessed 20 November 2023

White J (2012) Indirect Intervention in Syria: Crafting an Effective Response to the Crisis. The Washington Institute. https://www.washingtoninstitute.org/policy-analysis/indirect-interv ention-syria-crafting-effective-response-crisis. Accessed 24 November 2023

Cases

ICTY, *Prosecutor v. Dusko Tadić a/k/a "Dule"*, Tadić Decision on the Defence Motion for Interlocutory Appeal on Jurisdiction, 2 October 1995, Case. No. IT-94-1

ICTY, *Prosecutor v. Dusko Tadić*, Appeals Chamber judgment, 15 July 1999, Case No. IT-94-1-A

ICJ, *Military and Paramilitary Activities in and against Nicaragua (Nicaragua v. United States of America)*, Judgment, 27 June 1986, ICJ Rep. 14

ICJ, *Legality of the Threat or Use of Nuclear Weapons*, Advisory Opinion, 8 July 1996, ICJ Rep. 226

ICJ, *Case Concerning Application of the Convention on the Prevention and Punishment of the Crime of Genocide (Bosnia and Herzegovina v Serbia and Montenegro)*, Judgment, 26 February 2007, ICJ Rep. 43

ICC, *Prosecutor v Thomas Lubanga Dyilo*, Judgment Pursuant to Article 74 of the Statute, 14 March 2012, Case No. ICC-01/04-01/06-2842

The District Court of The Hague, *MH17 criminal case*, Judgment, 17 November 2022, ECLI:NL:RBDHA:2022:12218

Treaties

Charter of the United Nations, opened for signature 26 June 1945 (entered into force 24 October 1945)

Fourth Geneva Convention relative to the Protection of Civilian Persons in Time of War, opened for signature 12 August 1949, 75 UNTS 287 (entered into force 21 October 1950)

Hague Convention V Respecting the Rights and Duties of Neutral Powers and Persons in Case of War on Land, opened for signature 18 October 1907 (entered into force 26 January 1910)

Hague Convention XIII Concerning the rights and Duties of Neutral Powers in Naval War, opened for signature 18 October 1907 (entered into force 26 January 1910)

Protocol Additional to the Geneva Conventions of 12 August 1949, and relating to the Protection of Victims of International Armed Conflicts, opened for signature 8 June 1977, 1125 UNTS 3 (entered into force 7 December 1978)

Protocol Additional to the Geneva Conventions of 12 August 1949, and relating to the Protection of Victims of Non-International Armed Conflicts, opened for signature 8 June 1977, 1125 UNTS 609 (entered into force 7 December 1978)

Treaty on Principles Governing the Activities of States in the Exploration and Use of Outer Space, including the Moon and Other Celestial Bodies, opened for signature 27 January 1967, 610 UNTS 205 (entered into force 10 October 1967)

Part III
Year in Review

Chapter 5
Year in Review 2023

Belén Guerrero Romero, Wamika Sachdev and Baptiste Beurrier

Contents

5.1 Armed Conflicts and Related Developments 158
    5.1.1 Armenia/Azerbaijan 161
    5.1.2 Burkina Faso 165
    5.1.3 Democratic Republic of Congo 174
    5.1.4 Israel/Palestine 178
    5.1.5 Mali 190
    5.1.6 Myanmar 194
    5.1.7 Nigeria 200
    5.1.8 Sudan 202
    5.1.9 Ukraine/Russia 209
5.2 Courts and Tribunals 222
    5.2.1 International Tribunals 222
    5.2.2 Hybrid and Regional Courts and Tribunals 233
    5.2.3 Human Rights Courts and Bodies 238
    5.2.4 National Courts 242
5.3 Arms Control and Disarmament 251
    5.3.1 Arms Trade 252
    5.3.2 Conventional Weapons 252
    5.3.3 Non-conventional Weapons 253
    5.3.4 Other Developments 256
References 258

Abstract The aim of the Year in Review is to present an overview of significant developments that occurred in 2023 with notable relevance to international humanitarian law (IHL). Firstly, the Year in Review evaluates armed hostilities that occurred throughout the year in selected states, assessing their legal classification as either

---

B. Guerrero Romero (✉)
Civitas Maxima, Geneva, Switzerland
e-mail: belen.guerreroromero@civitas-maxima.org

W. Sachdev
Project Baala, New Delhi, India

B. Beurrier
The Hague, Netherlands
e-mail: B.Beurrier@asser.nl

© T.M.C. ASSER PRESS and the authors 2025
H. Krieger et al. (eds.), *Yearbook of International Humanitarian Law, Volume 26 (2023)*,
Yearbook of International Humanitarian Law 26,
https://doi.org/10.1007/978-94-6265-663-5_5

international or non-international armed conflicts, belligerent occupation, or situations not meeting the relevant legal criteria for the application of IHL. Secondly, the Year in Review provides a summary of relevant proceedings and developments in the prosecution of serious violations of IHL, such as war crimes, before international, hybrid, and domestic courts and tribunals. Lastly, the Year in Review highlights developments in the fields of arms control and disarmament related to IHL.

Keywords International humanitarian law · Non-state armed groups · Belligerent occupation · War crimes · Investigations · Prosecutions · Universal jurisdiction · Courts and tribunals · Arms control · Disarmament · Conventional weapons · Unconventional weapons · Outer space · Cyberspace · Strategic litigation

5.1 Armed Conflicts and Related Developments

The year 2023 saw the beginning and continuation of ongoing armed violence, belligerent occupation, peace talks, and other related developments. The purpose of this section is to review armed hostilities in new international and non-international armed conflicts as well as in those that saw significant developments in 2023. Specifically, it will organize IHL-related developments under the relevant state(s) involved and overview the classification of the armed hostilities at issue as international armed conflicts (IACs), including belligerent occupation, or non-international armed conflicts (NIACs). It is important to acknowledge that the legal classification of armed conflicts can be subjected to debate and may evolve. Therefore, the conflict classifications presented in this section should not be regarded as absolute assertions, but rather as conclusions drawn on the basis of currently available information.

In line with previous Year in Reviews, this section substantiates its assessments of the various conflicts using relevant news sources (both local and international), reports of international organisations and non-governmental organisations (NGOs), as well as academic commentaries where relevant. Whenever possible, priority has been given to open-access resources to ensure that the Year in Review can serve as a valuable tool for additional research.

The first type of armed conflicts overviewed in this review are IACs, which are triggered when one or more states have recourse to armed force in situations of "declared war or of any other armed conflict (…), even if the state of war is not recognized by one of them", in accordance with Common Article 2 to the four 1949 Geneva Conventions (GCs).[1] The threshold of violence necessary to trigger an IAC,

---

[1] Geneva Convention for the Amelioration of the Condition of the Wounded and Sick in Armed Forces in the Field, 75 UNTS 31, opened for signature 12 August 1949 (entered into force 21 October 1950) (GCI); Geneva Convention for the Amelioration of the Condition of Wounded, Sick and Shipwrecked Members of Armed Forces at Sea, 75 UNTS 85, opened for signature 12 August 1949 (entered into force 21 October 1950) (GCII); Geneva Convention relative to the Treatment of Prisoners of War, 75 UNTS 135, opened for signature 12 August 1949 (entered into force 21 October 1950) (GCIII); Geneva Convention relative to the Protection of Civilian Persons in Time

5 Year in Review 2023

as opposed to NIACs, is considerably low, involving any form of unilateral and intentional resort to armed force against another state, "even if the latter does not or cannot respond by military means".[2]

It is controversial whether the resort to armed force by a State against a non-State armed group (NSAG) on the territory of another state whose consent has not been obtained triggers an IAC between the two States. Consistent with previous issues, this Year in Review follows the approach of the International Committee of the Red Cross (ICRC) and considers that such a breach of the latter state's sovereignty triggers an IAC between both States.[3] Other situations can also trigger an IAC, including when a State exercises the requisite level of control over a NSAG which, in turn, engages in armed violence with another State. It remains controversial whether such level of control should be 'overall', as submitted by the ICRC[4] and the International Criminal Tribunal for the former Yugoslavia (ICTY) in *Tadić*,[5] or 'effective', as stated by the International Court of Justice (ICJ) in the *Nicaragua* case.[6] This Year in Review follows the ICRC's approach and abides by the 'overall control' test.

Situations of belligerent occupation also trigger the application of IHL to IACs, including provisions unique to situations of occupation better known as the law of occupation. For a territory to be considered as occupied, it must be actually placed under the authority of a hostile army.[7] This concept has been equated with the 'effective control' test, which implies the exercise of authority by the hostile army over the territory of another State without the latter's consent, effectively impairing its exercise of authority.[8] The law of occupation applies even when situations of occupation

---

of War, 75 UNTS 287, opened for signature 12 August 1949 (entered into force 21 October 1950) (GCIV), Article 2.

[2] ICTY, *The Prosecutor v. Dusko Tadić*, Appeals Chamber, Decision on the Defence Motion for Interlocutory Appeal on Jurisdiction, 2 October 1995, Case No. IT-94-1-AR72 (*Tadić* 1995), para 70; ICRC (2016) Commentary of 2016 on GC I, Article 2: Application of the Convention. https://ihl-dat abases.icrc.org/en/ihl-treaties/gci-1949/article-2/commentary/2016#49_B. Accessed 23 May 2024.

[3] See ICRC (2020) Commentary of 2020 on Convention (III) relative to the Treatment of Prisoners of War. Article 2: Application of the Convention. https://ihl-databases.icrc.org/applic/ihl/ ihl.nsf/Comment.xsp?action=openDocument&documentId=0D46B7ADFC9E8219C1258584004 64543#_Toc42429662. Accessed 12 May 2024.

[4] ICRC (2016) Commentary on the GCs of 1949. International Committee of the Red Cross. https://ihl-databases.icrc.org/en/ihl-treaties/gci-1949/toc/commentary/2016?activeTab=und efined. Accessed 30 June 2024, paras 271–273.

[5] ICTY, *Prosecutor v. Dusko Tadić*, Judgement, 15 July 1999, IT-94-1-A (*Tadić* 1999), paras 115–144.

[6] ICJ, *Case Concerning Military and Paramilitary Activities In and Against Nicaragua (Nicaragua v. United States of America)*, 27 June 1986, ICJ Rep 1986 (*Nicaragua v United States of America* 1986), para 115.

[7] See Hague Convention (IV) respecting the Laws and Customs of War on Land and its annex: Regulations concerning the Laws and Customs of War on Land (opened for signature 18 October 1907, entered into force 26 January 1910) U.S.T.S. 539, 2 A.J.I.L. Supp. 90, Annex to the Convention ('*Hague Regulations*'), Article 42.

[8] Rule of Law in Armed Conflicts (RULAC) Project, Geneva Academy of International Humanitarian Law and Human Rights (2023) Military occupation. https://www.rulac.org/classification/mil itary-occupations#collapse1accord. Accessed 30 June 2024.

are met with no armed resistance, and also to cases in which the status of the occupied territory is unclear, as long as the hostile army was not the rightful sovereign over the occupied territory at the start of the conflict.[9] The law of occupation ceases to apply when the hostile army no longer meets the 'effective control' test.[10] However, according to the theory of functional occupation abided by the ICRC, if the hostile army continues to retain some key elements of authority, it can be considered that the law of occupation still applies within the territorial and functional extent of that authority, even if the foreign forces are no longer physically present.[11]

For their part, NIACs occur when at least one side of the belligerent parties to an armed conflict exclusively involves one or more NSAGs. That basically includes two types of conflicts, namely conflicts involving state(s) against NSAG(s) and conflicts between two or more NSAGs. For a NIAC to be triggered in accordance with Common Article 3 to the 1949 GCs, two conditions need to be met: the NSAGs involved must be sufficiently 'organised' and armed violence between warring parties must reach a sufficient degree of intensity.[12] These requirements must be assessed on a case-by-case basis. Criteria that suggest that a NSAG is organized enough to "cause violence that is of humanitarian concern" and partake in a NIAC include, *inter alia*, the presence of some kind of command structure, the existence of internal disciplinary mechanisms, the ability to speak with one voice, to participate in the negotiation of agreements, to plan, coordinate and carry out military operations, or to engage in protracted armed violence.[13] Considerations relevant to establishing whether the required level of intensity to trigger a NIAC has been met include, among others, the number, duration, and intensity of individual confrontations, the type of military equipment and weapons used, the number of casualties and the extent of material destruction, the number of civilians fleeing the zone of hostilities, or the number of persons and types of forces partaking in the fighting.[14]

---

[9] ICRC (2016) Commentary on the GCs of 1949. International Committee of the Red Cross. https://ihl-databases.icrc.org/en/ihl-treaties/gci-1949/toc/commentary/2016?activeTab=und efined. Accessed 30 June 2024, paras 323 ff; ICJ, *Legal Consequences of the Construction of a Wall in the Occupied Palestinian Territory*, Advisory Opinion, 9 July 2004, ICJ Rep 2004, para 95.

[10] Protocol Additional to the Geneva Conventions of 12 August 1949, and relating to the Protection of Victims of International Armed Conflicts, 1125 UNTS 3 (opened for signature 8 June 1977, entered into force 7 December 1978) (API), Article 3(b).

[11] ICRC (2016) Commentary on the GCs of 1949. International Committee of the Red Cross. https://ihl-databases.icrc.org/en/ihl-treaties/gci-1949/toc/commentary/2016?activeTab=und efined. Accessed 30 June 2024, paras 307 ff.

[12] *Tadić* 1995, para 70; ICTY, *The Prosecutor v. Ramush Haradinaj and others*, Trial Chamber, Judgement, 3 April 2008, Case No. IT-04-84-T (*Prosecutor v Haradinaj and others* 2008), para 60; ICRC (2021) Why Engaging with Non-State Armed Groups? https://www.icrc.org/en/document/why-engaging-non-state-armed-groups. Accessed 25 May 2024.

[13] *Prosecutor v Haradinaj and others* 2008, para 60.

[14] ICTY, *The Prosecutor v. Ljube Boškoski and Johan Tarčulovski*, Trial Chamber, Judgement, 10 July 2008, Case No. IT-04-82-T, para 177.

The protections afforded under Additional Protocol II to the four 1949 GCs ('APII') apply only when several cumulative conditions are met. On the one hand, the State partaking in the armed conflict needs to be a party to the Protocol, and the armed conflict must take place within its territory. On the other hand, the forces of the NSAG(s) must act under responsible command and exercise a level of control over the State's territory that enables them to "carry out sustained and concerted military operations", as well as to implement APII.[15]

The law of IACs generally ceases to apply on the 'general close of military operations',[16] which include any hostile troop movements regardless of whether they involve actual hostilities. As formerly stated above, the law of occupation represents one of the exceptions to this rule. For its part, the law of NIACs generally becomes inapplicable at the 'end of the armed conflict'.[17] While the ICTY required the existence of a 'peaceful settlement' to the conflict to establish such end,[18] many scholars consider that a 'general close of military operation' suffice.[19]

5.1.1 Armenia/Azerbaijan

Developments happening in Nagorno-Karabakh in 2023 constitute an important change from last year's situation.

The fragile 2020 Russian-backed ceasefire agreement between Azerbaijan and Armenia did not hold. In September 2022, nearly 200 Armenian soldiers and 80 Azerbaijani soldiers were killed in an Azerbaijani military operation in Armenia.[20] While it is true that Armenia and Azerbaijan are fighting, therefore leading to the application of the law of IAC to govern their conduct, the Statute of the *Republic of Artsakh* remain a difficult but key point in the application of IHL.

---

[15] Protocol Additional to the Geneva Conventions of 12 August 1949, and relating to the Protection of Victims of Non-International Armed Conflicts, opened for signature 8 June 1977, 1125 UNTS 609 (entered into force 7 December 1978) (APII), Article 1(1).

[16] GCIV, above n 1, Article 6(2) and (3); API, Article 3(b).

[17] APII, above n 15, Article 2(2).

[18] *Tadić* 1999, above note 5, para 70.

[19] Sassòli M (2024) International Humanitarian Law: Rules, Controversies, and Solutions to Problems Arising in Warfare (Edward Elgar, Cheltenham), p. 211.

[20] De Waal T (2022) More Storm Clouds Gather Over Armenia, Azerbaijan. https://carnegieendowment.org/europe/strategic-europe/2022/09/more-storm-clouds-gather-over-armenia-azerbaijan?lang=en&center=europe. Accessed 9 June 2024.

For the purpose of this work, this review adopts the same view as the previous Year in Review. Namely, Armenian forces were present in Nagorno-Karabakh without Azerbaijan's consent, and the Armenian forces established their own authority through the separatist forces, i.e., the Republic of Artsakh.

The Artsakh forces were originally formed in 1992 to defend the region against Azerbaijan's military operations, and was formally distinct from Armenian forces. Nevertheless, as highlighted in the previous Year in Review, and despite the lack of information on "the functioning of armed groups of Nagorno-Karabakh" persisting in 2023, this review submitted that the separatist forces, being cited as "Armenia-backed" and the de facto army of Armenia, were indeed in overall control by Armenia and thus still occupying certain areas. In 2020, evidence of Armenia's overall control was the connection between the Armenian armed forces and those of the Republic of Artsakh. Before the outbreak of the war in 2020, the Armenian occupation of Azerbaijan was called upon by the General Assembly and the Security Council.

As such, the developments of 2023 happened within an ongoing IAC. Fighting between the two States resumed in February, during which Armenian and Artsakh forces fired in the direction of Azerbaijani positions.

5.1.1.1 Azerbaijan's Blockade

2023 started with the blockade by Azerbaijan of the Lachin Corridor, the only road connecting Armenia to Nagorno-Karabakh. Blocking the sole road connecting the region to Armenia had grave consequences for the Nagorno-Karabakh inhabitants. Azerbaijan banned all humanitarian transportation from entering the region.[21] Food-stuff was not allowed to enter the region, resulting in starvation, which is banned as a method of warfare under IHL customary international law.[22] The cut in gas supplies also caused the dysfunction of schools and hospitals. Additionally, medical patients transported by the Red Cross were prevented from leaving the region in order to receive medical treatment.[23] Finally, robbing civilians of their right to free passage violated the GCIV and API.[24] On 23 April 2023, Azerbaijan opened a checkpoint on the highway, which closed days later. Azerbaijan agreed to reopen the corridor

---

[21] France 24 (2023) Azerbaijan closes only road linking breakaway Nagorno-Karabakh region to Armenia. https://www.france24.com/en/europe/20230711-azerbaijan-closes-only-road-linking-breakaway-nagarno-karabakh-region-to-armenia. Accessed 9 June 2024.

[22] APII, above n 15, Article 14; ICRC Database (Undated) Customary IHL, Starvation as a Method of Warfare Rule 53. https://ihl-databases.icrc.org/en/customary-ihl/v1/rule53. Accessed 9 June 2024; Crisis Group (2023) The Nagorno-Karabakh Conflict: A Visual Explainer https://www.crisisgroup.org/content/nagorno-karabakh-conflict-visual-explainer. Accessed 9 June 2024.

[23] Radar Armenia (2023) Azerbaijan has banned all humanitarian transportation through the Lachin Corridor. https://radar.am/en/news/nagorno-karabakh-2573628899/. Accessed 9 June 2024.

[24] GCIV, above n 1, Article 23; API, above n 10, Article 18.

later that year in September—a few days before launching a military offensive in Nagorno-Karabakh, during which Azerbaijan took control of the region.

Attacks on Civilians

In March 2023, it was reported by an Armenian newspaper and the *Caucasian Knot* that Azerbaijani forces repeatedly opened fire in the direction of Artsakh civilians in the villages of Machkalashen, Taghavard, Sos, and Martakert. No casualties were reported until 12 April, when Azerbaijani servicemen shot and killed an employee of the Zangezur Copper-Molybdenum Combine in Shgharshik, Syunik region.[25] Shots were fired towards Nagorno-Karabakh civilians, spanning from January to September, totalising around 60 attacks.[26] No casualties were recorded. Close to the 19 September Azerbaijani offensive, one civilian was wounded after the Azerbaijani forces targeted a water truck near Chankatagh in the Martakert region with HAN-17 grenade launchers.

The 19 September military incursion constitutes an escalation in the 2023 hostilities. Several attacks were reported. Azerbaijani forces shelled Shushikend, Shusha, Khnatsakh and Sarnaghbyur, wounding at least twenty civilians, killing six civilians, including three children, and capturing four.[27] The next days, it was reported that Azerbaijani forces shelled an ambulance car, wounding its driver, and, in a different event, killed a civilian in Hartek.[28]

The summer has been marked by an increasing number of armed clashes between parties. While hostilities between Azerbaijan and Armenia forces across the year did not incur major casualties, September marked a concrete change in the clash between parties. Azerbaijani forces fired shots 321 times at Armenian and Artsakh forces between early May and the end of September, while Armenian and Artsakh forces fired shots 342 times during the same period.[29]

In March 2023, Azerbaijan's military multiplied its offensive towards Artsakh forces. Azerbaijani forces opened fire in Martakaret, Martuni, Askeran, Gegharkunik, and Syunik regions. On 5 March, a subversive group of the Azerbaijani armed forces shot at the car belonging to the Police forces of Artsakh that were transferring the members of the passport and visa department at the location called Khaipalu near Shusha, Azerbaijan. A shootout took place as a result of which three Artsakh policemen and two Azerbaijani servicemen were killed and one Artsakh policeman was wounded.[30] Additionally, one Armenian serviceman was killed on 22 March near Yearaskh in the Ararat region.[31]

---

[25] ACLED (2024) ACLED Data Export Tool. https://acleddata.com/data-export-tool/. Accessed 22 May 2024.

[26] Ibid.

[27] Ibid.

[28] Ibid.

[29] Ibid.

[30] Ibid.

[31] Ibid.

On 11 April, Azerbaijan's forces opened fire on Armenian servicemen near the Tegh village in the Syunik region. Armenia reported four killed and six wounded servicemen, while Azerbaijan claimed that three servicemen were killed.[32] From this date until the end of September, Azerbaijani forces' fires were reported almost every two days towards Artsakh and/or Armenian forces.[33] While Azerbaijan's forces mostly relied on various caliber firearms, the military weapons used in May raised the intensity of the assaults.

On 11 May 2023, Azerbaijani forces fired with mortars and artillery in the direction of Armenian positions near Sotk in the Gegharkunik region. Azerbaijani sources reported that Armenian forces fired mortars in the direction of Azerbaijani positions. Armenian sources report that Azerbaijani forces shelled an ambulance car that was transporting wounded servicemen. Azerbaijani sources reported that Armenian forces used Iranian-made kamikaze drones to fire at Azerbaijani positions. However, the Ministry of Defense of Armenia refuted this report, stating that the Armenian military does not own such drones. The clash resulted in the death of one Azerbaijani serviceman, and four Armenian servicemen were wounded. The next day, battles resumed in Sotk. Azerbaijani forces fired with drones, mortars, and artillery in the direction of Armenian positions. Azerbaijani sources reported that Armenian forces fired mortars in the direction of Azerbaijani positions. One Azerbaijani and one Armenian serviceman were killed, and four Armenian servicemen were wounded. On 17 May 2023, Azerbaijani forces opened fire in the direction of Armenian positions near Sotk, after which they shelled an ambulance car that was transporting a wounded serviceman. One Armenian serviceman was killed, and the doctor who was in the ambulance car was wounded. Targeting medical transports is prohibited under IHL unless they are used to commit acts harmful to the enemy.[34]

However, the month of September is marked by a repeat use of artillery by the Azerbaijani forces, enabling them to claim control over Nagorno-Karabakh at the end of the month. Azerbaijani forces shelled Artsakh positions and used mortars, drones, and various calibre firearms. September constituted the peak of casualties in the year. On 19 September, Azerbaijani forces heavily shelled the Askeran region and, in the length of one week, took control of Nagorno Karabakh.

On 20 September, and according to Azerbaijani sources, Artsakh forces fired at a KAMAZ truck belonging to the Russian Peacekeeping contingent near Chankatagh—resulting in the death of one peacekeeper and wounding another. As of 27 September, Artsakh forces announced 336 fatalities, and Azerbaijani forces announced 192 fatalities.

In May, Armenian forces opened fire several times in the Tovuz, Kashatag and Shahumyan regions. While these regions were still the theatre of Armenian fights in June, the Armenian fire assault also extended to the Gadabay, Sadarak and Ordubad

---

[32] Ibid.

[33] Ibid.

[34] ICRC Database (Undated) Customary IHL, Medical Transports, Rule 53. https://ihl-databases. icrc.org/en/customary-ihl/v1/rule29. Accessed 9 June 2024. See also GCI, above n 1, Article 35; GCIV, above n 1, Article 21; AP 1, above n 10, Article 21.

regions during the same period. In June, Artsakh forces attacked several Azerbaijani positions in the Shusha region, the Martuni region, and the Askeran region. In July, they expanded their attack to the Shahumyan and Kashatagh regions, and lastly, in August, they fired at Azerbaijani positions in the Fizuli region.

Between 19 July and 11 August, the Armenian forces and the Artsakh forces did not fire a shot. During this period, it has been reported that Artsakh forces tried to install long-term fortification devices in front of the positions of Azerbaijani forces—resulting in fires shot by Azerbaijani forces towards them.

Since 11 August, the Shahumyan region witnessed several Armenian assaults. While Armenian attacks have mostly been shaped by the use of calibre firearms, on 2 September, Armenian forces fired with 60- and 82-mm mortars at Azerbaijani positions located in front of the Armenian positions near Sotk, Gegharkunik region. Similar to the Armenian forces, the Artsakh forces used artillery twice against Azerbaijan when the latter attacked the region on 19 September. Artsakh forces shelled Shusha City, killing one civilian—and the next day, fired at the same city with large calibre guns and mortars, damaging and interrupting the electricity supply.

On 21 September, Azerbaijan claimed to have regained full control of the territory.[35] Thousands of ethnic Armenians fled the Nagorno-Karabakh region to Armenia, to the extent that the United Nations (UN) Karabakh mission said that this exodus means as few as 50 ethnic Armenians remained.[36] Azerbaijan's control of the region constituted the beginning of a decreasing number of attacks between Armenia and Azerbaijan. It also marked the start of peace talks at the year's end. The end of hostilities by the end of the year leaned towards the end of the conflict between the two States.

5.1.2 Burkina Faso

For years, the Central Sahel Region—comprising Mali (see Sect. 5.1.5), Burkina Faso and Niger—has been engulfed in prolonged armed conflicts involving various States, transnational entities, NSAGs, self-defence groups and ethnic militias. This violence has also spread, albeit to a lesser extent, to the northern regions of Benin, Togo, Ghana, and Côte d'Ivoire.[37] Burkina Faso has been home to different (potential) NIACs since 2015, when the NIACs confronting neighbouring Mali with NSAGs affiliated with

---

[35] AP News (2023) Azerbaijan claims full control of breakaway region and holds initial talks with ethnic Armenians. https://apnews.com/article/azerbaijan-armenia-explosions-nagorno-karabakh-russia-2964483a95121dfdccd0e6e4d220fb12. Accessed 10 June 2024.

[36] BBC (2023) Nagorno-Karabakh: Thousands flee as Armenia says ethnic cleansing under way. https://www.bbc.com/news/world-europe-66905581. Accessed 10 June 2023; UN News (2023) UN Karabakh mission told 'sudden' exodus means as few as 50 ethnic Armenians may remain. https://news.un.org/en/story/2023/10/1141782#:~:text=. Accessed 10 June 2023.

[37] Amnesty International (2023) Burkina Faso: "Death was slowly creeping on us": Living under siege in Burkina Faso. https://www.amnesty.org/en/documents/afr60/7209/2023/en/. Accessed 8 May 2024.

the Islamic State (IS) and al-Qaeda since 2012 spilled over into Burkinabe territory.[38] In Burkina Faso, the most active NSAGs are Jama'at Nasr al-Islam wal Muslimin (JNIM), associated with al-Qaeda, and the Islamic State Sahel Province (IS Sahel), linked to the IS. These groups operate across the entire Central Sahelian region, which adds a layer of complexity to the anti-Jihadi fight due to their transnational reach and operations.

In 2023, Burkina Faso has replaced Mali as the primary hotspot of the Jihadist crisis in Central Sahel, following the surge in violence in Burkinabe territory since 2019.[39] The year was characterized by numerous offensives initiated by interim President Ibrahim Traoré, countered by robust NSAGs counter-operations. As a result, in many regions across Burkina Faso, power often shifted between Jihadist groups and the state.[40] Fatalities linked to acts of political violence surpassed 8000 in 2023, doubling those of 2022 and positioning Burkina Faso second in West Africa only after Nigeria.[41] During 2023, NSAGs like JNIM and IS Sahel exerted control over at least 35% and as much as 60% of the Burkinabe territory, particularly in the countryside, and besieged more than 40 locations nationwide—approximately affecting one million persons.[42] NSAGs not only engaged in violence against the State, but also sporadically against each other.[43] There were reports of localized détentes being agreed to by JNIM and IS Sahel in different parts of Central Sahel in 2023, raising concerns over the creation of 'terrorist sanctuaries'.[44] In Burkina Faso, no clashes between JNIM and IS Sahel have been registered since October 2023.[45]

---

[38] See Rule of Law in Armed Conflicts project (RULAC) (2023) Non-International Armed Conflicts in Burkina Faso. https://www.rulac.org/browse/conflicts/non-international-armed-conflicts-in-bur kina-faso#collapse1accord. Accessed 28 May 2024.

[39] International Institute for Strategic Studies (IISS) 2023, p. 172.

[40] Ibid., pp. 173–174.

[41] ACLED (2024) Conflict Watchlist 2024: Sahel. https://acleddata.com/conflict-watchlist-2024/ sahel/. Accessed 8 May 2024.

[42] Human Rights Watch (2024) Country chapter: Burkina Faso. https://www.hrw.org/world-report/ 2024/country-chapters/burkina-faso. Accessed 8 May 2024; International Rescue Committee (IRC) Crisis in Burkina Faso: What you need to know and how you can help. https://www.rescue.org/ eu/article/crisis-burkina-faso-what-you-need-know-and-how-you-can-help. Accessed 8 May 2024; Amnesty International (2023) Burkina Faso: "Death was slowly creeping on us": Living under siege in Burkina Faso. https://www.amnesty.org/en/documents/afr60/7209/2023/en/. Accessed 8 May 2024.

[43] Rule of Law in Armed Conflicts project (RULAC) (2023) Non-International Armed Conflicts in Burkina Faso. https://www.rulac.org/browse/conflicts/non-international-armed-conflicts-in-bur kina-faso#collapse1accord. Accessed 28 May 2024. Considering that clashes between JNIM and IS Sahel as well as between JNIM and Islamic State West African Province constitute NIACs.

[44] See UN Security Council (2024) Eighteenth report of the Secretary-General on the threat posed by ISIL (Da'esh) to international peace and security and the range of United Nations efforts in support of Member States in countering the threat, UN Doc. S/2024/117, para 23; Institute for the Study of War (2023) Salafi-Jihadi Movement Weekly Update: December 1, 2023. https://www.unders tandingwar.org/backgrounder/salafi-jihadi-movement-weekly-update-december-1-2023. Accessed 8 May 2024.

[45] Calculations based on ACLED (2024) ACLED Data Export Tool. https://acleddata.com/data-exp ort-tool/. Accessed 22 May 2024.

5 Year in Review 2023

For space considerations, this Year in Review will exclusively focus on developments pertaining to the two conflicts that were most active during 2023, namely those featuring Burkinabe forces against JNIM and IS Sahel, respectively. Previous Year in Reviews determined that a NIAC existed between Burkina Faso and JNIM, whereas it was deemed inconclusive that IS Sahel met the necessary level of organization to trigger a NIAC with Burkinabe forces. This section will additionally provide an overview of political developments relevant to the progression of the aforementioned NIACs.

5.1.2.1 Relevant Political Developments in Burkina Faso

The ascension to power of Captain Ibrahim Traoré in September 2022, after the second coup d'état witnessed in Burkina Faso that year, had profound implications for the trajectory of the NIACs over 2023.[46] Initially, in January 2023, Traoré gave a one month-notice of withdrawal to French military troops, who had been assisting the government in the fight against NSAGs under *Operation Sabre*.[47] This move was widely interpreted as part of a broader shift among coup governments in Central Sahel to distance themselves from Western powers and strengthen ties with Russia.[48] Reports emerged in November indicating the deployment of 20 Russian soldiers to protect the President and support the anti-jihadist fight. Likewise, it has been suggested that a military base for Russian troops is under construction since December 2023.[49]

In December 2023, Burkina Faso, alongside Niger, made the decision to partially sever ties with other Sahelian States by withdrawing from the Group of Five for the Sahel (G5 Sahel), an alliance created in 2014 to promote development and security in Central Sahel, Mali and Mauritania.[50] This move mirrored the action taken by

---

[46] European Parliament 2022.

[47] Reuters (2023) Burkina Faso confirms end of military accord with France. https://www.reuters.com/world/africa/burkina-faso-confirms-end-military-accord-with-france-2023-01-23/. Accessed 8 May 2024; Le Monde (2023) Opération Sabre au Burkina Faso: d'une arrivée discrète à une fin amère. https://www.lemonde.fr/afrique/article/2023/02/21/operation-sabre-au-burkina-faso-d-une-arrivee-discrete-a-une-fin-amere_6162704_3212.html. Accessed 8 May 2024.

[48] IISS 2023, p. 174.

[49] Le Monde (2023) Le Burkina Faso resserre son alliance avec la Russie. https://www.lemonde.fr/afrique/article/2023/11/15/le-burkina-faso-resserre-son-alliance-avec-la-russie_6200216_3212.html. Accessed 8 May 2024; Olivier M and Roger B (2023) En Afrique, Poutine reprend la main sur Wagner, orphelin de Prigojine. Jeune Afrique. https://www.jeuneafrique.com/1515879/politique/en-afrique-poutine-reprend-la-main-sur-wagner-orphelin-de-prigojine/. Accessed 8 May 2024.

[50] Burkina 24 (2023) Le Burkina Faso et le Niger se retirent du G5 Sahel et de la Force conjointe. https://burkina24.com/2023/12/02/le-burkina-faso-et-le-niger-se-retirent-du-g5-sahel-et-de-la-force-conjointe/. Accessed 8 May 2024; Convention Portant Creation du G5 Sahel, Burkina Faso, Mali Niger, Mauritania, Chad, opened for signature 19 December 2014; Desgrais N (2018) La Force conjointe du G5 Sahel ou l'émergence d'une architecture de défense collective propre au Sahel [The G5 Sahel Joint Force or the emergence of a collective defense architecture specific to the Sahel]. Les Champs de Mars: 30 + Supplément.1: 211–220.

Malian authorities in May 2022, which marked a stalemate in operations of the G5 Sahel Joint Force.[51] Established in 2017 with 5000 police, military and civilian effectives, the Joint Force aimed at combatting jihadism, amongst other locations, in the tri-border area between Burkina Faso, Mali and Niger.[52]

The three junta-led governments had established in September 2023 the Alliance of Sahel States under the Liptako-Gourma charter.[53] This treaty committed them to mutual defence in the event of an attack, as well as to cooperation in the prevention of and fight against armed rebellions.[54] The intervention of third States in support of the Burkinabe government and to the detriment of the NSAGs operating in Burkina Faso does not change the classification of the existing NIAC, given that the third States at issue would be operating alongside the government with its consent.

The last major change implemented by Interim President Traoré pertained to the greater relevance given to the institution of the Volunteers for the Defense of the Homeland (VDPs), initially created in 2020 to undertake self-defence duties at the village level.[55] Authorities mobilised from 30,000 to 60,000 VDPs since Traore's assumption of power through several nationwide rounds of mass recruitment. In 2023, VDPs were present in 10 out of 13 regions, primarily deployed in urban areas.[56] Following a modification of the legislation governing VDPs in December 2022, the latter could during 2023 operate either at the commune level—encompassing a broader area than the formerly envisioned village level—or nationwide.[57] National VDPs were described by Traoré as "practically soldiers", as they are integrated with army forces in mixed battalions, act under the latter's orders, and receive the same equipment. All VDPs are trained and paid by the State. In light of the close relationship between the army forces and VDPs, this Year in Review considers VDPs,

---

[51] Africanews (2022) Mali withdraws from the regional anti-jihadist force G5 Sahel. https://www.africanews.com/2022/05/16/mali-withdraws-from-the-regional-anti-jihadist-force-g5-sahel/. Accessed 8 May 2024.

[52] G5 Sahel (2017) Résolutions de la Force Conjointe du G5 Sahel [Resolutions of the G5 Sahel Joint Force]. https://www.g5sahel.org/wp-content/uploads/2017/04/images_Docs_Resolutions_force_c onjointe__05_02_20171.pdf. Accessed 8 May 2024; African Union Peace and Security Council (2017) Communiqué, Doc. PSC/PR/COMM(DCLXXIX).

[53] *See* Charte du Liptako-Gourma instituant l'Alliance des États du Sahel entre le Burkina Faso, la République du Mali, la République du Niger, opened for signature 16 September 2023.

[54] Ibid., Articles 5 and 6.

[55] Loi N°002-2020/AN portant institution de volontaires pour la défense de la patrie, adopted by the National Assembly of Burkina Faso on 21 January 2020 [Law No. 002-2020/AN instituting volunteers for the defense of the homeland, adopted by the National Assembly of Burkina Faso on 21 January 2020]; International Crisis Group (2023) Armer les civils au prix de la cohésion sociale [Arming civilians at the expense of social cohesion]. https://www.crisisgroup.org/africa/sahel/bur kina-faso/burkina-faso/313-armer-les-civils-au-prix-de-la-cohesion-sociale. Accessed 8 May 2024.

[56] Ibid.

[57] Amnesty International (2023) Burkina Faso: "Death was slowly creeping on us": Living under siege in Burkina Faso. https://www.amnesty.org/en/documents/afr60/7209/2023/en/. Accessed 8 May 2024; International Crisis Group 2023, above n 55.

or at least the national ones, as part of the State party's forces in the NIACs against Jihadist NSAGs.[58]

VDPs have been accused of committing serious violations of IHL with impunity against Fulani civilians, who are protected under Common Article 3. Fulani individuals are associated in the Burkinabe common imaginary with jihadist groups, as the latter's main leaders and most of their ranks tend to be ethnically Fulani.[59] Particularly relevant was the massacre allegedly committed by VDPs and regular armed forces in April 2023 in the town of Karma and its surroundings, where 136 civilians were reportedly killed on suspicion of collaborating with JNIM in a matter of hours.[60] It is remarkable that many attacks against civilians or State forces and VDPs remain unattributable. In this regard, in early November, the Centre-North region witnesses the burning down of many properties, as well as the killing of at least 70 and as many as 100 civilians by unknown perpetrators.[61]

Jama'at Nasr al-Islam wal Muslimin (JNIM)

Organization of the Group

JNIM emerged as the Sahelian branch of al-Qaeda following the merger of Salafijihadist groups Ansar Dine, al-Qaeda in the Islamic Maghreb's Sahara region, al-Murabitun, and Katiba Macina in March 2017. Despite certain differences between the subgroups, JNIM has evolved overtime from a loose business-like coalition of NSAGs to a unified and cohesive entity.[62] While JNIM's influence used to be confined to northern and central Mali, it has expanded over the last years through the west and south of Mali, most regions in Burkina Faso, some areas in Niger, and the north of Benin, Ghana, Ivory Coast and Togo.[63] Currently, JNIM is the most notable NSAG in the Sahelian conflict, including Burkina Faso, where it has unofficially absorbed the

---

[58] The same conclusion is reached by Amnesty International in Amnesty International (2023) Burkina Faso: "Death was slowly creeping on us": Living under siege in Burkina Faso. https://www.amnesty.org/en/documents/afr60/7209/2023/en/. Accessed 8 May 2024.

[59] International Crisis Group 2023, above n 55.

[60] International Crisis Group (2023) CrisisWatch Database: Burkina Faso. https://www.crisisgroup.org/crisiswatch/database?location%5B0%5D=21&created=&page=1. Accessed 8 May 2024; ACLED (2024) Actor Profile: Volunteers for the Defense of the Homeland (VDP). https://acleddata.com/2024/03/26/actor-profile-volunteers-for-the-defense-of-the-homeland-vdp/. Accessed 8 May 2024.

[61] Office of the United Nations High Commissioner for Human Rights (OHCHR) (2023) Burkina Faso: Killing of civilians. https://www.ohchr.org/en/statements/2023/11/burkina-faso-killing-civilians#:~:text=The%20authorities%20have%20confirmed%20at,villagers%20to%20flee%20the%20area. Accessed 8 May 2024.

[62] ACLED (2023) Actor Profile: Jama'at Nusrat al-Islam wal Muslimin (JNIM). https://acleddata.com/2023/11/13/actor-profile-jamaat-nusrat-al-islam-wal-muslimin-jnim/. Accessed 8 May 2024; Global Initiative against Transnational Crime (2022) JNIM in Burkina Faso: A strategic criminal actor. https://globalinitiative.net/wp-content/uploads/2022/08/Burkina-Faso-JNIM-29-Aug-web.pdf. Accessed 10 May 2024.

[63] ACLED (2023) Actor Profile: Jama'at Nusrat al-Islam wal Muslimin (JNIM). https://acleddata.com/2023/11/13/actor-profile-jamaat-nusrat-al-islam-wal-muslimin-jnim/. Accessed 8 May 2024.

primary locally based NSAG, Ansaroul Islam.[64] Although the majority of JNIM's members are of Fulani ethnicity, this group welcomes in its ranks militants from various ethnic backgrounds.

JNIM's objective is to establish its own form of Islamist governance and operates under the leadership of Iyad Ag Ghaly, who also heads Ansar Dine. The NSAG functions through a hierarchical structure featuring a central leadership, regional commanders, and zone commanders.[65] JNIM operates through targeted assassinations, kidnappings, and large-scale military operations characterized by a notable use of artillery, explosives, and mortar fire.[66] It also sustains itself through various licit and illicit economic activities, such as mining, cattle theft, extorsion, fundraising, or the collection of taxes in areas under its control.[67] In these zones, JNIM also undertakes certain governance functions, such as the provision of security services, dispute resolution mechanisms, or the regulation of certain aspects of social life—including through the institutionalisation of gender segregation and dress codes.[68]

Development of Hostilities

Clashes between the Burkinabe army forces and JNIM in 2023 have been exceptionally intense, constituting the most active and widespread conflict in the year. While JNIM's areas of operation used to be concentrated in the Soum province, in 2023 JNIM was present or active in eleven out of thirteen Burkinabe regions.[69] The withdrawal of French forces significantly impacted areas where JNIM held strongholds, such as the Northern region, resulting in heightened peaks of violence.[70]

During the first two months of 2023, JNIM launched different attacks against Burkinabe forces, VDPs, and especially civilians. Particularly notable were the clashes in the East Region which led to JNIM's capture of the town of Partiaga,

---

[64] Global Initiative against Transnational Crime (2022) JNIM in Burkina Faso: A strategic criminal actor. https://globalinitiative.net/wp-content/uploads/2022/08/Burkina-Faso-JNIM-29-Aug-web.pdf. Accessed 10 May 2024.

[65] ACLED (2023) Actor Profile: Jama'at Nusrat al-Islam wal Muslimin (JNIM). https://acleddata.com/2023/11/13/actor-profile-jamaat-nusrat-al-islam-wal-muslimin-jnim/. Accessed 8 May 2024; Global Initiative against Transnational Crime (2022) JNIM in Burkina Faso: A strategic criminal actor. https://globalinitiative.net/wp-content/uploads/2022/08/Burkina-Faso-JNIM-29-Aug-web.pdf. Accessed 10 May 2024.

[66] ACLED (2023) Actor Profile: Jama'at Nusrat al-Islam wal Muslimin (JNIM). https://acleddata.com/2023/11/13/actor-profile-jamaat-nusrat-al-islam-wal-muslimin-jnim/. Accessed 8 May 2024.

[67] Ibid.

[68] Lyammouri R (2022) Centre Du Mali: Mobilisation Communautaire Armée Face À La Crise [Central Mali: Armed Community Mobilization in Response to the Crisis]. https://www.resolvenet.org/research/centre-du-mali-mobilisation-communautaire-armee-face-la-crise. Accessed 12 May 2024.

[69] International Crisis Group 2023, above n 55.

[70] IISS (2023) From Global Jihad to Local Insurgencies: the Changing Nature of Sub-Saharan Jihadis. https://www.iiss.org/publications/armed-conflict-survey/2023/from-global-jihad-to-local-insurgencies/. Accessed 12 May 2024.

reportedly killing 60 civilians and 5 VDPs, and burning down the Gendarmerie, town hall and telephone installations of the town.[71] In the subsequent months of March, April and May, Burkinabe forces and VDPs led military offensives against JNIM in the North, Center-North, East, Sahel and Boucle du Mouhoun regions, albeit results were unclear.[72]

The period ranging from June to October was marked by an important decline in Burkinabe offensives. In stark contrast, JNIM intensified its operations against State forces, VDPs and civilians. Among the deadliest incidents, JNIM attacked a civilian convoy escorted by soldiers and VDPs in the region of Center North on 26 June 2023, in which at least 31 soldiers—100 according to JNIM—3 VDPs and 40 JNIM militants died.[73] On the same day, JNIM struck positions of soldiers and VDPs in another village in the Center-North region, resulting in the death of 42 VDPs and around 50 militants.[74]

November and December witnessed an increase in offensives carried out by the Burkinabe forces and VDPs. These included multiple attacks in the Hauts-Bassins region that left 68 militants dead and prompted the resettlement of 10 villages, as well as airstrikes in the Center-North and Center-East regions, respectively killing around 40 and 60 JNIM members.[75] Notably, the area of Djibo—the capital of the Soum province in the North region, which had been subject to a blockade by JNIM for almost two years—became the site of heavy fighting after JNIM took control over a Burkinabe military base and VDPs' positions in late November. Burkinabe forces responded with airstrikes that reportedly killed more than 400 JNIM members, although non-governmental sources suggest a lower figure of around 50 militants.[76] At least 40 civilians and 22 members of the police, armed forces and VDPs also

---

[71] Africa News (2023) Burkina: At least 60 dead in Partiaga attack. https://www.africanews.com/2023/03/08/burkina-at-least-60-dead-in-partiaga-attack/. Accessed 28 June 2024; US Department of State (2023) 2023 Country Reports on Human Rights Practices: Burkina Faso. https://www.state.gov/reports/2023-country-reports-on-human-rights-practices/burkina-faso/. Accessed 28 June 2024.

[72] International Crisis Group 2023, above n 55.

[73] Ibid., ACLED (2024) ACLED Data Export Tool. https://acleddata.com/data-export-tool/. Accessed 22 May 2024.

[74] Ibid.

[75] Ibid.

[76] France 24 (2023) Armed groups carry out major attack in northern Burkina Faso, say security sources. https://www.france24.com/en/africa/20231128-armed-groups-carry-out-major-attack-in-northern-burkina-faso-say-security-sources. Accessed 28 June 2024.

perished.[77] In late December, JNIM militants took control over a Burkinabe military base in the North region, claiming the lives of at least 60 soldiers.[78]

Islamic State Sahel Province

Organization of the Group

IS Sahel is a Salafi-jihadist NSAG, which operates as the Sahelian branch of the IS. It was born in 2015 as a splinter from the Al-Qaeda affiliated group al-Mourabitoun, and it formally integrated into the IS structure as the separate Greater Sahara faction of the IS West African Province (see Sect. 5.1.7) in March 2019.[79] In 2022, IS Sahel was granted provincial status by IS, which prompted the change of its name to Islamic State Sahel Province. Like JNIM, IS Sahel hosts different ethnic groups within its ranks, with Fulani members accounting for its majority.

IS Sahel primarily operates in the Central Sahelian tri-border area along with neighbouring regions, such as the Burkinabe Sahel region, Malian Gao and Menaka regions, and Nigerien Tillabéri and Tahoua regions.[80] However, it has also sporadically engaged in violent activity in Algeria, Benin, and Nigeria.[81] IS Sahel is the dominant NSAG in Burkinabe Oudalan and Seno provinces and has varying levels of presence in other regions like Center-North, East, Boucle du Mouhoun, South-West, Center-South and Cascades.[82]

Under the leadership of the self-proclaimed emir Abu al-Bara al-Sahrawi and a range of commanders primarily deployed at the local level, IS Sahel generally operates through swarming tactics and ambushes.[83] Its increasing sophistication and rise

---

[77] Agence d'Information du Burkina (AIB) (2023) Burkina: Plus de 400 terroristes décimés à Djibo, bilan provisoire. https://www.aib.media/regions/2023/11/27/burkina-plus-de-400-terror istes-decimes-a-djibo-bilan-provisoire/. Accessed 8 May 2024; Radio France Internationale (RFI) (2023) Burkina Faso: Une attaque terroriste d'ampleur vise la ville de Djibo dans le Sahel. https://www.rfi.fr/fr/afrique/20231128-burkina-faso-une-attaque-terroriste-d-ampleur-vise-la-ville-de-djibo-dans-le-sahel. Accessed 8 May 2024.

[78] VOA News (2023) Dozens killed in week of Burkina Faso attacks: Security sources. https://www.voanews.com/a/dozens-killed-in-week-of-burkina-faso-attacks-security-sources/7419473.html. Accessed 28 June 2024.

[79] Thompson J (2021) Examining Extremism: Islamic State Greater Sahara. Center for Strategic and International Studies (CSIS). https://www.csis.org/blogs/examining-extremism/examining-ext remism-islamic-state-greater-sahara. Accessed 8 May 2024.

[80] Amnesty International (2023) Burkina Faso: "Death was slowly creeping on us": Living under siege in Burkina Faso. https://www.amnesty.org/en/documents/afr60/7209/2023/en/. Accessed 8 May 2024.

[81] ACLED (2023) Actor Profile: The Islamic State Sahel Province. https://acleddata.com/2023/01/13/actor-profile-the-islamic-state-sahel-province/. Accessed 8 May 2024.

[82] Ibid., IISS 2023, p. 175.

[83] Ibid.

in capabilities suggests aspirations of establishing a Sahelian caliphate, with quasi-administrative capitals located in the Malian Gao and Menaka regions.[84] In areas under its control, IS Sahel provides governance services to some extent, including various forms of dispute resolution, the provision of security services, the implementation of social welfare schemes, the delivery of food and medicines, and the collection of taxes.[85]

Former Year in Reviews found that it was not possible to conclude that IS Sahel fulfilled the organization criteria necessary to trigger a NIAC.[86] However, as of 2023, IS Sahel exhibits some forms of command structure and a strong operational capacity that allow the group to exercise territorial control, undertake governmental functions over important parts of Central Sahel, and engage in protracted armed violence with various States and NSAGs. Thus, at least since 2023, it seems plausible to conclude that IS Sahel was organized enough to trigger a NIAC under IHL.

Development of Hostilities

During 2023, the conflict confronting State forces and VDPs with IS Sahel was primarily confined to the Burkinabe Sahel region. The intensity of the clashes was lower than that of the conflict involving JNIM, although there were occasional peaks of violence during the year.

The period ranging from January to April 2023 was the deadliest of the year. In February, attacks perpetrated by IS Sahel against military forces, along with those carried out by JNIM, led to the highest death toll among military forces since the jihadist insurgency started in Burkina Faso in 2015.[87] Among others, on 17 February 2023, IS Sahel militants attacked the relief unit of a military detachment in Oudalan province, killing at least 51 and potentially up to 80 soldiers and capturing 5 soldiers. State forces killed from 60 to 160 militants in retaliatory airstrikes.[88] On 20 February 2023, IS Sahel attacked another military detachment in the town of Tin-Akoff in Oudalan, taking control over the base and village, as well as over many vehicles

---

[84] ACLED (2023) Actor Profile: The Islamic State Sahel Province. https://acleddata.com/2023/01/13/actor-profile-the-islamic-state-sahel-province/. Accessed 8 May 2024; US Department of State (2022) Country Reports on Terrorism 2022. https://www.state.gov/reports/country-reports-on-terrorism-2022/. Accessed 29 June 2024.

[85] Thompson J (2021) Examining Extremism: Islamic State Greater Sahara. Center for Strategic and International Studies (CSIS). https://www.csis.org/blogs/examining-extremism/examining-extremism-islamic-state-greater-sahara. Accessed 8 May 2024; International Crisis Group (2023) Sidelining Islamic State in Niger's Tillabery. https://www.crisisgroup.org/africa/sahel/niger/289-sidelining-islamic-state-nigers-tillabery. Accessed 8 May 2024; The Guardian (2019) Kalashnikovs and no-go zones: east Burkina Faso falls to militants. https://www.theguardian.com/global-development/2019/apr/22/kalashnikovs-and-no-go-zones-east-burkina-faso-falls-to-militants. Accessed 8 May 2024.

[86] See Gregoire et al. 2023, pp. 203–295; Sexton et al. 2023, pp. 193–277.

[87] International Crisis Group 2023, above n 55.

[88] US Department of State (2023) 2023 Country Reports on Human Rights Practices: Burkina Faso. https://www.state.gov/reports/2023-country-reports-on-human-rights-practices/burkina-faso/. Accessed 28 June 2024; ACLED (2024) ACLED Data Export Tool. https://acleddata.com/data-export-tool/. Accessed 22 May 2024.

and weapons.[89] At least 50 civilians and 19 soldiers and VDPs were killed, and 30 soldiers and VDPs were reported missing.

From May 2023 onwards, the conflict witnessed a general decrease in violence. In May 2023, Burkinabe military forces carried out airstrikes in Oudalan province killing at least 20 militants.[90] In July, VDPs clashed with IS Sahel in Seno, killing 13 militants and seizing 6 motorcycles.[91] IS Sahel continued allegedly perpetrating massacres against civilians, including one in an IDP camp in Seno province in September, resulting in 8 deaths, and another in October in the commune of Sampelga in Seno province, where 17 civilians were killed.[92] During the last months of 2023, the army kept launching airstrikes against IS Sahel positions in Seno and neighbouring localities in Niger in coordination with the Nigerien armed forces, notably leading to at least 10 deaths of militants on 9 November 2023.[93]

Conclusion

Various factors, such as the number and intensity of confrontations, the high number of casualties, the resources and weapons mobilized by the Burkinabe and Nigerien states to fight IS Sahel in Burkina Faso, the extent of control exercised by the group in certain parts of the Sahel region, as well as the blockades maintained in different towns and villages, suggest that violence between IS Sahel and the Burkinabe state was protracted during 2023. Therefore, it is plausible to establish the existence of a NIAC between Burkina Faso and IS Sahel at least since 2023.

5.1.3 Democratic Republic of Congo

Since 2012, rebel groups multiplied in Democratic Republic of Congo (DRC),[94] and their number is considerable. For the purpose of this study, we will focus on the armed group *March 23 Movement* (M23) and the Allied Democratic Forces (ADC). The M23 directly threatened the DRC ruling power, to the extent that they managed to seize Goma, the largest city of the North Kivu Province in the eastern region. In 2022, M23 resurfaced and, through violent attacks, seized several towns in North Kivu. In April 2022, the East African Community launched the Nairobi Peace Process to restore peace in the DRC's eastern region. As a result, M23 withdrew from occupied towns in January 2023. However, a peak of violence was still observed during that period—M23 shelled both Karton Hill and a village south of Mushaki, and the Armed

---

[89] Ibid.

[90] Ibid.

[91] Ibid.

[92] International Crisis Group 2023, above n 60.

[93] ACLED (2024) ACLED Data Export Tool. https://acleddata.com/data-export-tool/. Accessed 22 May 2024.

[94] See notably UN Security Council (2013) Resolution 2098 (2013), UN Doc. S/RES/2098, para 8 (e.g. M23, the FDLR, the ADF, the APCLS, the LRA, the National Force of Liberation (FNL)).

Forces of the DRC shelled M23 positions.[95] Violence went on until the official break of the ceasefire in October 2023. The ADF, affiliated with the IS, also operates in the North Kivu and Ituri regions. The ADF has reportedly killed thousands of civilians and hundreds of soldiers in DRC since 2014, in addition to conducting deadly attacks against civilians in Uganda.[96] The violence in North Kivu, Ituri and Mai Ndombe provinces led to the internal displacement of almost seven million people across the country in 2023—one of the most significant internal displacement crises in the world.[97]

Under the mandate of the UN Organization Stabilization Mission in the DRC (MONUSCO), the Security Council called for the creation of an Intervention Brigade composed of three infantry battalions, one artillery unit, one Special force, and one Reconnaissance company under the direct command of the MONUSCO Force Commander.[98] On 20 December, 2022, the UN Security Council passed resolution 2666, extending MONUSCO's mandate for another year and, "on an exceptional basis," renewing the mandate of its intervention brigade.

5.1.3.1 Rwanda's Involvement in the Conflict

The Rwandan military reportedly supported the M23 in 2012 and 2013. UN reports provide aerial footage, photographs, and FARDC testimony showing soldiers in Rwandan army uniforms within M23 camps in the DRC.[99] Since May 2022, as the M23 has engaged in mortar and artillery shelling, with their growing military capacity, NGOs analysed such facts as further Rwandan support.[100]

The UN expert reports illuminated the relationship between the Rwandan army and the M23 movement. On 13 June 2023, the group of Experts on the DRC addressed the Security Council, asserting that the M23 group is supported by the Rwandan Defence Force (RDF)—the Rwandan army. Despite Rwanda's denial of supporting

---

[95] ACLED (2024) ACLED Data Export Tool. https://acleddata.com/data-export-tool/. Accessed 22 May 2024.

[96] TV5 Monde (2023) Qui sont les rebelles ADF alliés à l'EI qui sèment la terreur en Afrique centrale ? [Who are the ADF rebels allied with the EI who are sowing terror in Central Africa?]. https://information.tv5monde.com/afrique/qui-sont-les-rebelles-adf-allies-lei-qui-sement-la-terreur-en-afrique-centrale-2649263. Accessed 22 June 2024.

[97] International Organisation for Migration (2023) Record High Displacement in DRC at Nearly 7 Million. https://www.iom.int/news/record-high-displacement-drc-nearly-7-million. Accessed 23 June 2024.

[98] UN Security Council (2013) Resolution 2098 (2013), UN Doc. S/RES/2098, para 12(b).

[99] UN Security Council (2022) Letter dated 16 December 2022 from the Group of Experts on the Democratic Republic of the Congo addressed to the President of the Security Council, UN Doc. S/2022/967, pp. 11–12.

[100] See notably HRW (2022) DR Congo: Resurgent M23. https://www.hrw.org/news/2022/07/25/dr-congo-resurgent-m23-rebels-target-civilians. Accessed 22 June 2024; ACLED (2023) Actor Profile: The March 23 Movement (M23). https://acleddata.com/2023/03/23/actor-profile-m23-drc/. Accessed 22 June 2024.

the M23, the group of experts found evidence of direct interventions and troop reinforcements by the RDF in Massi, Rutshuru and Nyiarango territories.[101] This finding is to be added to the ones of the previous letter issued in June, in which the expert reported that "the objective of the RDF military actions on the Democratic Republic of the Congo territory [...] was to reinforce M23 by providing troops and materiel and to use them to secure control over mine sites, gain political influence in the Democratic Republic of the Congo and decimate FDLR."[102] To date, the information gathered on their relationship leans more towards two entities fighting alongside than one unique command structure.

In October 2023, UN Special Envoy to the Great Lakes Region Xia Huang cautioned that rising tensions between the two countries might escalate into an open military conflict. The UN Special envoy highlighted his concerns about the military buildup in both countries, the lack of direct, high-level dialogue, and the ongoing hate speech.[103] By late November 2023, the two nations agreed to a US-mediated pact to mutually reduce military presence near the border, curb hate speech, and avoid actions to influence each other's political systems.

5.1.3.2   The M23 Movement

The M23 movement is equipped with tactical material. It has been reported that the armed group can conduct an attack against the armed forces of the DRC (FARDC) at night and to attack from long range.[104] The armed group also benefits from the Rwandan Army's expertise and sees its faction reinforced by trained militaries leaving the FARDC to join them.[105] In March, M23 fired a bomb in Masisi, North Kivu, killing several civilians.[106] In October and November, M23 shelled FARDC positions, most notably dropping bombs in the ceasefire zone of the FARDC in the Buhumba Groupement.[107] The RDC army used heavy weaponry against both the M23 and the ADF in 2023.

---

[101] UN Security Council (2023) Letter dated 13 June 2023 from the Group of Experts on the Democratic Republic of the Congo addressed to the President of the Security Council, UN Doc. S/2023/431, paras 55–61.

[102] Ibid., para 60.

[103] UN Security Council (2023) Implementation of the Peace, Security and Cooperation Framework for the Democratic Republic of the Congo and the Region, UN Doc. S/2023/730.

[104] The Conversation (2023) M23: Four things you should know about the rebel group's campaign in Rwanda-DRC conflict. https://theconversation.com/m23-four-things-you-should-know-about-the-rebel-groups-campaign-in-rwanda-drc-conflict-195020. Accessed 20 June 2024.

[105] ChimpReports (2023) DRC Army Colonels Defect to M23 Movement. https://chimpreports.com/drc-army-colonels-defect-to-m23-movement/. Accessed 20 June 2024.

[106] ACLED (2024) ACLED Data Export Tool. https://acleddata.com/data-export-tool/. Accessed 22 May 2024.

[107] Ibid.

In March, M23 fired a bomb in Masisi, North Kivu, killing several civilians.[108] In October and November, M23 shelled FARDC positions, most notably dropping bombs in the ceasefire zone of the FARDC in the Buhumba Groupement.[109] The RDC army used heavy weaponry against the M23 and the ADF in 2023. ACLED reported that the fights between the FARDC and the M23 movement also affected civilians—looting and property destruction activity being a central aspect of the report published in 2022 and 2023.[110] Civilian objects are protected as long as they do not constitute military objectives. Parties, either to an IAC or NIAC, must make a "careful assessment" of the nature of the object, as it cannot automatically be assumed that any object that appears dubious may constitute a lawful target.[111] Pillage is forbidden in both international and internal conflicts by the GCs and their Additional Protocols, as well as by customary IHL.[112] Lately, the M23 movement found alliances with political figures in DRC and Kenya by creating a new political-military platform named *Congo River Alliance*.[113] On the other hand, the DRC concluded a military alliance with South Africa, which deployed 2900 foot soldiers on the territory of the DRC to fight against the M23 movement in December 2023.[114]

5.1.3.3 The Allied Democratic Forces

Not much information has been disclosed on this group in the past few years, rendering any assessment of their organisation difficult. It has been reported that the ADF is the deadliest threat to civilians in the DRC, causing over 1000 reported deaths in 2023.[115] On 18 April 2023, ADF clashed against FARDC in Samboko (Beni, Nord-Kivu) after ADF killed and abducted civilians in the same area earlier that day.[116] Two days later, FARDC clashed with ADF on the Butembo-Karuruma road, coded to Karuruma (Beni, Nord-Kivu), as ADF was trying to ambush civilians.

---

[108] Ibid.

[109] Ibid.

[110] ACLED (2023) Actor Profile: The March 23 Movement (M23). https://acleddata.com/2023/03/23/actor-profile-m23-drc/. Accessed 22 June 2024.

[111] ICRC Database (Undated) Customary IHL, Civilian Objects' Loss of Protection from Attack, Rule 10. https://ihl-databases.icrc.org/en/customary-ihl/v1/rule10. Accessed 21 June 2024.

[112] ICRC Database (Undated) Customary IHL, Pillage, Rule 52. https://ihl-databases.icrc.org/en/customary-ihl/v1/rule52. Accessed 21 June 2024.

[113] Reuters (2023) Congo recalls envoys to Kenya and Tanzania over alliance launch in Nairobi. https://www.reuters.com/world/africa/congo-recalls-envoys-kenya-tanzania-over-alliance-launch-nairobi-2023-12-16/. Accessed 22 June 2024.

[114] Anadolu Ajansi (2024) 2 South African soldiers killed, 20 injured in DR Congo. https://www.aa.com.tr/en/africa/2-south-african-soldiers-killed-20-injured-in-dr-congo/3258931. Accessed 21 June 2024.

[115] ACLED (2024) Conflict Watchlist 2024: DRC. https://acleddata.com/conflict-watchlist-2024/drc/. Accessed 22 June 2024.

[116] ACLED (2024) ACLED Data Export Tool. https://acleddata.com/data-export-tool/. Accessed 22 May 2024.

Casualties are unknown.[117] Again, on 1 June 2023, ADF clashed with FARDC in Lumalisa (Mambasa, Ituri), as FARDC averted an attack by ADF on the village. Casualties remain unknown. ADF attacks on civilians also marked the end of the year. On 12 November 2023, ADF clashed with FARDC in Kitshanga, near Nobili (Beni, Nord-Kivu), as ADF assaulted the village. ADF elements and civilians were killed. A few abductees were liberated the next day. Civil society claimed a new toll of 42 deaths a week after the incident.[118]

5.1.4 Israel/Palestine

The year 2023 witnessed the greatest peak in hostilities between Gaza-based armed groups and Israel in history, turning 2023 into the most violent year for both Israel and Palestine in recent decades.[119] Hostilities between the aforementioned contingents that broke out on 7 October 2023, when Hamas launched a multi-stage attack against Israel that triggered a fierce counteroffensive, will be separately addressed in Sect. 5.1.4.2.

5.1.4.1 Belligerent Occupation

West Bank

Under Article 42 of the 1907 Hague Regulations, a territory of a State is considered to be occupied when it is actually placed under the authority of a hostile State. Considering that 139 out of 193 UN member States recognized Palestine as a State by 2023, as well as the fact that Palestine has UN status of 'non-member observer State',[120] this Year in Review considers Palestine as a State for the purposes of international law.[121] In the West Bank, despite the Palestinian National Authority exercising governmental control in Areas A and B—fully and partially, respectively—in line with the 1995 Oslo Interim Agreement, Israel continues to wield

---

[117] Ibid.

[118] Ibid.

[119] Diakonia IHL Resource Centre (2023) Legal Brief: Hostilities in Israel and Gaza. https://apidia koniase.cdn.triggerfish.cloud/uploads/sites/2/2023/12/Legal-Brief-2023-Hostilities-in-Israel-and-Gaza.pdf. Accessed 30 March 2024.

[120] Permanent Observer Mission of the State of Palestine to the United Nations (Undated) Diplomatic Relations. http://palestineun.org/about-palestine/diplomatic-relations/. Accessed 30 March 2024.

[121] Regardless, it is worth noting that the application of the GCs in the Occupied Palestinian territories derives from the fact that the occupation occurred as a consequence of an IAC between High Contracting Parties, in line with the ICJ, *Legal Consequences of the Construction of a Wall in the Occupied Palestinian Territory*, Advisory Opinion, 9 July 2004, ICJ Rep 2004, paras 92–101.

5 Year in Review 2023

significant leverage.[122] During 2023, Israel retained full governmental and security control over area C—which comprises 60% of the West Bank territory and all Israeli settlements operating with the acquiescence of the government.[123] In areas A and B, during 2023 Israel controlled the exit and entry of persons and goods through more than 700 checkpoints that curtailed the freedom of movement of Palestinians, retained the military court system and applied military law, and frequently entered the areas for law enforcement purposes, e.g. conducting search-and-arrest operations.[124] Further, Israel continued its annexation of East Jerusalem over 2023. Accordingly, it is possible to conclude that Israel continued its occupation over the West Bank during 2023.

During 2023, a total number of 507 Palestinians—of which 503 were civilians—were reportedly killed in the West Bank, including East Jerusalem, by Israeli forces and civilian settlers, spanning the record since OCHA began reporting fatalities in 2005.[125] 190 of them reportedly perished during search-and-arrest operations.[126] The Jenin refugee camp was particularly affected, most notably by the killing of 12 Palestinians, temporary displacement of 3500 persons, and damage to 460 houses in July 2023. For its part, 36 Israelis—of which six were IDF soldiers and 18 were civilian settlers—were killed by Palestinians from the West Bank in Israel and the West Bank during 2023, which also marks a record of violence.[127] Most notably, in January 2023 seven civilians were killed by a Palestinian in the Israeli settlement of Neve Yaakouv in occupied East Jerusalem.[128]

During 2023, more than 4000 Palestinians were forcibly displaced by Israeli forces or Israeli settlers in the West Bank and East Jerusalem.[129] These numbers raise

---

[122] RULAC (2023) Military Occupation of Palestine by Israel. https://www.rulac.org/browse/confli cts/military-occupation-of-palestine-by-israel#collapse2accord. Accessed 28 March 2024; Israel Policy Forum (Undated) West Bank Settlements Explained. https://israelpolicyforum.org/west-bank-settlements-explained/. Accessed 30 March 2024; UN General Assembly (2023) Note by the Secretary-General: Situation of human rights in the Palestinian territories occupied since 1967, UN Doc. A/78/545.

[123] Ibid.

[124] Ibid.

[125] UN Office for the Coordination of Humanitarian Affairs (OCHA) (Undated) Data on Casualties. https://www.ochaopt.org/data/casualties. Accessed 30 March 2024; UN OCHA (2024) Hostilities in Gaza Strip and Israel: Flash Update #94. https://www.unocha.org/publications/report/occupied-palestinian-territory/hostilities-gaza-strip-and-israel-flash-update-94. Accessed 30 March 2024.

[126] UN OCHA (2024) Hostilities in Gaza Strip and Israel: Flash Update #94. https://www.unocha.org/publications/report/occupied-palestinian-territory/hostilities-gaza-strip-and-israel-flash-upd ate-94. Accessed 30 March 2024.

[127] UN OCHA (Undated) Data on Casualties. https://www.ochaopt.org/data/casualties. Accessed 30 March 2024; Ibid.

[128] Al Jazeera (2023) Gunman Wounds at Least 5 People in East Jerusalem Attack. https://www.aljazeera.com/news/2023/1/27/gunman-wounds-at-least-5-people-in-east-jerusalem-attack. Accessed 1 April 2024.

[129] UN OCHA (2023) About 4,000 Palestinians Displaced in the West Bank in 2023. https://www.ochaopt.org/content/about-4000-palestinians-displaced-west-bank-2023?_gl=1*1a9clm k*_ga*MTc3NDk4NzA1OC4xNzEwMzI4Mzk5*_ga_E60ZNX2F68*MTcxMTU0NzU0Ni42Lj AuMTcxMTU0NzU1NC41Mi4wLjA. Accessed 30 March 2024.

concerns of individual and mass forcible transfers, which are prohibited in occupied territories under IHL.[130] For its part, according to the NGO Peace Now, 2023 saw the promotion of construction plans by the Israeli government for 12,349 housing units in settlements located in the West Bank, excluding East Jerusalem, and the legalization of 10 settler outputs therein.[131] Also, in 2023, Israeli settlers established at least 26 new settler outputs in the West Bank, with an average of three settler incidents per day, and 5 after 7 October 2023.[132] During that year, Israeli authorities reportedly provided services, security and infrastructure to over 710,000 settlers in the West Bank, including East Jerusalem.[133] These actions violate the prohibition of an occupying power to transfer its population into occupied territory.[134] Although the deliberate and individual resettlement of a person from the territory of the occupying power to occupied territory is not forbidden under IHL, "any measures taken by an occupying Power in order to organize or encourage transfers of parts of its own population into the occupied territory" breach GCIV.[135]

Gaza Strip

The question of whether the Gaza strip is an occupied territory has sparked much controversy since the disengagement of Israeli troops from Gazan soil in 2005. However, in line with the ICRC's approach, "in some specific and exceptional cases – in particular when foreign forces withdraw from occupied territory (or parts thereof) while retaining key elements of authority or other important governmental functions that are typical of those usually taken on by an Occupying Power – the law of occupation might continue to apply".[136] In Gaza, Israel maintains a naval and air blockade regime since 2007.[137] During 2023, Israel also controlled land crossings and the supply of civilian infrastructure, and it retained control over different governmental functions, including the administration of the Palestinian population

---

[130] GCIV, Article 49(1); Rule 129 CIHL.

[131] Peace Now (2024) A Good Year for Settlements, A Bad Year for Israel: Settlement Watch Peace Now Report 2023. February 2024. http://peacenow.org.il/wp-content/uploads/2024/02/A-Good-year-for-settlements-A-Bad-Year-for-Israel-Settlement-Watch-Peace-Now-Report-2023-February-2024-1.pdf. Accessed 30 March 2024.

[132] Ibid.; Human Rights Watch (2024) Israel and Palestine - World Report 2024. https://www.hrw.org/world-report/2024/country-chapters/israel-and-palestine. Accessed 2 April 2024.

[133] Human Rights Watch (2024) Israel and Palestine - World Report 2024. https://www.hrw.org/world-report/2024/country-chapters/israel-and-palestine. Accessed 2 April 2024.

[134] GCIV, Article 49(5). The ICJ already considered that Israel is in breach of this prohibition in ICJ, *Legal Consequences of the Construction of a Wall in the Occupied Palestinian Territory*, Advisory Opinion, 9 July 2004, ICJ Rep 2004, paras 120–121.

[135] Ibid., para 120.

[136] ICRC (2016) Commentary on Article 2 of the Geneva Conventions of 1949, paras 307–308. https://ihl-databases.icrc.org/en/ihl-treaties/gci-1949/article-2/commentary/2016?activeTab=1949GCs-APs-and-commentaries. Accessed 2 April 2024.

[137] RULAC (2023) Military Occupation of Palestine by Israel. https://www.rulac.org/browse/conflicts/military-occupation-of-palestine-by-israel#collapse2accord. Accessed 28 March 2024.

registry.[138] Accordingly, this Year in Review considers that the Gaza Strip was occupied by Israel during 2023. However, it is evident that Israel does not exercise effective control over all aspects of the Gaza Strip, as it can be inferred from the preparation of the 7 October 2023 attacks and their aftermath (see Sect. 5.1.4.2). In light of the theory of functional occupation, this Year in Review considers the applicability of the law of occupation exclusively to the extent that Israel retains effective control over specific functions and portions of territory. This control can fluctuate over time, as it has been the case for territories which have been placed under complete control of IDF soldiers after the Israeli ground invasion of the Gaza strip (see Sect. 5.1.4.2).

Before 7 October 2023, tensions gave rise to occasional hostilities between Gaza-based NSGAs and Israel.[139] For space considerations, only the classification of the armed conflicts confronting Israel respectively with armed groups Hamas and Palestinian Islamic Jihad (PIJ)—which has been the subject of much debate over the years[140]—will be studied in this Year in Review. Unlike previous Year in Reviews,[141] this Year in Review considers these conflicts to be of an international character. This is the case since it is possible to argue that both groups fall under the scope of Article 4(2)(a) GCIII, constituting armed resistance movements belonging to Palestine—even if they do not meet the collective conditions listed therein to be granted prisoner of war status. According to the ICRC, in order to determine that an armed group belongs to a State, a *de facto* relationship between both entities is needed, albeit this might be built upon tacit agreement. Some of the elements pointing in that direction would be where "a group is involved in combat operations alongside the State and claims to be fighting on behalf of the State, and when given a formal, public or other opportunity to deny this link, the State does not or declines to do so". Indeed, many scholars consider as the determining factor the absence of denial by a State that a group fights on its behalf.[142] While both NSAGs repeatedly affirm that they fight for Palestine, the Palestinian National Authority has failed to clearly refuse that they fight on behalf of the Palestinian nation and people.[143] Accordingly, this Year in Review classifies the conflicts confronting Israel respectively with NSAGs Hamas and the PIJ as IACs.

---

[138] Ibid.

[139] See, for example, Al Jazeera (2023) Israel airstrikes hit Gaza after 10 Palestinians killed in Jenin. https://www.aljazeera.com/news/2023/1/27/israel-airstrikes-hit-gaza-after-10-palestinians-killed-in-jenin. Accessed 29 March 2024.

[140] For a detailed account on different possible classifications of the situation in Gaza, *see* de Hemptinne J (2024) Classifying the Gaza Conflict under International Humanitarian Law: A Complicated Matter. https://www.ejiltalk.org/classifying-the-gaza-conflict-under-international-humanitarian-law-a-complicated-matter/?utm_source=mailpoet&utm_medium=email&utm_campaign=ejil-talk-newsletter-post-title_2. Accessed 2 April 2024.

[141] *See* for example Sexton et al. 2023, pp. 212–213.

[142] RULAC (2023) Military Occupation of Palestine by Israel. https://www.rulac.org/browse/conflicts/military-occupation-of-palestine-by-israel#collapse2accord. Accessed 28 March 2024; Cameron L and Chetail V (2013) Privatizing war: Private Military and Security Companies under Public International Law. Cambridge University Press, Cambridge, pp. 396–397.

[143] For a further consideration of this issue, see RULAC (2023) Military Occupation of Palestine by Israel. https://www.rulac.org/browse/conflicts/military-occupation-of-palestine-by-israel#collapse2accord. Accessed 28 March 2024.

Over the first half of 2023, the IDF and Gaza-based PIJ newly engaged in hostilities on 2 May 2023, when the latter fired 104 rockets into Israel in response to PIJ member Khader Adnan's death in an Israeli prison after a hunger strike.[144] Israel responded with airstrikes in Gaza that killed one person, and the parties agreed to a ceasefire on 3 May 2023 brokered by Egypt, Qatar and UN officials.[145] From 9 to 13 May 2023, hostilities resumed when Israel launched its Operation 'Shield and Arrow' in Gaza, resulting in a death toll of 33 individuals therein—including 18 PIJ members—and injuring around 200 civilians.[146] PIJ launched more than 1000 rockets over that period, reportedly killing two and injuring around 40 in Israel.[147] On 13 May 2023, the parties agreed to a ceasefire brokered by Egypt.

5.1.4.2 Armed Hostilities Unfolding Since 7 October 2023

Operation 'al-Aqsa Flood'

On 7 October 2023, during the Jewish festivity of Simchat Torah, the Islamist group Hamas—purportedly in collaboration with other 5 NSAGs based in Gaza, including PIJ, the al-Aqsa Martyrs' Brigades and Mujahideen Brigades[148]—unleashed Operation al-Aqsa Flood, a multipronged attack on Israel which revealed a glaring failure in Israel's intelligence services.[149] The toll of the 7 October 2023 attacks, described as "the bloodiest in Israel's history",[150] was of over 1200 killed—including more than 800 civilians, among which 29 children—and 4834 wounded.[151]

---

[144] International Crisis Group (2024) CrisisWatch Database: Israel/Palestine. https://www.crisis group.org/crisiswatch/database?location%5B%5D=91&crisis_state=&created=&from_month=1&from_year=2024&to_month=1&to_year=2024. Accessed 2 April 2024.

[145] Al Jazeera (2023) Palestinian groups, Israeli forces agree to Gaza truce: Report. https://www.alj azeera.com/news/2023/5/3/palestinian-groups-israeli-forces-agree-to-gaza-truce-report. Accessed 28 March 2024.

[146] International Crisis Group 2024, above n 146.

[147] Ibid.; United Nations OCHA (2023) Flash Update: 15 May 2023. https://www.ochaopt.org/con tent/flash-update-5-15-may-2023. Accessed 2 April 2024.

[148] BBC (2023) How Hamas built a force to attack Israel on 7 October. https://www.bbc.com/news/world-middle-east-67480680#. Accessed 28 March 2024.

[149] For a deeper insight onto the Israeli security failure, see The Conversation (2023) Why Israel's intelligence chiefs failed to listen to October 7 warnings and the lessons to be learned. https://theconversation.com/why-israels-intelligence-chiefs-failed-to-listen-to-october-7-warnings-and-the-lessons-to-be-learned-219346. Accessed 28 March 2024.

[150] The Economist (2023) Hamas's attack was the bloodiest in Israel's history. https://www.eco nomist.com/briefing/2023/10/12/hamass-attack-was-the-bloodiest-in-israels-history. Accessed 30 March 2024.

[151] Office of the Special Representative of the Secretary-General on Sexual Violence in conflict (2024) Mission report: Official visit of the Office of the SRSG-SVC to Israel and the occupied West Bank (29 January–14 February 2024). https://www.un.org/sexualviolenceinconflict/wp-con tent/uploads/2024/03/report/mission-report-official-visit-of-the-office-of-the-srsg-svc-to-israel-and-the-occupied-west-bank-29-january-14-february-2024/20240304-Israel-oWB-CRSV-report. pdf. Accessed 1 June 2024; UN General Assembly (2024) Report of the United Nations High

5 Year in Review 2023

The attack started at 6:30 a.m. when at least 2000 and as many as 5000 rockets were indiscriminately fired towards Southern and Central Israel, in what amounts to a breach of the principle of distinction under IHL. Consequently, an estimate of up to 3000 NSAGs fighters entered adjacent Israeli territory by land and water using cars, motorcycles, parachutes, and motorboats.[152] 22 communities in the Southern Israeli Gaza Envelope were attacked, whilst seven of them, three military bases and one police station were taken over by militants.[153] The IDF only regained full control of all Israeli territory on 9 October 2023, after purportedly killing 1500 Palestinian fighters and detaining dozens.[154]

In the raids against Southern Israeli communities, among others, it was reported that militants gunned down unarmed civilians—often while sheltering in safe rooms installed in their homes—tortured civilians and mutilated their bodies, ransacked and burned down houses with residents inside, and killed unarmed soldiers in their power.[155] It is also believed that acts of sexual violence, including rape and gang rape, were perpetrated in different locations.[156] The deadliest incident was the massacre at the Supernova Sukkot music festival near kibbutz Re'im, attended by up to 4000

Commissioner for Human Rights: Human rights situation in the Occupied Palestinian Territory, including East Jerusalem, and the obligation to ensure accountability and justice, UN Doc. A/HRC/55/28, para 12; AOAV (2023) An analysis of the 7th October 2023 casualties in Israel as a result of the Hamas attack. https://aoav.org.uk/2023/an-analysis-of-the-7th-of-october-2023-casualties-in-israel-as-a-result-of-the-hamas-attack/. Accessed 28 March 2024.

[152] Le Monde (2023) Hamas attack October 7: A day of hell on earth in Israel. https://www.lem onde.fr/en/international/article/2023/10/30/hamas-attack-october-7-a-day-of-hell-on-earth-in-isr ael_6213560_4.html. Accessed 27 March 2024; The Times of Israel (2023) IDF estimates 3,000 Hamas terrorists invaded Israel in Oct 7 onslaught. https://www.timesofisrael.com/idf-estimates-3000-hamas-terrorists-invaded-israel-in-oct-7-onslaught/. Accessed 28 March 2024; AOAV (2023) An analysis of the 7th of October 2023 casualties in Israel as a result of the Hamas attack. https://aoav.org.uk/2023/an-analysis-of-the-7th-of-october-2023-casualties-in-israel-as-a-result-of-the-hamas-attack/. Accessed 28 March 2024

[153] AOAV (2023) An analysis of the 7th of October 2023 casualties in Israel as a result of the Hamas attack. https://aoav.org.uk/2023/an-analysis-of-the-7th-of-october-2023-casualties-in-israel-as-a-result-of-the-hamas-attack/. Accessed 28 March 2024.

[154] BBC (2023) How Hamas built a force to attack Israel on 7 October. https://www.bbc.com/news/world-middle-east-67480680#. Accessed 28 March 2024; Diakonia IHL Resource Centre (2023) Hostilities in Gaza and Israel: Factual account of events. https://www.diakonia.se/ihl/news/2023-hostilities-in-gaza-and-israel-factual-account-of-events/. Accessed 26 March 2024.

[155] *See* Diakonia IHL Resource Centre (2023) Legal Brief: Hostilities in Israel and Gaza, 27–34. https://apidiakoniase.cdn.triggerfish.cloud/uploads/sites/2/2023/12/Legal-Brief-2023-Hos tilities-in-Israel-and-Gaza.pdf. Accessed 30 March 2024.

[156] *See* Office of the Special Representative of the Secretary-General on Sexual Violence in conflict (2024) Mission report: Official visit of the Office of the SRSG-SVC to Israel and the occupied West Bank (29 January–14 February 2024). https://www.un.org/sexualviolenceinconflict/wp-con tent/uploads/2024/03/report/mission-report-official-visit-of-the-office-of-the-srsg-svc_to-israel-and-the-occupied-west-bank-29-january-14-february-2024/20240304-Israel-oWB-CRSV-report. pdf. Accessed 1 June 2024.

persons, in which 332 individuals were reportedly killed while fleeing or hiding.[157] For its part, the most affected localities within Israel were Kibbutz Be'eri and Kfar Azza—both populated by less than 1500 persons—in which 86 and 53 persons were respectively killed during the attacks.[158] Acts committed by Islamist militants during 7 October 2023 likely constitute violations of IHL that amount to grave breaches of the GCs, including that of wilful killing, torture and inhuman treatment of civilians and persons *hors de combat*, acts of pillage, or the destruction of property not justified by military necessity.[159]

As a result of the ground attacks, around 242 individuals—including Israeli citizens, foreigners, and dual nationals, of which around 30 were children—were taken hostages and brought to Gaza by the militants. The arbitrary deprivation of liberty and the taking of hostages are prohibited under IHL, the latter amounting to a grave breach under GCIV.[160] By the end of 2023, 109 hostages had been freed or rescued; 1105 of them had been exchanged for 240 Palestinians held in Israeli detention centres as part of an agreement leading to the six-day truce in late November 2023, 4 had been released in October 2023, and one IDF soldier had been freed in a ground operation conducted in the same month.[161] By the end of December 2023, the death of 21 hostages had been confirmed by the IDF.[162] These included three hostages reportedly killed by IDF soldiers on 16 December 2023 in Gaza City while they were holding a stick with a white flag that read "SOS" and "Help, three hostages" in Hebrew.[163]

Operation '**Swords of Iron**'

In the wake of the attacks, Israeli launched an aerial counteroffensive, the Security Cabinet of Israel—composed by Prime Minister Netanyahu and different ministers—passed a formal declaration of war under Article 40 of the Basic Law, and the Israeli government announced the mobilization of up to 360,000 reservists.[164] This marked

---

[157] AOAV (2023) An analysis of the 7th of October 2023 casualties in Israel as a result of the Hamas attack. https://aoav.org.uk/2023/an-analysis-of-the-7th-of-october-2023-casualties-in-israel-as-a-result-of-the-hamas-attack/. Accessed 28 March 2024.

[158] Ibid.

[159] See GCIV, Article 147.

[160] See GCIV Articles 34 and 147; Rules 96, 99 CIHL.

[161] Al Jazeera (2024) How many Israeli captives have been released or rescued? https://www.aljazeera.com/news/2024/2/14/how-many-israeli-captives-have-been-released-or-rescued. Accessed 29 March 2024.

[162] The Times of Israel (2023) Daily Briefing, Dec 22: Day 77, How does IDF determine hostages' deaths without bodies? https://www.timesofisrael.com/daily-briefing-dec-22-day-77-how-does-idf-determine-hostages-deaths-without-bodies/. Accessed 28 March 2024.

[163] Al Jazeera (2024) How many Israeli captives have been released or rescued? https://www.aljazeera.com/news/2024/2/14/how-many-israeli-captives-have-been-released-or-rescued. Accessed 29 March 2024.

[164] The Insider (2023) Israel officially declares war for first time since 1973. https://theins.ru/en/news/265689. Accessed 28 March 2024; Institute for National Security Studies (INSS) (2023) The Reserve Forces in the Gaza War: Challenges for the Continuation of the Fighting. https://www.inss.org.il/publication/reserve-october-7/. Accessed 28 March 2024.

the beginning of the Israeli Operation 'Swords of Iron' aimed at destroying Hamas, which entailed thousands of strikes and a ground operation across the Gaza strip. Over this period, Hamas and other Gaza-based NSAGs also continued firing rockets into Israel and fighting IDF soldiers on ground combats. Since 7 October 2023, the fierce fighting was only interrupted for a seven day-long humanitarian pause held between 24 November and 1 December 2023. By the end of December 2023, according to the Gazan Ministry of Health, 21,822 individuals had been killed and 56,451 wounded in the Gaza Strip.[165] IDF had reportedly killed by the end of 2023 around 5000 Hamas militants—that might amount to one sixth of the NSAG's forces—including various military leaders.[166] The Israeli offensive has been notorious for being extremely lethal for children and journalists, with 5350 and 74 respectively being reportedly killed from 7 October 2023 until the end of December 2023.[167]

On 27 October 2023, Israel launched its ground operation in Northern Gaza with a focus on Gaza city, after urging more than 1 million residents to move south within a tight deadline. This has raised concerns that the duty to provide an "effective advance warning" to civilians under the principle of precautions in IHL has been violated. Ground operations expanded to Khan Younis and surrounding areas in central Gaza in December 2023.[168] By the end of December, around 1.9 million persons—over 85% of the Gazan population—had been internally displaced at least once,[169] raising alarms over acts of mass forced displacement, which is forbidden under IHL. Since the ground invasion started and until the end of 2023, 172 IDF soldiers were killed and 937 were wounded in combat.[170] Although Israel had managed to establish ground control over diverse parts of northern and middle Gaza by the end of the

---

[165] The Guardian (2023) Israel-Gaza war live: Netanyahu targets control of Gaza-Egypt border in many months of war on Hamas. https://www.theguardian.com/world/live/2023/dec/31/israel-gaza-war-live-netanyahu-targets-control-of-gaza-egypt-border-in-many-months-of-war-on-hamas?page=with:block-65913d668f083c8fda16c65d#block-65913d668f083c8fda16c65d. Accessed 28 March 2024.

[166] The Washington Post (2023) Israel begins military offensive aimed at Hamas and destruction of Gaza. https://www.washingtonpost.com/world/2023/12/05/israel-military-offensive-hamas-des truction-gaza/. Accessed 28 March 2024; The New York Times (2023) Israel-Hamas War: Israel Says 5 Hamas Military Leaders Have Been Killed. https://www.nytimes.com/live/2023/12/06/world/isr ael-hamas-war-gaza-news. Accessed 28 March 2024.

[167] Committee to Protect Journalists (CPJ) (2024) Israel-Gaza War Brings 2023 Journalist Killings to Devastating High. https://cpj.org/reports/2024/02/israel-gaza-war-brings-2023-journalist-killings-to-devastating-high/. Accessed 3 April 2024. According to the CPJ, the Israeli offensive has killed more journalists over the course of three months than any other conflict over a whole year.

[168] Reuters (2023) EU calls for humanitarian pauses in Gaza for aid after Israel raids enclave. https://www.reuters.com/world/middle-east/eu-calls-humanitarian-pauses-gaza-aid-israel-raids-enclave-2023-10-26/. Accessed 26 March 2024.

[169] United Nations Relief and Works Agency for Palestine Refugees in the Near East (UNRWA) (2023) UNRWA Situation Report #58: Situation in Gaza Strip and West Bank, including East Jerusalem. https://www.unrwa.org/resources/reports/unrwa-situation-report-58-sit uation-gaza-strip-and-west-bank-including-east-Jerusalem. Accessed 2 April 2024.

[170] The Times of Israel (2023) IDF: Deaths of 29 of 170 soldiers in Gaza op were 'so-called friendly fire' accidents. https://www.timesofisrael.com/idf-deaths-of-29-of-170-soldiers-in-gaza-op-were-so-called-friendly-fire-accidents/. Accessed 28 March 2024.

year, hostilities were still ongoing, among others, in some districts of major cities like Gaza city, Khan Younis, Dayr al-Balah or Jabalya.[171]

The harsh military counteroffensive of the IDF against NSAGs in the densely populated Gaza Strip has damaged or destroyed by the end of December 2023 about 70% of Gazan homes and 50% of Gazan buildings, and claimed the lives of thousands of persons.[172] This campaign has raised suspicions over violations of the laws regulating the conduct of hostilities, especially when considered in conjunction with statements issued by different Israeli authorities purportedly showing disregard for the existence of legal limitations on the use of force.[173] As such, the high number of attacks conducted during a shelling campaign described by experts as the "most destructive of this century"[174] raise suspicions of an Israeli "overexpansive approach in the selection of the targets" in contravention with the principle of distinction under IHL.[175]

One of the most notable examples lies in the surprisingly high number of attacks against medical units, personnel and transports—the protection of which under IHL ceases under very concrete and special conditions.[176] As such, by December 2023, only 4 out of 22 hospitals in Northern Gaza were reportedly functioning, as 14 of them had been directly hit in hostilities, and 20 were reportedly damaged or destroyed while thousands of persons were shielding therein.[177] Since 7 October 2023, hospitals have been subject to numerous shelling, weeks-long sieges and raids by IDF soldiers which have claimed the lives of hundreds of civilians.[178] Israel has repeatedly denied that it targets hospitals, alleging that Hamas uses them to shield militants, weapons

---

[171] Authors' calculations based on ACLED (2024) ACLED Data Export Tool. https://acleddata.com/data-export-tool/. Accessed 22 May 2024.

[172] The Wall Street Journal (2023) Gaza destruction deepens as bombing by Israel continues. https://www.wsj.com/world/middle-east/gaza-destruction-bombing-israel-aa528542. Accessed 27 March 2024.

[173] For a detailed account on these, see Diakonia IHL Resource Centre (2023) Legal Brief: Hostilities in Israel and Gaza. https://apidiakoniase.cdn.triggerfish.cloud/uploads/sites/2/2023/12/Legal-Brief-2023-Hostilities-in-Israel-and-Gaza.pdf. Accessed 30 March 2024.

[174] CBC News (2023) Israel's Gaza bombing campaign is the most destructive of this century, analysts say. https://www.cbc.ca/news/politics/israel-gaza-bombing-hamas-civilian-casualties-1.7068647. Accessed 25 March 2024.

[175] Diakonia IHL Resource Centre (2023) Legal Brief: Hostilities in Israel and Gaza, 46. https://apidiakoniase.cdn.triggerfish.cloud/uploads/sites/2/2023/12/Legal-Brief-2023-Hostilities-in-Israel-and-Gaza.pdf. Accessed 30 March 2024.

[176] CIHL Rules 25, 28, 29.

[177] CNN (2024) Gaza hospitals destroyed: An investigation. https://edition.cnn.com/interactive/2024/01/middleeast/gaza-hospitals-destruction-investigation-intl-cmd/. Accessed 26 March 2024.

[178] Ibid.; Front Line Defenders (2023) Israel must cease targeting human rights defenders, healthcare sector in Gaza. https://www.frontlinedefenders.org/en/statement-report/israel-must-cease-targeting-human-rights-defenders-healthcare-sector-in-gaza. Accessed 28 March 2024; UN OCHA (2023) Hostilities in Gaza Strip and Israel: Flash Update 66. https://www.ochaopt.org/content/hostilities-gaza-strip-and-israel-flash-update-66. Accessed 8 May 2024.

and command centres—albeit this is vehemently rejected by the NSAG.[179] The worst single incident affecting a hospital during 2023 was the explosion targeting al-Ahli Arab Hospital in Gaza City on 17 October 2023, in which reportedly 471 people died and 342 were injured according to the Gazan Ministry of Health.[180] However, the authorship of this attack remains contested and both parties attribute it to each other.[181]

The principle of proportionality has also been repeatedly put in question during the Israeli counteroffensive, considering the extremely high number of civilian victims and the extensive damage to civilian objects caused by various attacks. One such alarming incident was the 31 October bombing of the premises of the Jabalya refugee camp allegedly targeting an underground command centre of Hamas, in which over 110 Palestinians were reportedly killed and 300 injured.[182] Reports have also raised concerns over purported mistreatment of Palestinians detained both during the ground operation in Gaza and in the West Bank after 7 October 2023, including accounts of sexual violence,[183] torture and inhumane treatment.[184]

---

[179] CNN (2024) Gaza hospitals destroyed: An investigation. https://edition.cnn.com/interactive/2024/01/middleeast/gaza-hospitals-destruction-investigation-intl-cmd/. Accessed 26 March 2024.

[180] Palestinian Ministry of Health/Gaza (2023) Statements by the spokesperson of the Ministry of Health, Dr. Ashraf Al-Qudra: During a press conference on the serious repercussions of the ongoing Israeli aggression on the Gaza Strip for the twelfth day. https://www.facebook.com/MOHGaza1994/posts/pfbid02VihLzssMVKvwphaoxK71rs9X4f UtNFaXBj9nFamjZ4Z9A56Vu6SZ7GcTLS2yo23fl. Accessed 28 May 2024.

[181] For claims attributing the attack failed missiles launched by Palestinian NSAGs, see Human Rights Watch (2023) Gaza: Findings on October 17 Al-Ahli Hospital Explosion. https://www.hrw.org/news/2023/11/26/gaza-findings-october-17-al-ahli-hospital-explosion. Accessed 28 March 2024.

[182] The Washington Post (2023) Israel-Gaza: Refugee camp strike causes death and destruction. https://www.washingtonpost.com/world/2023/11/01/israel-gaza-refugee-camp-strike-death-destruction/. Accessed 28 June 2024. For different views on Israeli compliance with the principle of proportionality, see Manea A (2023) Too Early To Tell? The (Un)lawfulness of Israeli Attacks: The Case of the Jabalia Refugee Camp. https://www.ejiltalk.org/too-early-to-tell-the-unlawfuln ess-of-israeli-attacks-the-case-of-the-jabalia-refugee-camp/. Accessed 18 May 2024; Schack M (2023) In Defence of Preliminary Assessments: Proportionality and the 31 October Attack on the Jabalia Refugee Camp. https://www.ejiltalk.org/in-defence-of-preliminary-assessments-proportionality-and-the-31-october-attack-on-the-jabalia-refugee-camp/. Accessed 18 May 2024; Lattimer M (2023) Assessing Israel's Approach to Proportionality in the Conduct of Hostilities in Gaza. https://www.lawfaremedia.org/article/assessing-israel-s-approach-to-proportionality-in-the-conduct-of-hostilities-in-gaza. Accessed 18 May 2024.

[183] See The Public Committee Against Torture in Israel Adalah, The Legal Center for Arab Minority Rights in Israel Hamoked, Center for the Defence of the Individual Physicians for Human Rights – Israel (2024) Systemic torture and inhumane treatment of Palestinian detainees in Israeli prison facilities since October 7, 2023. https://itnewsletter.itnewsletter.co.il/sending/webpage.aspx?d=JN2gYjxKpACTdVMvYyH47vjFN6VuSGCb&w=1&ar=0&isDe=True&rfl=False&pl=0&l=9369918&sll=0&mlt=True. Accessed 18 May 2024; UN General Assembly (2024) Report of the UN High Commissioner for Human Rights: Human rights situation in the Occupied Palestinian Territory, including East Jerusalem, and the obligation to ensure accountability and justice, UN Doc. A/HRC/55/28, para 73.

[184] See Euro-Mediterranean Human Rights Monitor (2023) "They brought Israeli civilians to watch our nude torture": IDF torture of Palestinian prisoners is turned into entertainment for Israeli

Lastly, the dire humanitarian situation in Gaza has also raised suspicions of violations of the rules on the provision and safe passage of humanitarian relief, as well as on the prohibition of collective punishment, and even of the use of starvation as a method of warfare.[185] Indeed, on 9 October 2023, Israel's Defence Minister Gallant announced a complete siege over Gaza, impeding the entry of food, water, fuel and electricity.[186] This restriction was partially lifted from 21 October 2023 onwards, when the first aid trucks entered Gaza through the Rafah crossing. On 15 November 2023, the first fuel imports were allowed exclusively for UNRWA activities, and the Kerem Shalom crossing opened for the delivery of aid on 17 December 2023.[187] However, resources entering Gaza have been extremely far from enough to meet the needs of a population at risk of famine, displaced in its majority, and already extremely dependent on humanitarian aid before October 2023.[188] Indeed, by December 2023, the approximately 2.2 million inhabitants of the Gaza Strip were facing high levels of acute food insecurity, with more than half a million being subject to "extreme lack of food, starvation and exhaustion of coping capacities".[189]

Reactions Prompted by Operations 'al-Aqsa Flood' *and* 'Swords of Iron'

In October and December 2023, the UN General Assembly passed two resolutions respectively calling for immediate humanitarian truces and ceasefires.[190] In November 2023, UN Security Council Resolution 2712 was adopted, urging for, *inter*

---

viewers. https://euromedmonitor.org/en/article/6153. Accessed 27 March 2024; Al Jazeera (2023) Video, photos appear to show detainees stripped to underwear in Gaza. https://www.aljazeera.com/news/2023/12/8/video-photos-appear-to-show-detainees-stripped-to-underwear-in-gaza. Accessed 25 March 2024.

[185] Human Rights Watch (2023) Israel: Starvation used as weapon of war in Gaza. https://www.hrw.org/news/2023/12/18/israel-starvation-used-weapon-war-gaza. Accessed 25 March 2024; Khan K (2023) https://x.com/KarimKhanQC/status/1732573843980480736. Accessed 24 March 2024.

[186] International Crisis Group 2024, above n 147; UN OCHA (2023) Hostilities in the Gaza Strip and Israel: Flash Update #9. https://www.ochaopt.org/content/hostilities-gaza-strip-and-israel-flash-update-9. Accessed 28 March 2024; UN OCHA (2023) Hostilities in the Gaza Strip and Israel: Flash Update #33. https://www.ochaopt.org/content/hostilities-gaza-strip-and-israel-flash-update-33. Accessed 28 June 2024.

[187] Reuters (2023) Israel to allow two fuel trucks a day into Gaza, official says. https://www.reuters.com/world/middle-east/israel-allow-two-fuel-trucks-day-into-gaza-official-says-2023-11-17/. Accessed 28 March 2024; UN OCHA (2023) Hostilities in the Gaza Strip and Israel: Flash Update #43. https://www.ochaopt.org/content/hostilities-gaza-strip-and-israel-flash-update-43. Accessed 29 March 2024; Reuters (2023) Aid enters Gaza through Israel's Kerem Shalom crossing for the first time since war. https://www.reuters.com/world/middle-east/aid-enters-gaza-through-israels-kerem-shalom-crossing-first-time-war-2023-12-17/. Accessed 29 March 2024.

[188] *See* The Guardian (2023) In Gaza, the fuel has gone and now the trees are running out. https://www.theguardian.com/global-development/2023/dec/16/in-gaza-the-fuel-has-gone-and-now-the-trees-are-running-out. Accessed 28 March 2024.

[189] IPC (Integrated Food Security Phase Classification) (2023) IPC Country Analysis - State of Palestine. https://www.ipcinfo.org/ipc-country-analysis/details-map/en/c/1156749/. Accessed 1 April 2024.

[190] UN General Assembly (2023) Resolution adopted by the General Assembly on 27 October 2023, UN Doc. A/RES/ES-10/21, para 1.

alia, urgent humanitarian pauses and corridors to ensure the provision of humanitarian aid and essential goods and supplies.[191] For their part, two other UN Security Council draft resolutions were vetoed by the US in October and December 2023, which would have respectively called for a humanitarian pause and a ceasefire in Gaza.[192] Numerous international experts have voiced concerns over credible evidence pointing to the commission of a genocide against Palestinians in Gaza,[193] which by the end of the year led to the case brought by South Africa against Israel before the ICJ for alleged violations of the Convention on the Prevention and Punishment of the Crime of Genocide.

5.1.4.3 Other Related International and Non-international Armed Conflicts involving Israel

In addition, Israel was involved in other related international and non-international armed conflicts which, for space considerations, will not be analysed in-depth in this Year in Review. On 8 October 2023, the Iran-backed NSAG Hezbollah based in Lebanon fired rockets and shells against Israeli occupied Shebaa Farms in support of the Hamas-led attacks.[194] Ever since, Israel has engaged in numerous air strikes against Hezbollah's strongholds, to which the latter has replied by launching rocket and drone attacks against Israeli targets.[195] Hostilities have additionally involved Hezbollah positions in Syria, and Israel has targeted Syrian airports in Aleppo and Damascus on several occasions since October 2023.[196]

During 2023, these hostilities took the lives of at least four IDF soldiers, a hundred Hezbollah members, one Israeli civilian and dozens of civilians in Southern Lebanon—including Reuters journalist Issam Abdallah during an attack reportedly

---

[191] UN Security Council (2023), Resolution 2712(2023), UN Doc. S/RES/2712(2023), para 2.

[192] UN News (2023) Israel-Gaza crisis: US vetoes Security Council resolution. https://news.un.org/en/story/2023/10/1142507. Accessed 28 June 2024; UN News (2024) Security Council Fails to Adopt Draft Resolution on Situation in Middle East, Marking Longest Deadlock on Text Since Early December 2023. https://press.un.org/en/2024/sc15595.doc.htm#:~:text=The%20Security%20Council%20today%20failed,text%20since%20early%20December%202023. Accessed 3 April 2024.

[193] See, for example, OHCHR (2023) Gaza: UN Experts Call on International Community to Prevent Genocide. https://www.ohchr.org/en/press-releases/2023/11/gaza-un-experts-call-international-community-prevent-genocide-against. Accessed 2 April 2024.

[194] BBC (2023) How Hamas built a force to attack Israel on 7 October. https://www.bbc.com/news/world-middle-east-67480680#. Accessed 28 March 2024.

[195] See, for example, Reuters (2023) Lebanon's Hezbollah fires drones, Israel mounts air strikes. https://www.reuters.com/world/middle-east/lebanons-hezbollah-fires-drones-israel-mounts-air-strikes-2023-12-10/. Accessed 30 June 2024; VOA News (2023) Airstrikes to Intensify, Israel Warns, as Israel-Hezbollah Attacks Ramp Up. https://www.voanews.com/a/airstrikes-to-intensify-israel-warns-israel-hezbollah-attacks-ramp-up-/7321198.html. Accessed 30 June 2024.

[196] Diakonia IHL Resource Center (2023) Hostilities in Gaza and Israel: Factual account of events. https://www.diakonia.se/ihl/news/2023-hostilities-in-gaza-and-israel-factual-account-of-events/. Accessed 26 March 2024.

found to violate IHL by the UN Interim Forces of Lebanon.[197] Around 150,000 civilians over the Israeli-Lebanese border have been purportedly displaced.[198] Clashes most likely trigger a NIAC between Israel and Hezbollah, albeit a detailed study of the intensity of hostilities and the level of organization of Hezbollah falls outside the scope of this Year in Review for space constraints.[199] To the extent that the use of force by Israel in Lebanon and Syria were not consented by the latter States, they would also propel respective IACs between these countries.[200]

5.1.5 Mali

The Central Sahel Region has been privy to armed conflict in the States of Mali, Burkina Faso and Niger for many years.[201] Multiple NIACs have existed in these regions with the involvement of the States, NSAGs and ethnic militias since 2012.[202] The clashes are arguably mainly between the Malian armed forces with the support of the Wagner group, JNIM and IS Sahel.

The year 2023 has shown significant deterioration in Mali with massive-scale attacks against civilians by the NSAGs and the Malian Junta. Efforts to achieve lasting peace and stability have not gained success in the year, and the clashes between the armed groups continually grow. Thus, this Year in Review will focus on developments in Mali that majorly shaped its humanitarian crisis in 2023 including 8.8 million people in need of assistance, and more than 575,000 internally displaced people and refugees.[203] According to Human Rights Watch reports, clashes in 2023

---

[197] Human Rights Watch (2024) UN report: Israeli killing of journalist in Lebanon. https://www.hrw.org/news/2024/03/29/un-report-israeli-killing-journalist-lebanon#:~:text=We%2C%20the%20undersigned%20victims%2C%20survivors,south%20Lebanon%2C%20which%20killed%20Reuters. Accessed 27 March 2024.

[198] Arab Gulf States Institute in Washington (AGSIW) (2023) Lebanese Hezbollah fatalities since the beginning of the war in Gaza. https://agsiw.org/lebanese-hezbollah-fatalities-since-the-beginning-of-the-war-in-gaza/. Accessed 26 March 2024; The New York Times (2024) Israel and Lebanon: Civilians caught in the crossfire with Hezbollah. https://www.nytimes.com/2024/01/04/world/middleeast/israel-lebanon-hezbollah-civilians.html. Accessed 24 March 2024.

[199] For further information, see RULAC (2023) Military Occupation of Palestine by Israel. https://www.rulac.org/browse/conflicts/military-occupation-of-palestine-by-israel#collapse2accord. Accessed 28 March 2024.

[200] See ICRC (2020) Commentary of 2020 on Convention (III) relative to the Treatment of Prisoners of War. Article 2: Application of the Convention. https://ihl-databases.icrc.org/applic/ihl/ihl.nsf/Comment.xsp?action=openDocument&documentId=0B46B7ADFC9E8219C125858400464543#_Toc42429662. Accessed 12 May 2024.

[201] See generally Clingendael March 2015 Report 'Roots of Conflict Mali', Executive Summary https://www.clingendael.org/pub/2015/the_roots_of_malis_conflict/executive_summary/ Accessed 30 May 2024.

[202] RULAC (2023) Mali: Non-international armed conflicts in Mali. https://www.rulac.org/browse/conflicts/non-international-armed-conflits-in-mali#collapse1accord.

[203] HRW (2023) Mali, Events of 2023. https://www.hrw.org/world-report/2024/country-chapters/mali. Accessed 30 May 2024.

5   Year in Review 2023   191

between IS Sahel, JNIM and their rivalry are adding to the brutal consequences of humanitarian emergencies against civilians.[204] The operations of JNIM and IS Sahel have a presence in Burkina Faso, thus making the analysis carried out in that section sufficient for the NIACs discussed here.[205] ACLED attributed the increase in violence to JNIM, the Malian State (with the support of Wagner) and IS Sahel.[206] For this Year in Review, the focus will remain on the NIACS between the Malian Junta and JNIM, the Malian Junta and IS Sahel, and a potential NIAC between JNIM and IS Sahel.[207]

5.1.5.1   Major Armed Hostilities

There is a reported 38% increase in civilian targeting and violence in 2023 in the same period compared to 2022.[208] ACLED accounted for over 27 civilians killed in the Mopti Region in December, calling it the deadliest period since the beginning of the crisis in 2012.[209] For the first half of the year, clashes between IS Sahel and JNIM resulted in the deaths of more than 100 civilians in the region of Menaka, Tegurert, Konga and Essaylal.[210] JNIM claimed responsibility for two major incidents in April in the Nara and Mopti regions, destroying infrastructure and civilian casualties of more than 10.[211] In June and August, ISGS fighters attacked the regions of Dangabari and Bodio, killing more than 20 civilians.[212]

---

[204] HRW (2003) Mali: Mounting Islamist Armed Group Killings, Rape. https://www.hrw.org/news/2023/07/13/mali-mounting-islamist-armed-group-killings-rape. Accessed 30 May 2024.

[205] See Sect. 5.1.2 on Burkina Faso.

[206] ACLED (2023) Mali: Fact Sheet Attacks on Civilians Spike in Mali as Security Deteriorates Across the Sahel. https://acleddata.com/2023/09/21/fact-sheet-attacks-on-civilians-spike-in-mali-as-security-deteriorates-across-the-sahel/. Accessed 30 May 2024.

[207] ISPI 90 (2021) The Conflict Between Al-Qaeda and the Islamic State in Sahel, A Year on https://www.ispionline.it/en/publication/conflict-between-al-qaeda-and-islamic-state-sahel-year-29305. Accessed 30 May 2024.

[208] Ibid.

[209] Ibid.

[210] France 24 (2023) Mali: le groupe Etat islamique augmente son emprise à Ménaka et opère tout autour de son chef-lieu [Mali: the Islamic State group increases its grip in Menaka and operates all around its capital]. https://www.france24.com/fr/vidéo/20230413-mali-le-groupe-etat-isl amique-augmente-son-emprise-à-ménaka-et-opère-tout-autour-de-son-chef-lieu. Accessed 30 May 2024.

[211] HRW (2023) Mali, Events of 2023. https://www.hrw.org/world-report/2024/country-chapters/mali. Accessed 30 May 2024.

[212] Ibid.

5.1.5.2 Malian Junta, CMA and Political Climate

Military coups have failed to implement security measures and have resulted in political violence increasing by 5%.[213] The Coordination of Azawad Movements (CMA) is an alliance of the Tuareg groups that signed a peace agreement with the Malian Junta in 2015. 2023 is a year where violent CMA's 'ex-rebels' were called to contribute to the hostilities against the State.[214] The CMA consists of fractions of many liberation and separatist groups that have fulfilled the organization criterion.[215] However, there is no clarity regarding which NSAG they supported this year. It is therefore difficult for this Year in Review to include them in any specific NIAC despite there being evidence of their inclusion that resulted in violence in 2023.[216]

5.1.5.3 JNIM's Attacks on Passenger Ferry

On 7 September, JNIM attacked a military camp and the vessel Timbuktu in Mali, resulting in the deaths of around 50 civilians and 15 soldiers.[217] The attack's location was in the territory of Rarhous, which is in the central part of the State.[218] A group led by Al-Qaeda has claimed the credit for this attack, which gives reason to attribute it to JNIM.[219] Mopti and Segou regions saw the highest number of civilian casualties.[220] UNICEF further condemned the attack for causing the death of 24 children.[221] September witnessed attacks on boats along the region, frequent shelling and attacks

---

[213] ACLED (2023) Mali: Fact Sheet Attacks on Civilians Spike in Mali as Security Deteriorates Across the Sahel. https://acleddata.com/2023/09/21/fact-sheet-attacks-on-civilians-spike-in-mali-as-security-deteriorates-across-the-sahel/. Accessed 30 May 2024.

[214] Africanews (2023) Mali: ex-CMA rebels say they are in wartime with the junta. https://www.africanews.com/2023/09/12/mali-ex-cma-rebels-say-they-are-in-wartime-with-the-junta/. Accessed 30 May 2024.

[215] RULAC (2023) Mali: Non-international armed conflicts in Mali. https://www.rulac.org/browse/conflicts/non-international-armed-conflits-in-mali#collapse1accord. Accessed 30 May 2024.

[216] Ibid.

[217] Ibid.

[218] Aljazeera (2023) Attack on boat, army base in Mali kills at least 49 civilians, 15 soldiers. https://www.aljazeera.com/news/2023/9/7/attack-on-boat-army-base-in-mali-kills-at-least-49-civilians-15-soldiers#:~:text="On%20September%207%2C%202023%2C,central%20part%20of%20the%20country. Accessed 30 May 2024.

[219] Ibid.

[220] ACLED (2023) Mali: Fact Sheet Attacks on Civilians Spike in Mali as Security Deteriorates Across the Sahel. https://acleddata.com/2023/09/21/fact-sheet-attacks-on-civilians-spike-in-mali-as-security-deteriorates-across-the-sahel/. Accessed 30 May 2024.

[221] UNICEF (2023) UNICEF calls for the protection of children affected by violence in Mali https://www.unicef.org/wca/press-releases/unicef-calls-protection-children-affected-violence-mali%C2%A0. Accessed 30 May 2024.

on the airport, including targets at the UN Humanitarian Air Service and the flights of Malian Airlines in Timbuktu.[222]

5.1.5.4 The Untimely Withdrawal of the United Nations Multidimensional Integrated Stabilization Mission in Mali (MINUSMA)

The UN peacekeeping force MINUSMA has operated in Mali for a decade.[223]

On 16 June 2023, the Malian Junta demanded the immediate withdrawal of MINUSMA peacekeepers from Mali. The Crisis Group identified UN clashes with the military Junta over human rights abuses by Malian forces and Wagner Group mercenaries.[224] The UN Security Council approved the removal of the peacekeepers on 30 June 2023.[225] The claims for this withdrawal range from a failure to protect civilians to a lack of a role in formal peace processes. This withdrawal came when only 30% of the necessary funding for humanitarian aid was accessible in 2023. The result is millions of people left without basic needs in a climate where there is further deterioration of access owing to the escalation in conflict specifically in northern and central regions of Mali that are under blockade by the military junta.[226] Overall, it reflects poorly on the status and stability of these missions, and their future looks arguably bleak.[227]

5.1.5.5 Wagner's Association with Mali's Conflict

As discussed before, the Wagner armed group has been part of various atrocities in Ukraine and the African region.[228] The organization of the Wagner group will be analyzed in depth in Sect. 5.1.9. The deployment of this Russian private military

---

[222] ACLED (2023) Mali: Fact Sheet Attacks on Civilians Spike in Mali as Security Deteriorates Across the Sahel. https://acleddata.com/2023/09/21/fact-sheet-attacks-on-civilians-spike-in-mali-as-security-deteriorates-across-the-sahel/. Accessed 30 May 2024.

[223] IRC (2024) Crisis in Mali: What you need to know and how to help. https://www.rescue.org/eu/article/crisis-mali-what-you-need-know-and-how-help. Accessed 30 May 2024.

[224] International Crisis Group (2023) Ten Challenges for the UN in 2023–2024. https://www.crisisgroup.org/global/sb11-ten-challenges-un-2023-2024. Accessed 30 May 2024.

[225] IRC (2024) Crisis in Mali: What you need to know and how to help. https://www.rescue.org/eu/article/crisis-mali-what-you-need-know-and-how-help. Accessed 30 May 2024.

[226] Ibid.

[227] International Crisis Group (2023) Ten Challenges for the UN in 2023–2024. https://www.crisisgroup.org/global/sb11-ten-challenges-un-2023-2024. Accessed 30 May 2024.

[228] ACLED (2023) Moving Out of the Shadows Shifts in Wagner Group Operations Around the World https://acleddata.com/2023/08/02/moving-out-of-the-shadows-shifts-in-wagner-group-operations-around-the-world/#exec. Accessed 30 May 2024.

company (PMC) began in December 2021 upon an invitation from the Malian government.[229] The departure of the MINUSMA has negatively added to the issue.[230] Many Western States have condemned Wagner's involvement in Mali, saying that it can only worsen problems of security and human rights.[231] On 23 and 24 March 2023, villagers claimed they saw "white" foreign soldiers accompanied by the Malian army in the Mopti region where they killed approximately 20 civilians. On 15 June 2023, another attack in the Nara region took place where these foreign soldiers killed at least 5 civilians.[232] ACLED has recorded Wagner violating IHL and committing potential war crimes employing torture, summary executions, booby-trapping of corpses and ejection of prisoners from aircrafts.[233] Indeed, the already precarious security situation has been worsened by the UN's departure and has encouraged the NIAC in all of its clusters to continue.

5.1.6 *Myanmar*

5.1.6.1 History of Burma—A Non-international Armed Conflict with No End

Myanmar (or Burma) has been the centre of colossal levels of violence and humanitarian catastrophe owing to the scattered armed conflicts since they gained independence from British rule in 1948.[234] Particularly, the military coup in 2021 initiated another one of the most intense NIACs between the Tatmadaw and the Arakan Army (and many others) facilitating an ethnic-cleansing regime against the Rohingya Muslims.[235]

The main actors of the conflict include the State in the form of the Myanmar armed forces (Tatmadaw), ethnic armed groups, such as the Arakan Army, Arakan Rohingya Salvation Army, Myanmar National Democratic Alliance Army, the

---

[229] Sexton et al. 2023, p. 216.

[230] Ibid.

[231] Aljazeera (2021) Western powers slam 'deployment' of Russian mercenaries in Mali. https://www.aljazeera.com/news/2021/12/24/western-powers-slam-russian-mercenary-presence-in-mali. Accessed 30 May 2024.

[232] HRW (2023) Mali, Events of 2023. https://www.hrw.org/world-report/2024/country-chapters/mali. Accessed 30 May 2024.

[233] ACLED (2023) Mali: Fact Sheet Attacks on Civilians Spike in Mali as Security Deteriorates Across the Sahel. https://acleddata.com/2023/09/21/fact-sheet-attacks-on-civilians-spike-in-mali-as-security-deteriorates-across-the-sahel/. Accessed 30 May 2024.

[234] Council on Foreign Relations (2022) Myanmar's Troubled History: Coups, Military Rule, and Ethnic Conflict. https://www.cfr.org/backgrounder/myanmar-history-coup-military-rule-ethnic-conflict-rohingya. Accessed 30 May 2024.

[235] Center for Preventive Action Global Conflict Tracker (2024) Civil War in Myanmar https://www.cfr.org/global-conflict-tracker/conflict/rohingya-crisis-myanmar. Accessed 30 May 2024.

Ta'ang National Liberation Army, and the People's Defence Force.[236] After sporadic clashes throughout 2021 and 2022, the Arakan Army and the State Administration Council (SAC) agreed to a temporary ceasefire, brokered by the Nippon Foundation. Despite the attempt, tensions remained high, with both sides maintaining forces within the northern Rakhine State. In 2023, Myanmar remained in a state of civil war resulting in the death of 15,759.[237] A report by Action on Armed Violence (AOAV) realized a 122% rise in global civilian fatalities in 2023 worldwide compared to the previous year, attributing a chunk of this rise to the situation in Myanmar.[238] Additionally, casualties from landmines and explosions increased by 270% as compared to 2022.[239] Though this Year in Review discusses landmines in a separate section, it is important to note that UNICEF attributed over 1052 civilian deaths to them in Myanmar in 2023.[240]

Overall, Myanmar showcased continued violence, increased causalities, destruction, and displacement of civilians. Myanmar retains its status as hosting multiple NIACs in 2023, among which the one confronting the Tatmadaw and the Arakan Army is the most notorious.[241] One of the most tragic spillovers of the NIAC in Myanmar is the Rohingya refugee crisis, the relevant developments of which will be discussed in Sect. 5.1.6.6. The scope of this Year in Review will be the clashes between the Myanmar State and the Arakan Army (and the manifestations of its collaborations) that potentially qualify as a NIAC.

5.1.6.2 Political Developments, Military Regime and Contributors of Conflict

In early March, the Myanmar Junta dissolved all 40 political parties including the National League for Democracy (NLD)—its singular plausible (and former) opposition, for the apparent failure of meeting a deadline they set out under the new Political

---

[236] RULAC (2023) Countries: Myanmar. https://www.rulac.org/browse/countries/myanmar#collapse1accord. Accessed 30 May 2024.

[237] ACLED (2024) ACLED Data Export Tool. https://acleddata.com/data-export-tool/. Accessed 22 May 2024.

[238] Action on Armed Violence January (2024) 122% rise in global civilian fatalities from explosive weapons in 2023: a year of harm reviewed. https://reliefweb.int/report/world/122-rise-global-civilian-fatalities-explosive-weapons-2023-year-harm-reviewed. Accessed 30 May 2024.

[239] UN Press (2024) As Crisis in Myanmar Worsens, Security Council Must Take Resolute Action to End Violence by Country's Military, Address Humanitarian Situation, Speakers Urge https://press.un.org/en/2024/sc15652.doc.htm. Accessed 30 May 2024.

[240] Aljazeera (2023) Myanmar: Myanmar anti-coup forces claim 'success' in Naypidaw drone attack' https://www.aljazeera.com/news/2024/4/4/myanmar-opposition-launches-drone-attack-on-militarys-stronghold-capital. Accessed 30 May 2024.

[241] UN Press (2024) As Crisis in Myanmar Worsens, Security Council Must Take Resolute Action to End Violence by Country's Military, Address Humanitarian Situation, Speakers Urge https://press.un.org/en/2024/sc15652.doc.htm. Accessed 30 May 2024.

Party Registration Law.[242] This is the fourth 'state of emergency' declared by the Junta since the coup in 2021. Owing to the climate of political oppression, it has been ominously claimed that democratic elections in Myanmar will not take place in the foreseeable future.[243]

In addition, the following major incidents of hostilities took place between the Tatmadaw and the NSAGs: a drone attack on 31 January and 1 February led by the Karen National Defense Organisation, south of Myawaddy town; the Battle of Messe on 13 June in Kayah State conducted by the Karenni National People's Liberation Front (KNPLF); Operation Kanuang from July to September in the Mandalay region; and the Battle of Laukkai in November and December, which led to the Myanmar National Democratic Alliance Army (MNDAA) to take strategic control of the region of Laukkai.[244]

5.1.6.3 Air Strikes and the Junta's Violations Against the Civilian Population

The previously mentioned report by AOAV pointed to a 226% rise in air-launched attacks globally.[245] Thus, the increase in airstrikes being carried on in Myanmar in 2023 has been monumental and has caused reasonable worry in terms of non-compliance with norms of IHL when exercising this means of warfare.[246] The main regions affected are Rakhine, Kachin, Shan, Kayin and Mandalay.

Firstly, on 11 April 2023, airstrikes by the government's military killed more than 50 people, including civilians when they attacked an event organized by its opponents.[247] On the same day, the Junta attacked a building in the Sagaing Region using a thermobaric munition killing over 160 people. The usage of this kind of munition caused indiscriminate casualties in violation of IHL.[248] On 9 October, the military carried out an airstrike on a village in Kachin State killing around 40 civilians including children. On 11 October artillery fire hit a refugee camp and caused the death of around 30 internally displaced people. Though the Junta refuses to take

---

[242] HRW (2023) Myanmar Junta Dissolves Political Parties. https://www.hrw.org/news/2023/03/29/myanmar-junta-dissolves-political-parties. Accessed 30 May 2024.

[243] Ibid.

[244] Center for Preventive Action Global Conflict Tracker (2024) Civil War in Myanmar https://www.cfr.org/global-conflict-tracker/conflict/rohingya-crisis-myanmar. Accessed 30 May 2024.

[245] Action on Armed Violence January (2024) 122% rise in global civilian fatalities from explosive weapons in 2023: a year of harm reviewed. https://reliefweb.int/report/world/122-rise-global-civilian-fatalities-explosive-weapons-2023-year-harm-reviewed. Accessed 30 May 2024.

[246] ACLED (2024) ACLED Data Export Tool. https://acleddata.com/data-export-tool/. Accessed 30 May 2024.

[247] Reuters (2023) At least 50 killed as Myanmar military attacks rebel gathering, say media and militias. https://www.reuters.com/world/asia-pacific/multiple-casualties-after-myanmar-military-attacks-rebel-group-event-media-2023-04-11/. Accessed 30 May 2024.

[248] GC IV, Article 51(4).

responsibility for the attacks, several States condemn the government of Myanmar nonetheless.[249] It has been called the "deadliest attack on civilians" since the coup.[250]

5.1.6.4 Emerging Retaliation—Three Brotherhood Alliance and Operation 1027

Although Myanmar is not a signatory of APII, customary obligations of IHL apply regardless.[251] The Arakan Army, the Myanmar National Democratic Alliance Army and the Ta'ang National Liberation Army, who created the Three Brotherhood Alliance and other armed organizations, joined stronger forces in October 2023.[252] These ethnic armed organizations have a specific command structure and possess the ability to carry out sustained military operations.[253] According to an ACLED report, the alliance and other anti-coup forces gained significant territory in Chin, Rakhine, northern Shan and Mandalay. Accordingly, the alliance has become the highest level of threat Myanmar's military junta has faced since its coup in 2021.[254] The creation of this coalition led to many clashes.[255] On 27 October, they began Operation 1027. It was a coordinated offensive targeted against the Junta in the Shan State region. It came with the aim of "eradicating oppressive military dictatorship".[256]

The Junta has responded with airstrikes and artillery shelling that has caused civilian causalities.[257] The counteroffensives, including Operation 1111, renewed armed confrontations in northern Rakhine and Chin regions. On 19 November, airstrikes were carried out outside of the battle zone. A UN Report also elaborated on the alleged escalation of clashes in November in northern Shan and the Southeast. The armed confrontations between the Myanmar military, ethnic armed groups and

---

[249] Reuters (2023) Women, children among 29 killed as artillery hits Myanmar refugee camp. https://www.reuters.com/world/asia-pacific/many-killed-artillery-strike-northern-myanmar-media-local-sources-2023-10-10/. Accessed 30 May 2024.

[250] The Irrawaddy (2023) Myanmar: 'Midnight Massacre' at IDP Camp in Myanmar a War Crime: KIA https://www.irrawaddy.com/news/burma/midnight-massacre-at-idp-camp-in-mya nmar-a-war-crime-kia.html#google_vignette. Accessed 30 May 2024.

[251] See common Article 3 of the Geneva Conventions.

[252] Aljazeera (2024) What is Myanmar's Three Brotherhood Alliance that's resisting the military? https://www.aljazeera.com/news/2024/1/16/what-is-myanmars-three-brotherhood-alliance-thats-resisting-the-military. Accessed 30 May 2024.

[253] Ibid.

[254] ACLED (2024) ACLED Data Export Tool. https://acleddata.com/data-export-tool/. Accessed 22 May 2024.

[255] France 24 (2023) Myanmar rebels seize town from military junta despite China-backed ceasefire. https://www.france24.com/en/asia-pacific/20231216-myanmar-s-three-brotherhood-alliance-seizes-town-from-military-despite-china-backed-ceasefire. Accessed 30 May 2024.

[256] Aljazeera (2023) Myanmar military admits facing heavy assaults from anti-coup forces. https://www.aljazeera.com/news/2023/11/16/myanmar-military-admits-facing-heavy-assaults-from-anti-coup-forces. Accessed 30 May 2024.

[257] ACLED (2024) ACLED Data Export Tool. https://acleddata.com/data-export-tool/. Accessed 30 May 2024.

the People's Defence Forces resulted in an alleged displacement of approximately 23,000 people in the region.[258]

The nature of the attacks by the Junta wavers from the principle of distinction, which requires the ability to distinguish between military targets and civilians.[259] To that effect, facts suggest that none of the IHL rules required to be respected for the protection of civilians during an armed conflict have been followed.[260] The humanitarian situation has certainly worsened since the increase in these confrontations.[261] Amnesty International discussed the counter-response of the Junta to Operation 1027—recounting the attacks on and the displacement of civilians.[262] The UN estimated more than 900 civilians to be affected, whilst adding 660,000 to the two million already internally displaced.[263] Additionally, the events in October led to a considerable blow to the authority of the SACs, with a loss of more than 5500 soldiers, 10 generals and the capture of 30 towns.[264]

5.1.6.5 China's Intervention in Myanmar

China's involvement in the instability of Myanmar has been discussed owing to its border ties affecting the economy, trade and energy security of both states. The Three Brotherhood Alliance's announcement that one of their main objectives was to eliminate the scam syndicates, apparently fuelled China's support in their operation. China had previously mediated peace dialogues between officials of the regime and the Three Brotherhood Alliance on 2 June 2023. The diplomatic engagement has

---

[258] OCHA (2023) Myanmar: Escalation of clashes in northern Shan and the Southeast https://reliefweb.int/attachments/5ec2df68-8035-4751-ad19-1d4724bb4a21/Flash%20Update%202_Escalation%20in%20Clashes%20in%20Northern%20Shan%20and%20the%20Southeast_FINAL.pdf. Accessed 30 May 2024.

[259] Amnesty International (2023) Myanmar: Military should be investigated for war crimes in response to 'Operation 1027'. https://www.amnesty.org/en/latest/news/2023/12/myanmar-military-should-be-investigated-for-war-crimes-in-response-to-operation-1027/. Accessed 30 May 2024.

[260] Ibid.

[261] OCHA (2023) Myanmar: Escalation of clashes in northern Shan and the Southeast https://reliefweb.int/attachments/5ec2df68-8035-4751-ad19-1d4724bb4a21/Flash%20Update%202_Escalation%20in%20Clashes%20in%20Northern%20Shan%20and%20the%20Southeast_FINAL.pdf. Accessed 30 May 2024.

[262] Amnesty International (2023) Myanmar: Military should be investigated for war crimes in response to 'Operation 1027'. https://www.amnesty.org/en/latest/news/2023/12/myanmar-military-should-be-investigated-for-war-crimes-in-response-to-operation-1027/. Accessed 30 May 2024.

[263] Ibid.

[264] The Irrawaddy (2023) Dozens of Myanmar Junta Forces Killed in Four Days of Resistance Attacks. https://www.irrawaddy.com/news/war-against-the-junta/dozens-of-myanmar-junta-forces-killed-in-four-days-of-resistance-attacks-2.html. Accessed 30 May 2024.

5 Year in Review 2023

however not been fruitful. As such, Operation 1027's feasibility and success are largely tied to China's support.[265]

5.1.6.6 The Rohingya Refugee Crisis, Maritime Law Intersecting with International Humanitarian Law

The Rohingya crisis, originating in Myanmar, has resulted in a significant humanitarian disaster invoking massive-scale violations of international law. The exodus of Rohingya Muslims, fleeing from persecution, violence and abuse has led to the creation of the world's largest refugee crisis.[266]

In 2023, more than 500 Rohingyas died while trying to cross the sea. This is the highest recorded number in the past 9 years.[267] According to the UNHCR, approximately 4,500 people travelled across the Bay of Bengal in order to flee from Myanmar and the overcrowded camps of Bangladesh. They are termed 'boat people' (or Refugees at Sea) and are offered protection under the intersection of IHL, international human rights law (IHRL) and international maritime law.[268] Common Article 3 of the GCs, and more specifically Article 3 of the Convention against Torture invoke a responsibility in States to act on the customary principle of non-refoulement showcasing the complimentary application of IHL and IHRL.[269] In December, a joint statement issued by the civil society actors in Bangladesh referred to Bangladesh, Malaysia, India, Indonesia and Thailand as hosting the world's largest stateless population. There are more than 600,000 Rohingya still in Rakhine state in Myanmar. The joint report of statistics in collaboration with the UNHCR also read that 52% of the registered refugees are children.[270] The plea of the civil society was directed at UN Member states to support funding and humanitarian aid to the Rohingya people by cooperating with the host countries.[271]

---

[265] International Crisis Group (2024) Scam Centres and Ceasefires: China-Myanmar Ties Since the Coup. https://www.crisisgroup.org/asia/north-east-asia/china-myanmar/b179-scam-cen tres-and-ceasefires-china-myanmar-ties-coup Accessed 30 May 2024.

[266] HRW (2020) World Court Rules Against Myanmar on Rohingya. https://www.hrw.org/news/ 2020/01/23/world-court-rules-against-myanmar-rohingya. Accessed 30 May 2024.

[267] Aljazeera (2024) UNHCR: 569 Rohingya died at sea in 2023, highest in nine years. https:// www.aljazeera.com/news/2024/1/24/unhcr-569-rohingya-died-at-sea-in-2023-highest-in-nine-years. Accessed 30 May 2024.

[268] Medecins Sans Frontieres (Undated) Guide to Humanitarian Law - Boat People, Refugee at sea, Search and Rescue at Sea. https://guide-humanitarian-law.org/content/article/3/boat-people/. Accessed 30 May 2024.

[269] Ibid.

[270] UNHCR 2023.

[271] Ibid.

5.1.7 Nigeria

In Nigeria, decades-long ethnic and religious tensions coupled with political instability and disparities between the northern and southern regions have resulted in a violent and volatile environment in the State.[272]

The Nigerian State has been facing two major NIACs—one with Boko Haram and the other with IS in West Africa Province (ISWAP). The Nigerian military faced its first confrontation with Boko Haram in 2011 and ISWAP in 2019.[273] In 2023, RULAC added a potential NIAC between ISWAP and Boko Haram.[274] ISWAP broke off from Boko Haram in 2016, resulting in clashes and what has been widely classified as a NIAC between them with grave ongoing repercussions in 2023.[275] The Nigerian military has been collaborating with troops from Niger, Chad, Cameroon and Benin as the Multinational Joint Task Force (MNJTF) to support the fight against Boko Haram.[276]

ACLED has recorded an approximate number of 4431 civilian casualties for the year 2023, owing to the multiple existing NIACs in Nigeria and attributable to the clashes between the NSAGs and the Nigerian government's forces.[277] Furthermore, the International Organization for Migration (IOM) saw a massively high surge of internally displaced people because of the violence, covering the North-central and Northwestern regions of Nigeria.[278] There has been a series of unlawful killings, torture and attacks such as soldiers of the Nigerian army shooting three youth protestors in the Edo state on 29 June 2023 and the death in police custody of a student after being tortured during interrogation on 3 July 2023. Additionally, around 12,000 people were forcibly evicted from their properties on 27 July 2023 by the authorities.[279] As of 2023, more than 2.4 million people have remained internally displaced in the northeast regions of the state.[280]

---

[272] Ibid.

[273] RULAC (2023) Non-International Armed Conflicts in Nigeria. https://www.rulac.org/browse/conflicts/non-international-armed-conflict-in-nigeria. Accessed 30 May 2024.

[274] Ibid.

[275] Ibid.

[276] Ibid.

[277] ACLED (2024) ACLED Data Export Tool. https://acleddata.com/data-export-tool/. Accessed 30 May 2024.

[278] IOM Displacement Report (2023) Nigeria: North-Central and North-West Zones. https://dtm.iom.int/sites/g/files/tmzbdl1461/files/reports/DTM%20Nigeria%20-%20North-west%2C%20North-central%20Round%2011%20-%20Needs%20Monitoring%20Report_final%20%282%29.pdf. Accessed 30 May 2024.

[279] Amnesty International (2023) Nigeria. https://www.amnesty.org/en/location/africa/west-and-central-africa/nigeria/report-nigeria/. Accessed 20 May 2024.

[280] Ibid.

5.1.7.1 Political Violence

Elections in Nigeria took place on 25 February 2023 in an unstable political environment. In the months preceding the final election, there have been more than 200 recorded violent events during electoral rallies between party members and supporters of the opposing party. In the lead-up to 2023 around 109 deaths occurred, and they resulted in many streaks of violent incidents at the polls.[281] The north-western region saw clashes in Katsina and Kaduna state including the kidnapping of 8 civilians in Kagarko village.[282]

5.1.7.2 Boko Haram, ISWAP and the MNJTF

Boko Haram has declared allegiance to the IS and the Al-Qaeda. Over the years, it has successfully carried out military attacks against the Nigerian army and controls a significant amount of territory in the northern region of Nigeria.[283] ISWAP is a splinter of Boko Haram separated due to internal disturbances and differences in leadership. The result was a functional armed group with effective control in the region of Lake Chad.[284] Although it is difficult to attribute specific events to ISWAP and Boko Haram, the NIACs confronting the State with both insurgencies represent the greatest cause of armed clashes in Nigeria. In March, 30 civilians were tortured and killed by ISWAP in the Mukdolo village of Borno State, which is the birthplace of Boko Haram.[285] In June too, on several dates, at least 36 farmers in the Borno State were killed by Boko Haram.[286] They also abducted over 40 women and girls in Mafa, Borno State on 22 August 2023.[287]

The National Human Rights Commission has also launched an investigation related to forced abortions in the Boko Haram conflict. The allegations of these war crimes are directed at the Nigerian military.[288]

Airstrikes in Nasarawa

Multiple events of alleged disproportionate civilian harm were carried out by the government by way of airstrikes in 2023. In December, a drone strike allegedly

---

[281] Ibid.

[282] Aljazeera (2023) Rivalry among Boko Haram factions compounds violence in northern Nigeria. https://www.aljazeera.com/features/2023/9/8/rivalry-among-boko-haram-factions-compounds-violence-in-northern-nigeria. Accessed 30 May 2024.

[283] RULAC (2023) Non-International Armed Conflicts in Nigeria. https://www.rulac.org/browse/conflicts/non-international-armed-conflict-in-nigeria. Accessed 30 May 2024.

[284] Ibid.

[285] Ibid.

[286] Daily Trust (2023) Farmers On the Run As Boko Haram Killings Return. https://dailytrust.com/farmers-on-the-run-as-b-haram-killings-return/. Accessed 30 May 2024.

[287] HRW (2023) Nigeria. https://www.hrw.org/world-report/2024/country-chapters/nigeria. Accessed 30 May 2024.

[288] Ibid.

carried out by the Nigerian military resulted in the death of approximately 85 to 120 civilians. The President, Bola Tinubu, along with the spokesperson issued a statement expressing regret over the mishap and directed an investigation into it.[289] Retaliation attacks by the Nigerian armed forces against Boko Haram resulted in military airstrikes in the Nasarawa region in January killing around 39 civilians.[290] On 24 January 2022, civilians were allegedly killed by the Nigerian air force in Niger too.[291]

5.1.7.3 Vigilantes and the Recognition of Subgroups

The bandit groups and so-called 'vigilantes' are debated to be the highest cause of violence and unrest in Nigeria in its current circumstances.[292] The Northwest region has witnessed violence and hostilities in the form of killings and kidnappings owing these armed groups. In February, the 'bandits' carried out widespread killings and other serious crimes in the Katsina region. April saw the kidnappings of approximately 80 women and children in Zamfara.[293] Theories relative to the bandits are mainly three—that they are out-of-control farmers in the volatile confrontations stemming from the farmers in conflict, that it is a form of 'terrorism' continuing the Fulani Jihad or that they are sanctioned by the government and are sub-groups of already existing organizations.[294]

5.1.8 Sudan

During 2023, Sudan became one of the global epicentres of armed violence after fierce fighting broke out between the Sudanese Armed Forces (SAF) and the NSAG Rapid Support Forces (RSF) in April. Clashes, which first started in Sudan's capital Khartoum, spread throughout the year nationwide, leading to an estimated loss of life of around 13,000 persons.[295]

---

[289] HRW (2023) Nigeria. https://www.hrw.org/world-report/2024/country-chapters/nigeria. Accessed 30 May 2024.

[290] Amnesty International (2023) Nigeria. https://www.amnesty.org/en/location/africa/west-and-central-africa/nigeria/report-nigeria/. Accessed 20 May 2024.

[291] Ibid.

[292] Ibid.

[293] Reuters (2023) Gunmen kidnap 80, including children, in northwest Nigeria. https://www.reuters.com/world/africa/gunmen-kidnap-80-including-children-northwest-nigeria-2023-04-08/. Accessed 30 May 2024.

[294] Osasona T 2023.

[295] ACLED (2024) Sudan Situation Update, January 2024: The Rapid Support Forces (RSF) Gains Ground in Sudan. https://acleddata.com/2024/01/12/sudan-situation-update-januar-2024-the-rapid-support-forces-rsf-gains-ground-in-sudan/. Accessed 8 May 2024.

5 Year in Review 2023

Armed violence in Sudan has also triggered an unprecedented humanitarian crisis. Sudan has become the country with the greatest number of displaced persons in the world, after more than 7.2 million Sudanese had to relocate within or outside Sudan.[296] By the end of 2023, unravelling conflict coupled with a strong economic decline nationwide had driven 37% of the Sudanese population, what amounts to 17.7 million persons, into high levels of acute food insecurity.[297] Among other after-effects, the conflict also led to the complete disruption of services in 70–80% of hospitals in conflict-affected areas, as well as to the loss of access to formal education for more than 12 million children.[298]

Likewise, the conflict between the RSF and the SAF has propelled an increase in ethnic fights, as both warrying parties have tried to exploit their ethnic alliances. Such has been the case in the Darfuri region, where the conflict has revived inter-ethnic wars between Darfuri Arabs—which represents the majoritarian ethnic group among RSF ranks—and non-Arabs groups like the Masalit, as well as Darfuri Arabs and Sudanese riverine communities.[299] One further layer of complexity is added to the Sudanese landscape by the presence of other NSAGs that have during 2023 fought the RSF and/or the SAF, including the Sudan Liberation Movement/Army–Abdel Wahid al-Nur and the Sudan People's Liberation Movement/Army–North (Abdelaziz al-Hilu faction).[300] For space constraints, this Year in Review will however exclusively address conflict dynamics between the SAF and RSF.

5.1.8.1 Political Developments Leading up to the Conflict

In April 2019, a months-long popular uprising prompted by rising fuel prices led to the ousting of President Omar al-Bashir, who had ruled the country in an autocratic fashion for three decades.[301] Months into the protest, the SAF and the paramilitary group RSF, long allies of the President, withdrew their support for al-Bashir and

---

[296] UN OCHA (2023) Sudan Humanitarian Update, 28 December 2023. https://www.unocha.org/publications/report/sudan/sudan-humanitarian-update-28-december-2023. Accessed 28 June 2024.

[297] UN OCHA (2023) Sudan: Seven Months of Conflict - Key Facts and Figures, 15 December 2023. https://www.unocha.org/publications/report/sudan/sudan-seven-months-conflict-key-facts-and-figures-15-december-2023. Accessed 28 May 2024.

[298] UN OCHA (2023) Sudan Humanitarian Update, 5 October 2023. https://www.unocha.org/publications/report/sudan/sudan-humanitarian-update-5-october-2023#:~:text=The%20Sudan%20Ministry%20of%20Health,and%20the%20Rapid%20Support%20Forces.&text=Disease%20outbreaks%20have%20been%20reported,malaria%2C%20dengue%20fever%20and%20cholera. Accessed 28 May 2024.

[299] International Crisis Group (2023) Sudan: A Year of War. https://www.crisisgroup.org/africa/horn-africa/sudan/sudan-year-war. Accessed 28 May 2024.

[300] *See* for example ACLED (2023) Sudan Situation Update, June 2023: Conflict intensifies following the breakdown of Jeddah talks. https://acleddata-com.translate.goog/2023/06/23/sudan-situation-update-june-2023-conflict-intensifies-following-the-breakdown-of-jeddah-talks/?x_tr_sl=en&_x_tr_tl=es&_x_tr_hl=es&_x_tr_pto=sc. Accessed 28 June 2024; IISS 2023, p 250.

[301] BBC News (2019) Sudan crisis: Military council arrests protesters' leaders. https://www.bbc.com/news/world-africa-47852496. Accessed 28 June 2024.

orchestrated a coup to overthrow him.[302] In October 2019, a civilian-military transitional government was created with the goal of ultimately yielding power to a civilian administration. Both the leaders of the SAF General Abdel Fattah al-Burhan and the RSF General Mohamed Hamdan 'Hemedti' held high ranks therein—respectively as Chair and Co-Chair of the transitional Sovereign Council, the government's most powerful organ.[303]

Cooperation between al-Burhan and Hemedti progressively deteriorated and ultimately stalemated after the signature of the framework agreement between military and civilian leaders on 5 December 2022. The latter, which was aimed at clearing the pathway for the transition to a fully civilian government, envisioned among others the absorption of the RSF into the SAF.[304] Discrepancies between al-Burhan and Hemedti led to a power struggle which eventually prompted the resort to arms and a definitive breakdown in the delicate situation of the civilian-military transitional government.

5.1.8.2 Level of Intensity of Hostilities Between the SAF and RSF

a. **Greater Khartoum Area**

Fighting broke out between the SAF and RSF on 15 April 2023 in the vicinity of a RSF military base located in the south of Khartoum and spread throughout the whole region and main urban areas along major east-west roadways between West Darfur and Kassala.[305] Caught amidst heavy fighting, the Khartoum Metropolitan Area quickly found itself facing dire food, water and electricity shortages.[306]

In the early days of the conflict, Hemedti's RSF gained control of the Greater Khartoum area—comprising Khartoum and its sister cities Bahri and Omdurman—thanks to its superiority in rapid movement.[307] Among others, between April and early June the RSF took control over the military weapons factories of Khartoum

---

[302] Council on Foreign Relations (CFR) (2024) Power Struggle in Sudan. https://www.cfr.org/global-conflict-tracker/conflict/power-struggle-sudan. Accessed 28 June 2024.

[303] Human Rights Watch (2024) "The Massalit Will Not Come Home": Ethnic Cleansing and Crimes Against Humanity in El Geneina, West Darfur, Sudan. https://www.hrw.org/sites/default/files/media_2024/05/sudan0524web_0.pdf. Accessed 13 June 2024.

[304] Political Framework Agreement (adopted 5 December 2022).

[305] ACLED (2023) Fact Sheet: Conflict surges in Sudan. https://acleddata.com/2023/04/28/fact-sheet-conflict-surges-in-sudan/. Accessed 28 June 2024; ACLED (2023) Sudan Situation Update, May 2023: Fighting rages amid ceasefire talks. https://acleddata.com/2023/05/26/sudan-situation-update-may-2023-fighting-rages-amid-ceasefire-talks/. Accessed 28 June 2024.

[306] OHCHR (2023) Sudan: Plight of civilians amid hostilities. https://www.ohchr.org/en/press-briefing-notes/2023/04/sudan-plight-civilians-amid-hostilities. Accessed 24 June 2024.

[307] International Crisis Group (2024) CrisisWatch Database: Sudan. https://www.crisisgroup.org/crisiswatch/database?location%5B0%5D=14&crisis_state=&created=&from_month=1&from_year=2024&to_month=1&to_year=2024&page=1. Accessed 28 June 2024.

5 Year in Review 2023

and the main oil refinery in the country.[308] Likewise, the RSF seized or sieged most SAF military bases in the Greater Khartoum area. In June and July 2023, the SAF launched multi-attack counteroffensives against the RSF in Khartoum and Bahri, albeit these were effectively repelled by the RSF.[309]

By August, the SAF only maintained two strongholds in the city of Khartoum, including its headquarters.[310] As the NIAC progressed, the RSF also gained control of villages that surround Khartoum. As such, on 6 October 2023, the RSF shelled Khartoum neighbouring city Jabal Awlia, including the SAF's Air Force base located there, killing at least 118 people and injuring as many as 600. However, during 2023, the RSF did not manage to defeat the SAF in the whole state of Khartoum, as the latter continued exercising control over certain areas and military bases.

The RSF's decentralization and high experience in urban and guerrilla warfare, as well as its effective resort to ground-to-air missiles has given it a comparative advantage over the SAF in the Khartoum state.[311] During 2023, most of the SAF's strategy in Khartoum's metropolitan area was limited to defending its military bases while resorting to airstrikes and artillery shelling.[312] The high use of heavy explosive weapons in densely populated areas has resulted in great civilian casualties and vast loss of civilian property and critical infrastructure.[313]

b. *Other Regions*

Since the beginning of the NIAC, the fighting spread to other Sudanese regions, especially those of Darfur and Kordofan.[314] In Darfur, both sides of the conflict have

---

[308] ACLED (2023) Sudan Situation Update, June 2023: Conflict intensifies following the breakdown of Jeddah talks. https://acleddata.com/2023/06/23/sudan-situation-update-june-2023-conflict-int ensifies-following-the-breakdown-of-jeddah-talks/. Accessed 26 June 2024; International Crisis Group (2023) Sudan: A Year of War. https://www.crisisgroup.org/africa/horn-africa/sudan/sudan-year-war. Accessed 28 May 2024; PAX (2024) Oil in the Crosshairs. https://paxforpeace.nl/news/oil-in-the-crosshairs/. Accessed 26 June 2024.

[309] ACLED (2023) Sudan Situation Update, June 2023: Conflict intensifies following the breakdown of Jeddah talks. https://acleddata.com/2023/06/23/sudan-situation-update-june-2023-conflict-int ensifies-following-the-breakdown-of-jeddah-talks/. Accessed 26 June 2024.

[310] Reuters (2023) Sudan: Army chief Burhan appears in public for first time since war started - statement. https://www.reuters.com/world/africa/sudan-army-chief-burhan-appears-public-first-time-since-war-started-statement-2023-08-24/. Accessed 28 June 2024.

[311] Jamestown Foundation (2024) Can the SAF Defeat the RSF in Sudan? https://jamestown.org/program/can-the-saf-defeat-the-rsf-in-sudan/. Accessed 29 June 2024.

[312] ACLED (2024) Sudan Situation Update, February 2024: Sudan - the SAF breaks the siege. https://acleddata.com/2024/02/16/sudan-situation-update-february-2024-sudan-the-saf-bre aks-the-siege/. Accessed 26 June 2024; ACLED (2023) Sudan Situation Update, June 2023: Conflict intensifies following the breakdown of Jeddah talks. https://acleddata.com/2023/06/23/sudan-situat ion-update-june-2023-conflict-intensifies-following-the-breakdown-of-jeddah-talks/. Accessed 26 June 2024.

[313] Human Rights Watch (2024) World Report 2024: Sudan. https://www.hrw.org/world-report/2024/country-chapters/sudan. Accessed 28 June 2024.

[314] ACLED (2023) Sudan Situation Update, May 2023: Fighting rages amid ceasefire talks. https://acleddata.com/2023/05/26/sudan-situation-update-may-2023-fighting-rages-amid-ceasef ire-talks/. Accessed 28 June 2024.

relied on affiliated local militias to engage in the fight. Different truces agreed at the local and regional level in Darfur quickly collapsed,[315] demonstrating the high instability of the region. Notable examples of clashes include the killing of at least 280 persons on 12–13 May 2023 in reported battles between Masalit and RSF-backed Arab militia in al-Geneina, the capital of West Darfur state.[316] This raises the issue that not all clashes held in Darfur during 2023 took place within the context of the NIAC confronting the SAF and RSF, albeit they obviously maintain a close relationship.

Of particular relevance is the RSF's conquer of South Darfur state on 27 October 2023 after seizing the last military base controlled by the SAF in the capital Nyala—the second biggest city in Sudan.[317] By the end of the year, the RSF virtually controlled all South, Central, West and East Darfur states.[318] Since November and until the end of 2023, intense clashes took place in the only state in the Darfuri region not controlled by the RSF, North Darfur, and especially in its capital El Fasher.[319] Some NSAGs signatories of the Juba Peace Agreement based in North Darfur decided to renounce neutrality and join the SAF in anticipation of the RSF offensive.

The RSF's operations in Darfur have faced numerous allegations of ethnic cleansing against the Masalit population, with widespread killings, sexual violence, torture, and other forms of ill-treatment having been documented during 2023.[320] Most notably, on 13 July 2023, the UN reported that the bodies of at least 87 Massalit individuals were found in a mass grave in the capital of West Darfur state al-Geneina.[321] Likewise, the Governor of West Darfur State, Khamis Abakar, was kidnapped and killed on 14 June 2023, hours after he had accused the RSF of committing genocide in Sudan.[322] While different factors point towards the responsibility

---

[315] ACLED (2023) Sudan Situation Update, June 2023: Conflict intensifies following the breakdown of Jeddah talks. https://acleddata.com/2023/06/23/sudan-situation-update-june-2023-conflict-int ensifies-following-the-breakdown-of-jeddah-talks/. Accessed 26 June 2024.

[316] International Crisis Group (2024) CrisisWatch Database: Sudan. https://www.crisisgroup.org/crisiswatch/database?location%5B%5D=14&crisis_state=&created=&from_month=1&from_y ear=2024&to_month=1&to_year=2024&page=1. Accessed 28 June 2024.

[317] Ibid.

[318] Ibid.

[319] Ibid.

[320] Human Rights Watch (2024) "The Massalit Will Not Come Home": Ethnic Cleansing and Crimes Against Humanity in El Geneina, West Darfur, Sudan. https://www.hrw.org/sites/default/files/media_2024/05/sudan0524web_0.pdf. Accessed 13 June 2024.

[321] OHCHR (2023) Sudan: At least 87 buried in mass grave in Darfur, Rapid Support Forces deny victims. https://www.ohchr.org/en/press-releases/2023/07/sudan-least-87-buried-mass-grave-darfur-rapid-support-forces-deny-victims. Accessed 24 June 2024.

[322] BBC (2023) Sudan conflict: West Darfur governor killed after genocide claim. https://www-bbc-com.translate.goog/news/world-africa-65914569?_x_tr_sl=en&_x_tr_tl=es&_x_tr_hl=es&_x_tr_pto=sc&_x_tr_hist=true. Accessed 25 June 2024.

of the RSF, the group has denied it. Moreover, high levels of looting, burning and destruction of civilian property have been reported.[323]

In the Kordofan region, fighting intensified in June 2023. In North Kordofan state, amidst clashes over its capital al-Obeid, 50 civilians were reportedly killed in the al-Humaira village by the RSF on 3 June 2023.[324] In North Kordofan, 2023 ended with continued clashes over the capital al-Obeid.[325] For its part, the last month of 2023 also saw the shocking capture of Wad Medani, capital of the Gezira state, by the RSF, which amounted to its first strike south east of Khartoum. Many of Khartoum's residents had fled to Wad Medani, as it constituted one of the most stable SAF's strongholds when the war broke out.[326]

c. *Peace Efforts*

Many uncoordinated peace initiatives involving numerous international actors have been launched to bring an end to the Sudanese conflict between the SAF and RSF, including the signature of at least nine failed ceasefire agreements.[327] In this regard, the seven-day nationwide ceasefire brokered by Saudi Arabia and the United States in Jeddah on 20 May 2023 was particularly relevant, although fighting escalated once again after its expiration.[328] By the end of May 2023, SAF envoys withdrew from negotiations, which have been intermittent ever since. On 27 August 2023, the RSF expressed its willingness to host talks and presented a ten-point plan to achieve 'lasting peace', which was rejected by al-Burhan.[329]

The parties signed the Jeddah Declaration of Commitment to Protect the Civilians of Sudan on 12 May 2023, committing to respect IHL and IHRL to enable humanitarian action and fulfil the needs of civilians in emergencies.[330] This agreement has

---

[323] ACLED (2023) Sudan Situation Update, May 2023: Fighting rages amid ceasefire talks. https://acleddata.com/2023/05/26/sudan-situation-update-may-2023-fighting-rages-amid-ceasef ire-talks/. Accessed 28 June 2024.

[324] International Crisis Group (2024) CrisisWatch Database: Sudan. https://www.crisisgroup.org/crisiswatch/database?location%5B0%5D=14&crisis_state=&created=&from_month=1&from_y ear=2024&to_month=1&to_year=2024&page=1. Accessed 28 June 2024.

[325] Ibid.

[326] International Crisis Group (2023) Sudan: A Year of War. https://www.crisisgroup.org/africa/horn africa/sudan/sudan year war. Accessed 28 May 2024.

[327] Jeffery J (2023) Sudan army says it has killed RSF leader in clashes. https://apnews.com/article/sudan-rsf-army-war-f3516c941335f0e21c01b15e30572ac1. Accessed 28 June 2024.

[328] ACLED (2023) Sudan Situation Update, June 2023: Conflict intensifies following the breakdown of Jeddah talks. https://acleddata-com.translate.goog/2023/06/23/sudan-situation-update-june-2023-conflict-intensifies-following-the-breakdown-of-jeddah-talks/?_x_tr_sl=en&_x_tr_tl= es&_x_tr_hl=es&_x_tr_pto=sc. Accessed 28 June 2024; BBC News (2023) Sudan ceasefire: Khartoum largely quiet, residents say. https://www.bbc.com/news/world-africa-65683681. Accessed 28 June 2024.

[329] Al Jazeera (2023) Sudan's RSF floats peace plan as rival army chief eyes regional trip. https://www.aljazeera.com/news/2023/8/28/sudans-rsf-floats-peace-plan-as-rival-army-chief-eyes-regional-trip. Accessed 28 June 2024.

[330] ReliefWeb (2023) Jeddah Declaration: Commitment to protect civilians in Sudan. https://rel iefweb.int/report/sudan/jeddah-declaration-commitment-protect-civilians-sudan. Accessed 29 June 2024.

however been qualified as 'meaningless' by various civil society actors.[331] During 2023, different agreements at the local level were also brokered generally with the help of local community leaders.

Level of Organization of the RSF

The RSF was formally created in 2013 with the support of back then President Omar al-Bashir and his National Intelligence and Security Services out of the loosely coordinated Arab-majority Janjaweed militia.[332] The RSF was well known for its involvement in the commission of atrocities in the Darfuri war against non-Arab populations in the early 2000s. RSF was given 'regular force' status in 2015 and in 2017 a law legitimizing the RSF as an independent security force was passed.[333] The group was used by the President, among others, to guard borders, repress citizen uprisings, fight in the Yemeni war for the Saudi coalition, and serve as a sort of presidential guard.[334]

Conservative estimates suggest that the RSF has a strength that ranges from 40,000 to 70,000 active fighters,[335] while other sources point towards a force between 70,000 and 150,000 recruits.[336] Beyond war-mongering activities, the RSF sustains itself through different economic initiatives, including gold mining in the Darfuri region, the taxation of commercial and agricultural trade in Darfur and the supply of mercenaries in different conflicts.[337]

In light of the description of the fight between the RSF and SAF, the former has also demonstrated a high capacity to engage in protracted armed violence and to carry multi-attack offensives in different parts of the country throughout 2023. In the course of peace efforts, the RSF has also proved its ability to speak with one voice and to engage in negotiations.

Conclusion

Considering the intensity of hostilities confronting the SAF and RSF since 15 April 2023 as well as the level of organization of the RSF, it seems clear that a NIAC between the two warring parties has been triggered in Sudan during 2023.

---

[331] Middle East Eye (2023) Sudan crisis: Jeddah agreement no ceasefire, more fighting. https://www.middleeasteye.net/news/sudan-crisis-jeddah-agreement-no-ceasefire-more-fighting. Accessed 28 June 2024.

[332] Al Jazeera (2023) Who is Hemedti, the puppeteer behind Sudan's feared RSF fighters? https://www.aljazeera.com/news/2023/4/16/who-is-hemedti-the-puppeteer-behind-sudans-feared-rsf-fighters. Accessed 27 June 2024.

[333] Al Jazeera (2023) Sudan unrest: What is the Rapid Support Forces? https://www.aljazeera.com/news/2023/4/16/sudan-unrest-what-is-the-rapid-support-forces. Accessed 28 June 2024.

[334] Center for Preventive Action (2024) Civil War in Sudan. https://www.cfr.org/global-conflict-tracker/conflict/power-struggle-sudan#:~:text=The%20conflict%20is%20primarily%20a,Rapid%20Support%20Forces%20(RSF). Accessed 26 June 2024.

[335] IISS 2023, p. 251.

[336] RULAC (2023) Non-International Armed Conflicts in Sudan. https://www.rulac.org/browse/conflicts/non-international-armed-conflicts-in-sudan#collapse4accord. Accessed 28 June 2024.

[337] IISS 2023, p. 251.

5 Year in Review 2023

5.1.9 Ukraine/Russia

The full-scale invasion of Ukraine in February 2022 became a matter of positional warfare in 2023. Since the August 2022 Ukrainian counter-offensive,[338] both sides favoured the construction of trench systems and made heavy use of artillery, which was, as will be discussed below, helped by third-state supplies. As a result, the frontline became more static, and the increasing use of heavy explosive weapons resulted in an aggravation of civilian and military casualties.[339] The frontline as of December 2023 did not drastically change compared to the one of December 2022. Russian attacks were not only on the frontlines but also targeted the cities of Kyiv, Dnipro, Kharkiv, Odesa, Smila, Lviv and Sumy. Almost 6.5 million Ukrainians fled the country, and around 3.5 million were displaced within Ukraine.

Despite the counter-offensive launched against Russian positions in mid-2022 by Ukrainian forces in Eastern Ukraine, the Russians' control over the region was expanded at the end of 2023. The first months were marked by the Russian launch of large-scale strikes in Vinnytsia and Odesa blasts, targeting civilian buildings. Russian forces targeted energy infrastructure in Kyiv, Khmelnytskyi, Dnipropetrovsk, Pavlohrad, Vinnytsia, Zaporizhia, Odesa, Mykolaiv, Poltava, Zhytomyr, Kirovohrad, and Kharkiv. Such conduct is likely to violate the prohibition to target civilian objects.[340]

Ukrainian forces lost control of Soledar in the east after attacks by the Wagner forces, a private military organisation fighting alongside the Russian army, whose command will be examined below. Bakhmut and its surroundings have been the theatre of fierce fighting since March, with each party claiming to control the city. The

---

[338] Reuters (2023) Mapping Ukraine's counteroffensive. https://www.reuters.com/graphics/UKR AINE-CRISIS/MAPS/klvygwawavg/. Accessed 13 June 2024.

[339] As a result of the use of explosive weapons, the OHCHR reported that 1851 civilians were killed and 6274 were injured in 2023. *See* OHCHR (2023) Report on the Human Rights Situation in Ukraine 1 February–31 July 2023.https://www.ohchr.org/sites/default/files/documents/hrbodies/ hrcouncil/coiukraine/23-10-04-OHCHR-36th-periodic-report-ukraine-en.pdf. Accessed 15 March 2024; OHCHR (2023) Report on the Human Rights Situation in Ukraine 1 August 2023– 30 November 2023. https://www.ohchr.org/sites/default/files/2023-12/23-12-12-OHCHR-37th-per iodic-report-ukraine-en.pdf. Accessed 15 March 2024. A declassified US report in December 2023 found that 315,000 Russian troops, "or about 87% of the total with which it started the war in 2022, have been killed or injured." *See* Reuters (2023) U.S. intelligence assesses Ukraine war has cost Russia 315,000 casualties -source. https://www.reuters.com/world/us-intelligence-assesses- ukraine-war-has-cost-russia-315000-casualties-source-2023-12-12/. Accessed 15 March 2024. As of August 2023, the New York Times shared that, according to U.S. officials, 70,000 Ukrainians militaries were killed and 100,000 to 120,000 were wounded. *See* New York Times (2023) Troop Deaths and Injuries in Ukraine War Near 500,000, U.S. Officials Say. https://www.nytimes.com/ 2023/08/18/us/politics/ukraine-russia-war-casualties.html. Accessed 15 March 2024.

[340] API, above n 10, Article 48 and Article 52(2).

Russian forces attempted to seize Ukraine's positions with foot soldiers' movements, and the aim was to outnumber Ukrainian forces.[341]

Battles taking place in the Black Sea have considerably escalated in 2023. The Russian Federation fleet has been pushed out of the northwestern Black Sea.[342] It has been reported that Ukraine has employed cutting-edge naval drones and Western-supplied missiles to damage or destroy an increasing number of Russian vessels and strike significant targets, including the headquarters of the Russian Black Sea Fleet. Satellite imagery and international media reports from early October 2023 confirmed that most of the Russian Black Sea Fleet had been relocated from Crimea to the relative safety of Russian ports.[343]

Several IHL-related developments happened in the conflict opposing the Federation of Russia to Ukraine. Specific focus has been given to the attacks against the environment during the conflict and the consequences of the fights on the Ukrainian ecosystems. In June 2023, the destruction of the Kakhovka Dam by Russian forces triggered an ecological and humanitarian disaster, endangering the survival of numerous species in the aquatic ecosystem.[344] It also reinforced the debate about recognising ecocide as an international crime.[345] For the purpose of conflict classification, this Year in Review proposes to address the topic of third-state participation and the related question to what extent a third state can be considered a party to an ongoing IAC. Likewise, this Year in Review covers new developments on the status of the para-military group Wagner in 2023.

5.1.9.1 Conflict Classification and Third State Support

The 2022 Year in Review identified the existence of an IAC between Ukraine and the Russian Federation. The 2023 developments reaffirm this assessment. Continuing the defensive military aid sent in 2022, the US and European countries provided

---

[341] *See notably* Al-Jazeera (2023) Russia seizes more ground in Ukraine's east as Kyiv's forces await supplies. https://www.aljazeera.com/news/2024/5/1/russia-seizes-more-ground-in-ukraines-east-as-kyivs-forces-await-supplies. Accessed 10 June 2024.

[342] Oleksiy Goncharenko (2023) 2023 review: Ukraine scores key victories in the Battle of the Black Sea. https://www.atlanticcouncil.org/blogs/ukrainealert/2023-review-ukraine-scores-key-victories-in-the-battle-of-the-black-sea/. Accessed 15 March 2024.

[343] Ibid.

[344] New York Times (2023) Why the Evidence Suggests Russia Blew Up the Kakhovka Dam. https://www.nytimes.com/interactive/2023/06/16/world/europe/ukraine-kakhovka-dam-collapse.html. Accessed 20 June 2024; European Civil Protection and Humanitarian Aid Operations – stories (2023) A disaster in photos: Nova Kakhovka dam breach in Ukraine. https://civil-protection-humanitarian-aid.ec.europa.eu/news-stories/stories/disaster-photos-nova-kakhovka-dam-breach-ukraine_en. Accessed 20 June 2024.

[345] *See* Jérôme de Hemptinne, Luigi Prosperi (2024) Prosecuting Ecocide Before the International Criminal Court: Concrete Possibility or Long-Term Aspiration? (Part 1). https://www.uu.nl/en/news/prosecuting-ecocide-before-the-international-criminal-court-concrete-possibility-or-long-term. Accessed 20 June 2024.

5 Year in Review 2023

Ukraine with ammunition, heavy weaponry, grenade launchers, and small arms.[346] A significant shift in military supply happened in January 2023, when the United Kingdom, the US, Norway, and Germany sent battle tanks to Ukraine, changing their defensive posture towards an offensive one.[347]

While depleting its missile arsenal, the Russian Federation received more than a thousand Shahed drones from Iran, and support extended through the year.[348] Ukrainian authorities have stated that the Russian Federation persisted in acquiring Iranian-produced Shahed drones and the Russian Federation established terms to produce them within Russia with the assistance of Iran.[349]

Determining the extent of third-state support capable of turning it into a party to the ongoing IAC is difficult. The ICRC argued that the application of IHL in the case of a third State intervention is clear.[350] Arguably, it is necessary to identify hostilities between the third State and one of the State parties to the ongoing IAC, and thus the acts of financing and equipping would not suffice to meet the required threshold.[351] Michael N. Schmitt argued that for a third State to become a party to an ongoing IAC, one must identify resort to armed force between States.[352] Instead of suggesting that a new conflict must appear between two States, Alexander Wentker recognises that a

---

[346] European Parliamentary Research Service (2023) Russia's war on Ukraine: Western-made tanks for Ukraine. https://www.europarl.europa.eu/RegData/etudes/ATAG/2023/739316/EPRS_A TA(2023)739316_EN.pdf. Accessed 26 April 2024.

[347] Ibid.

[348] Iran supplied Russian troops with ammunition, artillery shells, glide bombs. *See* Institute for the Study of War (2023) Russian Offensive Campaign Assessment, April 24, 2023. https://www.und erstandingwar.org/backgrounder/russian-offensive-campaign-assessment-april-24-2023. Accessed 25 April 2024; Institute for the Study of War (2023) Russian Offensive Campaign Assessment, November 22, 2023. https://www.understandingwar.org/backgrounder/russian-offensive-campaign-assessment-november-22-2023. Accessed 25 April 2024.

[349] Institute for the Study of War (2023) Russian Offensive Campaign Assessment, July 5, 2023. https://understandingwar.org/backgrounder/russian-offensive-campaign-assessment-july-5-2023. Accessed 25 April 2024. Institute for the Study of War (2023) Russian Offensive Campaign Assessment, June 9, 2023. https://www.understandingwar.org/backgrounder/russian-offensive-campaign-assessment-june-9-2023. Accessed 25 April 2024; Institute for the Study of War (2023) Russian Offensive Campaign Assessment, August 1, 2023. https://www.understandingwar.org/backgrounder/russian-offensive-campaign-assessment-august-1-2023. Accessed 25 April 2024.

[350] Ferraro T (2016) The ICRC's legal position on the notion of armed conflict involving foreign intervention and on determining the IHL applicable to this type of conflict. International Review of the Red Cross 97:1227–1252, p. 1228.

[351] Such a view is confirmed in *Tadić*, where the Appeals Chamber found that "equipping and financing" a non-State actor does not turn the NIAC into an IAC. As underlined by Michael N. Schmitt, "[i]f materiel assistance to a non-State group in a non-international armed conflict does not initiate IAC between the supporting State and the State against which the arms and equipment will be employed, there is no rationale for saying it would do so in an international armed conflict." *See* Micheal N. Schmitt (2022) Providing arms and materiel to Ukraine: Neutrality, Co-Belligerency, and the Use of Force. https://lieber.westpoint.edu/ukraine-neutrality-co-belligerency-use-of-force/. Accessed 14 June 2024.

[352] Ibid.

third State may become part to an ongoing IAC if its acts "form part of the hostilities or military operations that constitute the international armed conflict".[353]

A possible avenue to understand what conduct triggers third-state participation could be framed under the ICRC's interpretive guidance on direct participation in hostilities. Accordingly, the harm caused by the third State "must attain a certain threshold", that can be reached "either by causing harm of a specifically military nature or by inflicting death, injury, or destruction on persons or objects protected against direct attack".[354] Additionally, allied parties will have to coordinate their operations closely—but again, it is difficult to assess which degree of closeness is required. In 2022, US Press Secretary Jen Psaki stated that the US was sharing intelligence in real-time with the Ukrainian military, which had put under the spotlight a potential military cooperation between the two countries. However, this statement has not been backed by any subsequent findings on the US conduct. As a result, it hardly leads to the qualification of the US and the other third parties as participants in the existing conflict, as the nexus between the supply and the harm caused to the enemy is too remote.[355]

Conflict Classification

The 2022 Year in Review identified the existence of an IAC between Ukraine and the Russian Federation. The 2023 developments reaffirm this assessment. It must be highlighted that the frontline as of December 2023 did not drastically change compared to the one of December 2022.[356]

5.1.9.2 Assessing Wagner's Status Under IHL

The armed conflict, for the past year, is undoubtedly an IAC.[357] The mutiny of Wagner, namely Russian proxy forces, must be considered part of the discussion of the IHL regime that applies to PMC in the conflict. Indeed, one could argue that the

---

[353] Wentker A (2022) At War: When Do States Supporting Ukraine or Russia become Parties to the Conflict and What Would that Mean? https://www.ejiltalk.org/at-war-when-do-states-supporting-ukraine-or-russia-become-parties-to-the-conflict-and-what-would-that-mean/. Accessed 20 June 2024.

[354] ICRC (2009) Interpretive Guidance on the Notion of Direct Participation in Hostilities under International Humanitarian Law. https://www.icrc.org/en/doc/assets/files/other/icrc-002-0990.pdf. Accessed 24 April 2024.

[355] API, above n 10, Article 51(3); ICRC (2009) Interpretive Guidance on the Notion of Direct Participation in Hostilities under International Humanitarian Law. https://www.icrc.org/en/doc/ass ets/files/other/icrc-002-0990.pdf. Accessed 24 April 2024.

[356] Institute for the Study of War (2023) Russian Offensive Campaign Assessment, December 31, 2023. https://www.understandingwar.org/backgrounder/russian-offensive-campaign-assessment-december-31-2023. Accessed 25 April 2024. https://understandingwar.org/backgrounder/russian-offensive-campaign-assessment-december-31; Institute for the Study of War (2022) Russian Offensive Campaign Assessment, December 31, 2022. https://understandingwar.org/backgrounder/rus sian-offensive-campaign-assessment-december-31. Accessed 25 April 2024.

[357] Gregoire et al. 2023, pp. 203–295.

law of NIAC should be applied to these non-state actors, considering that they still participate in the hostilities and broke out from the Russian army's command. This, in line with the ICRC's opinion, considers that the overall control of State over a non-state party results in the application of the law of IAC.[358] While the relationship between Wagner and the Russian Military Command has been unclear since the group's appearance, developments in 2023 have shed light on their ties.

Evidence of Wagner Constituting Part of the Russian Armed Forces Before the Mutiny

The manifest opacity within the group led experts to be careful in their qualification of Wagner's troops as *combatants*. Such a conclusion is reached after observing that the private military group is under the command of a State party to the conflict.[359] To this end, the units to be analysed do not have to be formally part of the State military to be considered State forces.[360] Pursuant to Article 43 API, two layers of analysis are needed to assess (a) the organisation of Wagner's group and (b) the Russian Federation's command over Wagner.[361]

Wagner's Organisation

The ICRC Commentaries to API highlight the flexibility of the term 'organised' in determining an armed group's affiliation. Such assessment has to be distinguished from identifying organisation factors for conflict classification. As such, relying on the detailed ICTY case law on this matter could prove helpful.

In the *Tadić* case, the ICTY Appeal Chamber discussed the conditions under which armed forces fighting against a State in which they operate may be deemed to act on behalf of another State. Before turning on its lengthy discussion, the Court relied on the four conditions set out in Article 4(A)2 GCIII as one of the elements defining *legitimate combatants*, namely:

(a) that of being commanded by a person responsible for his subordinates;
(b) that of having a fixed distinctive sign recognisable at a distance;
(c) that of carrying arms openly and
(d) that of conducting their operations in accordance with the laws and customs of war.

This provision, reflecting customary international law, could be considered *replaced* by the one of Article 43(1) API.

> The armed forces of a Party to a conflict consist of all organized armed forces, groups and units which are under a command responsible to that Party for the conduct of its subordinates,

---

[358] Ferraro T (2016) The ICRC's legal position on the notion of armed conflict involving foreign intervention and on determining the IHL applicable to this type of conflict. International Review of the Red Cross 97:1227–1252, p. 1249.

[359] API above n 10, Article 43(1).

[360] API, above n 10, Article 43. *See also* ICRC Commentary of 1987, para 1672.

[361] For a similar analysis: Open Society, Justice initiative (2023) Accountability for Crimes of Personnel of the Wagner Group in Ukraine. https://www.justiceinitiative.org/uploads/a8de622f-bfbf-4cf5-99ba-f5b98b34f4ad/accountability-for-crimes-of-personnel-of-the-wagner-group-in-ukraine-en-20231108.pdf. Accessed 22 April 2024.

even if that Party is represented by a government or an authority not recognized by an adverse Party. Such armed forces shall be subject to an internal disciplinary system which, 'inter alia', shall enforce compliance with the rules of international law applicable in armed conflict.

As highlighted by the Appeal Chamber in a footnote, such replacement of a custom may only happen if Article 43(1) API has also reached the status of custom. Unfortunately, the Appeal Chamber did not discuss the status of this article further. The ICRC, in 2005, considered that the criteria of the GCIII, through Article 43(1) API, "have been reduced to two conditions, the main difference being the exclusion of the requirements of visibility for the definition of armed forces as such".[362]

The second organisational requirement under Article 43 API concerns the existence of an internal disciplinary system within the forces, enforcing compliance with international law. Such a disciplinary system covers both military disciplinary law and military penal law.[363] This requirement has to be understood as the need to identify a system that enforces minimum compliance with IHL provisions. The existence of a discipline must be identified, i.e., if a soldier receives an order, (s)he will execute it. Thus, the soldier will carry out any order to apply IHL rules. Secondly, respect for core IHL provisions must be observed, meaning the level of compliance must meet a minimum set of norms about core IHL principles, such as the principle of distinction, prohibition of killing protected persons.

Wagner appears to be quite organised. As it has been reported in 2023 by several think thanks[364] and newspapers, Wagner seems to possess some level of coordination between distinctive units. In July 2023, a former senior Russian army officer and Wagner operative sent the UK Parliamentary Committee evidence of Wagner's organisation. An anonymous source provided that:

> During military combat Wagner PMCs perform the functions of assault squads i.e. units that carry out frontal attack manoeuvres, while the regular armed forces remain behind the assault squads in a layered battle formation.[365]

Wagner's troops launched large-scale and organised operations, had a unified strategy, gathered thousands of recruits, provided military training, supplied weapons, used communications equipment, and wore specific clothes, distinguishing them from other armed groups and between Wagner's troops themselves.[366]

---

[362] ICRC Database (Undated) Customary IHL, Definitions of Armed Forces, Rule 4. https://ihl-databases.icrc.org/en/customary-ihl/v1/rule4. Accessed 21 June 2024.

[363] ICRC 1987 Commentaries of API, Article 43(1).

[364] Open Society, Justice initiative (2023) Accountability for Crimes of Personnel of the Wagner Group in Ukraine. https://www.justiceinitiative.org/uploads/a8de622f-bfbf-4cf5-99ba-f5b98b34f4ad/accountability-for-crimes-of-personnel-of-the-wagner-group-in-ukraine-en-20231108.pdf. Accessed 22 April 2024.

[365] UK Parliament (2023) Written evidence to Foreign Affairs Committee Inquiry into Wagner Group – Answers Provided by anonymous source to committee questions (WGN0026). https://committees.parliament.uk/writtenevidence/122628/html/. Accessed 21 April 2024.

[366] Open Society, Justice initiative (2023) Accountability for Crimes of Personnel of the Wagner Group in Ukraine. https://www.justiceinitiative.org/uploads/a8de622f-bfbf-4cf5-99ba-f5b98b34f4ad/accountability-for-crimes-of-personnel-of-the-wagner-group-in-ukraine-en-20231108.pdf. Accessed 22 April 2024.

Most notably, a key document drafted in May 2014 that leaked in June 2023 set the foundations of Wagner's purposes and highlighted its command structure.[367] The Institute for the Study of War shared that the document commits Yevgeny Prigozhin and Dimitry Utkin "to follow a set of rules for their new private military company's participation for combat in eastern Ukraine."[368] The document mentions a series of duties for both of them, according to which Yevgeny Prigozhin, the director, has the responsibility to, notably, provide weapons and funding to resolve all issues "collegially" and to participate in person.[369] Dimitry Utkin, the commander, was to select and train personnel, get rid of deserters, prohibit alcohol and drugs, resolve issues "collegially", implement lessons learned and complete tasks to the end.[370]

It is difficult to monitor the assessment of the level of discipline within Wagner's units. It has been reported that Wagner had a sense of military discipline, which quickly turned into high-ranking soldiers threatening low-ranking soldiers with being killed or physically hurt with a view to enforce superiors' orders. As Michael N. Schmitt underlined, the brutality of such discipline satisfies the ability to implement IHL.[371]

Under the Command of the Russian Federation

Determining what "responsible command" means under Article 43 API is complex. The 'effective control' test elaborated by the ICJ aims to attribute one's group conduct to a State. In contrast, the overall control test seeks to discuss the required State's involvement in an armed conflict with another State to characterise it as international.

Namely, the 'overall control' test required that a State party to the conflict "has a role in organizing, coordinating or planning the military actions of the military group, in addition to financing, training, and equipping or providing operational support to that group".[372]

The 'effective control' test was designed to question every wrongful act committed by the studied armed group to determine whether it is attributable to the State, which proved inappropriate in discussing whether the Wagner forces are to be understood as combatants under API. Indeed, if Wagner was to be recognised as acting under the command of the Russian Federation as defined in Article 43(1) API, not all of their conduct would necessarily be attributable to the Russian Federation under the rules

---

[367] See the original leak – Telegram Chanel (2023) Правила ЧВК "Вагнер" подписанные Пригожиным и Уткиным 1 мая 2014 года. Фото также сделано при обыске в доме Пригожина. [Rules of PMC "Wagner" signed by Prigozhin and Utkin on 1 May 2014. The photo was also taken during the search in Prigozhin's house]. https://t.me/boris_rozhin/91688. Accessed 21 April 2024.

[368] Institute for the Study of War (2023) Russian Offensive Campaign Assessment, July 9, 2023. https://www.understandingwar.org/backgrounder/russian-offensive-campaign-assessment-july-9-2023 Accessed 25 April 2024.

[369] Ibid.

[370] Ibid.

[371] Michael N. Schmitt (2023) Was Russia at War with the Wagner Group? https://lieber.westpoint.edu/was-russia-war-wagner-group/. Accessed 25 April 2024.

[372] *Tadić*, ICTY Judgment of July 15, 1999 (IT-94-1-A), para 137.

codified in the ILC's Articles on State Responsibility.[373] The 'overall control' test has been recognised as considering the specific needs of the IHL context. It is sufficient to say that the 'overall control' test imposes itself as the benchmark to discuss belonging to a Party in IHL—and will ultimately inform any other test that might be suitable to discuss the requirement of Article 43(1) API.[374] As such, our analysis will use the indicators set out in the 'overall control' test to determine Wagner's belonging to the Russian Federation. Several of the factual findings mentioned in the application of this test before 2023 were first mentioned by the Open Society Justice Initiative.[375]

Russia organised, coordinated, and planned military actions of the Wagner Group in Ukraine. The declaration of the Russian Federation over the role played by Wagner in capturing Soledar and Bakhmut is one element that needs to be added to the 2020 revelation of the close connection between Wagner and the Russian Ministry of Defence.[376] Such coordination was confirmed in early 2023.[377] On the other hand, the confirmation of the nonexistence of a *de jure* relation was made in early June 2023 through several statements by Yevgeny Prigozhin, testifying his disinterest in formally subordinating Wagner to the Russian Ministry of Defence.[378] Additionally, it has been reported that Prigozhin claimed that the Russian Ministry of Defence tried to dissolve the Organisation and attacked Wagner's positions in Ukraine in the past.[379]

Russia also financed, trained and equipped Wagner. The Russian Federation's Head of State declared that Wagner's financing was coming from the Defence Ministry, allocating around 1 billion USD to the group between May 2022 and

---

[373] It must be noted that the ICTY Appeal Chamber, in *Tadić*, affirms otherwise, i.e., that the overall control could be used for the purpose of attribution within the State Responsibility realm; *Tadić*, Appeal Judgement, para 131. This view was also endorsed by the ICRC. *See* ICRC, Commentary on GC I, para 271. Such determination was made contrary to what the ICJ ruled. *See* Application of the Convention on the Prevention and Punishment of the Crime of Genocide (Bosn. & Herz. v. Serb. & Montenegro), Judgment, 2007 I.C.J. Rep. 43, paras 404–406.

[374] Among others, Esti Tambay and Anna Khalfaoui have argued that the indicators of the overall control test should inform the applicable test under Article 43(1) API. *See* Open Society, Justice initiative (2023) Accountability for Crimes of Personnel of the Wagner Group in Ukraine. https://www.justiceinitiative.org/uploads/a8de622f-bfbf-4cf5-99ba-f5b98b34f4ad/acc ountability-for-crimes-of-personnel-of-the-wagner-group-in-ukraine-en-20231108.pdf. Accessed 22 April 2024, p. 42.

[375] Ibid.

[376] Bellingcat (2020) Putin Chef's Kisses of Death: Russia's Shadow Army's State-Run Structure Exposed. https://www.bellingcat.com/news/uk-and-europe/2020/08/14/pmc-structure-exposed/. Accessed 23 April 2024.

[377] Politico (2023) Inside the stunning growth of Russia's Wagner Group. https://www.politico.com/news/2023/02/18/russia-wagner-group-ukraine-paramilitary-00083553. Accessed 21 April 2024.

[378] Institute for the Study of War (2023) Russian Offensive Campaign Assessment, June 17, 2023. https://www.understandingwar.org/backgrounder/russian-offensive-campaign-ass essment-june-17-2023. Accessed 25 April 2024.

[379] Institute for the Study of War (2023) Russian Offensive Campaign Assessment, June 26, 2023. https://www.understandingwar.org/backgrounder/russian-offensive-campaign-ass essment-june-26-2023. Accessed 25 April 2024.

5 Year in Review 2023

May 2023.[380] In addition to identifying Wagner's piece of equipment belonging to the Russian armed forces,[381] Wagner's soldiers have been reported to bear Russian State decorations.[382]

Finally, Wagner received logistical support from the Russian State. Wagner recruited soldiers in Russian prisons, used transport infrastructure related to the Russian Ministry of Defence, and benefited from administrative support and assistance usually dedicated to the Ministry of Defence.[383]

Conclusion

A tenuous linkage between Wagner and the Russian Federation was established before the 2023 mutiny, setting indicators of Wagner possibly belonging to the Russian State. The fog over the exact control exercised by the Russian Federation and the difficulty in applying a proper test of command responsibility under Article 43(1) API certainly indicate a relation of belonging but prevents any definitive assessment.[384]

5.1.9.3 Mutiny within Russian Proxy Forces

There is no definition of mutiny within IHL. This phenomenon describes the break-up of part of the armed forces against superiors—and, therefore, a discontinuation of the command responsibility.

While capturing Soledar in early 2023, the Russian forces omitted to mention Wagner's troops' support. To justify this omission, the Ministry of Defence stated that a "heterogeneous grouping of troops" executed a "joint plan" and mentioned Wagner as the organisation that led the assault on residential areas.

After the attack on Soledar in early 2023, Yevgeny Prigozhin, Wagner's leader, made several statements against the Russian military strategy. In December 2023, the *World Street Journal* revealed that the Kremlin announced around the same time

---

[380] TASS (2023) Putin says Wagner group fully financed by Russian government. https://tass.com/defense/1639345. Accessed 23 April 2024.

[381] Forbes (2022) Why Are Mercenaries Driving Russia's Best T-90 Tanks? https://www.forbes.com/sites/davidaxe/2022/12/28/why-are-mercenaries-driving-russias-best-t-90-tank/. Accessed 23 April 2024; US Department of Defense (2020) Imagery – Wagner Equipment. https://www.defense.gov/Multimedia/Photos/igphoto/2002464197/. Accessed 23 April 2024.

[382] Jack Margolin (2023) Twitter Account – post of July 17, 2023. https://twitter.com/Jack_Mrgln/status/1681036854928318480?s=20. Accessed 23 April 2024.

[383] Bellingcat (2019) Wagner Mercenaries With GRU-issued Passports: Validating SBU's Allegation. https://www.bellingcat.com/news/uk-and-europe/2019/01/30/wagner-mercenaries-with-gru-issued-passports-validating-sbus-allegation. Accessed 23 April 2024.

[384] Justice Initiative (2023) Accountability for Crimes of Personnel of the Wagner Group in Ukraine. https://www.justiceinitiative.org/uploads/a8de622f-bfbf-4cf5-99ba-f5b98b34f4ad/accountability-for-crimes-of-personnel-of-the-wagner-group-in-ukraine-en-20231108.pdf. Accessed 22 April 2024, p. 47.

that they planned to dismantle Wagner as a fighting force by forcing all fighters to register with the Russian Minister of Defence by 1 July 2023.[385]

Ultimately, ISW asserted that this event led Prigozhin to declare on 23 June 2023 that he would lead a "march for justice" against the Russian military.[386] The next day, Vladimir Putin publicly stated that Wagner had committed an "armed mutiny", accusing Prigozhin of treason.[387] It appeared that Yevgeny Prigozhin launched an armed rebellion to force a leadership change within the Russian Ministry of Defence, which constituted a shift in the command responsibility between Wagner and the Russian military.[388] It has been reported that Wagner, in the following hours, killed over a dozen Russian personnel.[389]

The mutiny, however, wound down rather quickly after Prigozhin seemingly struck a deal with the Kremlin and Belarussian Head of State Alexander Lukashenko. The next day, Prigozhin released an audio message claiming his "march for justice" had achieved its goal. He ordered Wagner's forces to go back to their training grounds to prevent the situation from becoming bloody.[390]

Although signs of Wagner military's retreat and move toward the Russian capital were shown through the summer, Yevgeny Prigozhin's uprising did not result in a full-scale attack on Moscow. Vladimir Putin and Yevgeny Prigozhin had a face-to-face meeting. It was reported that the Russians asked whether the Wagner Commanders were prepared to serve under Alexei Troshev, founder of Wagner and chief staff of the

---

[385] Institute for the Study of War (2023) Russian Offensive Campaign Assessment, December 22, 2023. https://www.understandingwar.org/backgrounder/russian-offensive-campaign-assessment-december-22-2023. Accessed 25 April 2024.

[386] Al-Jazeera (2023) Timeline: How Wagner Group's revolt against Russia unfolded. https://www.aljazeera.com/news/2023/6/24/timeline-how-wagner-groups-revolt-against-russia-unfolded. Accessed 22 April 2023.

[387] Al-Jazeera (2023) Wagner mutiny reflects fault lines in Russia: Analysts. https://www.aljazeera.com/news/2023/6/24/wagner-mutiny-reflects-fault-lines-in-russia-analysts. Accessed 24 June 2023.

[388] Institute for the Study of War (2023) Russian Offensive Campaign Assessment, June 23, 2023. https://www.understandingwar.org/backgrounder/russian-offensive-campaign-assessment-june-23-2023. Accessed 25 April 2024.

[389] Institute for the Study of War (2023) Russian Offensive Campaign Assessment, June 24, 2023. https://www.understandingwar.org/backgrounder/russian-offensive-campaign-assessment-june-24-2023. Accessed 25 April 2024.

[390] Ibid.

5 Year in Review 2023

Group's operations in Syria.[391] Wagner's unit was then sent to Belarus. Prigozhin's plane crashed on the 27 August with him on board.[392]

A former BBC Russian Service investigative journalist, Andrey Zakharov, claimed that around this time, Putin told Prigozhin to deal with Wagner's involvement in African countries but not to be involved in Ukraine.[393] It appears that no fighting involving Wagner's forces and the Ukrainian forces was reported during 23–24 June 2023, ultimately preventing a shift from applying the law of IACs to the law of NIACs to Wagner's conduct against Ukrainian forces during this short period. Two weeks later, it was reported that Wagner was no longer engaged with Ukrainian troops. On 30 August 2023, the Russian Ministry of Defence was not allowing Wagner's forces to fight in Ukraine.[394]

New Developments Over Wagner Belonging to the Russian Federation Post-mutiny

Wagner's mutiny in late June marks a turning point in the organisation's statute. ISW assessed that the Russian Ministry of Defence and the Kremlin destroyed the Wagner Group since the June 24 rebellion.[395] Developments post-mutiny shed light on Wagner's affiliation with the Russian Federation.

They saw the break-up of Wagner's staff, who left this organisation to join others or join the Russian army. Precisely, the post-mutiny relationship confirms the tenuous nature of the *de facto* command of the Russian Federation, and constitutes evidence of a friction between the Wagner forces and the Ministry of Defence. Since the mutiny,

---

[391] Kommersant (2023) «ЧВК "Вагнер" не существует» Владимир Путин в коридорах ЦМТ рассказал о встрече 29 июня ["The PMC Wagner does not exist." Vladimir Putin in the corridors of the ITC spoke about the meeting on 29 June]. https://www.kommersant.ru/doc/6098488. Accessed 25 April 2024; Council of the European Union (2021) Regulation (EU) 2021/2194 of 13 December 2021 implementing Regulation No 36/2012 concerning restrictive measures in view of the situation in Syria. https://eur-lex.europa.eu/legal-content/EN/TXT/?uri=uriserv%3AOJ.LI. 2021.445.01.0007.01.ENG. Accessed 22 April 2024.

[392] The Guardian (2023) Yevgeny Prigozhin confirmed dead after plane crash, Russian investigators say. https://www.theguardian.com/world/2023/aug/27/wagner-boss-yevgeny-prigozhin-killed-in-plane-crash-russia-investigative-committee-confirms. Accessed 23 April 2024.

[393] Zakharov Telegram Chanel (2023) Post of August 27, 2023. https://t.me/zakharovchannel/1020;%C2%A0 https://t.me/bbcrussian/51479. Accessed 23 April 2024.

[394] Важные истории (2023) ЧВК «Вагнер» предложила бойцам найти другую работу из-за конкуренции с Минобороны и Росгвардией в Африке и на Ближнем Востоке [PMC "Wagner" offered fighters to find other jobs because of competition with the Ministry of Defence and Rosgvardiya in Africa and the Middle East]. https://storage.googleapis.com/istories/news/2023/08/30/chvk-vagner-predlozhila-boitsam-naiti-druguyu-rabotu-iz-za-konkurentsii-s-minoboroni-i-ros gvardiei-v-afrike-i-na-blizhnem-vostoke/index.html. Accessed 26 April 2024. Важные истории Telegram Chanel (2023) Post of August 30, 2023. https://t.me/istories_media/3518; Accessed 26 April 2024; Meduza (2023) В ЧВК Вагнера посоветовали своим бойцам искать «другие варианты заработка» [The Wagner PMC advised its fighters to look for "other options for earning money"]. https://meduza.io/news/2023/08/30/v-chvk-vagnera-posovetovali-svoim-boytsam-iskat-drugie-varianty-zarabotka. Accessed 26 April 2024.

[395] Institute for the Study of War (2023) Russian Offensive Campaign Assessment, August 23, 2023. https://www.understandingwar.org/backgrounder/russian-offensive-campaign-assessment-august-23-2023. Accessed 25 April 2024.

the Russian Federation has not funded Wagner's troops. In August, it was reported that the Kremlin refused to pay the Belarusian government for Wagner's deployment to Belarus. This added to the existing financial issues, ultimately leading to Wagner fighters' resignation.[396]

On 26 June 2023, Vladimir Putin stated that Wagner fighters who seek to continue "serving Russia" could sign a contract with the Russian Ministry of Defence.[397] Precisely, ISW has reported that several Wagner elements likely signed contracts with the Russian armed forces. At the same time, efforts from the Kremlin were observed to assume formal control over the Wagner Group, taking place in countries where Wagner was already involved.[398]

In mid-July, Putin asked the Wagner commanders to serve under another Wagner Commander, separating Yevgeny Prigozhin from Wagner's leadership and forces.[399] In the meantime, Prigozhin retained some command over Wagner's troops in African countries, and Wagner's troops in the Central African Republic were still not formally integrated into the Russian Army.[400] The ISW reported that Prigozhin recognised that former Wagner's elements would join other unspecified Russian security services— likely the Russian Ministry of Defence.[401] Concerns about Russia's capability to integrate irregular formations into its military arose when reports[402] revealed that

---

[396] Institute for the Study of War (2023) Russian Offensive Campaign Assessment, August 24, 2023. https://www.understandingwar.org/backgrounder/russian-offensive-campaign-assessment-august-24-2023. Accessed 25 April 2024.

[397] Institute for the Study of War (2023) Russian Offensive Campaign Assessment, June 26, 2023. https://www.understandingwar.org/backgrounder/russian-offensive-campaign-assessment-june-26-2023. Accessed 25 April 2024.

[398] Institute for the Study of War (2023) Russian Offensive Campaign Assessment, June 29, 2023. https://www.understandingwar.org/backgrounder/russian-offensive-campaign-assessment-june-29-2023. Accessed 25 April 2024; Reuters (2023) Syria brought Wagner fighters to heel as mutiny unfolded in Russia. https://www.reuters.com/world/syria-brought-wagner-group-fighters-heel-mutiny-unfolded-russia-2023-07-07/. Accessed 25 April 2024. "By June 24, Wagner fighters in Syria were asked to sign new contracts by which they report directly to Russia's defence ministry [...]." More than a month later, it was reported that private military companies controlled by the Russian Federation were trying to recruit Wagner's personnel to work in Africa instead of Ukraine. Путин рассказал «Ъ» подробности встречи с бойцами ЧВК «Вагнер».

[399] Kommersant (2023) Путин рассказал «Ъ» подробности встречи с бойцами ЧВК «Вагнер» [Putin told Kommersant details of his meeting with Wagner PMC fighters]. https://www.kommersant.ru/doc/6098572. Accessed 25 April 2024.

[400] Позывной Брюс Telegram Chanel (2023) Post of July 19 2023. https://t.me/brussinf/6352. Accessed 27 April 2024. https://t.me/prigozhin_2023_tg/2384; Пригожин 2023 Telegram Chanel (2023) Post of 19 July 2023. https://t.me/rusbrief/140246%C2%A0;%C2%A0 https://t.me/rusbrief/140280. Accessed 27 April 2024; NewsFrol (2023) Евгений Пригожин подтвердил приостановку набора в ряды ЧВК «Вагнер» [Yevgeny Prigozhin confirmed the suspension of recruitment in the ranks of PMC "Wagner"]. https://newsfrol.ru/24/12086/. Accessed 27 April 2024.

[401] Institute for the Study of War (2023) Russian Offensive Campaign Assessment, July 19, 2023. https://www.understandingwar.org/backgrounder/russian-offensive-campaign-assessment-july-19-2023. Accessed 27 April 2024.

[402] See notably AOCBE (2023) Как устроена ЧВК «Конвой» и кто ее финансирует [How the PMC "Convoy" is organised and who finances it]. https://dossier.center/konvoy/. Accessed 27 April 2024.

5 Year in Review 2023

financial and political backing for the Convoy private military company and its ongoing activities in Ukraine were detached from the Ministry of Defence's command structure.[403]

On 16 September 2023, it was reported that former Wagner's elements were going back to the Ukrainian battlefield either under an unidentified command, which is to be most likely coming from the Ministry of Defence,[404] or, as claimed by a Kremlin-affiliated milblogger, under the command of a private military company's banners, affiliated with the Russian Ministry of Defence.[405] Such information was confirmed on 28 October 2023—former Wagner's soldiers joined various detachments of the Chechnyan paramilitary organisation named Akhmat Spetsnaz and were sent to the Ukrainian battlefield.[406] Around the same date, several former Wagner' elements appeared to fight in the Avdiivka direction under the command of the Ministry of Defence.[407]

The Russian Federation's logistical support seems to have decreased since the mutiny. On 30 July 2023, Prigozhin announced that Wagner had enough soldiers and had no immediate plans for further recruitment until the need arose.[408] Subsequently, on the same day, a Telegram page associated with Wagner announced the indefinite suspension of regional recruitment centres in Russia, citing the organisation's existing reserves as sufficient.[409] Most importantly, it seems that the Russian Federation tried to disrupt Wagner's logistics.[410]

Conclusion

The involvement of the Russian Federation in organising, coordinating, and planning military actions of the remaining elements of the Wagner Group became more

---

[403] Institute for the Study of War (2023) Russian Offensive Campaign Assessment, August 14, 2023. https://www.understandingwar.org/backgrounder/russian-offensive-campaign-assessment-august-14-2023. Accessed 27 April 2024.

[404] Пригожин 2023 Telegram Chanel (2023) Post of September 16, 2023. https://t.me/prigozhin_2023_tg/3585. Accessed 28 April 2024.

[405] Institute for the Study of War (2023) Russian Offensive Campaign Assessment, September 26, 2023. https://www.understandingwar.org/backgrounder/russian-offensive-campaign-assessment-september-26-2023. Accessed 27 April 2024.

[406] Россия сегодня (2023) В "Ахмате" рассказали о массовом пополнении из экс-бойцов "Вагнера" [In "Akhmat" told about the mass replenishment from ex-fighters of "Wagner"]. https://ria.ru/20231028/akhmat-1905834455.html. Accessed 25 April 2024.

[407] ZOV (2023) Специальное подразделение ОБСпН "Арбат" в своей основе состоит из бывших сотрудников ЧВК Вагнер [The special OBSpN unit "Arbat" is composed of former employees of PMC Wagner]. https://dnr-news.ru/society/2023/10/25/516368.html. Accessed 27 April 2024; Собственный корреспондент Telegram Chanel (2023) Post of October 25, 2023. https://t.me/zovgrad/13922%C2%A0. Accessed 27 April 2024.

[408] Grey Zone Telegram Chanel (2023) Post of July 31, 2023. https://t.me/grey_zone/19764. Accessed 27 April 2024.

[409] ЧВК Вагнер I Объявления о работе Telegram Chanel (2023) Post of July 30, 2023. https://t.me/wagner_employment/88. Accessed 27 April 2024.

[410] Рыбарь Telegram Chanel (2023) Post of September 13, 2023. https://t.me/rybar/51872%C2%A0;%C2%A0 https://t.me/africaintel/5095%C2%A0. Accessed 27 April 2024.

tenuous, even to the extent that the Russian Federation tried to wreck Wagner's Group. As such, at the end of 2023, it is not possible to assert that Wagner's soldiers were to be considered combatants of the Russian Federation.

5.2 Courts and Tribunals

This section compiles IHL-related developments over 2023 stemming from judicial bodies with competence to investigate and adjudicate IHL violations or to interpret and apply this body of law. Developments outlined in this section refer *inter alia* to the investigation and adjudication of violations of IHL, including war crimes— namely, serious violations of customary or treaty IHL that give rise to individual criminal responsibility under international law.[411] It is worth noting that the 'Courts, Tribunals and other Bodies' section is not intended to provide an exhaustive overview of the IHL-related judicial and quasi-judicial developments in 2023. Instead, it is aimed at shedding light over the most outstanding developments and to constitute a valuable resource for deeper research.

This section is divided into three subsections. The first one highlights the developments occurred within International Courts, with a special focus on the International Criminal Court (ICC). The second subsection focuses on the IHL-related developments at hybrid criminal tribunals and regional human rights courts and bodies. The third section focuses on the investigation and adjudication of war crimes cases in national courts, many of them under the principle of universal jurisdiction.

5.2.1 International Tribunals

The following section focuses on the IHL-related developments at international tribunals during 2023, focusing on the ICC and the International Residual Mechanism for Criminal Tribunals.

5.2.1.1 International Criminal Court

Overview

The ICC was established in July 2002 when its founding treaty, the Rome Statute, entered into force following its sixtieth ratification since it was adopted in July 1998. The ICC, which seats in The Hague, has jurisdiction over the international crimes of genocide, crimes against humanity and war crimes, as well as the crime of aggression

---

[411] *Tadić* 1995 above n 2, para 94.

in specific circumstances. The ICC plays a crucial role in the interpretation and development of IHL.

The year 2023 also saw the ratification of this treaty by the Republic of Armenia, which would become the 124th State Party after the entry into force of the Statute on 1 February 2024.[412] During 2023, the Assembly of States Parties to the Rome Statute elected six new judges—one third of the 18 judges sitting at the Court—for a term of nine years during its twenty-second session held in December 2023 at the UN Headquarters in New York.[413]

The Situation in the Islamic Republic of Afghanistan

In March 2020, the Appeals Chamber authorized the start of an investigation into alleged crimes committed in the Islamic Republic of Afghanistan since 1 May 2003 and other related crimes with a nexus to the armed conflict in Afghanistan committed in the territory of other State Parties since 1 July 2002.[414] The Appeals Chamber overturned Pre-Trial Chamber II's decision dating from April 2019 rejecting the Prosecutor's request for authorization to start an investigation in December 2017 on the basis that such investigation would not be in the interest of justice. After the Government of Afghanistan requested a deferral of the investigation in March 2020, the Office of the Prosecutor (OTP) requested an authorization to resume its investigation in September 2021 in light of the Talibans' takeover of power.[415]

In October 2022, Pre-Trial Chamber II authorized the resumption of the investigation, considering that Afghanistan is not presently carrying out genuine investigations that justify a deferral.[416] In April 2023, the Appeals Chamber issued its Judgement on the Prosecutor's appeal to amend the scope of the investigation set in Pre-Trial Chamber II's decision, aligning it with the scope that had been set by the Appeals Chamber back in March 2020.[417] Pre-Trial Chamber II had found that the scope of the investigation only concerned "the crimes [and parties] falling within the situation

---

[412] ICC (2023) International Criminal Court welcomes Armenia as a new State Party. https://www.icc-cpi.int/news/international-criminal-court-welcomes-armenia-new-state-party#:~:text=Background%3A%20On%2014%20November%202023,European%20group%20to%20do%20so. Accessed 28 June 2024.

[413] ICC (2024) Six newly elected ICC judges to be sworn in on 8 March 2024. https://www.icc-cpi.int/news/six-newly-elected-icc-judges-be-sworn-8-march-2024. Accessed 28 June 2024.

[414] ICC, *Situation in the Islamic Republic of Afghanistan*, Judgment on the appeal against the decision on the authorisation of an investigation into the situation in the Islamic Republic of Afghanistan, 5 March 2020, ICC-02/17 OA4.

[415] ICC (2022) Statement by Prosecutor of the International Criminal Court, Karim Khan QC, following application. https://www.icc-cpi.int/news/statement-prosecutor-international-criminal-court-karim-khan-qc-following-application. Accessed 28 June 2024.ICC.

[416] ICC, *Situation in the Islamic Republic of Afghanistan*, Decision pursuant to article 18(2) of the Statute authorising the Prosecution to resume investigation, 31 October 2022, ICC-02/17.

[417] ICC, *Situation in the Islamic Republic of Afghanistan*, Judgment on the Prosecutor's appeal against the decision of Pre-Trial Chamber II entitled "Decision pursuant to article 18(2) of the Statute authorising the Prosecution to resume investigation", 4 April 2023, ICC-02/17 OA5.

and the conflict, as it existed at the time of the decision authorising the investigation and based on the request to open it".[418]

The investigation focuses on crimes against humanity and war crimes committed in the armed conflict between pro and anti-Government forces.[419] War crimes investigated include murder, cruel treatment, outrages upon personal dignity, the passing of sentences and carrying out of executions without proper judicial authority, intentional attacks against civilians, civilian objects and humanitarian assistance missions, and treacherously killing or wounding an enemy combatant.

The Situation in the Central African Republic (CAR) I

The Prosecutor opened an investigation in the CAR in May 2007, focusing on alleged war crimes and crimes against humanity committed in the context of a conflict in the CAR since 1 July 2002, with the peak of violence in 2002 and 2003.

The Situation in the CAR II

On December 10, 2018, an arrest warrant for war crimes and crimes against humanity was issued under seal for Maxime Jeoffroy Eli Mokom Gawaka. He was accused of serving as the National Coordinator of Operations for the Anti-Balaka group in the CAR. In this role, he allegedly committed numerous war crimes and crimes against humanity across various regions in CAR, including Bangui, Bossangoa, the Lobaye Prefecture, Yaloké, Gaga, Bossemptélé, Boda, Carnot, and Berberati, from at least 5 December 2013, to at least December 2014. After being surrendered to the ICC by Chad authorities on 14 March 2022, Mr. Mokom made his initial appearance before Pre-Trial Chamber II on 22 March 2022.

The confirmation of charges hearing began on 22 August 2023, but had not yet concluded as the parties still needed to submit written arguments on the case's merits. On 17 October 2023, Pre-Trial Chamber II ended the proceedings in the *Mokom* case and ordered Mr. Mokom's immediate release from ICC detention on the same day. This decision followed the Prosecution's notice of withdrawal of charges against Mr. Mokom on 16 October 2023. The notice indicated significant changes in the evidence, leading the Prosecution to believe that, even if the charges were confirmed by Pre-Trial Chamber II, there was no reasonable prospect of securing a conviction at trial.

An arrest warrant for Mahamat Said Abdel Kani was issued under seal on 7 January 2019, for war crimes (torture and cruel treatment) and crimes against humanity (imprisonment or other severe deprivation of liberty, torture, persecution, enforced disappearance, and other inhumane acts) allegedly committed in Bangui, CAR in 2013. After being surrendered to the ICC by the CAR authorities in January 2021, Mr. Said appeared before Judge Rosario Salvatore Aitala of Pre-Trial Chamber II at the end of that month. The confirmation of charges hearing took place in October 2021,

---

[418] ICC, *Situation in the Islamic Republic of Afghanistan*, Decision pursuant to article 18(2) of the Statute authorising the Prosecution to resume investigation, 31 October 2022, ICC-02/17, para 59.

[419] ICC (Undated) Afghanistan: Situation in the Islamic Republic of Afghanistan. https://www.icc-cpi.int/afghanistan. Accessed 28 June 2024.

and in December 2021, Pre-Trial Chamber II partially confirmed the charges against Mr. Said. The Chamber concluded that there was sufficient evidence to establish substantial grounds that Mr. Said was a senior member of the Séléka coalition and that he bears criminal responsibility for crimes against humanity and war crimes (including torture, cruel treatment, and outrages upon personal dignity) under Articles 25(3)(a) and 25(3)(b) of the Rome Statute.

These crimes were allegedly committed against detainees believed to be supporters of former President Bozizé between 12 April and 30 August 2013. On 26 September 2022 the trial in the case of The Prosecutor v. Mahamat Said Abdel Kani opened before Trial Chamber VI of the ICC.

In late January 2023, Mr. Said underwent scheduled medical treatment, and on 7 February 2023, the Chamber convened a status conference in closed session. During the status conference, the Registry informed the Chamber, parties and participants, inter alia, that Mr. Said was not capable of appearing at hearings for medical reasons and that he would likely be unable to participate in hearings for at least six months.[420] On 12 June 2023, following a period in which the Chamber received updates from the Medical Officer at the Detention Centre regarding Mr. Said's health, the Registry filed a report from the Medical Officer indicating that Mr. Said had ceased to give his consent for his medical information to be disclosed to the Chamber.[421] On 17 November 2023, Mr. Said was examined by medical experts appointed by the Court to determine whether he was able to attend trial.[422] On 15 December 2023, the Trial Chamber VI found that Mr. Said was fit to attend trial.[423]

Situation in the DRC

The situation in the DRC was referred to the ICC by the DRC's government in 2004 and the Prosecutor chose to open an investigation. The investigation focuses on alleged war crimes and crimes against humanity committed in the context of armed conflict in the DRC since 1 July 2002.

In July 2019, Trial Chamber VI of the ICC found Bosco Ntaganda guilty of war crimes and crimes against humanity.[424] On 7 November 2019, Mr. Ntaganda was sentenced to 30 years in prison.[425] Following the sentencing, the defence and prosecution appealed the judgement, and the defence also submitted an appeal against the

---

[420] ICC, Decision on Mr Said's Fitness to Stand Trial, 15 December 2023, ICC-01/14-01/21.

[421] Annex A to the Registry Transmission of the Medical Officer's Report, 12 June 2023, ICC-01/14-01/21-615-SECRET-Exp-Anx.

[422] ICC, Decision on Mr Said's Fitness to Stand Trial, 15 December 2023, ICC-01/14-01/21, p. 10.

[423] Ibid., p. 44.

[424] ICC, The Prosecutor v. Bosco Ntaganda, Judgement, 8 July 2019, ICC-01/04-02/06.

[425] ICC, The Prosecutor v. Bosco Ntaganda, Sentencing judgement, 7 November 2019, ICC-01/04-02/06.

sentence.[426] On 30 March 2021, the appeal chamber upheld the Trial Chamber Judgement and confirmed the sanction order issued by the Trial Chamber.[427] In September 2022, the Appeals Chamber directed the Trial Chamber to issue a new reparations order, citing several errors in the Trial Chamber's decision.[428] On 14 July 2023, the Chamber issued the Addendum to the Reparations Order of 8 March 2022, in which it ruled on a sample of 171 victims' dossiers and set out the procedure for carrying out the eligibility assessment of victims at the implementation stage. On 11 August 2023, the Chamber issued its First Decision on the Trust Fund for Victims' Draft Implementation Plan for Reparations.[429] The Appeal Chamber found that the proposed overall objective and outcomes of the Draft Implementation Plan for Reparations responded adequately to the Reparations Order.[430] Nevertheless, the Appeals Chamber emphasised the lack of clarity of the project.[431] The Appeals Chambers directed the Trust Fund for Victims to update the methods of implementation given the time that has passed since the Updated Draft Implementation Plan was submitted.[432] Finally, the Appeals Chamber detailed its conclusions as to the steps and responsible organs for the execution of the administrative eligibility process, according to which the eligibility process should be conducted and lead to the identification of the eligible victims by 31 December 2025.[433]

The Situation in the Republic of Mali

In January 2013, the Prosecutor opened an investigation into alleged crimes committed on the territory of Mali since January 2012 after the government of Mali referred the situation to the ICC in July 2012.[434] The investigations have focused on alleged war crimes committed in the three northern Malian regions of Gao, Kidan and Timbuktu, as well as on some incidents that occurred in the south in Bamako and Sévaré. The Prosecutor alleged that there are reasonable grounds to believe that the war crimes of "murder; mutilation, cruel treatment and torture; intentionally directing

---

[426] ICC (2021) Ntaganda Case: ICC Appeals Chamber to deliver appeals judgement on 30 March 2022 - Practical information. https://www.icc-cpi.int/Pages/item.aspx?name=MA263. Accessed 28 June 2024.

[427] ICC, The Prosecutor v. Bosco Ntaganda, Public redacted version of Judgement on the appeals of Mr Bosco Ntaganda and the Prosecutor against the decision of Trial Chamber VI of 8 July 2019 entitled 'Judgement', 30 March 2021, ICC-01/04-02/06 A A2.

[428] ICC, The Prosecutor v. Bosco Ntaganda, Judgment on the appeals against the decision of Trial Chamber VI of 8 March 2021 entitled "Reparations Order", 12 September 2022, ICC-01/04-02/06 A4-A5. *See* also Gregoire et al. 2023, pp. 240–241.

[429] First Decision on the Trust Fund for Victims' Draft Implementation Plan for Reparations ('First DIP Decision'). 11 August 2023, ICC-01/04-02/06-2860-Conf.

[430] ICC, Prosecutor v Bosco Ntaganda, First Decision on the Trust Fund for Victims' Draft Implementation Plan for Reparations, ICC-01/04-02/06-2860-Conf, para 26.

[431] Ibid., pp. 14, 16, 17, 27, 37.

[432] Ibid., para 124.

[433] Ibid., paras 183–188.

[434] ICC (Undated) Mali: Situation in the Republic of Mali. https://www.icc-cpi.int/situations/mali. Accessed 28 June 2024.

attacks against protected objects; the passing of sentences and the carrying out of executions without previous judgement pronounced by a regularly constituted court; pillaging; and rape" have been committed there.[435] So far, the Situation in Mali has led to the opening of two cases.

The Prosecutor v. Al Hassan Ag Abdoul Aziz Ag Mohamed Ag Mahmoud ("Al Hassan")

In July 2020, the trial against Mr. Al Hassan, alleged member of NSAG Ansar Eddine and *de facto* chief of Islamic police in Tumbuktu, started for alleged crimes committed between 1 April 2012 and 28 January 2013.[436] Charges included numerous counts on alleged crimes against humanity as well as the war crimes of torture, cruel treatment, outrages upon personal dignity, passing of sentences without previous judgement pronounced by a regularly constituted court affording all judicial guarantees which are generally recognized as indispensable, intentionally directing attacks against buildings dedicated to religion and historic monuments, rape and sexual slavery.[437] In February 2023, Trial Chamber X declared the closure of the submission of evidence and the parties and participants issued their closing statements in May 2023.[438] The Court marked 18 January 2024 as the date on which it would render its trial decision.[439]

The Situation in the State of Palestine

In March 2021, the OTP opened an investigation into the Situation in Palestine after Palestine referred the situation to the ICC in May 2018.[440] In January 2020, the Prosecutor had requested Pre-Trial Chamber I to clarify the territorial scope of the Court's jurisdiction, which the Chamber did in February 2021, referring to Gaza

---

[435] Ibid.

[436] ICC (2020) Al Hassan trial opens - International Criminal Court. https://www.icc-cpi.int/news/al-hassan-trial-opens-international-criminal-court. Accessed 28 June 2024; ICC (Undated) Al Hassan Case: The Prosecutor v. Al Hassan Ag Abdoul Aziz Ag Mohamed Ag Mahmoud. https://www.icc-cpi.int/mali/al-hassan. Accessed 28 June 2024.

[437] ICC, *The Prosecutor v. Al Hassan Ag Abdoul Aziz Ag Mohamed Ag Mahmoud*, Public redacted version of the "Corrected Version of the *'Décision portant modification des charges confirmées le 30 septembre 2019 à l'encontre d'Al Hassan Ag Abdoul Aziz Ag Mohamed Ag Mahmoud, 23 avril 2020, ICC-01/12-01/18-767-Conf'"* ["Decision Amending the Charges Confirmed on September 30, 2019, Against Al Hassan Ag Abdoul Aziz Ag Mohamed Ag Mahmoud, April 23, 2020, ICC-01/12-01/18-767-Conf"] With a Public Redacted Annex Containing the Full List of Charges Confirmed against the Accused, 1 May 2020, ICC-01/12-01/18.

[438] ICC (Undated) Mali: Situation in the Republic of Mali. https://www.icc-cpi.int/situations/mali. Accessed 28 June 2024.

[439] ICC (2024) Trial Judgment in the Al Hassan case - 18 January 2024: Practical information. https://www.icc-cpi.int/news/trial-judgment-al-hassan-case-18-january-2024-practical-inform ation#:~:text=On%20Thursday%2C%2018%20January%202024,Aziz%20Ag%20Mohamed% 20Ag%20Mahmoud. Accessed 28 June 2024.

[440] ICC (Undated) Palestine Situation. https://www.icc-cpi.int/palestine. Accessed 28 June 2024.

and the West Bank, including East Jerusalem.[441] Following the events that unfolded in Israel/Palestine since 7 October 2023, the States of South Africa, Bangladesh, Bolivia, Comoros, and Djibouti referred the situation in Palestine to the ICC in November 2023.[442] The Prosecutor replied that the investigation "is ongoing and extends to the escalation of hostilities and violence since the attacks that took place on 7 October 2023".[443] Ever since the commencement of the last round of hostilities in Israel/Palestine, the Prosecutor has issued several statements repeatedly calling for the respect of IHL.[444]

The Situation in Darfur, Sudan

In June 2005, the Prosecutor opened an investigation into allegations of genocide, war crimes and crimes against humanity committed in Darfur, Sudan, since 1 July 2002 after the referral of the situation in Darfur to the ICC by the UN Security Council in its Resolution 1593 (2005).[445] The investigation has so far led to the issuance of seven arrest warrants and the opening of six cases. The Prosecutor issued statements before the UN Security Council on the situation in Darfur, pursuant to Resolution 1593 (2005) in January and July 2023, updating it on the progress of the investigation, and ensuring that the most recent round of hostilities affecting Darfur since 15 April 2023 is also being investigated.[446]

The Prosecutor v. Ali Muhammad Ali Abd-Al-Rahman ("Ali Kushayb")

The trial against Ali Kushayb, alleged leader of the militia Janjaweed, opened in April 2022 for crimes allegedly committed between August 2003 and, at least, April 2004 in Darfur, Sudan.[447] Aly Kushayb is accused of 31 counts of crimes against

---

[441] ICC, *Situation in the State of Palestine*, Decision on the 'Prosecution request pursuant to article 19(3) for a ruling on the Court's territorial jurisdiction in Palestine', 5 February 2021, ICC-01/18.

[442] ICC (2023) Statement by Prosecutor of the International Criminal Court, Karim A.A. Khan KC, on the Situation in the State of Palestine. https://www.icc-cpi.int/news/statement-prosecutor-intern ational-criminal-court-karim-aa-khan-kc-situation-state-palestine. Accessed 28 June 2024.

[443] Ibid.

[444] *See* ICC (2023) Statement by ICC Prosecutor Karim Khan KC in Cairo on the Situation in the State of Palestine and Israel. https://www.icc-cpi.int/news/statement-icc-prosecutor-karim-khan-kc-cairo-situation-state-palestine-and-israel. Accessed 28 June 2024; ICC (2023) ICC Prosecutor Karim Khan KC concludes first visit to Israel and the State of Palestine - ICC Prosecutor. https://www.icc-cpi.int/news/icc-prosecutor-karim-khan-kc-concludes-first-visit-israel-and-state-palestine-icc-prosecutor. Accessed 28 June 2024.

[445] ICC (Undated) Darfur, Sudan: Situation in Darfur, Sudan. https://www.icc-cpi.int/darfur. Accessed 28 June 2024.

[446] *See* ICC (2023) Statement by ICC Prosecutor Karim Khan KC to the United Nations Security Council on the Situation in Darfur. https://www.icc-cpi.int/news/statem ent-icc-prosecutor-karim-khan-kc-united-nations-security-council-situation-darfur. Accessed 28 June 2024; https://www.icc-cpi.int/news/statement-icc-prosecutor-karim-khan-kc-united-nations-security-council-situation-darfur-0

[447] ICC (2022) Abd Al-Rahman trial opens - International Criminal Court. https://www.icc-cpi.int/news/abd-al-rahman-trial-opens-international-criminal-court. Accessed 28 June 2024.

humanity and war crimes.[448] Alleged war crimes include intentionally directing attacks against the civilian population, murder, attempted murder, pillaging, destruction of the property of an adversary without military necessity, outrages upon personal dignity, rape, torture, and cruel treatments. In February 2023, the Prosecution notified Trial Chamber I that it had concluded its evidence presentation and in June 2023, the common Legal Representatives of Victims commenced presenting their views and concerns.[449] In October 2023, the Defence of the accused began presenting its case.

The Situation in Uganda

In July 2004, the OTP opened an investigation into the situation in Uganda after the Government of Uganda referred it to the Court in December 2003.[450] The OTP's investigation concerned alleged crimes against humanity and war crimes committed in Northern Uganda between 1 July 2022 and 31 December 2005 in the context of a NIAC between the Lord's Resistance Army (LRA) and the national authorities. After years of investigation which led to the issuance of five arrest warrants and the opening of two cases, the Prosecution decided to conclude the Situation in Uganda in December 2023 except for the outstanding case against Joseph Kony.[451]

The Prosecutor v. Joseph Kony and Vincent Otti

In November 2023, Pre-Trial Chamber II terminated proceedings against Vincent Otti, alleged former Vice-Chairman and Second-in-Command of the Lord's Resistance Army (LRA).[452] This decision followed the Prosecution's third request to terminate proceedings against Vincent Otti, in which it explained that "all available evidence indicates that Mr. Otti was killed in a remote area of the Democratic Republic of Congo in October 2007".[453] An arrest warrant had been issued against Mr. Otti in July 2005, who was suspected of 11 counts of crimes against humanity and 21 counts of war crimes allegedly committed in northern Uganda after 1 July 2002.

Concerning proceedings against Joseph Kony, following the Prosecution's "Request to Hold a Hearing on the Confirmation of Charges against Joseph Kony in his Absence" filed in November 2022, Pre-Trial Chamber II issued, in November

---

[448] ICC, Situation in Darfur, Sudan, Decision on the confirmation of charges against Ali Muhammad Ali Abd-Al-Rahman ('Ali Kushayb'), 9 July 2021, ICC-02/05-01/20.

[449] ICC (Undated) Darfur, Sudan: Situation in Darfur, Sudan. https://www.icc-cpi.int/darfur. Accessed 28 June 2024.

[450] ICC (Undated) Uganda: Situation in Uganda. https://www.icc-cpi.int/situations/uganda. Accessed 28 June 2024.

[451] ICC (2023) Statement by Prosecutor of the International Criminal Court, Karim A.A. Khan KC, announcing his decision. https://www.icc-cpi.int/news/statement-prosecutor-international-cri minal-court-karim-aa-khan-kc-announcing-his-decision. Accessed 28 June 2024.

[452] ICC (2023) ICC terminates proceedings against Vincent Otti following his passing. https://www.icc-cpi.int/news/icc-terminates-proceedings-against-vincent-otti-following-his-passing. Accessed 28 June 2024.

[453] ICC, *The Prosecutor vs. Joseph Kony and Vincent Otti*, Third Request to Terminate Proceedings against Vincent Otti, 15 November 2023, ICC-02/04-01/05.

2023, a preliminary decision ordering the Prosecutor to file a public "Document containing the charges" if he wished to continue with his request.[454] After that, the Chamber would evaluate whether "all reasonable steps to inform the suspect of the charges" had been taken, which is a prerequisite to decide if a confirmation of charges hearing can take place *in absentia*. Mr. Kony was suspected of 33 counts of crimes against humanity and war crimes, including the latter inducing rape, directing attacks against the civilian population, enlisting children, cruel treatment, pillaging, and murder.[455]

The Prosecutor v. Dominic Ongwen

After the Appeals Chamber confirmed Trial Chamber IX's decision on Dominic Ongwen's guilt and sentence in December 2022, a phase concerning the reparation of the victims began.[456] On 18 December 2023, Ongwen was transferred to Norway to serve his 25-year-long imprisonment term for the commission of 61 counts of crimes against humanity and war crimes committed in Northern Uganda between 1 July 2002 and 31 December 2005.[457]

The Situation in Ukraine

On 2 March 2022, the Prosecutor announced that he had opened an investigation into the situation in Ukraine based on the referrals received. The scope of the situation includes any past and present allegations of war crimes, crimes against humanity or genocide committed on any part of the territory of Ukraine by any person from 21 November 2013 onwards.[458]

In March 2023, the ICC Prosecutor concluded its fourth visit to Ukraine, leading to the approval of the Agreement on the Establishment of the Country Office of the International Criminal Court in Ukraine by the Cabinet of Ministers of Ukraine.[459] On 17 March 2023, ICC Pre-Trial Chamber II issued arrest warrants for Vladimir

---

[454] ICC, *The Prosecutor vs. Joseph Kony*, Decision on the Prosecution's request to hold a confirmation of charges hearing in the *Kony* case in the suspect's absence, 23 November 2023, ICC-02/04-01/05; ICC (2023) ICC judges issue preliminary decision on holding confirmation of charges hearing in absence of Joseph Kony. https://www.icc-cpi.int/news/icc-judges-issue-preliminary-decision-holding-confirmation-charges-hearing-absence-joseph-kony. Accessed 28 June 2024.

[455] ICC, *Situation in Uganda*, Warrant of Arrest for Joseph Kony Issued on 8 July 2005 as Amended on 27 September 2005, 27 September 2005, ICC-02/04-01/05.

[456] *See* ICC, The Prosecutor v. Dominic Ongwen, Judgment on the appeal of Mr Dominic Ongwen against the decision of Trial Chamber IX of 6 May 2021 entitled "Sentence", 15 December 2022, ICC-02/04-01/15 A2.

[457] ICC (2023) Dominic Ongwen transferred to Norway to serve his sentence of imprisonment. https://www.icc-cpi.int/news/dominic-ongwen-transferred-norway-serve-his-sentence-imprisonment. Accessed 28 June 2024.

[458] ICC (Undated) Ukraine: Situation in Ukraine. https://www.icc-cpi.int/situations/ukraine. Accessed 26 May 2024.

[459] ICC (Undated) Ukraine: Statement, ICC Prosecutor Karim A. A. Khan KC concludes fourth visit to Ukraine: "Amidst this darkness, the light of justice is emerging". https://www.icc-cpi.int/news/icc-prosecutor-karim-khan-kc-concludes-fourth-visit-ukraine-amidst-darkness-light-justice. Accessed 26 May 2024.

Vladimirovich Putin, President of the Russian Federation, and Maria Alekseyevna Lvova-Belova, Commissioner for Children's Rights in the Office of the President of the Russian Federation. Based on the Prosecutor application dated 22 February 2023, the Pre-Trial Chamber II considered that there are reasonable grounds to believe that each suspect bears responsibility for the war crime of unlawful deportation of population (children) and that of unlawful transfer of population (children) from occupied areas of Ukraine to the Russian Federation, in prejudice of Ukrainian children.[460]

On 23 March 2023, the Prosecutor General of Ukraine and the Registrar of the ICC signed a cooperation agreement to establish an ICC country office in Ukraine.[461]

5.2.1.2 International Residual Mechanism for Criminal Tribunals (IRMCT)

The IRMCT was established by the UN Security Council Resolution 1966 (2010) to carry out essential residual functions for the International Criminal Tribunal for Rwanda (ICTR) and the International Criminal Tribunal for the former Yugoslavia (ICTY), which were respectively expected to close in 2015 and 2017. The IRMCT's branch located in Arusha assumed functions stemming from the ICTR, whereas the IRMCT's branch in The Hague followed suit with the ICTY. Both started operating respectively in July 2012 and July 2013.

On 8 August 2023, the in-court activity of the IRMCT came to an end after the Appeals Chamber of the IRMCT confirmed that Félicien Kabuga, the last suspect, was unfit to stand trial, and that it was very unlikely that he would regain fitness in the future.[462] The Chamber also rejected the possibility suggested by the Trial Chamber of continuing proceedings through an "alternative finding procedure that resembles a trial as closely as possible, but without the possibility of a conviction".[463] Kabuga had been accused of genocide, direct and public incitement to commit genocide, conspiracy to commit genocide and various crimes against humanity allegedly committed in Rwanda in 1994.[464]

Prosecutor v. Jovica Stanišić and Franko Simatović

Jovica Stanišić and Franko Stanišić, former senior officials in the State Security Service of the Ministry of Internal Affairs of Serbia, were originally tried by the

---

[460] ICC (Undated) Ukraine: Situation in Ukraine. https://www.icc-cpi.int/situations/ukraine. Accessed 26 May 2024.

[461] ICC (Undated) Ukraine: Press Release, Ukraine and International Criminal Court sign an agreement on the establishment of a country office. https://www.icc-cpi.int/news/ukraine-and-internationonal-criminal-court-sign-agreement-establishment-country-office. Accessed 26 May 2024.

[462] IRMCT, *Prosecutor v. Félicien Kabuga*, Decision on Appeals of Further Decision on Félicien Kabuga's Fitness to Stand Trial, 7 August 2023, MICT-13-38-AR80.3.

[463] Ibid., para 68; *Prosecutor v. Félicien Kabuga*, Case No. MICT-13-38-T, Further Decision on Félicien Kabuga's Fitness to Stand Trial, 6 June 2023, MICT-13-38-T, 6 June 2023, paras 45, 57.

[464] IRMCT (Undated) KABUGA, Félicien (MICT-13-38). https://www.irmct.org/en/cases/mict-13-38. Accessed 28 June 2024.

ICTY between June 2009 and January 2013.[465] They had been accused of aiding and abetting, planning and ordering, and committing crimes against humanity of persecution, murder, deportation and inhumane acts in the form of forcible transfer, as well as the war crime of murder. Concerning the direct perpetration of crimes, both accused were charged for their participation in a joint criminal enterprise (JCE) with the objective to forcibly and permanently remove the majority of Croats, Bosnian Muslims and Bosnian Croats from Serb-claimed areas of Bosnia and Herzegovina and Croatia that led to the commission of the aforementioned crimes. Mr. Stanišić and Mr. Simatović were acquitted on all grounds by the Trial Chamber in May 2013.[466]

Following the Prosecution's appeal, the Appeals Chamber found in December 2015 that the Trial Chamber had failed to adjudicate and provide a reasoned opinion on essential elements of JCE liability and ordered that the accused be retried on all counts of the indictment in light of Rule 117(C) of the ICTY Rules of Procedure and Evidence.[467] Indeed, the Appeals Chamber considered that the Trial Chamber had erred by failing to make findings on the existence and scope of a common criminal purpose shared by a plurality of people prior to finding that the intent of Mr. Stanišić and Mr. Simatović to further that criminal purpose had not been established. In December 2015, Mr. Stanišić and Mr. Simatović were brought before the IRMCT, where they both pleaded not guilty.[468] The retrial took place from June 2017 to April 2021, in what amounted to the first retrial held before the IRMCT.[469]

In June 2021, the Trial Chamber delivered its judgement, convicting Mr. Stanišić and Mr. Simatović's of aiding and abetting crimes against humanity and war crimes committed in ethnic cleansing campaigns by Bosnian Serb forces in 1992 in Bosnia and Herzegovina, sentencing them to a prison term of 12 years.[470] On 31 May 2023, the Appeals Chamber of the IRMCT issued its judgement on the case against Mr. Stanišić and Mr. Simatović, increasing their sentence to 15 years of imprisonment.[471] This decision represented the last appeals judgement involving core crimes from cases originating before the ICTY.

---

[465] IRMCT (2013) Trial Chamber Judgement in the *Stanišić* and Simatović case to be rendered on 30 May 2013. https://www.icty.org/en/sid/11299. Accessed 25 April 2023.

[466] IRMCT, *The Prosecutor v. Jovica Stanišić and Franko* Simatović, Judgement, 30 May 2013, IT-03-69-T.

[467] IRMCT, *The Prosecutor v. Jovica Stanišić and Franko* Simatović, Judgement, 9 December 2015, IT-03-69-A.

[468] UN IRMCT (2015) Initial appearance of *Stanišić* and Simatović before the Mechanism. https://www.irmct.org/en/news/initial-appearance-stani%C5%A1i%C4%87-and-simatovi%C4%87-mechanism Accessed 25 April 2023.

[469] UN IRMCT (2021) Conclusion of closing arguments in Prosecutor v. Jovica Stanišić and Franko Simatović. https://www.irmct.org/en/news/21-04-23-conclusion-closing-arguments-prosecutor-v-jovica-stanisic-and-franko-simatovic. Accessed 25 April 2023.

[470] IRMCT, *The Prosecutor v. Jovica Stanišić and Franko* Simatović, Judgement, 30 June 2021, MICT-15-96-T (*Stanišić and Simatović* 2021).

[471] IRMCT, *The Prosecutor v. Jovica Stanišić and Franko* Simatović, Judgement, 31 May 2023, MICT-15-96-A (*Stanišić and Simatović* 2023).

The Appeals Chamber dismissed Mr. Stanišić and Mr. Simatović's 12 grounds of appeals against their conviction for different crimes, including aiding and abetting murder as a violation of the laws and customs of war committed in connection with and following the takeover of Bosanski Šamac in April 1992.[472] For its part, it partially granted the Prosecution's appeal, finding that the Trial Chamber had erred in not convicting the accused under the liability mode of JCE for crimes committed by Serb forces in different locations of Bosnia and Herzegovina in 1992 and 1995 as well as of a murder committed in 1992 in Croatia. While the Trial Chamber had found that a JCE existed with a common criminal purpose of forcibly and permanently removing the majority of non-Serbs from large areas in Croatia and Bosnia and Herzegovina, it found that it had not been proven that the accused shared the intent to further the common criminal purpose, in spite of their contributions thereto.[473] The Appeals Chamber considered that they shared the intent to further the common criminal purpose and found that they had contributed to this purpose.[474]

5.2.2 Hybrid and Regional Courts and Tribunals

Overview

For the purpose of this review, hybrid tribunals are defined as criminal tribunals that contain both national and international features. Numerous developments relating to IHL occurred at hybrid criminal tribunals during 2023. This section focuses on the tribunals which witnessed the most relevant IHL-related developments over 2023, namely: the Special Criminal Court (Cour Pénale Spéciale or CPS in French) for CAR, the Kosovo Specialist Chambers (KSC) and Specialist Prosecutor's Office (SPO), the Special Tribunal for Lebanon (STL) and the Extraordinary Chambers in the Courts of Cambodia (ECCC).

5.2.2.1 Special Criminal Court CAR

The very first final decision of the SCC's Appeals Chamber was handed in July 2023, against Issa Sallet Adoum alias Bozizé, Ousman Yaouba and Mahamat Tahir. They were members of the armed group *Retour, Réclamation et Réhabilitation*, who attacked the villages of Koundjili and Lemouna in the Ouham-Pendé prefecture in the north-west of CAR. The Court found that all of them were acting as co-perpetrators for several counts of crimes against humanity.[475]

---

[472] Ibid, para 664.

[473] See footnote 507.

[474] *Stanišić and Simatović* 2023, paras 378–516; 567.

[475] Cour Pénal Spéciale, Judgment no. 9 on the appeals against judgment no. 003-2022 of 31 October 2022 of Trial Chamber I, 20 July 2023.

The Appeals Chamber found several flaws in the Trial Chamber's reasoning. More precisely, the Chamber found that the reasoning on the required intensity to identify an IAC at the time of the commission of the crimes was unclear.[476] Additionally, the Appeals Chamber found that the Trial Chamber erred in its application of the category "other inhumane acts" constituting crimes against humanity. Accordingly, the Appeals Chamber found that "the particularly cruel circumstances of a murder can be taken into account in determining the appropriate sentence", but do not require a separate conviction—misqualified by the Trial Chamber as "other inhumane acts."[477] Finally, reviewing the Trial Chamber's sentencing of Issa Sallet, the Appeals Chamber found that the imposition of the maximum sentence (life imprisonment) without retaining the identified mitigating circumstances was disproportionate.[478]

5.2.2.2 Kosovo Specialist Chambers and Specialist Prosecutor's Office

In August 2015, the Kosovo Assembly modified Article 162 of the Kosovo Constitution and adopted the law on Specialist Chambers and Specialist Prosecutor's Office after an international agreement between Kosovo and the EU had been signed.[479] The KSC and SPO started operating in April 2016 at The Hague with a view to respectively investigate and adjudicate crimes against humanity, war crimes and other crimes under Kosovo law that commenced or committed in Kosovo between January 1998 and 31 December 2000 by or against citizens of Kosovo or the Federal Republic of Yugoslavia.[480]

In 2023, numerous developments took place within the KSC. On 2 February 2023, the appeal judgement against Hysni Gucati and Nasim Haradinaj, respectively former Chairman and Deputy Chairman of the Kosovo Liberation Army (KLA) Army War Veteran's Association was rendered.[481] At the trial stage, both accused had been found guilty of obstructing official persons in performing official duties, of intimidation during criminal proceedings, and violations of the secrecy of proceedings by the Trial Panel of the KSC on 18 May 2022.[482] On appeal, all charges were confirmed except for the obstruction of official persons in performing official duties.[483] Consequently, the Appeals Panel reduced by majority the trial sentences of four and a half years to four years and three months of imprisonment, affirming the additional sentence of

---

[476] Ibid., para 38.

[477] Ibid., paras 54–55.

[478] Ibid., para 74.

[479] KSC (2022) Kosovo Specialist Chambers & Specialist Prosecutor's Office. https://www.scp-ks.org/en Accessed 25 June 2024.

[480] Ibid.

[481] KSC, *Specialist Prosecutor v. Hysni Gucati and Nasim Haradinaj*, Appeal Judgement, 2 February 2023, KSC-CA-2022-01 (*Gucati and Haradinaj* 2023).

[482] KSC, *Specialist Prosecutor v. Hysni Gucati and Nasim Haradinaj*, Public Redacted Version of the Trial Judgment, 18 May 2022, KSC-BC-2020-07, paras 1012–1016.

[483] *Gucati and Haradinaj* 2023, para 442.

5 Year in Review 2023

paying a fine of 100 euros each.[484] As found in both stages, the accused had revealed, without authorization, protected information, including the identity of (potential) witnesses, and had further made accusations against them.

In February 2023, the trial against the former member of the KLA Pjetër Shala started before the Trial Panel of the KSC.[485] Mr. Shala is charged with the commission of war crimes of arbitrary detention, cruel treatment, torture and murder allegedly committed between approximately 17 May 1999 and 5 June 1999 against civilians nationals of the Federal Republic of Yugoslavia detained at the Kukës Metal Factory (Albania).[486] The SPO closed its case on 6 July 2023. On 21 August 2023, the Victims' Counsel presented evidence, and the Defence Preparation Conference took place on 24 and 25 August 2023. A Defence motion to dismiss the charge of murder against Mr. Shala was denied by the Panel on 15 September, after which the Defence commenced presenting its case on 20 September 2023.

In April 2023, the trial against former senior KLA officials Hashim Thaçi, Kadri Veseli, Rexhep Selimi and Jakup Krasniqi opened.[487] The accused are charged with six counts of crimes against humanity and four counts of war crimes, namely illegal detentions, cruel treatment, torture and murder, allegedly committed in several locations across Kosovo and Northern Albania from at least March 1998 through September 1999.[488] The trial preparation conference had previously been held on 18 January 2023, later followed by the Specialist Prosecutor's Preparation Conference, which took place on 15 February 2023. On 27 February 2023, the SPO filed its lesser redacted version of the indictment, which is the currently operative indictment in the case.[489]

On 5 October 2023, Sabit Januzi and Ismet Bahtijari were arrested in Kosovo and transferred to the KSC after an indictment against them was confirmed on 2 October 2023.[490] The indictment sustains that Januzi and Bahtijari met with a witness who had or was likely to provide information to relevant authorities about crimes falling under the KSC jurisdiction to induce them to withdraw evidence or refrain from providing it before the court.[491] The accused allegedly threatened the witness and promised some benefits, for which they were indicted with two counts for criminal offences against public order and one count for a criminal offence against the administration

---

[484] Ibid.

[485] KSC (Undated) Case of Pjeter Shala. https://www.scp-ks.org/en/cases/pjeter-shala. Accessed 26 June 2024.

[486] Ibid.

[487] KSC (Undated) Case of Hashim Thaçi et al. https://www.scp-ks.org/en/cases/hashim-thaci-et-al. Accessed 30 June 2024.

[488] Ibid.

[489] KSC (Undated) Case of Sabit Januzi, Ismet Bahtijari, Haxhi Shala. https://www.scp-ks.org/en/cases/sabit-januzi-ismet-bahtijari-haxhi-shala. Accessed 30 June 2024; KSC, *Specialist Prosecutor v. Hashim Thaçi, Kadri Veseli, Rexhep Selimi And Jakup Krasniqi*, Public Lesser Redacted Version of Amended Indictment, 27 February 2023, KSC-BC-2020-06.

[490] KSC, *Specialist Prosecutor v. Sabit Januzi and Ismet Bahtjari*, Public redacted Indictment, KSC-BC-2023-10, 4 October 2023 (*Januzi and Bahtjari* 2023).

[491] *Januzi and Bahtjari* 2023, para 30.

of justice and public administration.[492] The accused would have allegedly acted upon instructions from Haxhi Shala, who was himself arrested on 11 December 2023 in Kosovo after the indictment against him had been made public on 12 December 2023.[493] Mr. Shala was accused of the same counts as Januzi and Bahtijari.[494]

On 2 November 2023, Isni Kilaj was arrested in Kosovo after an arrest order had been issued by the SPO for offences against the administration of justice, including obstructing official persons in performing official duties and violating the secrecy of the proceedings.[495] The initial indictment against Mr. Kilaj was submitted to the Single Judge by the SPO on 15 December 2023.[496]

On 14 December 2023, the Appeals Panel of the KSC delivered its appeal judgement in the case of Salih Mustafa. Mr. Mustafa was the Commander of the 'BIA' guerrilla unit, which operated within the Llap Operational Zone of the KLA.[497] He had been convicted in December 2022 for counts of war crimes of arbitrary detention, torture and murder, and was sentenced to 26 years of imprisonment for acts committed by KLA members against detainees in detention centers in the village of Zllash, in the Gollak region of Kosovo.[498] The Appeals Panel affirmed Mr. Mustafa's conviction on all counts but reduced his overall single sentence from 26 years to 22 years of imprisonment in light of the fact that sentences for comparable war crimes before international tribunals and Kosovo courts tend to be shorter.[499]

5.2.2.3 Special Tribunal for Lebanon

The STL was established by the UN Security Council Resolution 1757 in 2007, and was inaugurated in 2009 with the mandate to hold persons responsible "for the attack of 14 February 2005 resulting in the death of former Lebanese Prime Minister Rafiq Hariri and in the death or injury of other persons", as well as for attacks which "are connected in accordance with the principles of criminal justice and are of a nature and gravity similar to the attack of 14 February 2005" and that were committed "between 1 October 2004 and 12 December 2005, or any later date decided by the

---

[492] Ibid.

[493] KSC (Undated) Case of Sabit Januzi, Ismet Bahtijari, Haxhi Shala. https://www.scp-ks.org/en/cases/sabit-januzi-ismet-bahtijari-haxhi-shala. Accessed 30 June 2024; KSC, *Specialist Prosecutor v. Haxhi Shala*, Public redacted Indictment, 6 December 2023, KSC-BC-2023-11 (*Haxhi Shala* 2023).

[494] *Haxhi Shala* 2023, para 30.

[495] KSC (Undated) Case of Isni Kilaj. https://www.scp-ks.org/en/cases/isni-kilaj. Accessed 25 June 2024.

[496] Ibid.

[497] KSC, *Specialist Prosecutor v. Salih Mustafa*, Public Redacted Version of Appeal Judgment, 14 December 2023, KSC-CA-2023-02 (*Mustafa* 2023).

[498] KSC, *Specialist Prosecutor v. Salih Mustafa*, Further redacted version of Corrected version of Public redacted version of Trial Judgement, 16 December 2022, KSC-BC-2020-05, para 831.

[499] *Mustafa* 2023, para 484.

5 Year in Review 2023

Parties and with the consent of the Security Council".[500] In the attack committed on 14 February 2025, 21 persons other than the former Prime Minister perished and 226 were injured after explosives equivalent to 2500–3000 kg of dynamite detonated, leaving a 11-m-wide crater.[501]

The STL applied the Lebanese Criminal Code and Lebanese law of 11 January 1958 on "Increasing the penalties for sedition, civil war and interfaith struggle".[502] However, the tribunal was not part of Lebanon's justice system; instead, it was located in The Hague and relied on national and international judges—although it did not constitute a UN tribunal either. The Tribunal, which had exclusively been entrusted since July 2022 with non-judicial residual functions, definitively closed its doors on 31 December 2023.[503]

Over its life span, it convicted Samil Jamil Ayyash for crimes including the commission of a terrorist act by an explosive device and the intentional homicide of Mr. Hariri.[504] The Appeals Chamber of the STL also convicted Hassan Habib Merhi and Hussein Hassan Oneissi by reversing their initial acquittal for crimes including being accomplices to the felony of committing a terrorist act and co-perpetrating a conspiracy aimed at committing a terrorist act.[505] Proceedings against these men were held *in absentia* and they remain at large.

5.2.2.4 Extraordinary Chambers in the Courts of Cambodia

The ECCC were established in 2001 under Cambodian law to adjudicate on crimes under Cambodian and international law committed from 17 April 1975 to 6 January 1979, when Cambodia was ruled by the Communist Party of Kampuchea, known as 'Khmer Rouge'.[506] In June 2003, the Cambodian government and the UN signed an agreement regulating the cooperation between both entities, which entered into force in April 2005.[507] The Court had jurisdiction over Khmer Rouge senior leaders

---

[500] UN Security Council (2007), Resolution 1757 (2007) - Attachment; Statute of the Special Tribunla for Lebanon, UN Doc. S/RES/1757(2007), Article 1.

[501] UN News (2023). Justice served: Lebanon's Special Tribunal closes. https://news.un.org/en/story/2023/12/1145217. Accessed 30 June 2024.

[502] UN Security Council (2007), Resolution 1757 (2007) - Attachment; Statute of the Special Tribunal for Lebanon, UN Doc. S/RES/1757(2007), Article 1, Article 2.

[503] UN News (2023). Justice served: Lebanon's Special Tribunal closes. https://news.un.org/en/story/2023/12/1145217. Accessed 30 June 2024.

[504] Justice Info (2020) Lebanon: STL Symbolically Sentences Ayyash to Life Imprisonment. https://www.justiceinfo.net/en/46228-lebanon-stl-symbolically-sentences-ayyash-to-life-imprisonment.html. Accessed 30 June 2024.

[505] Justice Info (2020) Special Tribunal for Lebanon's Second Best Justice. https://www.justiceinfo.net/en/88918-special-tribunal-for-lebanons-second-best-justice.html. Accessed 30 June 2024.

[506] Law on the Establishment of Extraordinary Chambers in the Courts of Cambodia for the Prosecution of Crimes Committed During the Period of Democratic Kampuchea (2004), Article 2.

[507] Agreement between the United Nations and the Royal Government of Cambodia concerning the prosecution under Cambodian law of crimes committed during the period of Democratic Kampuchea, 41723 UNTS 2329(117) (adopted 29 April 2005).

and "those believed to be most responsible for grave violations of national and international law", under whose rule at least 1.7 million persons are believed to have perished from executions, forced labour, torture and starvation.[508] The ECCC relied on a mix of Cambodian and international judges, prosecutors, and defence lawyers.

On 1 January 2023, the ECCC commenced its residual functions, after having put an end to its judicial work with the confirmation of Khieu Samphan's conviction for genocide, war crimes and crimes against humanity in the Case 002/02 on 22 September 2022.[509] Consequently, the ECCC has relocated to new premises in the heart of Phnom Penh to better fulfil its function of raising awareness on the work through a newly created Resource Centre, which will host an international archive repository.[510] During 2023, the ECCC also continued its work in the field of reparations for civil parties of the cases.

5.2.3   Human Rights Courts and Bodies

Overview

This section outlines developments of particular relevance to IHL that occurred during 2023 at human rights courts, bodies, and other entities with a mandate over acts that might amount to war crimes, namely the European Court of Human Rights (ECtHR), the UN Human Rights Council (HRC), the Independent Institution on Missing Persons in Syria and the UN Investigative Team to Promote Accountability for Crimes Committed by Da'esh/ISIL (UNITAD).

5.2.3.1   European Court of Human Rights

Narayan and Others v. Azerbaijan

On 19 December 2023, the European Court of Human Rights (ECtHR) issued its judgment in the case of *Narayan and Others v. Azerbaijan*. The Court established Azerbaijan's extraterritorial jurisdiction concerning the substantive aspect of the right to life of soldiers acting in an official capacity.[511] The Court subsequently found a violation of this right.[512] The case stemmed from military clashes between Azerbaijan

---

[508] Law on the Establishment of Extraordinary Chambers in the Courts of Cambodia for the Prosecution of Crimes Committed During the Period of Democratic Kampuchea (2004), Article 2.

[509] ECCC (2023) The Court Report 2023. https://eccc.gov.kh/sites/default/files/publications/THE%20COURT%20REPORT%202023_EN.pdf. Accessed 29 June 2024.

[510] Ibid.

[511] ECtHR, Narayan and others v. Azerbaijan, 19 December 2023, Applications Nos. 54363/17 and two others, para 119.

[512] Ibid., para 122.

and Armenia on 29 December 2016, which resulted in the deaths of one Azerbaijani and three Armenian soldiers.[513]

The ECtHR noted that the Azerbaijani soldier had entered the Armenian military post and fired upon Armenian soldiers. The attack led to the deaths of two unarmed Armenian soldiers, one while using the toilet and the other while attempting to fill a water tank.[514] The Azerbaijani soldier and a third Armenian soldier who repelled the attack were killed during the exchange of gunfire.[515]

The ECtHR determined that Azerbaijan exercised extraterritorial jurisdiction through state agent authority and control over the first two soldiers,[516] but not over the third Armenian soldier, who had fired his gun at the enemy before being shot shortly afterward.[517] The Court's reasoning was based on the fact that the distance between the Azerbaijani soldier and the third Armenian soldier was around 60–70 m, the crossfire occurred under conditions of reduced visibility due to fog and drizzle, and the third Armenian soldier was not an unarmed target.[518]

This decision has triggered an academic debate as to whether the ECtHR applied IHL correctly. It has been argued that even though the first two soldiers did not constitute a threat, they constituted legitimate targets.[519] Therefore, one could argue that the ECtHR did not analyse the alleged attack of the Azerbaijani soldier in light of IHL norms, which resulted in "a controversial finding of a violation of the substantive limb of the right to life."[520] On the other hand, it has been argued that combatants *hors de combat* cannot be killed. Combatants *hors de combat* have been rendered "defenceless… whether or not he has laid down his arms", including soldiers who have been "surprised in [their] sleep by the adversary."[521] As such, the ECtHR's conclusion regarding Azerbaijan's violation of the right to life is compatible with IHL.

5.2.3.2 Human Rights Council

The HRC passed resolutions during 2023 urging belligerent parties to comply with IHL and condemning violations thereto in the context of the armed conflicts active

---

[513] Ibid., para 4.

[514] Ibid., paras 92, 94, 95, 101, 105.

[515] Ibid., paras 92, 94, 95, 105.

[516] Ibid., para 108.

[517] Ibid., paras 108, 109, 110.

[518] Ibid., para 109.

[519] Musayev 2024, p. 9; see also Rule 3 CIHL and API, above n 10, Article 43(2).

[520] ECtHR did not analyse the alleged attack of the Azerbaijani soldier in light of IHL norms and found a controversial finding of a violation of the substantive limb of the right to life, p. 9.

[521] ICRC commentary Art 41 of API, p. 484. See Mischa Gureghian Hall, Who's Afraid of Human Rights in War? (Part II): On the Place of the ECHR during Armed Conflict in Response to a Misguided Critique of Narayan and Others v. Azerbaijan, Völkerrechtsblog, 18.04.2024.

in Afghanistan,[522] Central African Republic,[523] Democratic Republic of Congo,[524] Israel/Palestine,[525] Mali,[526] Myanmar,[527] Somalia,[528] South Sudan,[529] Sudan,[530] Syria,[531] Ukraine,[532] and Yemen.[533]

Likewise, on 11 October 2023, the HRC adopted Resolution 54/2, establishing an independent international fact-finding mission for Sudan to investigate and establish the facts of human rights violations and abuses, as well as violations of IHL, including those committed against refugees, and related crimes in the context of the conflict between the SAF and RSF in Sudan since 15 April 2023.[534] The resolution, which grants further competences to the mechanism to support potential future legal proceedings, was adopted with 19 votes in favour, 16 against and 12 abstentions.

5.2.3.3 Independent Institution on Missing Persons in Syria

On 29 June 2023, the UN General Assembly passed Resolution A/77/L.79, providing for the establishment of an independent UN body dedicated to "clarifying the fate and whereabouts of missing persons in the Syrian Arab Republic and to providing

---

[522] UN General Assembly (2023) Situation of human rights in Afghanistan, UN Doc. A/HRC/RES/54/1.

[523] UN General Assembly (2023) Technical assistance and capacity-building in the field of human rights in the Central African Republic, UN Doc. A/HRC/RES/54/31.

[524] UN General Assembly (2023), Technical assistance and capacity-building in the field of human rights in the Democratic Republic of the Congo, UN Doc. A/HRC/RES/54/34.

[525] UN General Assembly (2023), Israeli settlements in the Occupied Palestinian Territory, including East Jerusalem, and in the occupied Syrian Golan, UN Doc. A/HRC/RES/52/35.

[526] UN General Assembly (2023), Technical assistance and capacity-building for Mali in the field of human rights, UN Doc. A/HRC/RES/52/42.

[527] UN General Assembly (2023), Situation of human rights of Rohingya Muslims and other minorities in Myanmar, UN Doc. A/HRC/RES/53/26; UN General Assembly (2023), Situation of human rights in Myanmar, UN Doc. A/HRC/RES/52/31.

[528] UN General Assembly (2023), Assistance to Somalia in the field of human rights, UN Doc. A/HRC/RES/54/32.

[529] UN General Assembly (2023), Advancing human rights in South Sudan, UN Doc. A/HRC/RES/52/1.

[530] UN General Assembly (2023), The human rights impact of the ongoing conflict in Sudan, UN Doc. A/HRC/RES/S-36/1.

[531] UN General Assembly (2023), Situation of human rights in the Syrian Arab Republic, UN Doc. A/HRC/RES/53/18. UN General Assembly (2023), Situation of human rights in the Syrian Arab Republic, A/HRC/RES/52/30.

[532] UN General Assembly (2023), Situation of human rights in Ukraine stemming from the Russian Aggression, UN Doc. A/HRC/RES/52/32.

[533] UN General Assembly (2023), Technical assistance and capacity-building for Yemen in the field of human rights, UN Doc. A/HRC/RES/54/29.

[534] UN General Assembly (2023), Responding to the human rights and humanitarian crisis caused by the ongoing armed conflict in the Sudan, UN Doc. A/HRC/RES/54/2.

adequate support to victims, survivors and the families of those missing".[535] This institution is also expected to meaningfully integrate in its efforts victims, survivors and the families of missing persons, who outnumber the figure of 100,000 since the Arab Spring revolution started in Syria and degenerated into very deadly NIACs.[536] The initial phase of this institution was due to run from 1 April to 31 December 2024.[537]

5.2.3.4 United Nations Investigative Team to Promote Accountability for Crimes Committed by Da'esh/ISIL

UNITAD was established by the UN Secretary General pursuant to UN Security Council Resolution 2379 (2017) as an investigative body with the mandate of "collecting, preserving and storing evidence in Iraq of acts that may amount to war crimes, crimes against humanity and genocide committed by ISIL (Da'esh) in Iraq (…) to ensure the broadest possible use before national courts, and complementing investigations being carried out by the Iraqi authorities or investigations carried out by authorities in third countries at their request".[538]

UNITAD relies on international experts, Iraqi investigative judges and other criminal experts working under the authority of a Special Adviser.[539] During 2023, Christian Ritscher served as Special Adviser and Head of UNITAD. On 15 September 2023, the UN Security Council adopted Resolution 2697(2023), setting 17 September 2024 as the date of the completion of the mandate of UNITAD.[540] In light of the sudden decision to close the investigative team in the close future, Special Adviser Ritscher highlighted that UNITAD "will not be able to deliver final outputs on all lines of inquiry it has initiated, but will only be able to deliver preliminary findings for those lines of investigations rather than comprehensive reports".[541]

---

[535] UN General Assembly (2023), Independent Institution on Missing Persons in the Syrian Arab Republic, UN Doc. A/77/L.79, para 2.

[536] Baranowska G and Citroni G (2023) The UN Independent Institution on Missing Persons in the Syrian Arab Republic A marathon, a sprint, or a hurdle race? https://www.ejiltalk.org/the-un-independent-institution-on-missing-persons-in-the-syrian-arab-republic-a-marathon-a-sprint-or-a-hurdle-race/. Accessed 27 June 2024.

[537] Committee on Enforced Disappearances (2024) Summary record (partial)* of the 472nd meeting, UN Doc. CED/C/SR.472, para 3.

[538] UN Security Council (2018) Letter dated 9 February 2018 from the Secretary-General addressed to the President of the Security Council, UN Doc. S/2018/118, para 2.

[539] Ibid, para 14.

[540] UN Security Council (2023), Resolution 2697(2023), UN Doc. S/RES/2697(2023), para 2.

[541] UN News (2023) Sudden End to Team Investigating Da'esh Crimes in Iraq Could Impact Ongoing Inquiries, Justice for Victims, Special Adviser Warns Security Council. https://press.un.org/en/2023/sc15514.doc.htm. Accessed 26 June 2024.

5.2.4 National Courts

This section provides a brief overview of the most significant developments relevant for the investigation and prosecution of war crimes in specific domestic courts and tribunals throughout 2023. Several of the cases highlighted below were prosecuted using the principle of universal jurisdiction, which grants national courts the authority to try international crimes regardless of the location where they were committed and the nationality of either the victim(s) or the perpetrator(s). Universal jurisdiction worldwide was on the rise in 2023, with total cases open for any international crime reaching record of 84.[542]

5.2.4.1 Argentina

On 19 December 2023, the opening of an investigation under the grounds of universal jurisdiction for crimes allegedly committed by former Colombian President Álvaro Uribe in the context of the 'false positives' policy was announced.[543] Although the charges have not been formally announced, the investigation focuses on the war crime of murder, as well as on the crimes against humanity of murder and enforced disappearance allegedly committed between 8 August 2002 and 31 December 2008.[544] Argentinian authorities have reportedly asked the ICC for relevant information, as well as launched proceedings of mutual legal assistance with Colombian authorities.[545]

5.2.4.2 Australia

In November 2020, the Inspector General of the Australian Defence Force released a report documenting credible evidence of war crimes allegedly committed by members of the Australian Defence Forces throughout their operations in Afghanistan from 2005 to 2016.[546] Consequently, the Office of the Special Investigator was established in 2021 to investigate the alleged crimes. In March 2023, the Office of the Special Investigator announced that former member of the Australian Defence Force Oliver Schulz had been charged with the war crime of murder for

---

[542] Trial International 2024.

[543] Infobae (2023) La justicia argentina abrió una investigación contra un ex presidente de Colombia por crímenes y desapariciones. https://www.infobae.com/judiciales/2023/12/19/la-jus ticia-argentina-abrio-una-investigacion-contra-un-ex-presidente-de-colombia-por-crimenes-y-des apariciones/. Accessed 25 June 2024.

[544] Ibid.

[545] Trial International 2024.

[546] Ibid.

allegedly shooting an Afghan civilian who was not directly participating in hostilities in the head and chest in 2012.[547] Charges in this case, which represents the first time in which an Australian national has been indicted for alleged war crimes committed in Afghanistan, have not been confirmed yet.

5.2.4.3 Belgium

2023 saw various developments on war crimes cases in Belgian courts. On 28 March 2023, a Syrian national who reportedly belonged to IS was arrested during investigations over alleged executions of civilians who did not swear allegiance to IS in the surroundings of the Syrian city of Palmyra.[548] The case, brought under the framework of universal jurisdiction against a suspect who had been granted refugee status in Belgium in 2015, focuses on potential charges for war crimes and participation in the activities of a terrorist group.[549]

On 3 May 2023, Iraqi national O.Y.T. was arrested in Belgium for his alleged membership in an Al-Qaeda cell that launched various bombing attacks in Baghdad against governmental buildings between 2009 and 2010, with a toll of 376 killed and over 2300 injured.[550] O.Y.T., who had been granted asylum as a refugee in Belgium in 2015, was indicted for charges of murder with terrorist intent, participation in a terrorist group, war crimes and crimes against humanity.[551] The investigation against O.Y.T. had been opened in 2020 under grounds of universal jurisdiction after a request for extradition issued by Iraqi authorities for the same charges was denied on account of the refugee status of O.Y.T. and the existence of death penalty sentences in Iraq.[552]

On 21 June 2023, Rwandan national and former businessman V.K. was arrested in Belgian soil and indicted over charges of war crimes and genocide allegedly perpetrated in the Rwandese Butare region against members of the Tutsi community over the course of the 1994 Rwandan genocide.[553] The suspect, whose acts are investigated under the framework of universal jurisdiction, remains detained on remand.

On 19 December 2023, the popular jury of the Brussels Criminal Court convicted Rwandan businessman Pierre Basabosé and leader of an *Interhamwe* militia Séraphin Twahirwa for war crimes and acts of genocide committed in 1994 in Rwanda.[554] Basabosé was sentenced to indefinite internment in a medical facility, whereas Twahira

---

[547] Ibid.

[548] JusticeInfo.net (2024) Belgium probes refugee status of Syrian war crimes suspect. https://www.justiceinfo.net/en/114527-belgium-probes-refugee-status-of-syrian-war-crimes-supect.html. Accessed 30 June 2024.

[549] Ibid.

[550] Trial International 2024.

[551] Ibid.

[552] Ibid.

[553] Ibid.

[554] The Brussels Times (2023) Seraphin Twahirwa and Pierre Basabose found guilty of genocide and war crimes. https://www.brusselstimes.com/846674/seraphin-twahirwa-and-pierre-basabose-found-guilty-of-genocide-and-war-crimes. Accessed 30 June 2024.

followed suit with life imprisonment.[555] In June 2023, Basabosé's lawyers attempted to halt the start of the trial on the basis of the memory problems and fragile state of health faced by 76-year-old Basabosé.[556] The court however found that Basabosé was able to understand what he was accused of and to defend himself, declaring him fit to stand trial.[557]

5.2.4.4 Bosnia Herzegovina

On 8 June 2023, the Bosnian state court in Sarajevo convicted on trial stage five former Serbian police officers of committing the war crime of torture against Bosnian Muslim civilians in the area of the Bosnian locality of Janja from 1992 to 1994.[558] The accused Milan Djokic and Branislav Trisic were sentenced to a prison term of 3 years, whereas Zoran Tanasic, Zarko Milanovic and Mladen Krajisnik followed suit with an imprisonment sentence of 2 years.[559] All defendants were found responsible for having beaten civilians, except for Djokic, who was convicted for failing to prevent the abuse of detained civilians by persons under his command as then chief of the police station of Janja.[560]

On 8 August 2023, 13 former commanders and members of the Army of the Republic of Bosnia and Herzegovina were indicted by the Special Department for War Crimes in Bosnia and Herzegovina for charges of war crimes, crimes against humanity and incitement to genocide.[561] According to the Special Department for War Crimes, the accused would be responsible for acts allegedly committed against Serbian victims in the Bosnian town of Jošanica in December 1992, in which over 50 Serbian civilians were killed and a dozen wounded, amidst severe burning and destruction of civilian property.[562] Commanders Ahmet Sejdić and Ferid Buljubasic were additionally charged for alleged war crimes allegedly committed in other areas.[563]

---

[555] Ibid.

[556] JusticeInfo.net (2024) Pierre Basabose is mentally absent but will be tried. https://www.justic einfo.net/en/120450-pierre-basabose-is-mentally-absent-but-will-be-tried.html. Accessed 30 June 2024.

[557] Ibid.

[558] Balkan Insight4 (2023) Bosnia Convicts Serb Ex-Policemen of Torturing Civilians. https://bal kaninsight.com/2023/06/08/bosnia-convicts-serb-ex-policemen-of-torturing-civilians/. Accessed 25 June 2024.

[559] Ibid.

[560] Ibid.

[561] Sarajevo Times (2023) Indictment issued for war crimes near Foca. https://sarajevotimes.com/ indictment-issued-for-war-crimes-near-foca/. Accessed 25 June 2024.

[562] Ibid.

[563] Ibid.

5.2.4.5 Colombia

The Special Jurisdiction for Peace (Jurisdicción Especial para la Paz or JEP in Spanish) was established in March 2017 to investigate, prosecute and punish individuals responsible for the most serious human rights violations, including war crimes committed before 1 December 2016 in the context of the armed conflict between Colombia and the NSAG Fuerzas Armadas Revolucionarias de Colombia-Ejército Pueblo (FARC-EP).[564] It started working on 2018 and was first envisioned in the Final Peace Accord signed in 2016 between the government and the FARC as one of the pillars of the integral system of truth, justice, reparation and no repetition to be implemented in Colombia.

In 2023, the JEP underwent important developments. Among others, on 8 March 2023, the JEP issued its first indictment against ten former FARC-EP fighters for war crimes charges concerning the recruitment of child soldiers.[565] Likewise, the accused also faced war crimes charges for acts of murder, executions without trials, displacement and destruction of the environment, as well as crimes against humanity charges for the alleged use of anti-personnel landmines and the kidnapping of indigenous persons.[566]

On 27 September 2023, the JEP opened the stage of acknowledgment of truth, responsibility, and determination of facts and conduct for Macro case 11 focusing on gender-based violence, including sexual and reproductive violence and crimes committed based on sexual orientation and gender identity prejudices.[567] The JEP has already identified three subcases falling within Macro case 11: two of them respectively involving acts of violence committed against civilians by members of the FARC-EP and State forces, and another one focusing on intra-party violence within the FARC-EP and State forces.[568] The JEP also confirmed that Macro case 11 will be the last one opened under the mandate of the special tribunal.

---

[564] Coljuristas (2019) Boletin #1 del Observatorio sobre la JEP. https://www.coljuristas.org/observ atorio_jep/documentos/documento.php?id=1#:~:text=El%2029%20de%20marzo%20de,Acto% 20Legislativo%2001%20de%202017. Accessed 8 May 2024.

[565] JusticeInfo.net (2023) First child soldier charges against ex-FARC guerrillas: tribunal. https:// www.justiceinfo.net/en/113474-first-child-soldier-charges-against-ex-farc-guerrillas-tribunal. html. Accessed 30 June 2024.

[566] Ibid.

[567] JEP (2023) La JEP abre macrocaso 11 que investiga la violencia basada en género, incluyendo violencia sexual y reproductiva, y crímenes cometidos por prejuicio [The JEP opens Macrocase 11 to investigate gender-based violence, including sexual and reproductive violence, and crimes committed out of prejudice]. https://www.jep.gov.co/Sala-de-Prensa/Paginas/-la-jep-abre-macroc aso-11-que-investiga-la-violencia-basada-en-genero-incluyendo-violencia-sexual-y-reproductiva-y-crimenes.aspx. Accessed 30 June 2024.

[568] Ibid.

246 B. Guerrero Romero et al.

5.2.4.6 Croatia

On 21 March 2023, the Osijek County Court convicted *in absentia* Aleksandar Vasiljevic, the former head of the Yugoslav People's Army's Counterintelligence Service, for war crimes committed during 1991 against Croatian civilians and prisoners of war detained in camps in Serbia and Croatia.[569] The Court found that Vasiljevic had ordered the setting up of the camps in Serbian localities Begejci, Stajicevo, Sremska Mitrovica, Nis and Stara Gradiska. There, at least 19 Croats were killed, whereas many more were tortured and subjected to acts of sexual violence.[570] According to the Court, Vasiljevic knew and failed to prevent the abovementioned mistreatments, as well as to ensure adequate conditions of life for the prisoners detained in the camps.[571]

5.2.4.7 Finland

From 10 January to 8 September 2023, the appeal proceedings against Sierra Leonean national Gibril Massaquoi, former Lieutenant Colonel and spokesperson of the armed group Revolutionary United Front (RUF), were held before the Turku Court of Appeal.[572] In the trial judgement, Massaquoi had been acquitted of charges for aggravated war crimes and violations of human rights in a state of emergency for acts including murder, rape, torture, assault, forced labour and mistreatment of the dead, allegedly committed between 2001 and 2003 in Liberia.[573] Interestingly, the Court of Appeal hosted most of its hearings in Liberia.[574] The decision was expected in early 2024.

5.2.4.8 France

French courts witnessed various significant developments concerning the investigation, prosecution and adjudication of war crimes during 2023. On 29 March 2023, the investigative judge ordered the indictment of high ranking Syrian senior officials Ali Mamluk, Jamil Hassan and Abdel Salam Mahmoud before the Paris Criminal Court for charges of the war crimes of extortion and concealment of extortion of property, as well as complicity in the crimes against humanity of deliberate attacks on life, torture, enforced disappearance and imprisonment or other serious deprivation of

---

[569] Sarajevo Times (2023) Indictment issued for war crimes near Foca. https://sarajevotimes.com/indictment-issued-for-war-crimes-near-foca/. Accessed 25 June 2024.

[570] Ibid.

[571] Ibid.

[572] Trial International 2024.

[573] JusticeInfo.net (2024) Massaquoi case: Finnish Court of Appeal. https://www.justiceinfo.net/en/111661-massaquoi-case-finnish-court-of-appeal-liberia.html. Accessed 30 June 2024.

[574] Ibid.

liberty.[575] The facts giving rise to the opening of this case under the extraterritorial principle of passive nationality are the death of Syrian-French nationals Patrick Dabbagh and his father Mazen Dabbagh following their arrest in November 2013 by Syrian Air Force Intelligence officials in the Al-Mezzeh detention centre.[576]

On 10 May 2023, a war crimes investigation was launched by the French National Prosecutor's Office into the killing of French Agence France-Presse journalist Arman Soldin near Bakhmout on 9 May 2023 after being hit by a salvo of a Grad rocket.[577] Later in the year, preliminary investigations were also opened into the killings of French journalists Pierre Zakrzewski, who perished during an attack against his car on 14 March 2023, and Frédéric Leclerc-Imhoff, who died during a humanitarian mission in East Ukraine on 30 May 2023.[578]

On 19 July 2023, investigative judges of the specialized unit for the prosecution of international crimes sent Majdi Nema alias Islam Alloush, former spokesperson of the Syrian armed group Jaysh al-Islam to trial for complicity in war crimes and enforced disappearances, as well as for charges of participation in a group formed for the purpose of committing war crimes.[579] The war crimes-related charges at issue included complicity in the war crimes of recruiting child soldiers, wilful killings, wilfully causing great suffering or serious injury to body or health, and deliberate attacks against civilians.[580] On 20 November 2023, the Court of Appeal of Paris confirmed the previous decision after the defence of Nema had appealed it, although only for the charges of complicity in the war crime of recruiting child soldiers and participation in a group formed for the purpose of preparing war crimes.[581] The group Jays al-Islam is believed to be responsible for different crimes, including the abduction, torture and enforced disappearance of human rights lawyers Razan Zaitouneh, Nazem al-Hammadi and Wael Hamada, and of the political activist Samira al-Khalil.[582]

On 18 October 2023, French investigative judges issued arrest warrants against four Syrian former high ranking officials, including former minister of defence Fahed Jassem al-Fraij for charges of the war crimes of deliberate attack against civilians

---

[575] Trial International 2024.

[576] Ibid.

[577] CBS News (2023) Arman Soldin: Reporter killed in Ukraine, France opens war crime investigation. https://www.cbsnews.com/news/arman-soldin-reporter-killed-ukraine-france-war-crime-investigation/. Accessed 27 May 2024.

[578] Trial International 2024.

[579] International Federation for Human Rights (FIDH) (2023) Syria: French judges send Majdi Nema to trial before the criminal court. https://www.fidh.org/en/region/north-africa-middle-east/syria/syria-french-judges-send-majdi-nema-to-trial-before-the-criminal. Accessed 26 May 2024.

[580] Ibid.

[581] JusticeInfo.net (2023) Crimes de guerre en Syrie: procès aux assises confirmé en France pour un ex-rebelle salafiste. https://www.justiceinfo.net/fr/125108-crimes-de-guerre-en-syrie-proces-aux-assises-confirme-en-france-pour-un-ex-rebelle-salafiste.html. Accessed 27 May 2024.

[582] Trial International 2024.

and murder of protected persons.[583] The accused, namely al-Fraij, Ali Abdallah Ayoub, Ahmad Balloul and Ali Safetli are suspected of being responsible for the attack allegedly targeting civilian infrastructure on 7 June 2017 in the city of Deraa in which French-Syrian national Salah Abou Nabout was killed.[584]

On 14 November 2023, French investigative judges issued an international arrest warrant against Syrian President Bashar al-Assad as well as high ranking officials Maher al-Assad—the brother of Bashar al-Assad—and Generals Ghassan Abbas and Bassam al-Hassan for their alleged responsibility in attacks using chemical weapons committed against citizens including French nationals in 2013 in Syria.[585] The accused are charged with complicity in the war crimes of wilful killings, wilfully causing great suffering or serious injury to body or health and deliberate attacks against civilians, as well as in the crimes against humanity of wilful killings and other inhumane acts.[586] On 21 December 2023, the prosecutor appealed the arrest warrant against President al-Assad on the basis of the alleged personal immunity he is entitled to as the back then Head of State of Syria.[587]

5.2.4.9 Germany

On 23 February 2023, a Syrian national and former member of the Free Palestine armed group, Moafak D. was sentenced to life imprisonment by the Higher Regional Court of Berlin for the war crimes of attacking civilians, as well as for other offenses under domestic law.[588] The Court found that Moafak D. had fired a grenade into a crowd of persons queuing for humanitarian relief in Damascus on 23 March 2014, which killed at least seven people and injured at least three others.[589]

On 2 August 2023, an alleged member of Syrian regime-affiliated Shabiha militia, Ahmad H. was arrested in Bremen following an arrest warrant of the investigating judge of the Federal Court of Justice, which was issued on 26 July 2023.[590] Ahmad H. is suspected of having committed crimes against humanity and war crimes, including through acts of torture and enslavement.[591] On 3 August 2023, the investigating

---

[583] JusticeInfo.net (2023) Crimes de guerre en Syrie: procès aux assises confirmé en France pour un ex-rebelle salafiste. https://www.justiceinfo.net/fr/125108-crimes-de-guerre-en-syrie-proces-aux-assises-confirme-en-france-pour-un-ex-rebelle-salafiste.html. Accessed 25 June 2024.

[584] Ibid.

[585] The Guardian (2023) French court issues arrest warrant for Bashar al-Assad over crimes against humanity in Syria. https://www.theguardian.com/world/2023/nov/15/french-court-arrest-warrant-bashar-al-assad-crimes-against-humanity-syria. Accessed 30 June 2024.

[586] Trial International 2024.

[587] Ibid.

[588] Trial International 2024.

[589] Ibid.

[590] Deutsche Welle (2023) Alleged former Syrian militia leader arrested in Germany. https://www.dw.com/en/alleged-former-syrian-militia-leader-arrested-in-germany/a-66433893. Accessed 27 June 2024.

[591] Ibid.

judge who had issued the arrest warrant against Ahmad H. ordered his detention on remand.[592]

On 12 December 2023, alleged former member of Hezbollah Ammar A. was arrested in the Rhein-Neckar region after an arrest warrant against him had been issued by the Federal Court of Justice on 27 November 2023.[593] Ammar A. is suspected of having committed crimes against humanity of torture and deprivation of liberty as well as war crimes against protected persons and property in the Syrian locality of Busra al-Sham between 2012 and 2013.[594]

5.2.4.10 The Netherlands

On 17 January 2023, Syrian security chief for Jabhat Al-Nusra and IS, Ayham al-S. was arrested in Arkel under charges of alleged participation in a criminal organization aimed at committing war crimes.[595] According to the prosecution, al-S. would have held a senior role in the security services of IS between 2015 and 2018, and of Jabhat Al-Nusra from 2013 to 2015, where he would have been in charge of detentions around the Yarmouk refugee camp south of Damascus.[596]

In early 2023, Dutch alleged former IS member Krista van T. was arrested in the Netherlands after having been repatriated from a detention camp located in Northern Syria in November 2022.[597] Charges against her included the war crime of pillage, the crime against humanity of slavery and membership in a foreign terrorist organization.[598]

From 30 November to 4 December 2023, the trial of Syrian national Mustafa A. took place before the Hague District Court for charges of war crimes of serious deprivation of liberty and torture, as well as for crimes against humanity and participation in an organization aimed at committing international crimes.[599] Mustafa A., who had been living in the Netherlands since 2020 as an asylum-seeker, faced a 17 year-long imprisonment term for acts committed in Syria in 2013 while he was an

---

[592] Ibid

[593] Baladi E (2023) Germany: Arrest of Hezbollah suspect charged with war crimes in Syria. https://english.enabbaladi.net/archives/2023/12/germany-arrest-of-hezbollah-suspect-charged-with-war-crimes-in-syria/. Accessed 26 May 2024.

[594] Ibid.

[595] DW (2024) Dutch police arrest alleged IS security chief for war crimes. https://www.dw.com/en/dutch-police-arrest-alleged-is-security-chief-for-war-crimes/a-64426831. Accessed 30 June 2024.

[596] Trial International 2024.

[597] National Public Prosecution Service of the Netherlands (Date of retrieval) Syria cases prosecuted. https://www.prosecutionservice.nl/topics/international-crimes/what-cases-have-been-prosecuted/syria. Accessed 30 June 2024.

[598] Trial International 2024.

[599] Just Security (2023) Syrian Regime Crimes on Trial in the Netherlands. https://www.justsecurity.org/90225/syrian-regime-crimes-on-trial-in-the-netherlands/. Accessed 30 June 2024.

alleged member of pro-regime militia Liwa al-Quds.[600] The verdict was expected by early 2024.

5.2.4.11 Sweden

On 19 December 2023, the Svea Court of Appeal confirmed the conviction and life imprisonment sentence that the Stockholm District Court had issued for the Iranian national Hamid Noury for war crimes on 14 July 2022.[601] Both courts found that Noury, who served as the former assistant to the deputy prosecutor at the Gohardasht prison in Karaj, Iran, was involved in the mass execution of different left-wing sympathizers who had been deemed as apostates.[602]

On 5 September 2023, the trial of Swiss Orrön Energy CEO Alex Schneiter and Swedish Chairman of Orrön Energy Ian Lundin started before the Stockholm District Court for their alleged complicity in war crimes purportedly committed between 1999 and 2003 in the context of the Second Sudanese war.[603] According to the indictment, the company Orrön Energy, now Lundin Petroleum, allegedly paid the Sudanese army as well as various NSAGs to displace local communities from oil-rich areas in Southern Sudan in order to ensure the viability of their operations.[604] The prosecutor has also requested the confiscation of around 117 million euros, allegedly corresponding to the profit made by Lundin Oil in 2003, to secure reparations.[605] Schneiter appealed the indictment alleging that Swedish courts did not have jurisdiction over him as a Swiss national, which was rejected by both the Stockholm District and the Svea Court of Appeal.[606]

5.2.4.12 Switzerland

On 1 June 2023, the Appeals Chamber of the Swiss Federal Criminal Court rendered its verdict in the case concerning former commander of the armed group United Liberation Movement of Liberia for Democracy Alieu Kosiah.[607] In it, the Chamber

---

[600] Trial International 2024.

[601] Reuters (2023) Swedish court upholds guilty verdict in Iran executions case. https://www.reuters.com/world/swedish-court-upholds-guilty-verdict-iran-executions-case-2023-12-19/. Accessed 30 June 2024.

[602] Trial International 2024.

[603] JusticeInfo.net (2023) Oil and war crimes in Sudan: Lundin trial opens in Sweden. https://www.justiceinfo.net/en/121068-oil-and-war-crimes-in-sudan-lundin-trial-opens-in-sweden.html. Accessed 30 June 2024.

[604] Trial International 2024.

[605] Ibid.

[606] Ibid.

[607] Swissinfo.ch (2024) Swiss court upholds ruling against former Liberian warlord. https://www.swissinfo.ch/eng/politics/swiss-court-upholds-ruling-against-former-liberian-warlord/48558426. Accessed 30 June 2024.

5 Year in Review 2023

confirmed the conviction by the Trial Chamber for counts of crimes against humanity and war crimes including for acts of rape, murder, inhumane treatment, and use of child soldiers.[608]

5.2.4.13 Ukraine

Three months after the full-scale invasion of Ukraine, a Kyiv Court sentenced a Russian soldier to life imprisonment (under Article 438(2) of the Ukrainian Criminal Code) for killing a civilian.[609] This conviction for having committed a war crime is the first of a long series of trials for crimes related to the conflict between Ukraine and the Russian Federation that happened in 2023. Most of the judgements taking place to adjudicate war crimes in 2023 were conducted *in absentia*. District criminal courts also rendered judgements over counts of incitement to commit genocide in 2023. Among the trials that took place in 2023, the elements of the crime of incitement were not applied consistently to the facts of the cases. Under Ukrainian legislation, incitement to genocide does not need to be *direct*. Additionally, under Ukrainian legislation, incitement to genocide is to be considered *a minor offence*,[610] which suggests that it is not possible to prosecute Russians when the incident occurred in Russia.

5.2.4.14 United Kingdom

During 2023, an Angolan national was arrested in the United Kingdom during the course of an investigation into alleged war crimes allegedly committed between 1991 and 1994 in Angola.[611] This person is suspected to have been responsible for the murder and torture of various victims. On another note, 2023 witnessed the closure of investigations into alleged war crimes in Liberia, Iraq and Sierra Leone due to insufficient evidence.[612]

5.3 Arms Control and Disarmament

The purpose of this section is to summarize developments related to treaties and conventions dealing with arms control and disarmament and briefly highlight important progression in the field in the year 2023. Amongst significant global trends was

---

[608] Ibid.

[609] Trial International 2024.

[610] Ukrainian Criminal Code, Articles 8 and 12.

[611] Trial International 2024.

[612] Ibid.

India becoming the world's biggest arms importer in 2023 with Russia being its main supplier, and Russia and China supporting Myanmar through arms export.[613]

5.3.1 Arms Trade

On 25 August 2023, the Final Report of the Ninth Conference of State Parties to the Arms Trade Treaty (ATT) came to various interesting conclusions.[614] The focus was on the theme of "The Role of Industry in Responsible International Transfers of Conventional Arms" and its relationship with the ATT both in the international and national context. State Parties decided that they would share industry-related information about ATT, integrate the UN Guiding Principles on Business and Human Rights and IHL to the application of arms trade, and actively include private industries showing accountability to their nation-states in acting responsibly for matters of arms trade and transfer.

5.3.2 Conventional Weapons

In November, the Annual Conference of Protocol V on Explosive Remnants of War (ERW) highlighted the requirements of the Convention on Prohibitions or Restrictions on the Use of Certain Conventional Weapons.[615] The State Parties discussed the previously submitted agenda which included the "consideration of matters about national implementation of this Protocol, including national reporting or updating annually".[616] The main recommendations addressed to States concerned the strengthened universalization of the Protocol, the recording, retaining and transmission of information as required by Article 4, national reporting, victim assistance, and clearance of explosive remnants of war.[617] During the Conference, the ICRC stressed the importance of the universalization of the working paper given that only half of the world's States are party to Protocol V.[618]

---

[613] SIPRI (2023) Trends in International Arms Transfers. https://www.sipri.org/publications/2024/sipri-fact-sheets/trends-international-arms-transfers-2023. Accessed 30 May 2024.

[614] Ibid.

[615] Seventeenth Annual Conference of the High Contracting Parties to Protocol V on Explosive Remnants of War to the Convention on Prohibitions or Restrictions on the Use of Certain Conventional Weapons Which May Be Deemed to Be Excessively Injurious or to Have Indiscriminate Effects (2023) Final document, UN. Doc CCW/P.V/CONF/2023/5.

[616] Ibid.

[617] Ibid.

[618] ICRC (2023) Statement for delivery under the General Debate. https://docs-library.unoda.org/Convention_on_Certain_Conventional_Weapons_-Protocol_V_Annual_Conference_(2023)/ICRC_-_Statement_Protocol_V.pdf. Accessed 30 May 2024.

5 Year in Review 2023

5.3.2.1 Cluster Munitions

The 2008 Convention on Cluster Munitions saw the ratification of Nigeria and South Sudan in February and August 2023 respectively.[619] According to the Cluster Munition Monitor Report of 2023, countries who used this form of weaponry in the year included Russia, Myanmar and Syria.[620]

The Eleventh Meeting of State Parties to the Convention took place in September. The meeting served as a reminder of the responsibility States have not to use cluster munitions given their role in the increase of civilian casualties and humanitarian impact as documented in the previous conference. The State of particular concern in this regard was Ukraine.[621]

5.3.2.2 Landmines

UN Secretary General Antonio Guterres published "A New Agenda for Peace", urging member states to work toward "achieving universality of treaties banning inhumane and indiscriminate weapons" such as the Mine Ban Treaty.[622] Also, the 2023 Landmine Monitor reported usage of landmines by the State Party Ukraine and States not parties, Russia and Myanmar, as well as the usage by NSAGs in Colombia, India, Myanmar, Thailand, Tunisia and the Sahel region of Africa.[623]

5.3.3 Non-conventional Weapons

5.3.3.1 Biological Weapons

---

[619] International Campaign to Ban Landmines 2023, p. 1.

[620] Ibid.

[621] *See* Convention on Cluster Munitions, (opened for signature on 3 December 2008), 2688 UNTS 39 (entered into force 1 August 2010) (CCM) https://disarmament.unoda.org/convention-on-cluster-munitions/. Accessed 30 May 2024.

[622] Ibid.

[623] Ibid.

In December 2023, the third session of the Working Group on the Strengthening of the Biological Weapons Convention (BWC) was conducted.[624] It saw many positive Convention-related developments.[625] South Sudan acceded to the Convention in 2023, becoming the 185th State Party.[626] The agenda emphasized the universalization of the convention, which had a fruitful response from State Parties.[627] Norway's submission at the meeting was an update on the activities related to reducing biological risks. To that effect, they discussed the Workshop on International Cooperation and Assistance under the BWC which took place in Croatia during February and March, and the Capacity-building Course on Virus Detection and Biosecurity in June.[628] The Association of Southeast Asian Nations' (ASEAN) joint statement also eludes to efforts for the same objective, by pointing to the BWC Confidence Building Measures Workshop in Bangkok, which addressed officials of Southeast Asia.[629] Additionally, the G7's joint statement discussed the gendered impact of biological weapons.[630]

Notably, there were submission exchanges of Ukraine-Russia directly related to their conflict. The statement of the Ukrainian delegation highlighted "the breach by the Russian armed forces of the dam at Kakhovka hydroelectric plant on 6 June 2023 resulting in a heightened biohazard threat and a widespread and devastating impact on the environment and people of Ukraine".[631]

5.3.3.2 Chemical Weapons

2023 marked a significant year for the endeavours by the Organisation of the Prohibition of Chemical Weapons (OPCW) and States to put an end to the use of chemical weapons.

---

[624] Working Group on the Strengthening of the Convention on the Prohibition of the Development, Production and Stockpiling of Bacteriological (Biological) and Toxin Weapons and on Their Destruction (2023) Agenda of the Working Group on the Strengthening of the Convention, UN Doc. BWC/WG/1/1.

[625] Council on Strategic Risks (2023) The Biological and Toxin Weapons Convention 2023: Glimmers of Progress Set Against a Troubled Geopolitical Landscape. https://councilonstrate gicrisks.org/2023/12/14/the-biological-and-toxin-weapons-conventionin-2023-glimmers-of-pro gress-set-against-a-troubled-geopolitical-landscape/. Accessed 29 May 2024.

[626] Working Group on the Strengthening of the Convention on the Prohibition of the Development, Production and Stockpiling of Bacteriological (Biological) and Toxin Weapons and on Their Destruction (2023) Agenda of the Working Group on the Strengthening of the Convention, UN Doc. BWC/WG/1/1.

[627] Ibid.

[628] Ibid.

[629] Ibid.

[630] Ibid.

[631] Ibid.

On 7 July 2023, the US successfully destroyed its chemical weapons stockpile completing the destruction of all declared stockpiles in the world.[632] The OPCW Centre for Chemistry and Technology began its functioning in May 2023 owing to emerging threats of AI, toxic chemicals and a potential re-emergence that tests the boundaries of the Chemical Weapons Convention (CWC).[633]

Qatar and Zambia hosted a seminar on the CWC and Chemical Safety and Security Management for Asian States Parties and the African region respectively in March.[634] On 26 September, the EU prolonged the restrictive measures relative to chemical weapons for another year and extended the sanctions regime for three years.[635]

5.3.3.3 Nuclear Weapons

2023 saw unfortunate setbacks in terms of nuclear arms and disarmament. Russia withdrew from the Treaty on Measures for the Further Reduction and Limitation of Strategic Offensive Arms as the final arm after its previous withdrawal from all other nuclear control treaties.[636] The fourth session of the Conference on the Establishment of a Middle East Zone Free of Nuclear Weapons and Other Weapons of Mass Destruction hosted by the General Assembly in November stressed the necessity of Israel's participation to create a legally binding instrument for establishing a nuclear arms free Middle East. The fear arose from recent threats made by high-ranking officials and the Minister of Heritage of Israel, threatening to use nuclear force on Gaza.[637]

5.3.3.4 Lethal Autonomous Weapon Systems

The legality of employing autonomous weapon systems (AWS) remains highly controversial owing to their States increased usage in warfare, the debates on what treaty they fall under, as well as whether IHL is sufficiently equipped to ensure

---

[632] OPCW (2023) OPCW confirms: All declared chemical weapons stockpiles verified as irreversibly destroyed. https://www.opcw.org/media-centre/news/2023/07/opcw-confirms-all-dec lared-chemical-weapons-stockpiles-verified. Accessed 29 May 2024.

[633] Ibid.

[634] Ibid.

[635] Council of the European Union (2023) Chemical Weapons: EU restrictive measures prolonged for an additional year.
https://www.consilium.europa.eu/en/press/press-releases/2023/10/09/chemical-weapons-eu-restrictive-measures-prolonged-for-an-additional-year/. Accessed 29 May 2024.

[636] SIPRI Media (2024) Role of nuclear weapons grows as geopolitical relations deteriorate– new SIPRI Yearbook out now. https://www.sipri.org/media/press-release/2024/role-nuclear-weapons-grows-geopolitical-relations-deteriorate-new-sipri-yearbook-out-now. Accessed 29 May 2024.

[637] See Convention on Certain Conventional Weapons (opened for signature 10 April 1981), 1342 UNTS 137 (entered into force 2 December 1983) (CCW).

accountability for this new system of harm in armed conflict.[638] An agenda released in October by the General Assembly discussed the application of IHL and human rights to AWS, expressing concern about the ethical, legal and humanitarian risks of these developing systems.[639]

5.3.4 Other Developments

5.3.4.1 Cyberspace

As established in the previous Year in Reviews, cyberattacks can trigger the application of IHL.[640] The Tallinn Manual sets out the threshold for a cyberattack to amount to an illegal use of force.[641] Most States agreed in the General Assembly's session meeting in October 2023 that international law plays an undeniable role in cyber issues, which have become a grave threat and concern as a form of warfare.[642]

5.3.4.2 Outer Space

The Outer Space Security Conference takes place annually to discuss the international community's role in challenges that may arise due to increased technological development that could raise concerns.[643] In 2023, discussions were held in September in Geneva. Multilateral efforts to build space security was a common theme and the panellists elaborated on acknowledging the applicability of the UN Charter and IHL to space activities.[644] The imperative need to include IHL concerning space security arose out of humanitarian concerns over a potential eruption of conflict.[645] In the coming years, States will further deliberate upon the specific elements of IHL's applicability and how it can be tailored to space.[646]

---

[638] Jaime (2023) Discussions on autonomous weapons systems in 2023: Like it or not, the issue is already out of the CCW. https://www.forumarmstrade.org/uploads/1/9/0/8/19082495/munoz_15_december_2022.pdf. Accessed 29 May 2024.

[639] Ibid.

[640] Gregoire et al. 2023, p. 68.

[641] UN Press, 24 October 2023, 'Without Adequate Guardrails, Artificial Intelligence Threatens Global Security in Evolution from Algorithms to Armaments, Speaker Tells First Committee' https://press.un.org/en/2023/gadis3725.doc.htm. Accessed 29 May 2024.

[642] Ibid.

[643] UNIDIR Outer Space Security Conference 2023, https://unidir.org/event/outer-space-security-conference-2023-2/ Accessed 29 May 2024.

[644] Ibid.

[645] Ibid.

[646] Ibid.

5.3.4.3 Human Rights, Due Diligence, Corporate Responsibility

On 13 July 2023, the HRC adopted a resolution on the impact of arms transfer on human rights.[647] The ICRC states that businesses including arms-exporting companies should respect IHL if they carry out activities 'closely linked' to an armed conflict.[648]

There has been massive discussion towards adopting a human rights and due diligence approach to arms trade. Accordingly, the often overshadowed responsibility of private and corporate actors in the arms trade race has been brought to the forefront.[649] Policy suggestions from the main reports on this topic in 2023 include the potential of holding arms exporters liable in tort for a failure of their duty of care toward the victims of war crimes and violations of IHL.[650]

5.3.4.4 Strategic Litigation

The arms industry saw a rise in strategic litigation as a means adopted to curb trade and supply that leads to support of armed conflict.[651] An Arms Trade Litigation Monitor was set up in April 2023.[652]

In October 2023, a precedent was set in the Netherlands with a case brought forward by the Dutch NGOs Oxfam Novib, PAX and The Rights Forum. They called upon the State of the Netherlands to ban the transfer of F-35 parts to Israel. Although the appeals decision of 2024 which resulted in the court ruling in favour of the plaintiffs falls outside of the temporal scope of this Year in Review, it is nonetheless important to touch upon the initiation of the proceedings. The Dutch Court also recognized the ability of NGOs to bring civil suits as representing the interests of civilians and the general interest of compliance with IHL, IHRL and the prevention of genocide.[653]

---

[647] UN Human Rights Council (2023) (Impact of arms transfers on human rights), UN Doc. A/HRC/RES/53/15. https://documents.un.org/doc/undoc/gen/g23/150/41/pdf/g2315041.pdf. Accessed 30 May 2024.

[648] Ibid.

[649] Alwisheva (2024) The move towards human rights due diligence policies by the arms industry. https://www.forumarmstrade.org/blog/the-move-towards-human-rights-due-diligence-policies-by-the-arms-industry. Accessed 30 May 2024.

[650] Flemish Peace institute 2023.

[651] Atlantic Council (2024) Experts react: What the International Court of Justice said (and didn't say) in the genocide case against Israel. https://www.atlanticcouncil.org/blogs/new-atlanticist/experts-react/experts-react-what-the-international-court-of-justice-said-and-didnt-say-in-the-genocide-case-against-israel/#kmiotek-icj. Accessed 30 May 2024.

[652] Saferworld (2023) Launching the new Arms Trade Litigation Monitor website. https://www.saferworld-global.org/resources/news-and-analysis/post/1003-launching-the-new-arms-trade-litigation-monitor-website. Accessed 30 May 2024.

[653] Arms Trade Litigation Monitor (Undated) Dutch Arms and Palestine. https://armstradelitigationmonitor.org/overview/dutch-arms-and-the-occupied-palestinian-territories/ Accessed 30 May 2024.

In March 2023, Yemeni nationals brought a case in the District of Columbia challenging the legality of the US sending weapons to a Saudi and UAE coalition that allegedly attacked Yemen when the Houthi armed group took control of Yemen's capital in 2014. The Group of Eminent International and Regional Experts on Yemen concluded there are grounds to believe that the parties to the conflict are committing violations of IHL potentially amounting to war crimes.

In general, States are condemning the transfer of weapons and ammunition to Israel in light of the aggravated humanitarian catastrophe in Gaza. As such, this points to strategic diplomacy and litigation has taken major turns in 2023.

References

Articles, Books and Other Documents

ACLED (2023) Actor Profile: Jama'at Nusrat al-Islam wal Muslimin (JNIM). https://acleddata.com/2023/11/13/actor-profile-jamaat-nusrat-al-islam-wal-muslimin-jnim/

ACLED (2023) Actor Profile: The Islamic State Sahel Province. https://acleddata.com/2023/01/13/actor-profile-the-islamic-state-sahel-province/. Accessed 8 May 2024

ACLED (2023) Fact Sheet: Conflict surges in Sudan. https://acleddata.com/2023/04/28/fact-sheet-conflict-surges-in-sudan/. Accessed 28 June 2024

ACLED (2023) Sudan Situation Update, June 2023: Conflict intensifies following the breakdown of Jeddah talks. https://acleddata-com.translate.goog/2023/06/23/sudan-situation-update-june-2023-conflict-intensifies-following-the-breakdown-of-jeddah-talks/?_x_tr_sl=en&_x_tr_tl=es&_x_tr_hl=es&_x_tr_pto=sc. Accessed 28 June 2024

ACLED (2023) Sudan Situation Update, May 2023: Fighting rages amid ceasefire talks. https://acleddata.com/2023/05/26/sudan-situation-update-may-2023-fighting-rages-amid-ceasefire-talks/. Accessed 28 June 2024

ACLED (2024) ACLED Data Export Tool. https://acleddata.com/data-export-tool/. Accessed 22 May 2024

ACLED (2024) Actor Profile: Volunteers for the Defense of the Homeland (VDP). https://acledata.com/2024/03/26/actor-profile-volunteers-for-the-defense-of-the-homeland-vdp/. Accessed 8 May 2024

ACLED (2024) Conflict Watchlist 2024: DRC. https://acleddata.com/conflict-watchlist-2024/drc/. Accessed 22 June 2024

ACLED (2024) Conflict Watchlist 2024: Sahel. https://acleddata.com/conflict-watchlist-2024/sahel/. Accessed 8 May 2024

ACLED (2024) Sudan Situation Update, February 2024: Sudan - the SAF breaks the siege. https://acleddata.com/2024/02/16/sudan-situation-update-february-2024-sudan-the-saf-breaks-the-siege/. Accessed 26 June 2024

ACLED (2024) Sudan Situation Update, January 2024: The Rapid Support Forces (RSF) Gains Ground in Sudan. https://acleddata.com/2024/01/12/sudan-situation-update-januar-2024-the-rapid-support-forces-rsf-gains-ground-in-sudan/. Accessed 8 May 2024

ACLED 2 August 2023 'Moving Out of the Shadows Shifts in Wagner Group Operations Around the World' https://acleddata.com/2023/08/02/moving-out-of-the-shadows-shifts-in-wagner-group-operations-around-the-world/#exec Accessed 30 May 2024

ACLED Factsheet 21 September 2023 https://acleddata.com/2023/09/21/fact-sheet-attacks-on-civilians-spike-in-mali-as-security-deteriorates-across-the-sahel/. Accessed 30 May 2024

5 Year in Review 2023

African Union Peace and Security Council (2017) Communiqué, Doc. PSC/PR/COMM(DCLXXIX)

Agreement between the United Nations and the Royal Government of Cambodia concerning the prosecution under Cambodian law of crimes committed during the period of Democratic Kampuchea, 41723 UNTS 2329(117) (adopted 29 April 2005)

Amnesty International (2023) Burkina Faso: "Death was slowly creeping on us": Living under siege in Burkina Faso. https://www.amnesty.org/en/documents/afr60/7209/2023/en/. Accessed 8 May 2024

Amnesty Report 2023 Nigeria, https://www.amnesty.org/en/location/africa/west-and-central-africa/nigeria/report-nigeria/ Accessed 20 May 2024

AOAV (2023) An analysis of the 7th of October 2023 casualties in Israel as a result of the Hamas attack. https://aoav.org.uk/2023/an-analysis-of-the-7th-of-october-2023-casualties-in-israel-as-a-result-of-the-hamas-attack/. Accessed 28 March 2024

Arms Trade Litigation Monitor, Dutch Arms and Palestine, https://armstradelitigationmonitor.org/overview/dutch-arms-and-the-occupied-palestinian-territories/ Accessed 30 May 2024

ATT/CSP9/2023/SEC/773/Conf.FinRep.Rev2, 25th August 2023, https://thearmstradetreaty.org/hyper-images/file/ATT_CSP9_ATTS_Final%20Report_%20rev2_EN/ATT_CSP9_ATTS_Final%20Report_%20rev2_EN.pdf Accessed 28 May 2024

Cameron L and Chetail V (2013) Privatizing war: Private Military and Security Companies under Public International Law. Cambridge University Press, Cambridge, pp 396–397

Campaign to Ban Landmines, Landmine Monitor 2023, November 2023, pg 1 Main Findings https://backend.icblcmc.org/assets/reports/Landmine-Monitors/LMM2023/Downloads/Landmine-Monitor-2023_web.pdf Accessed 29 May 2024

CCW/GGE.1/2024/CRP.1, 1 March 2024 https://docs-library.unoda.org/Convention_on_Certain_Conventional_Weapons_-Group_of_Governmental_Experts_on_Lethal_Autonomous_Weapons_Systems_(2024)/CCW_GGE1_2024_CRP1.pdf. Accessed May 29 2024

CCW/P.V/CONF/2023/5, 23 November 2023, https://docslibrary.unoda.org/Convention_on_Certain_Conventional_Weapons_-Protocol_V_Annual_Conference_(2023)/CCW-P.V-CONF-2023-5_English.pdf Accessed 28 May 2024

Center for Preventive Action Global Conflict Tracker 23 March 2024, 'Civil War in Myanmar', https://www.cfr.org/global-conflict-tracker/conflict/rohingya-crisis-myanmar Accessed 30 May 2024

Chamber VI of 8 March 2021 entitled "Reparations Order", 12 September 2022, ICC-01/04-02/06

Clingendael March 2015 Report 'Roots of Conflict Mali', Executive Summary https://www.clingendael.org/pub/2015/the_roots_of_malis_conflict/executive_summary/ Accessed 30 May 2024

Clingendael Report March 2015, 'The Failed path to national unity', https://www.clingendael.org/pub/2015/the_roots_of_malis_conflict/1_the_failed_path_to_national_unity/ Accessed 30 May 2024

Convention on Cluster Munitions, CCM/MSP/2023/11 29 September 2023, https://docs-library.unoda.org/Convention_on_Cluster_Munitions_-EleventhMeeting_of_States_Parties_(2023)/CCM.MSP_.2023.11_AdvCopy.pdf Accessed 29 May 2024

Council on Foreign Relations (CFR) (2024) Power Struggle in Sudan. https://www.cfr.org/global-conflict-tracker/conflict/power-struggle-sudan. Accessed 28 June 2024

Council on Foreign Relations 31 January 2022, 'Myanmar's Troubled History: Coups, Military Rule, and Ethnic Conflict' https://www.cfr.org/backgrounder/myanmar-history-coup-military-rule-ethnic-conflict-rohingya Accessed 30 May 2024

Council on Strategic Risks 14 December 2023, 'The Biological and Toxin Weapons Convention 2023: Glimmers of Progress Set Against a Troubled Geopolitical Landscape', https://councilonstrategicrisks.org/2023/12/14/the-biological-and-toxin-weapons-convention-in-2023-glimmers-of-progress-set-against-a-troubled-geopolitical-landscape/ Accessed 29 May 2024

Crisis Group (2023) The Nagorno-Karabakh Conflict: A Visual Explainer https://www.crisisgroup.org/content/nagorno-karabakh-conflict-visual-explainer. Accessed 9 June 2024

De Hemptinne J, Prosperi L (2024) Prosecuting Ecocide Before the International Criminal Court: Concrete Possibility or Long-Term Aspiration? (Part 1). https://www.uu.nl/en/news/prosecuting-ecocide-before-the-international-criminal-court-concrete-possibility-or-long-term. Accessed 20 June 2024

De Waal T (2022) More Storm Clouds Gather Over Armenia, Azerbaijan, https://carnegieendowment.org/europe/strategic-europe/2022/09/more-storm-clouds-gather-over-armenia-azerbaijan?lang=en&center=europe

Democratic Republic of the Congo addressed to the President of the Security Council, UN Doc. S/2023/431

Diakonia IHL Resource Center (2023) Hostilities in Gaza and Israel: Factual account of events. https://www.diakonia.se/ihl/news/2023-hostilities-in-gaza-and-israel-factual-account-of-events/. Accessed 26 March 2024

Diakonia IHL Resource Centre (2023) Legal Brief: Hostilities in Israel and Gaza. https://apidiakoniase.cdn.triggerfish.cloud/uploads/sites/2/2023/12/Legal-Brief-2023-Hostilities-in-Israel-and-Gaza.pdf. Accessed 30 March 2024

ECCC (2023) The Court Report 2023. https://eccc.gov.kh/sites/default/files/publications/THE%20COURT%20REPORT%202023_EN.pdf. Accessed 29 June 2024

Euro-Mediterranean Human Rights Monitor (2023) "They brought Israeli civilians to watch our nude torture": IDF torture of Palestinian prisoners is turned into entertainment for Israeli viewers. https://euromedmonitor.org/en/article/6153. Accessed 27 March 2024

European Parliament Resolution of 20 October 2022 on the Situation in Burkina Faso Following the Coup D'état, adopted 20 October 2022, 2022/2865(RSP)

European Parliamentary Research Service (2023) Russia's war on Ukraine: Western-made tanks for Ukraine. https://www.europarl.europa.eu/RegData/etudes/ATAG/2023/739316/EPRS_ATA(2023)739316_EN.pdf. Accessed 26 April 2024

Ferraro T (2015) The ICRC's legal position on the notion of armed conflict involving foreign intervention and on determining the IHL applicable to this type of conflict International Review of the Red Cross 97:1227–1252

First Decision on the Trust Fund for Victims' Draft Implementation Plan for Reparations ('First DIP Decision')

Flemish Peace institute, Kanetake and Ryngaert 10 May 2023, Report on Due diligence and corporate liability of the defence industry: Arms exports, end use and corporate responsibility' https://vlaamsvredesinstituut.eu/wp-content/uploads/2023/05/VVI-Rapport-Due-Dilligence-WEB-new.pdf Accessed 30 May 2024

G5 Sahel (2017) Résolutions de la Force Conjointe du G5 Sahel [Resolutions of the G5 Sahel Joint Force]. https://www.g5sahel.org/wp-content/uploads/2017/04/images_Docs_Resolutions_force_conjointe__05_02_20171.pdf. Accessed 8 May 2024

Geneva Academy War Report 2017, 'Myanmar: A Battle For Recognition', https://www.geneva-academy.ch/joomlatools-files/docman-files/Myanmar%20A%20Battle%20for%20Recognition.pdf. Accessed 30 May 2024

Global Initiative against Transnational Crime (2022) JNIM in Burkina Faso: A strategic criminal actor. https://globalinitiative.net/wp-content/uploads/2022/08/Burkina-Faso-JNIM-29-Aug-web.pdf. Accessed 10 May 2024

Gregoire C et al. (2023) Year in Review 2022. In: Krieger H, Kalmanovitz P, Lieblich E, Pantazopoulos SE (eds) Yearbook of International Humanitarian Law 25, T.M.C. Asser Press, The Hague, 203–295

Human Rights Watch (2023) Israel: Starvation used as weapon of war in Gaza. https://www.hrw.org/news/2023/12/18/israel-starvation-used-weapon-war-gaza

Human Rights Watch (2024) "The Massalit Will Not Come Home": Ethnic Cleansing and Crimes Against Humanity in El Geneina, West Darfur, Sudan https://www.hrw.org/sites/default/files/media_2024/05/sudan0524web_0.pdf. Accessed 13 June 2024

Human Rights Watch (2024) Country chapter: Burkina Faso. https://www.hrw.org/world-report/2024/country-chapters/burkina-faso. Accessed 8 May 2024

Human Rights Watch (2024) Israel and Palestine - World Report 2024. https://www.hrw.org/world-report/2024/country-chapters/israel-and-palestine. Accessed 2 April 2024

Human Rights Watch (2024) World Report 2024: Sudan. https://www.hrw.org/world-report/2024/country-chapters/sudan. Accessed 28 June 2024

Human Rights Watch Mali Events of 2023, https://www.hrw.org/world-report/2024/country-chapters/mali Accessed 30 May 2024

ICC (2021c) Ntaganda Case: ICC Appeals Chamber to deliver appeals judgement on 30 March 2022 - Practical information. https://www.icc-cpi.int/Pages/item.aspx?name=MA263

ICC (2022) Statement by Prosecutor of the International Criminal Court, Karim Khan QC, following application. https://www.icc-cpi.int/news/statement-prosecutor-international-criminal-court-karim-khan-qc-following-application. Accessed 28 June 2024

ICC (2023) Dominic Ongwen transferred to Norway to serve his sentence of imprisonment. https://www.icc-cpi.int/news/dominic-ongwen-transferred-norway-serve-his-sentence-imprisonment. Accessed 28 June 2024

ICC (2023) ICC marks Rome Statute's 25th anniversary. https://www.icc-cpi.int/news/icc-marks-rome-statutes-25th-anniversary. Accessed 28 June 2024

ICC (2023) ICC Office of the Prosecutor launches public consultation on Policy on Complementarity and Cooperation. https://www.icc-cpi.int/news/icc-office-prosecutor-launches-public-consultation-policy-complementarity-and-cooperation. Accessed 28 June 2024

ICC (2023) ICC Prosecutor Karim A.A. Khan KC announces launch of Advanced Evidence Submission Platform (OTPLink). https://www.icc-cpi.int/news/icc-prosecutor-karim-aa-khan-kc-announces-launch-advanced-evidence-submission-platform-otplink. Accessed 28 June 2024

ICC (2023) International Criminal Court welcomes Armenia as a new State Party. https://www.icc-cpi.int/news/international-criminal-court-welcomes-armenia-new-state-party#:~:text=Background%3A%20On%2014%20November%202023,European%20group%20to%20do%20so. Accessed 28 June 2024

ICC (2023) Measures taken following unprecedented cyber attack - ICC. https://www.icc-cpi.int/news/measures-taken-following-unprecedented-cyber-attack-icc. Accessed 28 June 2024

ICC (2023) Statement by ICC Prosecutor Karim Khan KC in Cairo on the Situation in the State of Palestine and Israel. https://www.icc-cpi.int/news/statement-icc-prosecutor-karim-khan-kc-cairo-situation-state-palestine-and-israel. Accessed 28 June 2024

ICC (2023) ICC Prosecutor Karim Khan KC concludes first visit to Israel and the State of Palestine - ICC Prosecutor. https://www.icc-cpi.int/news/icc-prosecutor-karim-khan-kc-concludes-first-visit-israel-and-state-palestine-icc-prosecutor. Accessed 28 June 2024

ICC (2023) Statement by Prosecutor of the International Criminal Court, Karim A.A. Khan KC, on the Situation in the State of Palestine. https://www.icc-cpi.int/news/statement-prosecutor-international-criminal-court-karim-aa-khan-kc-situation-state-palestine. Accessed 28 June 2024

ICC (2024) Six newly elected ICC judges to be sworn in on 8 March 2024. https://www.icc-cpi.int/news/six-newly-elected-icc-judges-be-sworn-8-march-2024. Accessed 28 June 2024

ICC (2024) Trial Judgment in the Al Hassan case - 18 January 2024: Practical information. https://www.icc-cpi.int/news/trial-judgment-al-hassan-case-18-january-2024-practical-information#:~:text=On%20Thursday%2C%2018%20January%202024,Aziz%20Ag%20Mohamed%20Ag%20Mahmoud. Accessed 28 June 2024

ICC (Undated) Afghanistan: Situation in the Islamic Republic of Afghanistan. https://www.icc-cpi.int/afghanistan. Accessed 28 June 2024

ICC (Undated) Darfur, Sudan : Situation in Darfur, Sudan. https://www.icc-cpi.int/darfur. Accessed 28 June 2024

ICC (Undated) Mali: Situation in the Republic of Mali. https://www.icc-cpi.int/situations/mali. Accessed 28 June 2024

ICC (Undated) Palestine Situation. https://www.icc-cpi.int/palestine. Accessed 28 June 2024.

ICC (Undated) Uganda: Situation in Uganda. https://www.icc-cpi.int/situations/uganda. Accessed 28 June 2024

ICC OTP Statement 27 March 2024 https://www.icc-cpi.int/news/statement-icc-office-prosecutor-conclusion-deputy-prosecutor-mame-mandiaye-niangs-official Accessed 30 May 2024

ICRC (2009) Interpretative Guidance on the Notion of Direct Participation in Hostilities under International Humanitarian Law. https://www.icrc.org/en/doc/assets/files/other/icrc-002-0990.pdf. Accessed 24 April 2024

ICRC 2016, Commentary of 2016 on Convention (I) for the Amelioration of the Conditions of the Wounded and Sick in Armed Forces in the Field. Article 2: Application of the Convention. https://ihl-databases.icrc.org/en/ihl-treaties/gci-1949/article-2/commentary/2016#49_B. Accessed 23 May 202

ICRC 2016, Commentary on Article 2 of the Geneva Conventions of 1949, paras 307-308. https://ihl-databases.icrc.org/en/ihl-treaties/gci-1949/article-2/commentary/2016?activeTab=1949GCs-APs-and-commentaries. Accessed 2 April 2024

ICRC 2016, Commentary on the Geneva Conventions of 1949. International Committee of the Red Cross. https://ihl-databases.icrc.org/en/ihl-treaties/gci-1949/toc/commentary/2016?activeTab=undefined. Accessed 30 June 2024, paras 271–273

ICRC 2020, Commentary of 2020 on Convention (III) relative to the Treatment of Prisoners of War. Article 2: Application of the Convention. https://ihl-databases.icrc.org/applic/ihl/ihl.nsf/Comment.xsp?action=openDocument&documentId=0B46B7ADFC9E8219C125858400464543#_Toc42429662. Accessed 12 May 2024

ICRC 2021, Why Engaging with Non-State Armed Groups? https://www.icrc.org/en/document/why-engaging-non-state-armed-groups. Accessed 25 May 2024

ICRC 2006, 'Business and International Humanitarian Law: An Introduction to the Rights and Obligations of Business Enterprises Under International Humanitarian Law pg. 14.

ICRC Database (Undated) Customary IHL, Civilian Objects' Loss of Protection from Attack, Rule 10. https://ihl-databases.icrc.org/en/customary-ihl/v1/rule10. Accessed 21 June 2024

ICRC Database (Undated) Customary IHL, Medical Transports, Rule 53. https://ihl-databases.icrc.org/en/customary-ihl/v1/rule29. Accessed 9 June 2024

ICRC Database (Undated) Customary IHL, Pillage, Rule 52. https://ihl-databases.icrc.org/en/customary-ihl/v1/rule52. Accessed 21 June 2024

ICRC Database (Undated) Customary IHL, Starvation as a Method of Warfare ICRC Ferraro 2015, 'The ICRC's legal position on the notion of armed conflict involcing foreign intervention and determining the IHL applicable to this type of conflict' pg. 1234

Institute for the Study of War (2023) Russian Offensive Campaign Assessment, November 22, 2023. https://www.understandingwar.org/backgrounder/russian-offensive-campaign-assessment-november-22-2023. Accessed 25 April 2024

International Campaign to Ban Landmines (2023) Landmine Monitor 2023

Institute for the Study of War (2023) Russian Offensive Campaign Assessment, July 5, 2023. https://understandingwar.org/backgrounder/russian-offensive-campaign-assessment-july-5-2023. Accessed 25 April 2024

Institute for the Study of War (2023) Russian Offensive Campaign Assessment, June 9, 2023. https://www.understandingwar.org/backgrounder/russian-offensive-campaign-assessment-june-9-2023. Accessed 25 April 2024

Institute for the Study of War (2023) Russian Offensive Campaign Assessment, August 1, 2023. https://www.understandingwar.org/backgrounder/russian-offensive-campaign-assessment-august-1-2023. Accessed 25 April 2024

Institute for the Study of War (2023) Salafi-Jihadi Movement Weekly Update: December 1, 2023. https://www.understandingwar.org/backgrounder/salafi-jihadi-movement-weekly-update-december-1-2023. Accessed 8 May 2024

International Crisis Group (2023) Sudan: A Year of War. https://www.crisisgroup.org/africa/horn-africa/sudan/sudan-year-war. Accessed 28 May 2024

International Crisis Group (2023) Armer les civils au prix de la cohésion sociale [Arming civilians at the expense of social cohesion]. https://www.crisisgroup.org/africa/sahel/burkina-faso/burkina-faso/313-armer-les-civils-au-prix-de-la-cohesion-sociale. Accessed 8 May 202

5 Year in Review 2023

International Crisis Group (2023) CrisisWatch Database: Burkina Faso. https://www.crisisgroup. org/crisiswatch/database?location%5B0%5D=21&created=&page=1. Accessed 8 May 2024

International Crisis Group (2023) Sidelining Islamic State in Niger's Tillabery. https://www.cri sisgroup.org/africa/sahel/niger/289-sidelining-islamic-state-nigers-tillabery. Accessed 8 May 2024

International Crisis Group (2024) CrisisWatch Database: Israel/Palestine. https://www.crisisgroup. org/crisiswatch/database?location%5B%5D=91&crisis_state=&created=&from_month=1& from_year=2024&to_month=1&to_year=2024. Accessed 2 April 2024

International Crisis Group (2024) CrisisWatch Database: Israel/Palestine. https://www.crisisgroup. org/crisiswatch/database?location%5B%5D=91&crisis_state=&created=&from_month=1& from_year=2024&to_month=1&to_year=2024

International Crisis Group (2024) CrisisWatch Database: Sudan. https://www.crisisgroup.org/cri siswatch/database?location%5B0%5D=14&crisis_state=&created=&from_month=1&from_y ear=2024&to_month=1&to_year=2024&page=1. Accessed 28 June 2024

International Crisis Group 14 September 2023, Special Briefing 'Ten Challenges for the UN in 2023-2024', https://www.crisisgroup.org/global/sb11-ten-challenges-un-2023-2024 Accessed 30 May 2024

International Crisis Group Crisis Watch Nigeria https://www.crisisgroup.org/africa/west-africa/nig eria Accessed 30 May 2024

International Crisis Group Report 27 March 2024, 'Scam Centres and Ceasefires : China-Myanmar Ties Since the Coup' https://www.crisisgroup.org/asia/north-east-asia/china-myanmar/b179-scam-centres-and-ceasefires-china-myanmar-ties-coup 30 May 2024

International Federation for Human Rights (FIDH) (2023) Syria: French judges send Majdi Nema to trial before the criminal court. https://www.fidh.org/en/region/north-africa-middle-east/syria/ syria-french-judges-send-majdi-nema-to-trial-before-the-criminal. Accessed 26 May 2024

International Institute for Strategic Studies (2023) Armed Conflict Survey 2023, 1st ed. Routledge, Oxfordshire 2023

International Institute for Strategic Studies (2023) From Global Jihad to Local Insurgencies: the Changing Nature of Sub-Saharan Jihadis. https://www.iiss.org/publications/armed-conflict-sur vey/2023/from-global-jihad-to-local-insurgencies/. Accessed 12 May 2024

International Organisation for Migration (2023) Record High Displacement in DRC at Nearly 7 Million. https://www.iom.int/news/record-high-displacement-drc-nearly-7-million. Accessed 23 June 2024

International Rescue Committee (Undated) Crisis in Burkina Faso: What you need to know and how you can help. https://www.rescue.org/eu/article/crisis-burkina-faso-what-you-need-know-and-how-you-can-help. Accessed 8 May 2024

IOM UN Migration March 2023 Report, 'Nigeria – North Central and North West Displacement Report 11' https://dtm.iom.int/reports/nigeria-north-central-and-north-west-displacement-rep ort-11-march-2023 Accessed 30 May 2024

IPC (Integrated Food Security Phase Classification) (2023) IPC Country Analysis - State of Palestine. https://www.ipcinfo.org/ipc-country-analysis/details-map/en/c/1156749/. Accessed 1 April 2024

ISPI 90 Newsletter 15 February 2021, 'The Conflict Between Al-Qaeda and the Islamic State in Sahel, A Year on' https://www.ispionline.it/en/publication/conflict-between-al-qaeda-and-isl amic-state-sahel-year-29305 Accessed 30 May 2024

Israel Policy Forum (Undated) West Bank Settlements Explained. https://israelpolicyforum.org/ west-bank-settlements-explained/. Accessed 30 March 2024

Jaime, 'Discussions on autonomous weapons systems in 2023: Like it or not, the issue is already out of the CCW' https://www.forumarmstrade.org/uploads/1/9/0/8/19082495/munoz_15_dec ember_2022.pdf Accessed 29 May 2024

Jeffery J (2023) Sudan army says it has killed RSF leader in clashes. https://apnews.com/article/ sudan-rsf-army-war-f3516c941335f0e21c01b15e30572ae1. Accessed 28 June 2024

JEP (2023) La JEP abre macrocaso 11 que investiga la violencia basada en género, incluyendo violencia sexual y reproductiva, y crímenes cometidos por prejuicio [The JEP opens Macrocase 11 to investigate gender-based violence, including sexual and reproductive violence, and crimes committed out of prejudice]. https://www.jep.gov.co/Sala-de-Prensa/Paginas/-la-jep-abre-mac rocaso-11-que-investiga-la-violencia-basada-en-genero-incluyendo-violencia-sexual-y-reprod uctiva-y-crimenes.aspx. Accessed 30 June 2024

Joint Government of Bangladesh – UNHCR Population Factsheet (as of 31 October 2023), UNHCR Joint Registration Exercise

Joint Statement on the Rohingya Situation by the NGO Community in the Bangladesh Global Refugee Forum/December 2023

Just Security (2023) Syrian Regime Crimes on Trial in the Netherlands. https://www.justsecurity. org/90225/syrian-regime-crimes-on-trial-in-the-netherlands/. Accessed 30 June 2024

Justice Info (2020) Lebanon: STL Symbolically Sentences Ayyash to Life Imprisonment. https://www.justiceinfo.net/en/46228-lebanon-stl-symbolically-sentences-ayyash-to-life-imprisonment.html. Accessed 30 June 2024

Justice Info (2020) Special Tribunal for Lebanon's Second Best Justice. https://www.justiceinfo. net/en/88918-special-tribunal-for-lebanons-second-best-justice.html. Accessed 30 June 2024

JusticeInfo.net (2023) First child soldier charges against ex-FARC guerrillas: tribunal. https:// www.justiceinfo.net/en/113474-first-child-soldier-charges-against-ex-farc-guerrillas-tribunal. html. Accessed 30 June 2024

JusticeInfo.net (2024) Belgium probes refugee status of Syrian war crimes suspect. https://www. justiceinfo.net/en/114527-belgium-probes-refugee-status-of-syrian-war-crimes-supect.html. Accessed 30 June 2024

KSC (2022) Kosovo Specialist Chambers & Specialist Prosecutor's Office. https://www.scp-ks. org/en Accessed 25 June 2024

Law on the Establishment of Extraordinary Chambers in the Courts of Cambodia for the Prosecution of Crimes Committed During the Period of Democratic Kampuchea (2004), Article 2

Loi N°002-2020/AN portant institution de volontaires pour la défense de la patrie, adopted by the National Assembly of Burkina Faso on 21 January 2020 [Law No. 002-2020/AN instituting volunteers for the defense of the homeland, adopted by the National Assembly of Burkina Faso on 21 January 2020]

Lyammouri R (2022) Centre Du Mali: Mobilisation Communautaire Armée Face À La Crise [Central Mali: Armed Community Mobilization in Response to the Crisis]. https://www.resolv enet.org/research/centre-du-mali-mobilisation-communautaire-armee-face-la-crise. Accessed 12 May 2024

Medecins Sans Frontieres Guide to Humanitarian Law 'Article 3 Boat People' https://guide-hum anitarian-law.org/content/article/3/boat-people/ Accessed 30 May 2024.

Micheal N. Schmitt (2022) Providing arms and materiel to Ukraine: Neutrality, Co-Beligerency, and the Use of Force. https://lieber.westpoint.edu/ukraine-neutrality-co-belligerency-use-of-force/. Accessed 14 June 2024

Middle East Treaty Organization (METO), 'The Biological Weapons Convention and the Weapons of Mass Destruction Free Zone in the Middle East' https://rosalux.nyc/wp-content/uploads/ 2023/11/The-Biological-Weapons-Convention.pdf Accessed 29 May 2024

Mischa Gureghian Hall, Who's Afraid of Human Rights in War? (Part II): On the Place of the ECHR during Armed Conflict in Response to a Misguided Critique of Narayan and Others v. Azerbaijan, Völkerrechtsblog

Musayev T (2024) Is the Harmonisation of IHL and IHRL Eroding? Narayan and Others v. Azerbaijan, Völkerrechtsblog

National Public Prosecution Service of the Netherlands (Date of retrieval) Syria cases prosecuted. https://www.prosecutionservice.nl/topics/international-crimes/what-cases-have-been-prosecuted/syria. Accessed 30 June 2024

5 Year in Review 2023

Office of the Prosecutor of the ICC (2023) Draft Policy on Complementarity and Cooperation. https://www.icc-cpi.int/sites/default/files/2023-10/DRAFT-Complementarity-and-Cooperation-Policy-Paper_September-2023%20%281%29.pdf. Accessed 28 June 2024

Office of the Prosecutor of the ICC (2023) Policy on Children. https://www.icc-cpi.int/sites/default/files/2023-12/2023-policy-children-en-web.pdf. Accessed 28 June 2024

Office of the Prosecutor of the ICC (2023) Policy on Gender-based Crimes: Crimes involving sexual, reproductive and other gender-based violence. https://www.icc-cpi.int/sites/default/files/2023-12/2023-policy-gender-en-web.pdf. Accessed 28 June 2024

Office of the Special Representative of the Secretary-General on Sexual Violence in conflict (2024) Mission report: Official visit of the Office of the SRSG-SVC to Israel and the occupied West Bank (29 January - 14 February 2024). https://www.un.org/sexualviolenceinconflict/wp-content/uploads/2024/03/report/mission-reportofficial-visit-of-the-office-of-the-srsg-svc-to-israel-and-the-occupied-west-bank-29-january-14-february-2024/20240304-Israel-oWB-CRSV-report.pdf. Accessed 1 June 2024

OHCHR (2023) Gaza: UN Experts Call on International Community to Prevent Genocide. https://www.ohchr.org/en/press-releases/2023/11/gaza-un-experts-call-international-community-prevent-genocide-against. Accessed 2 April 2024

OHCHR (2023) Sudan: At least 87 buried in mass grave in Darfur, Rapid Support Forces deny victims. https://www.ohchr.org/en/press-releases/2023/07/sudan-least-87-buried-mass-grave-darfur-rapid-support-forces-deny-victims. Accessed 24 June 2024

OHCHR (2023) Sudan: Plight of civilians amid hostilities. https://www.ohchr.org/en/press-briefing-notes/2023/04/sudan-plight-civilians-amid-hostilities. Accessed 24 June 2024.

Osasona IRRC No. 923 June 2023, 'The question of definition: Armed banditry in Nigeria's North-West in the context of international humanitarian law' https://international-review.icrc.org/articles/the-question-of-definition-armed-banditry-in-nigeria-923#footnote2_umcct1d Accessed 30 May 2024

Palestinian Ministry of Health / Gaza (2023) Statements by the spokesperson of the Ministry of Health, Dr. Ashraf Al-Qudra: During a press conference on the serious repercussions of the ongoing Israeli aggression on the Gaza Strip for the twelfth day. https://www.facebook.com/MOHGaza1994/posts/pfbid02VihLzssMVKvwphaoxK71rs9X4fUtNFaXBj9nFamjZ4Z9A56Vu6SZ7GcTLS2yo23fl. Accessed 28 May 2024.

PAX (2024) Oil in the Crosshairs. https://paxforpeace.nl/news/oil-in-the-crosshairs/. Accessed 26 June 2024

Permanent Observer Mission of the State of Palestine to the United Nations (Undated) Diplomatic Relations. http://palestineun.org/about-palestine/diplomatic-relations/. Accessed 30 March 2024

Peterson, Derek R., ed., *Abolitionism and imperialism in Britain, Africa, and the Atlantic* (Ohio University Press, 2010)

Reliefweb 9 January 2024 Report, '122% rise in global civilian fatalities from explosive weapons in 2023. a year of harm reviewed', https://reliefweb.int/report/world/122-rise-global-civilian-fatalities-explosive-weapons-2023-year-harm-reviewed Accessed 30 May 2024

Resue organization Emergency Watchlist 2024, 'Crisis in Mali: What you need to know and how to help', https://www.rescue.org/eu/article/crisis-mali-what-you-need-know-and-how-help Accessed 30 May 2024

RULAC (2023) Military Occupation of Palestine by Israel. https://www.rulac.org/browse/conflicts/military-occupation-of-palestine-by-israel#collapse2accord. Accessed 28 March 2024

RULAC (2023) Non-International Armed Conflicts in Sudan. https://www.rulac.org/browse/conflicts/non-international-armed-conflicts-in-sudan#collapse4accord. Accessed 28 June 2024

Rule of Law in Armed Conflicts (RULAC) Project, Geneva Academy of International Humanitarian Law and Human Rights (2023) Military occupation. https://www.rulac.org/classification/military-occupations#collapse1accord. Accessed 30 June 2024

Rule of Law in Armed Conflicts project (RULAC) (2023) Non-International Armed Conflicts in Burkina Faso. https://www.rulac.org/browse/conflicts/non-international-armed-conflicts-in-bur kina-faso#collapse1accord. Accessed 28 May 2024

Saferworld News 19 April 2023, 'Launching the new Arms Trade Litigation Monitor website' https://www.saferworld-global.org/resources/news-and-analysis/post/1003-launching-the-new-arms-trade-litigation-monitor-website Accessed 30 May 2024

Sassòli M (2024) International Humanitarian Law: Rules, Controversies, and Solutions to Problems Arising in Warfare (Edward Elgar, Cheltenham)

Sexton JP et al. (2023) Year in Review 2021. In: Krieger H, Kalmanovitz P, Lieblich E, Mignot-Mahdavi R (eds) Yearbook of International Humanitarian Law 24. T.M.C. Asser Press, The Hague, 193–277

Statement of the Kingdom of the Netherlands concerning Protocol V, 13th November 2023, H.E. Robert in den Bosch, Permanent Representative of the Kingdom of the Netherlands to the Conference on Disarmament and Ambassador-at-large for Disarmament Affairs. https://docs-library.unoda.org/Convention_on_Certain_Conventional_Weapons-Protocol_V_Annual_Conference_(2023)/Netherlands_-_Statement_Protocol_V.pdf

The Public Committee Against Torture in Israel Adalah, The Legal Center for Arab Minority Rights in Israel Hamoked, Center for the Defence of the Individual Physicians for Human Rights UN General Assembly (2024) Report of the UN High Commissioner for Human Rights : Human rights situation in the Occupied Palestinian Territory, including East Jerusalem, and the obligation to ensure accountability and justice, UN Doc. A/HRC/55/28

Thompson J (2021) Examining Extremism: Islamic State Greater Sahara. Center for Strategic and International Studies (CSIS). https://www.csis.org/blogs/examining-extremism/examining-ext remism-islamic-state-greater-sahara. Accessed 8 May 2024

Trial International (2024) UJAR 2024_digital. https://trialinternational.org/wp-content/uploads/2024/04/UJAR-2024_digital.pdf. Accessed 26 May 2024

UN General Assembly (2023) Note by the Secretary-General: Situation of human rights in the Palestinian territories occupied since 1967, UN Doc. A/78/545

UN General Assembly (2023) Resolution adopted by the General Assembly on 27 October 2023, UN Doc. A/RES/ES-10/21

UN General Assembly (2023) Situation of human rights in Afghanistan, UN Doc. A/HRC/RES/54/1

UN General Assembly (2023) Technical assistance and capacity-building in the field of human rights in the Central African Republic, UN Doc. A/HRC/RES/54/31

UN General Assembly (2023), Advancing human rights in South Sudan, UN Doc. A/HRC/RES/52/1

UN General Assembly (2023), Assistance to Somalia in the field of human rights, UN Doc. A/HRC/RES/54/32

UN General Assembly (2023), Independent Institution on Missing Persons in the Syrian

UN General Assembly (2023), Israeli practices affecting the human rights of the Palestinian people in the Occupied Palestinian Territory, including East Jerusalem, UN Doc. A/RES/77/247

UN General Assembly (2023), Israeli settlements in the Occupied Palestinian Territory, including East Jerusalem, and in the occupied Syrian Golan, UN Doc. A/HRC/RES/52/35

UN General Assembly (2023), Situation of human rights in Myanmar, UN Doc. A/HRC/RES/52/31

UN General Assembly (2023), Situation of human rights in the Syrian Arab Republic, UN Doc. A/HRC/RES/53/18. UN General Assembly (2023), Situation of human rights in the Syrian Arab Republic, A/HRC/RES/52/30

UN General Assembly (2023), Situation of human rights in Ukraine stemming from the Russian Aggression, UN Doc. A/HRC/RES/52/32

UN General Assembly (2023), Situation of human rights of Rohingya Muslims and other minorities in Myanmar, UN Doc. A/HRC/RES/53/26

5 Year in Review 2023

UN General Assembly (2023), Technical assistance and capacity-building in the field of human rights

UN General Assembly (2023), The human rights impact of the ongoing conflict in Sudan, UN Doc. A/HRC/RES/S-36/1

UN General Assembly (2024) Report of the United Nations High Commissioner for Human Rights: Human rights situation in the Occupied Palestinian Territory, including East Jerusalem, and the obligation to ensure accountability and justice, UN Doc. A/HRC/55/28

UN IRMCT (2015) Initial appearance of *Stanišić* and Simatović before the Mechanism

UN IRMCT (2021) Conclusion of closing arguments in Prosecutor v. Jovica Stanišić and Franko Simatović

UN OCHA (2023) Hostilities in the Gaza Strip and Israel: Flash Update #33. https://www.ochaopt.org/content/hostilities-gaza-strip-and-israel-flash-update-33. Accessed 28 June 2024

UN OCHA (2023) Sudan Humanitarian Update, 28 December 2023. https://www.unocha.org/publications/report/sudan/sudan-humanitarian-update-28-december-2023. Accessed 28 June 2024

UN OCHA (2023) Sudan Humanitarian Update, 5 October 2023. https://www.unocha.org/publications/report/sudan/sudan-humanitarian-update-5-october-2023#:~:text=The%20Sudan%20Ministry%20of%20Health,and%20the%20Rapid%20Support%20Forces.&text=Disease%20outbreaks%20have%20been%20reported,malaria%2C%20dengue%20fever%20and%20cholera. Accessed 28 May 2024

UN OCHA (2023) Sudan: Seven Months of Conflict - Key Facts and Figures, 15 December 2023. https://www.unocha.org/publications/report/sudan/sudan-seven-months-conflict-key-facts-and-figures-15-december-2023. Accessed 28 May 2024

UN OCHA (2024) Hostilities in Gaza Strip and Israel: Flash Update #94. https://www.unocha.org/publications/report/occupied-palestinian-territory/hostilities-gaza-strip-and-israel-flash-update-94. Accessed 30 March 2024

UN Office for Disarmament Affairs, Convention on Certain Conventional Weapons (2023) –Protocol V Annual Conference, https://meetings.unoda.org/ccw-pv/convention-on-certain-conventional-weapons-seventeenth-protocol-v-annual-conference-2023 Accessed 28 May 2024

UN Office for the Coordination of Humanitarian Affairs (OCHA) (Undated) Data on Casualties. https://www.ochaopt.org/data/casualties. Accessed 30 March 2024

UN Security Council (2007), Resolution 1757 (2007) - Attachment; Statute of the Special Tribunal for Lebanon, UN Doc. S/RES/1757(2007)

UN Security Council (2013) Resolution 2098 (2013), UN Doc. S/RES/2098

UN Security Council (2018) Letter dated 9 February 2018 from the Secretary-General addressed to the President of the Security Council, UN Doc. S/2018/118

UN Security Council (2022) Letter dated 16 December 2022 from the Group of Experts on the Democratic Republic of the Congo addressed to the President of the Security Council, UN Doc. S/2022/967

UN Security Council (2023) Implementation of the Peace, Security and Cooperation Framework for the Democratic Republic of the Congo and the Region, UN Doc. S/2023/730

UN Security Council (2023), Resolution 2697(2023), UN Doc. S/RES/2697(2023)

UN Security Council (2023), Resolution 2712(2023), UN Doc. S/RES/2712(2023)

UN Security Council (2024) Eighteenth report of the Secretary-General on the threat posed by ISIL (Da'esh) to international peace and security and the range of United Nations efforts in support of Member States in countering the threat, UN Doc. S/2024/117

UNHCR (2023) Multi-Sector Needs Assessment: Northwest and Southwest Regions, Cameroon. https://data.unhcr.org/en/documents/details/106296. Accessed 8 May 2024

UNIDIR 13-14 September 2023 'Outer Space Security Conference Report', https://unidir.org/wp-content/uploads/2023/11/UNIDIR_2023_Outer_Space_SecurityConference_Report.pdf Accessed 29 May 2024

UNIDIR Outer Space Security Conference 2023, https://unidir.org/event/outer-space-security-conference-2023-2/ Accessed 29 May 2024

United Nations OCHA (2023) Flash Update: 15 May 2023. https://www.ochaopt.org/content/flash-update-5-15-may-2023. Accessed 2 April 2024

United Nations Relief and Works Agency for Palestine Refugees in the Near East (UNRWA) (2023) UNRWA Situation Report #58: Situation in Gaza Strip and West Bank, including East Jerusalem. https://www.unrwa.org/resources/reports/unrwa-situation-report-58-situation-gaza-strip-and-west-bank-including-east-Jerusalem. Accessed 2 April 2024

US Department of State (2022) Country Reports on Terrorism 2022. https://www.state.gov/reports/country-reports-on-terrorism-2022/. Accessed 29 June 2024

US Department of State (2023) 2023 Country Reports on Human Rights Practices: Burkina Faso. https://www.state.gov/reports/2023-country-reports-on-human-rights-practices/burkina-faso/. Accessed 28 June 2024 ; ACLED (2024) ACLED Data Export Tool. https://acleddata.com/data-export-tool/. Accessed 23 March 2024

Working Group on the Strengthening of the Convention on the Prohibition of the Development, Production and Stockpiling of the Bacteriological (Biological) and Toxin Weapons and on Their Destruction, BWC/WG/1/1, 17 March 2023 https://documents.un.org/doc/undoc/gen/g23/051/91/pdf/g2305191.pdf?token=2XdYiyGOyYS5ztWk6x&fe=true Accessed 29 May 2024

Treaties

Charte du Liptako-Gourma instituant l'Alliance des États du Sahel entre le Burkina Faso, la République du Mali, la République du Niger, opened for signature 16 September 2023

Geneva Convention for the Amelioration of the Condition of the Wounded and Sick in Armed Forces in the Field, 75 UNTS 31, opened for signature 12 August 1949 (entered into force 21 October 1950)

Geneva Convention for the Amelioration of the Condition of Wounded, Sick and Shipwrecked Members of Armed Forces at Sea, 75 UNTS 85, opened for signature 12 August 1949 (entered into force 21 October 1950)

Geneva Convention relative to the Protection of Civilian Persons in Time of War, 75 UNTS 287, opened for signature 12 August 1949 (entered into force 21 October 1950)

Geneva Convention relative to the Treatment of Prisoners of War, 75 UNTS 135, opened for signature 12 August 1949 (entered into force 21 October 1950)

Hague Convention (IV) respecting the Laws and Customs of War on Land and its annex: Regulations concerning the Laws and Customs of War on Land (opened for signature 18 October 1907, entered into force 26 January 1910) U.S.T.S. 539, 2 A.J.I.L. Supp. 90, Annex to the Convention

Protocol Additional to the Geneva Conventions of 12 August 1949, and relating to the Protection of Victims of International Armed Conflicts, 1125 UNTS 3 (opened for signature 8 June 1977, entered into force 7 December 1978)

Protocol Additional to the Geneva Conventions of 12 August 1949, and relating to the Protection of Victims of Non-International Armed Conflicts, 1125 UNTS 609 (opened for signature 8 June 1977, entered into force 7 December 1978)

Cases

ECtHR, Narayan and others v. Azerbaijan, 19 December 2023, Applications nos. 54363/17 and two others

ICC, *Situation in the Islamic Republic of Afghanistan*, Decision pursuant to article 18(2) of the Statute authorising the Prosecution to resume investigation, 31 October 2022, ICC-02/1

5 Year in Review 2023   269

ICC, *Situation in the Islamic Republic of Afghanistan*, Judgment on the appeal against the decision on the authorisation of an investigation into the situation in the Islamic Republic of Afghanistan, 5 March 2020, ICC-02/17 OA4

ICC, *Situation in the Islamic Republic of Afghanistan*, Judgment on the Prosecutor's appeal against the decision of Pre-Trial Chamber II entitled "Decision pursuant to article 18(2) of the Statute authorising the Prosecution to resume investigation", 4 April 2023, ICC-02/17 OA5

ICC, *Situation in the State of Palestine*, Decision on the 'Prosecution request pursuant to article 19(3) for a ruling on the Court's territorial jurisdiction in Palestine', 5 February 2021, ICC-01/18

ICC, *Situation in Uganda*, Warrant of Arrest for Joseph Kony Issued on 8 July 2005 as Amended on 27 September 2005, 27 September 2005, ICC-02/04-01/05

ICC, *The Prosecutor v. Al Hassan Ag Abdoul Aziz Ag Mohamed Ag Mahmoud*, Public redacted version of the "Corrected Version of the '*Décision portant modification des charges confirmées le 30 septembre 2019 à l'encontre d'Al Hassan Ag Abdoul Aziz Ag Mohamed Ag Mahmoud, 23 avril 2020, ICC-01/12-01/18-767-Conf'*" ["Decision Amending the Charges Confirmed on September 30, 2019, Against Al Hassan Ag Abdoul Aziz Ag Mohamed Ag Mahmoud, April 23, 2020, ICC-01/12-01/18-767-Conf"] With a Public Redacted Annex Containing the Full List of Charges Confirmed against the Accused, 1 May 2020, ICC-01/12-01/18

ICC, The Prosecutor v. Bosco Ntaganda, Judgement, 8 July 2019, ICC-01/04-02/06

ICC, The Prosecutor v. Bosco Ntaganda, Judgment on the appeals against the decision of Trial

ICC, The Prosecutor v. Bosco Ntaganda, Public redacted version of Judgement on the appeals

ICC, The Prosecutor v. Bosco Ntaganda, Sentencing judgement, 7 November 2019, ICC-01

ICC, The Prosecutor v. Dominic Ongwen, Judgment on the appeal of Mr Dominic Ongwen against the decision of Trial Chamber IX of 6 May 2021 entitled "Sentence", 15 December 2022, ICC-02/04-01/15 A2

ICC, *The Prosecutor vs. Joseph Kony and Vincent Otti*, Third Request to Terminate Proceedings against Vincent Otti, 15 November 2023, ICC-02/04-01/05

ICC, *The Prosecutor vs. Joseph Kony*, Decision on the Prosecution's request to hold a confirmation of charges hearing in the *Kony* case in the suspect's absence, 23 November 2023, ICC-02/04-01/05; I CC (2023) 28 June 2024

ICJ (2022) Application of the International Convention on the Elimination of All Forms of Racial Discrimination (Armenia v. Azerbaijan): Request for the modification of the Court's Order. https://www.icj-cij.org/sites/default/files/case-related/180/180-20220919-PRE-01-00-EN.pdf. Accessed 30 June 2024

ICJ (2023) *Application of the International Convention on the Elimination of All Forms of Racial Discrimination (Armenia v. Azerbaijan)*: Request for the modification of the Court's Order indicating provisional measures. https://www.icj-cij.org/sites/default/files/case-related/180/180-20230524-PRE-01-00-EN.pdf. Accessed 29 June 2024

ICJ (2023) Conclusion of the public hearings. https://www.icj-cij.org/sites/default/files/case-related/182/182-20230927-pre-01-00-en.pdf. Accessed 27 June 2024

ICJ (2024) Legal Consequences Arising from the Policies and Practices of Israel in the Occupied Palestinian Territory (Request for Advisory Opinion) : Public hearings to be held from Monday 19 to Monday 26 February 2024. https://www.un.org/unispal/document/legal-consequences-arising-from-the-policies-and-practices-of-israel-in-the-occupied-palestinian-territory-9feb-2024. Accessed 28 June 2024

ICJ (Undated) Legal Consequences arising from the Policies and Practices of Israel in the Occupied Palestinian Territory, including East Jerusalem. https://www.icj-cij.org/case/186. Accessed 28 June 2024

ICJ, *Allegations of Genocide Under the Convention on the Prevention and Punishment of the Crime of Genocide (Ukraine v. Russian Federation)*, Application Instituting Proceedings, 26 February 2022

ICJ, *Allegations of Genocide Under the Convention on the Prevention and Punishment of the Crime of Genocide (Ukraine v. Russian Federation)*, Request for the Indication of Provisional Measures

Submitted by Ukraine, 26 February 2022; ICJ, *Allegations of Genocide Under the Convention on the Prevention and Punishment of the Crime of Genocide (Ukraine v. Russian Federation)*, Order on the Request for the Indication of Provisional Measures, 16 March 2022

ICJ, *Allegations of Genocide Under the Convention on the Prevention and Punishment of the Crime of Genocide (Ukraine v. Russian Federation)*, Preliminary Objections Submitted by the Russian Federation, 3 October 2022

ICJ, *Allegations of Genocide Under the Convention on the Prevention and Punishment of the Crime of Genocide (Ukraine v. Russian Federation)*, Order on the Admissibility of the Declarations of Intervention, 5 June 2023

ICJ, Application of the Convention on the Prevention and Punishment of the Crime of Genocide in the Gaza Strip (South Africa v. Israel), Application Instituting Proceedings, 29 December 2023

ICJ, *Application of the International Convention on the Elimination of All Forms of Racial Discrimination (Armenia v. Azerbaijan)*, Application Instituting Proceedings, 16 September 2021

ICJ, *Application of the International Convention on the Elimination of All Forms of Racial Discrimination (Armenia v. Azerbaijan)*, Order on the Request for the Indication of Provisional Measures, 7 December 2021

ICJ, *Application of the International Convention on the Elimination of All Forms of Racial Discrimination (Armenia v. Azerbaijan)*, Order on the Request for the Modification of the Order Indicating Provisional Measures of 7 December 2021, 12 October 2022

ICJ, *Application of the International Convention on the Elimination of All Forms of Racial Discrimination (Armenia v. Azerbaijan)*, Request by the Republic of Armenia for the Indication of Provisional Measures, 27 December 2022

ICJ, *Application of the International Convention on the Elimination of All Forms of Racial Discrimination (Armenia v. Azerbaijan)*, Order on the Request for the Indication of Provisional Measures, 22 February 2023

ICJ, *Application of the International Convention on the Elimination of All Forms of Racial Discrimination (Armenia v. Azerbaijan)*, Preliminary Objections of the Republic of Azerbaijan, 21 April 2023

ICJ, *Application of the International Convention on the Elimination of All Forms of Racial Discrimination (Armenia v. Azerbaijan)*, Order on the Request for the Modification of the Order of 22 February 2023 Indicting Provisional Measures, 6 July 2023

ICJ, *Application of the International Convention on the Elimination of All Forms of Racial Discrimination (Armenia v. Azerbaijan)*, Request by the Republic of Armenia for the Indication of Provisional Measures, 28 September 2023

ICJ, *Application of the International Convention on the Elimination of All Forms of Racial Discrimination (Armenia v. Azerbaijan)*, Order on the Request for the Indication of Provisional Measures, 17 November 2023

ICJ, *Canada and The Kingdom of the Nethernalds v. The Syrian Arab Republic*, Order on the Request for the Indication of Provisional Measures Made by Canada and the Kingdom of the Netherlands, 16 November 2023

ICJ, *Case Concerning Application of the Convention Against Torture and Other Cruel, Inhuman or Degrading Treatment or Punishment (Canada and the Netherlands v. Syrian Arab Republic)*, Joint Application Instituting Proceedings Concerning a Dispute Under the Convention Against Torture and Other Cruel, Inhuman or Degrading Treatment or Punishment, 8 June 2023

ICJ, *Case Concerning Application of the Convention Against Torture and Other Cruel, Inhuman or Degrading Treatment or Punishment (Canada and the Netherlands v. Syrian Arab Republic)*, Request for the Indication of Provisional Measures Further to the Joint Application Instituting Proceedings Concerning a Dispute Under the Convention Against Torture and Other Cruel, Inhuman or Degrading Treatment or Punishment, 8 June 2023

ICJ, *Case Concerning Military and Paramilitary Activities In and Against Nicaragua (Nicaragua v. United States of America)*, 27 June 1986, ICJ Rep 1986 (*Nicaragua v United States of America* 1986)

5 Year in Review 2023

ICJ, *Legal Consequences of the Construction of a Wall in the Occupied Palestinian Territory*, Advisory Opinion, 9 July 2004, ICJ Rep 2004

ICTY, *The Prosecutor v. Dusko Tadić*, Appeals Chamber, Decision on the Defence Motion for Interlocutory Appeal on Jurisdiction, 2 October 1995, Case No. IT-94-1-AR72

ICTY, *Prosecutor v. Dusko Tadić*, Judgement, 15 July 1999, Case No. IT-94-1-A

ICTY, *The Prosecutor v. Ljube Boškoski and Johan Tarčulovski*, Trial Chamber, Judgement, 10 July 2008, Case No. IT-04-82-T

ICTY, *The Prosecutor v. Ramush Haradinaj and others*, Trial Chamber, Judgement, 3 April 2008, Case No. IT-04-84-T (*Prosecutor v Haradinaj and others* 2008)

IRMCT (Undated) KABUGA, Félicien (MICT-13-38). https://www.irmct.org/en/cases/mict-13-38. Accessed 28 June 2024

IRMCT, *Prosecutor v. Félicien Kabuga*, Decision on Appeals of Further Decision on Félicien Kabuga's Fitness to Stand Trial, 7 August 2023, MICT-13-38-AR80.3

IRMCT, *The Prosecutor v. Jovica Stanišić and Franko* Simatović, Judgement, 30 May 2013, IT-03-69-T

IRMCT, *The Prosecutor v. Jovica Stanišić and Franko* Simatović, Judgement, 9 December 2015, IT-03-69

IRMCT, *The Prosecutor v. Jovica Stanišić and Franko* Simatović, Judgement, 30 June 2021, MICT-15-96-T (*Stanišić and Simatović* 2021)

IRMCT, *The Prosecutor v. Jovica Stanišić and Franko* Simatović, Judgement, 31 May 2023, MICT-15-96-A (*Stanišić and Simatović* 2023)

KSC (Undated) Case of Hashim Thaçi et al. https://www.scp-ks.org/en/cases/hashim-thaci-et-al. Accessed 25 June 2024

KSC (Undated) Case of Isni Kilaj. https://www.scp-ks.org/en/cases/isni-kilaj. Accessed 25 June 2024

KSC (Undated) Case of Pjeter Shala. https://www.scp-ks.org/en/cases/pjeter-shala. Accessed 26 June 2024

KSC (Undated) Case of Sabit Januzi, Ismet Bahtijari, Haxhi Shala. https://www.scp-ks.org/en/cases/sabit-januzi-ismet-bahtijari-haxhi-shala. Accessed 30 June 2024

KSC, *Specialist Prosecutor v. Haxhi Shala*, Public redacted Indictment, 6 December 2023, KSC-BC-2023-11 (*Haxhi Shala* 2023)

KSC, *Specialist Prosecutor v. Hashim Thaçi, Kadri Veseli, Rexhep Selimi And Jakup Krasniqi*, Public Lesser Redacted Version of Amended Indictment, 27 February 2023, KSC-BC-2020-06

KSC, *Specialist Prosecutor v. Hysni Gucati and Nasim Haradinaj*, Appeal Judgement, 2 February 2023, KSC-CA-2022-01 (*Gucati and Haradinaj* 2023)

KSC, *Specialist Prosecutor v. Hysni Gucati and Nasim Haradinaj*, Public Redacted Version of the Trial Judgment, 18 May 2022, KSC BC 2020 07, paras 1012 1016

KSC, *Specialist Prosecutor v. Sabit Januzi and Ismet Bahtjari*, Public redacted Indictment, KSC-BC-2023-10, 4 October 2023 (*Januzi and Bahtjari* 2023)

KSC, *Specialist Prosecutor v. Salih Mustafa*, Further redacted version of Corrected version of Public redacted version of Trial Judgement, 16 December 2022, KSC-BC-2020-05

KSC, *Specialist Prosecutor v. Salih Mustafa*, Public Redacted Version of Appeal Judgment, 14 December 2023, KSC-CA-2023-02

Prosecutor v. Félicien Kabuga, Case No. MICT-13-38-T, Further Decision on Félicien Kabuga's Fitness to Stand Trial, 6 June 2023, MICT-13-38-T, 6 June 2023

Printed in the United States
by Baker & Taylor Publisher Services